ERIC WHITE

RIZZOLI
NEW YORK

New York · Paris · London · Milan

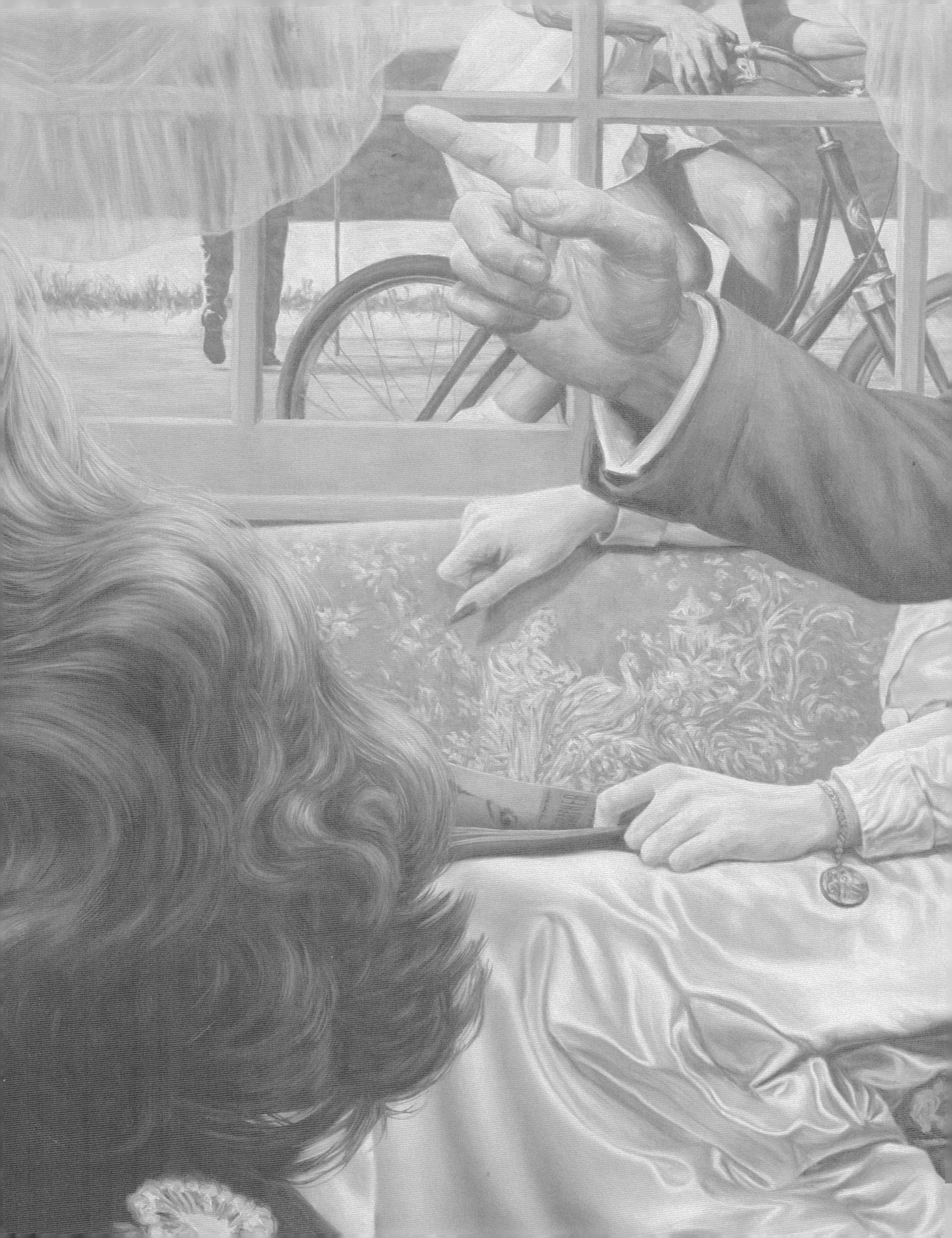

ERIC WHITE

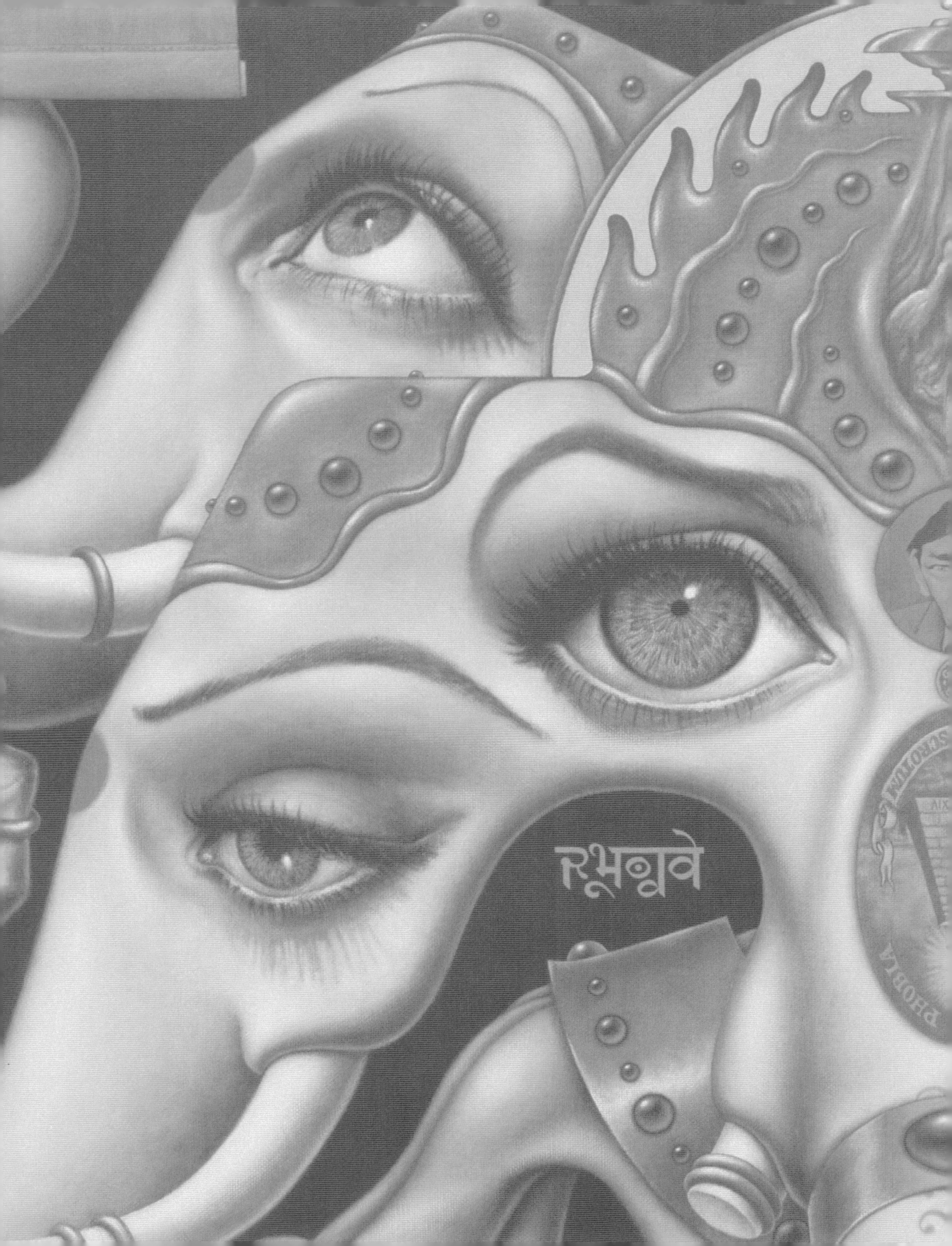

THE NEW REAL
ANTHONY HADEN-GUEST

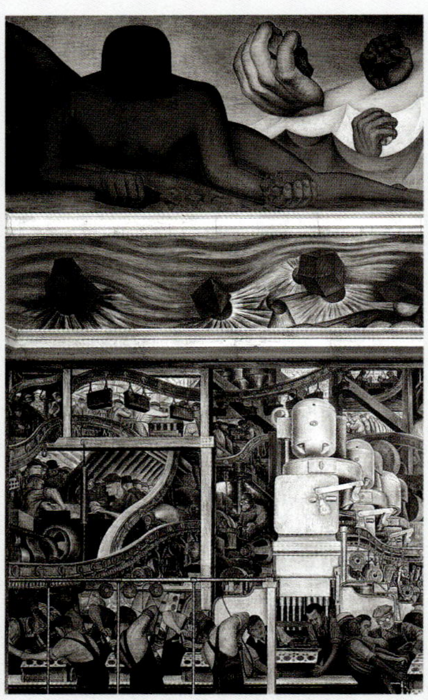

Diego Rivera (1886–1957)
Detroit Industry **(detail)**
1932–3
Fresco
Detroit Institute of Arts, Detroit, Michigan

Eric White is from Michigan. Detroit shaped him. One grandfather spent his life working at The Chrysler Dodge Main plant, the other was a mechanical engineer with twenty-five patents on auto components. Indeed, one of the strongest cards in White's hand—by which I mean that mix of talents, traits, and preoccupations that constitute an individual's makeup—is the whole-heartedness with which he embraces that background, that culture. The series of car interior paintings he's been making lately are a testament his reverence for where he came from. Seeing Diego Rivera's *Detroit Industry* murals at The Detroit Institute of Art as a child completely rocked White's world, and ultimately helped lead him to where he is today.

Yes, *that* Museum. The DIA, a world-class institution whose collection—one of the finest in the nation—was saved at the last moment from being pawned off to satisfy the city's creditors in December of 2014. This had been a dire emblem of Detroit's collapse into a dystopia, a situation belonging to a post-apocalyptic sci-fi story, not a real-world metropolis in the richest and most powerful country on earth. This sad state of affairs only intensified the grip of White's hometown on his imagination, a grip perhaps made stronger for being exerted from afar.

If an artist has a particularly strong talent for drawing, it will often emerge early, and so it was for White. He did his best to squeeze as much art instruction as possible from the Ann Arbor public school system, while working closely with a private teacher for many years. Out of high school his talent took him to The Rhode Island School of Design. Some of his artistic influences at that time included Salvador Dalí, René Magritte, and the American surrealist George Tooker. A freshman year assignment challenged students to design a deck of fifty-two playing cards, each representing a different artist. It would prove to be one of the most valuable assignments in his schooling, leading to introductions to many important artists and expanding his view of what was possible through art. One of the figures he encountered while rooting

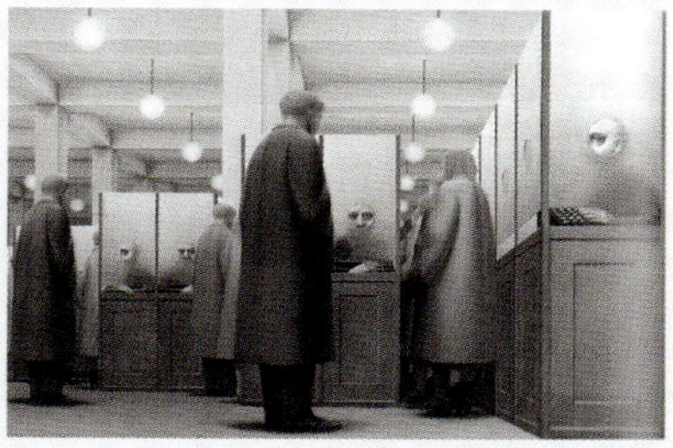

George Tooker (1920–2011)
Government Bureau
Egg tempera on wood
© 1956 The Metropolitan Museum of Art
Courtesy Art Resource, New York

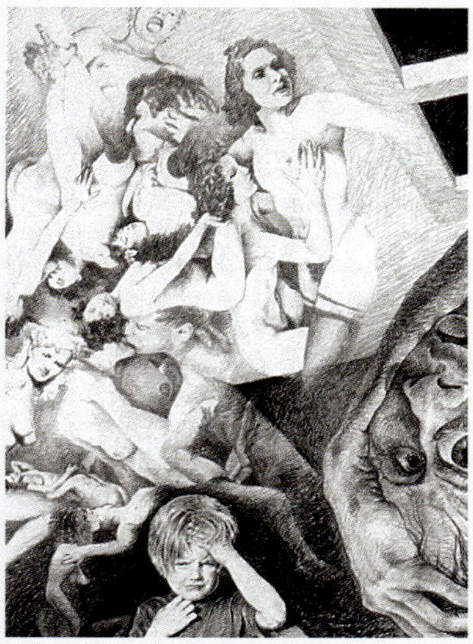

Eric White
***Self Portrait* (detail)**
1987
Graphite on board

through monographs in the RISD library was the British artist Peter Blake. Coming upon this particular book was a double whammy. For one thing, White realized that it was Blake who had created an image which he (and much of the world) had been fixated on for years: the cover of The Beatles' 1967 album *Sergeant Pepper's Lonely Hearts Club Band*. As an adult it occurred to White that in retrospect, along with Richard Hamilton's work for *The Beatles* (now referred to as simply *The White Album*), seeing the *Sergeant Pepper's* album as a small child was probably White's earliest exposure to "high art." And seeing Blake's *On The Balcony*—a 1955–1957 canvas that the artist had begun while still in college—sealed it for White. The work demonstrated that an artist could be a master of the most fastidious representational techniques imaginable and still make work as direct as a slap on the face. The picture is dense with meticulous detail and as intense as a fever dream. "Seeing that painting changed my life," White says. Moreover, *On The Balcony* is part of the permanent collection of the Tate Gallery in London, proving that artists with the skills of a Magic Realist did sit at the art world high table, alongside the hardcore Conceptualists, the second generation Minimalists, and other worthies of the Po-Mo menagerie.

A sophomore-year drawing class with the legendary RISD instructor Mahler Ryder resulted in another breakthrough. White had acquired some vintage 1950s-era pornography, and collaged some of the imagery together into a physically-impossible orgy, which he then integrated into a large graphite self-portrait. White says: "Somehow that piece foreshadowed what I was to do years later, and relates more to what I'm doing now than a lot of work I made in between." With his time at RISD coming to an end, White, like many of his friends, was considering a move to New York City. But his girlfriend at the time was set on returning to San Francisco, so in 1990, degrees in hand, they headed West.

White's appetite for retro had broadened, and he felt increasingly drawn to the aesthetic of 1940s Hollywood, so during down time he would compulsively watch old movies on television. One evening it was *A Place in the Sun* starring Elizabeth Taylor and Montgomery Clift:

> There's a pivotal romantic scene where she's staring at him and you see her face and the back of his head. The idea to deconstruct her beauty mark hit me out of nowhere. I drew a sketch of them, with a kind of diagrammatic thing radiating outward from the birthmark on her cheek in an attempt to extrapolate meaning. The moment was profound and very exciting—I can still picture exactly where I was, what the room looked like, how it felt, etc."

White recognized this as a breakout moment in his art-making; his approach was both a means to deploy his figurative strengths and charge the work with conceptual energy. The resulting painting, *A Place in the Sun (Explained)*, put the techniques he had been practicing to use, and magnified Taylor's features to such an extreme that without the painting's title, Liz Taylor's most devout fans would have been hard-pressed to identify her.

White segued into making art in which the fun-house-mirror distortions of the figure sometimes dominate, as with the woman and schoolchildren in his painting Czechsicle. Sometimes the subjects are refracted into multiple images or perspectives, creating pictures with a disorienting "fly's-eye" effect. In both cases, the figures retain an eerie, deadpan authenticity.

There is some kinship here to the work of the artists who had surfaced in the late 1980s and early 1990s in Los Angeles, where White first began to show his work. There is a significant difference, however: while these artists take pride in referencing and celebrating underground culture with garish and cartoonish imagery, White's

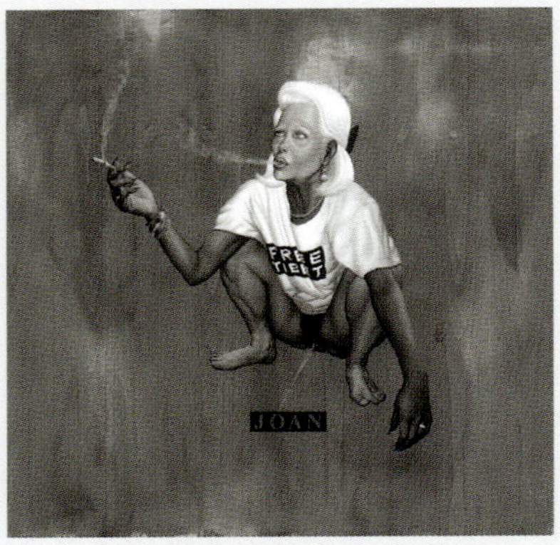

Ashley Bickerton (b. 1959)
Joan and the Cosmos
1996
Oil, acrylic, and pencil on wood
© 1996 Ashley Bickerton
Image courtesy Ashley Bickerton

work of this period strives to examine the insanity of "normal" American society, dissecting and reconstructing it with the precision and brutality of an Existentialist. It derives its manic energy not from channeling commercial culture but precisely from the exhilaration at shaking it off. White uses his technical skills and bits and pieces of familiar subject matter as raw materials with which to build obsessive, absurd, and sometimes scary worlds.

Another significant input came from the art world proper, which didn't quite yet have the culture of digital buzz it does today, and White's info about art world goings-on farther afield than California was spotty. "I knew about some mainstream contemporary artists at that point," he says. "But I wasn't aware of people like Ashley Bickerton until I started visiting New York." In 1996 he caught the Bickerton exhibition *Back to the Wall* at Sonnabend on West Broadway. Neo-Geometric Conceptualism was dead and gone and Bickerton, never shy of genial aggression, was on a tear of in-your-face ultra-realism: scary green-skinned demon-women and a squatting blonde in a FREE TIBET tee, smoking a ciggie and pissing. White says: "I'd never seen anything like it. They were just incredible. Demented, hilarious, and so technically unbelievable. It changed my perspective about the art world and what one could get away with. And to top it off, the last page of the show catalog read something like 'The artist formerly known as Ashley Bickerton is henceforth to be known as Cat Stevens,' which is one of the funniest things I've ever heard."

After a decade in San Francisco, and as if to regularize a major shift in his practice, no small part of which was the switch from acrylic to oil, White moved to New York in 2000. It is surely no coincidence that it was over this same period that, well, let's just say it was as if his fever broke. It was not that his skewed world became less hectic; rather, it was increasingly invaded by dark, buried psychological narratives that had perhaps been fermenting internally for a long while.

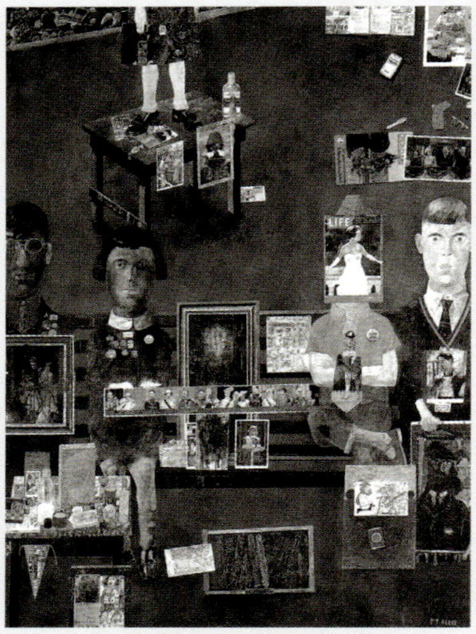

Peter Blake (b. 1932)
On the Balcony
1955–7
Oil on canvas
© 2015 Peter Blake. All rights reserved, DACS / Artists Rights Society (ARS), New York

Often when artists populate a picture space with human figures it's simply because they belong there, but there are artists who load their figures with specific meaning. So Edward Hopper's nighthawks exhale urban anomie and Magritte's figures are impenetrable blanks. The pictorial resonance to the figures in White's own pictures is often singular: that of characters in movies. Often, but by no means always. This is because they are based on a known actor—Robert Mitchum, Loretta Young, Shelley Duvall. But White is not using these familiar faces as Warhol used Marilyn, Liz, or Elvis. The narratives from which Warhol plucked their images is irrelevant, the subject of the work being their stardom, not the role they played. White uses his characters differently. They remain, so to speak, in character. Their presence signifies that they are playing a role, that their private emotions are available to us, so they command our attention and involve us in the story.

Sometimes, as when the actions depicted take place in automobiles (hello, Detroit) as in *1961 Ford Galaxie 500 Sunliner (Pierrot Le Fou)*, the characters are shown multiple times, compressing a stretch of time into a single image. The interactions in these automobile pictures take place in a shallow, artificial space—not the three-dimensional world that was opened up for us by the Renaissance, but which boxes us in after a fashion, an all-too-familiar sensation in our world of screens.

Then there are the single images, which can also be disorienting. Sometimes this is because of withheld information or incongruities of cropping and perspective. Jane, who is forefronted in the picture of the same name, is hanging her filmy pink knickers on a clothing line with a look of ethereal joy. Deep in the background a red van is parked. An apparently naked man with his back to us is confronting a mass of foliage. Is he relieving himself? The obvious narrative doesn't fit. In other canvases, White's figural world has been invaded by shapes of non-representational

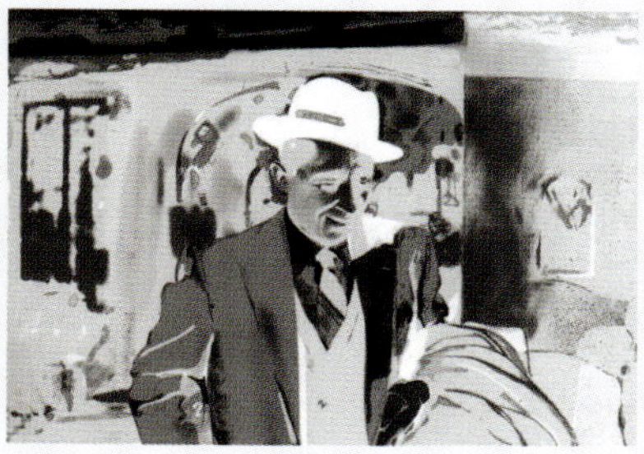

Richard Hamilton (1922–2011)
I'm Dreaming of a White Christmas
1967
Oil on canvas
© 2015 R. Hamilton. All Rights Reserved, DACS and ARS
Photo © 2015 Tate, London

otherness. The luminous gold circles in *Foyer*, the schematics in *Protocol*, or the black dots in *Albina*—all conceptual offspring of the spokes and whorls that emanated from Elizabeth Taylor's birthmark in *A Place In The Sun (Explained)*. There is nothing arbitrary here, nothing forced. The combination of meticulous craft and focused conceptual intensity brings to mind not only the influence of Peter Blake, but other maestros of Brit-Pop such as Richard Hamilton and Eduardo Paolozzi. Hamilton indeed made a painting based on a negative photographic still of Bing Crosby in *White Christmas*, which seems to salute White from a distant shore, as Paolozzi foreshadows White's obsession with the multiple worlds of the pulps.

In some of his more recent work White moves further into areas that might once have seemed overly bizarre, but which fit all too seamlessly into his evolving vision and our evolving world. In *Mommie Issues 2: The Reckoning* a few people sitting in a sparsely populated movie theater are texting while watching a film depicting a man at a desk defacing a magazine, while a woman on the phone stands naked before him and next to a television that broadcasts static. The painting *PENTAPLEX: Coming Attractions* prominently features the word "Vril" on one of the five movie screens (only three of which are visible). The word comes from *The Coming Race*, an 1881 novel by Edward Bulwer-Lytton, an English baron, better known for *The Last Days of Pompeii*. "Vril" was fluid energy, a power source for superior beings who inhabited subterranean caves. Bulwer-Lytton presented his belief-structure as fiction—unlike, say, L. Ron Hubbard—but believers in its truth included Madame Blavatsky, the founder of Theosophy, Rudolf Steiner, and Adolf Hitler. White says:

> According to an article I found a few years ago there was something called the 'Vril Society,' which grew out of a belief in the reality of that novel. The article referred to these five beautiful women who were psychic and were connected to some Nazi scientists who were working on the reverse engineering of UFO technology. The article was in German, and the English translation was horrendous, so maybe I misinterpreted some of that. But even if it's all complete bullshit it doesn't matter, because once I'm exposed to something like that it snaps my mind out of a habitual and lazy way of thinking and of viewing reality. It's really exciting to me, so sometimes I seek things like that out. It feels like it changes my brain chemistry a little bit—In a good way. So in *PENTAPLEX*, as well as in *The Lobby*, I decided to invent these fake movies with ridiculous or impossible subjects, or involving things or people hardly anyone gives a shit about but which are important to me. It's about imagining an alternate world in which these obscure things could exist in a mainstream way, and at the same time it's a reflection of how insane the world we inhabit is.

If White's artistic journey is only getting weirder and deeper and darker, that is perhaps because of the very nature of the New Real. Hence his references to sources as far-flung as the Multiverse, which is the theory—subscribed to by some physicists—that we inhabit only one of infinite universes. Or the equivalently modish notion that we may experience time in a linear way, but that from another standpoint everything is happening simultaneously. What with one thing and another, it doesn't look as if Eric White is going to be running out of strange ideas to make pictures about any time soon.

CINEMATOGRAPHER OF THE TRANSACTED IMAGE

DANIEL ROUNDS

In his paintings, drawings, and installations, Eric White uses the raw material of twentieth-century history and pop culture, including aspects of film and music, to subvert and recode the dominant narratives we tell ourselves about ourselves. In so doing, White strips away surface layers of social interaction to reveal what isn't said, showing us the appetites, drives, and desires that lurk beneath the machinery of our shared cultural iconography.

Here one might enter the familiar terrain of postmodern discourse and remark on the intertextual nature of his paintings while also referring to those aspects of the work that suggest "the play of signs, and the slippage of the signifier." One could also reference the Situationist International, the commodification of images, and refer, in turn, to White's strategic hijacking and reworking of shared cultural symbolism as a means to upend the hegemony of the capitalist cultural spectacle. Like other "culture-jammers," White regularly employs the tactic of *détournement* to rework the codes and texts found in pop culture, most specifically in his paintings appropriating imagery from cinema. Still, this sort of analysis falls short to the extent that it omits the disconcerting, primeval, and otherworldly aspects of White's oeuvre.

In painting after painting, White blurs the borders between the rational and irrational aspects of human behavior, as well as the civil and barbaric aspects of society, abutting and fusing, for example, the so-called technical-rational thinking characteristic of "advanced" western societies, with the sacred, violent, and erotic aspects of lived human experience.

For example, in the painting *The Sunday Funnies No. 1*, in a series of comic panels, White contrasts explicit pornographic imagery with meta-philosophic and mathematical discourses, situating thought and speech bubbles containing mathematical formulae and dialogue pertaining to "the reign of logic" above the naked and intertwined bodies of Charles Mingus and Katherine Hepburn. In one of the panels, Mingus performs cunnilingus on Hepburn while daydreaming about what appears to be an econometric function or a calculus equation. In another panel, Hepburn and Mingus

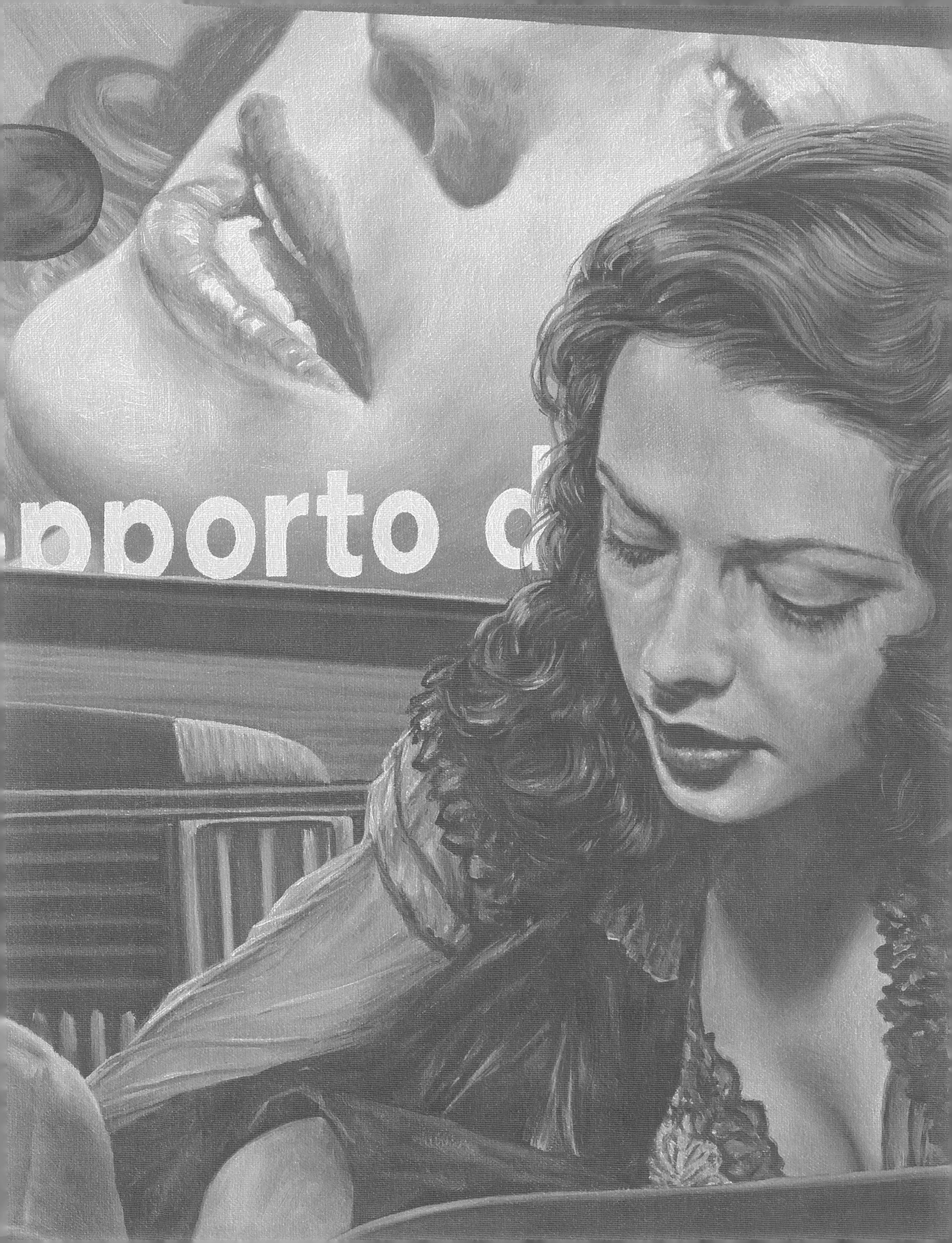
pporto d

express post-coital thoughts via André Breton's *Surrealist Manifesto*. They call into question whether our ability for logic and complex reasoning provides us with any respite to the problem of existential meaning.

In *Product (Anti-Love Expurgated)* White fuses the head of Eisenhower with the body of a deer and places a portrait of this Dwight-bambi-centaur-beast on a box of breakfast cereal that also contains a sequential diagram of moth pupas being subjected to scientific experiment.

Here White entwines the so-called rationalism of both science and the free market (represented graphically by the moth experiment and cereal box advertising) with the explicitly barbaric imagery of war. Whether intended or not, White's moth pupa seems to morph into mushroom clouds, phalluses, and two bombs dropping from the sky. By doing this, the artist channels the spirit of 1950s America by grounding its postwar economic power and pastoral domestic environs (the breakfast table) within the larger geo-political context of its growing military might. The imagery is rendered all the more poignant by the juxtaposition of mythic and/or "primitive" elements (the deer-centaur) with ratiocinative elements (the pupa experiment), implicitly problematizing mid-twentieth century notions of "civilizing" progress.

Sometimes the messaging is more subtle. In a series of paintings titled *Infinite Interior*, depicting scenes worthy of a Peter Nadas novel, White situates the naked bodies of men and women amid the interlocking salons and meeting rooms of the domestic quotidian.

In *No Neutral Thoughts*, a topless Gene Tierney in panties, with her face, hands, and thighs partially painted blue, sits in a leather chair, rolling her eyes toward the ceiling. Over her left shoulder, a vase of flowers coffee table and an enormous and eyeless Brando-esque head sit on a table. In *On The Air*, a group of naked middle-aged men can be seen through a window in the background, playing ball, while another unclothed woman wearing a mask of a man's head is positioned in the foreground, adjacent to what seems to be a working woman secretary. In *The Big Foist*, the viewer peers into a multi-paneled picture window at a woman in a pink chiffon dress holding
a long, flame-wicked matchstick. She stares back through the window while behind her, two men engage in conversation while a woman, fully dressed, passively looks on. Outside the room and to the immediate left and right of the window stand two nude women.

Does the imagery of the paintings comprising the series *Infinite Interior* offer a feminist critique of the everyday trafficking of the female body, or is White offering a critique of the domestication of the human animal amid the etiquette and cultural norms of the American bourgeoisie? Maybe he is doing both, while also expressing a degree of skepticism about our western view of individual subjectivity and our collective conceptions about Enlightenment progress. Maybe the self is not coherent or self-directed, but rather is something more like an amalgamated carnal vector of energy flows and appetites as Nietzsche and Deleuze and both theorized. Maybe the play of labyrinthian rooms and interlocking interiors and exteriors suggests an ever-changing map to the unseen-but-felt operative subconscious.

If the latter interpretation of the work has any purchase one might summarize the entire canon as offering a vision of the recent historical and contemporary landscape as somehow, "paramodern," by which I mean the work combines elements of the premodern, the modern and the postmodern, situating the human subjects of history in a jarring and paranormal atmosphere. As such, White then becomes a sort of Rabelaisian cinematographer of the transacted image, replaying and parodying reruns of times past on the screen of the eternal present.

In one of his most recent series of paintings, *Down In Front*, these tendencies come to the fore when White situates individuals and groups of famous actors, in scenes from famous movies, in cars, parked in front of movie screens at drive-ins. The backgrounds are awash with the great expanses of the American landscape while the paintings combine depictions of cinematic storytelling with performative yet partially censored acts of ongoing libidinal transactions.

The painting *Down in Front: Love in the Afternoon*, shows Harry Dean Stanton looking off into the distance of what appears to be a Southern California setting, as the sun sinks into an ocean somewhere not far off camera. To the right of Stanton, there is a billboard with German text, and on it we see a woman in high heels, legs held high above her shoulders by an unseen man, who presumably bears down on her. In the painting *Down In Front: Sedile Posteriore*, White repeats the same sort of content using different subjects from different eras in a nearly similar setting. Here we see, from the view of the backseat, two drive-in patrons, a couple in 1940s period style seated in the front seat, while through the windshield, we see a movie screen upon which is a woman's face, her mouth partially open, her lips lit-up by the director's lights and camera. The man in the front seat stares at the 1970s-era starlet on film, while his female partner faces away from the screen, looking down at what might be hands busily engaged in some sort of motion.

With these images, White casts the subjects of cinema as fetishized commodities employed by the culture industry as the raw material of both desire and myth-making. The sexed body is ever present and serves as a symbol for carnal reflexes, but it also represents itself as both totem and text, a sort of symbolic-yet-lived vehicle for the creative surplus energies surging around and across the surface of the painting's embodied social subjects.

The automobiles serve as a metaphor for the atomization and privatization of self in an era of American Empire. Individuals or couples, and even groups in some instances, are separated from one another by the walls of their cars. At the same time the movie screen is cast as the tabula rasa of the American mind. On its surface, desire is projected, constructed, and transacted in an ongoing dialogue between members of the viewing audience and the celebrity factotums that serve as the avatars of America's mythical narratives.

White thrusts his bodily subjects into an atopic landscape of boredom, alienation, and desire. Is it any wonder that White's paintings tend to disconcert the viewer, yet also leave him or her feeling somehow enlivened or even stimulated?

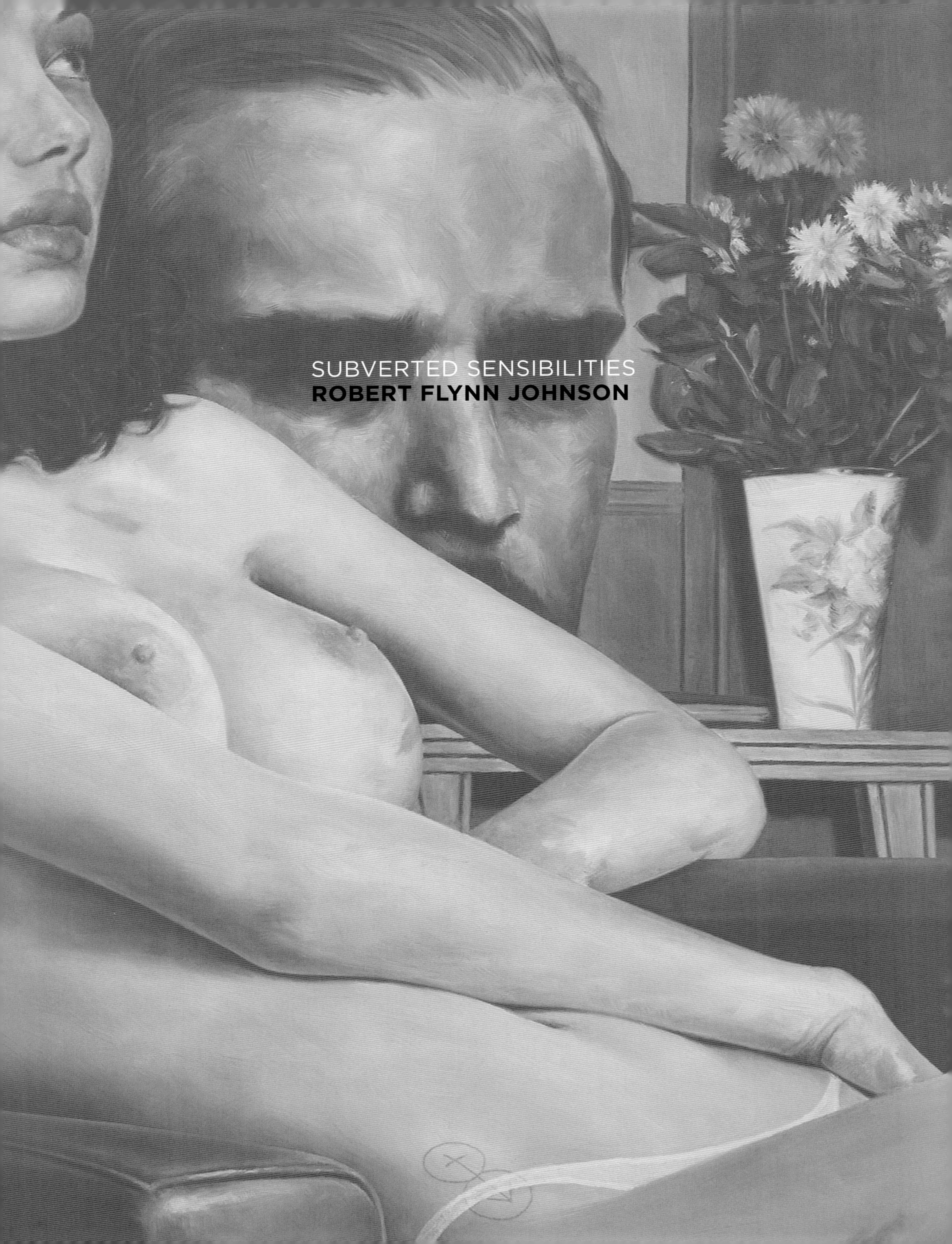

SUBVERTED SENSIBILITIES

ROBERT FLYNN JOHNSON

"All good art is an indiscretion."
—Tennessee Williams, *Memoirs* [1]

The art of Eric White forces us to view the world on his terms. His technical virtuosity and vivid imagery confront us with an unsettling and disorienting Through the Looking Glass vision of life.

The renowned English playwright Tom Stoppard ruefully remarked, "Skill without imagination is craftsmanship and gives us many useful objects such as wickerwork picnic baskets. Imagination without skill gives us modern art."[2] In many contemporary art circles today, the appearance of technical skill in drawing and painting is often grounds for the dismissive put-down that the artist is quaintly displaying mere craft. This woefully arrogant viewpoint unfairly uses the great Marcel Duchamp as the exemplar that "idea" is all one needs to triumph in art today. It is a bankrupt concept which is why the majority of educated individuals find so much of contemporary art devoid of meaning, increasingly irrelevant, and borderline ludicrous. Into this often-"emperor's new clothes" environment of style over substance comes the subversive art of Eric White. His painting and drawing bring reassurance to the notion that visual imagination in combination with consummate skill can produce a significant contribution to the art of our time and place.

Born in Ann Arbor, Michigan in 1968 into a middle-class family, White's first interaction with art came from his paternal grandfather who was an amateur artist. However, White's true artistic evolution began with his attendance at the Rhode Island School of Design. White majored in the seemingly conservative medium of illustration, bucking the fashionable trends of conceptualism at the time. This choice inadvertently provided him with the necessary technical skills to allow him to realize his extraordinarily complex representational imagery in his mature style. Emblematic of his generation in his unabashed receptiveness, White utilizes free associations of music, cars, women, and scenes of contemporary life. However, he is also highly individualistic if not downright quirky, often working in a monochromatic palette and with obsessive references to scenes in cinema from films made long before he was born. This mixture of new trends and old traditions makes White's art both perplexing and compelling.

White states:

> We all walk around in a hypnotized state and are conditioned to live with such a narrow view of the universe. I am interested in anything that shakes me out of this state of waking unconsciousness. I'm not saying my work necessarily does this; I just hope it somehow subconsciously conveys the notion that our perception of reality isn't necessarily the truth.[3]

White's paintings are populated by individuals both vaguely familiar yet totally foreign to our contemporary eyes. Like ghosts in a Charles Dickens novel, they glide in and out of his compositions seemingly real yet steadfastly apparitions from the past. Their presence, carrying with them a kind of melancholy, recalls the narrator of Nathaniel West's indelible observations of doomed inhabitants of Hollywood in his 1939 classic, *The Day of the Locust*:

> . . . He examined the evening crowd. A great many of the people wore sports clothes, which were not really sports clothes. Their sweaters, knickers, slacks, blue flannel jackets with brass buttons were fancy dress. The fat lady in the yachting cap was going shopping, not boating; the man in the Norfolk jacket and Tyrolean hat was returning not from a mountain, but from an insurance office; and the girl in slacks and sneaks with a bandana around her head had just left a switchboard, not a tennis court. . . . It's hard to laugh at the need for beauty and romance no matter how tasteless, even horrible the results of that need are. But it is easy to sigh. Few things are sadder than the truly monstrous.[4]

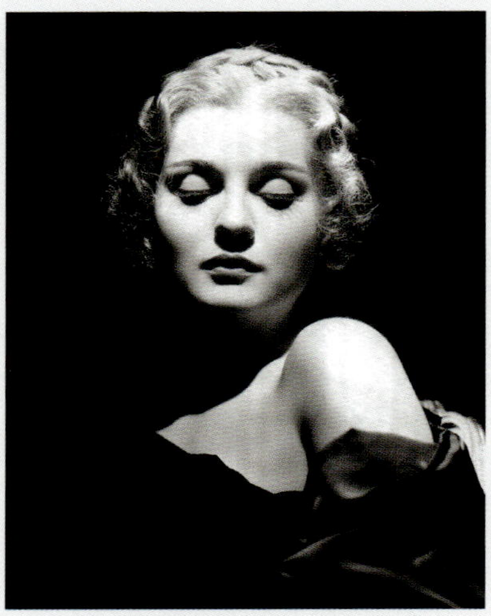

Portrait of Anna Sten
Anonymous
ca. 1935
Metro-Goldwyn-Mayer

In viewing Eric White's art there is an implication that one is catching a glimpse of an ongoing emotional interaction often at a critical, disquieting moment. The narrative is intriguing and mysterious, which is exactly the way White wishes it to remain. Picasso wisely said, "A picture is not thought out and settled beforehand. While it is being done it changes as one's thoughts change. And when it is finished it still goes on changing, according to the state of mind of whoever is looking at it."[5]

Eric White is expansive in his revelation of cultural influences. In the 2003 book *It Feeds Itself*, White created a list of more than seven hundred artists, writers, and musicians ranging from Jan van Eyck and H. P. Lovecraft to Billie Holiday and Jim Jarmusch. The list is an excessive yet fascinating outpouring of personal associations that White shares with us, allowing speculation as to how many of these diverse individuals worked their way into his artistic vision. The direct parallels to White's art, however, are not only among visual artists. Instead they seem more directly linked to the bleak assessment of life in the writings of authors that he lists such as Nathaniel West, George Orwell, Hunter S. Thompson, and Charles Bukowski. In turn, he also pays homage to the hallucinatory cinematic visions of filmmakers like John Cassavetes, Luis Buñuel, Nicolas Roeg, and David Lynch, along with the wry cynicism of Rainer Werner Fassbinder and Paul Thomas Anderson.

Eric White has made no secret of his love of cinema and its influence on his work, especially the symbol of the sultry femme fatale, a hallmark of film noir movies of the 1940s and '50s. His use of moments from classic films from that era, as well as more contemporary cinema, function as crucial compositional and contextual elements in White's recent work, folding their recognizable content effortlessly into his own. White commented:

> I really love the imagery from that era. I love the films, and have a large collection of books on the subject. I find it endlessly inspiring and

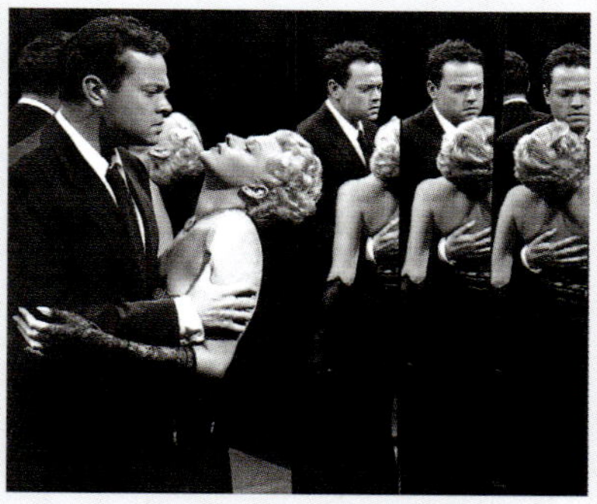

The Lady from Shanghai

Courtesy Columbia Pictures

> aesthetically compelling. The Hollywood starlet to me represents an idealized mother figure. I'm very interested in the unconscious mind and the way infantile psychology figures in, and how decisions made before the age of five, invariably involving the mother, can determine the direction and scope of our entire lives. Also, metaphysically speaking, I think of a movie as an invented reality, which I equate with the theory that our reality is some sort of illusory projection of consciousness.[6]

White's art is the shattered shards of our collective consciousness muddled by an ever-expanding visual and electronic overload of stimuli from all directions. Like the prescient vision of Orson Welles in the 1947 noir classic, *The Lady from Shanghai*, we are trapped in the crashing glass of a hall of mirrors where the dizzying fragmentation of shadows and reflections distorts reality and our emotions.

The environment of an artist is insightful as to their working method even though it does not necessarily collate directly to their finished work. Gerhard Richter's Cologne studio, for example, in keeping with his meticulous art, looks more like the orderly laboratory of a doctor or scientist. In turn, the rough hewed sculptures of Alberto Giacometti emerged out of the dust filled chaos of his decrepit Parisian hovel. Contrasting means versus ends, the London studio of Francis Bacon was engulfed by visual stimuli. A plethora of books, photographs, and reproductions littered the floor of his studio yet out of this clutter came paintings of consummate skill, elegant surface, and intellectual rigor. Similar to Bacon, Eric White embraces a riot of visual overload in his studio to stimulate and embolden his imagination. The walls and shelves display an array of imagery and objects harking back to adolescent obsessions and more recent mature preoccupations. White does not allow the seemingly visual confusion of his studio to distract him from his creativity but, instead, channels it into the complex but orderly nature of his finished work.

The successful reception of any contemporary art in our society today is highly problematic. Regardless of how original or well composed, art today seems sadly dependent on no more than twenty percent "execution" by the artist at best and eighty percent "perception" by an often uninformed and easily manipulated public. It is interesting that up to this point in his career, the most receptive critical and commercial response to Eric White's art has come from Los Angeles and Europe, among their galleries, collectors, and critics. This is puzzling in light of White's obvious talent and the fact that he made New York his home for a decade and a half. A possible explanation might be that the incorporation of cinematic imagery in White's work strikes a chord of recognition in the film community of Los Angeles, while the clearly intense, intellectually challenging content of his art, infused with overtones of nostalgic American cultural references, holds a fascination with Europeans. Regardless, it is only a matter of time before the East Coast art establishment truly recognizes and embraces the achievement of one who works in their midst.

The art of Eric White is a constantly-moving target of creative energy, a wellspring of dazzlingly yet often disorienting subject matter backed by consummate draftsmanship and painterly finesse. In the simplest of terms, Eric White's achievement is the art of now, capturing on canvas and paper the zeitgeist we inhabit. His art reflects his generation with all its talents, contradictions, anxieties, and aspirations. He has the heart of an iconoclast, the head of a historian, and the wickedly creative sleight of hand of a magician—so you would not want to bet against what artistic cards he will next lay down upon the table.

Robert Flynn Johnson
Curator Emeritus
Achenbach Foundation for Graphic Arts, Fine Arts Museums of San Francisco

Footnotes

1 Tennessee Williams. *Memoirs* (New York: New Directions, 2006), p. 144.
2 Tom Stoppard. *Artist Descending a Staircase* (1972).
3 J. L. Schnabel. Interview with Eric White, *The New Contemporary Art Magazine*, September 17, 2011.
4 Nathaniel West. *The Day of the Locust* (New York: Random House, 1939), pp. 5, 7.
5 Dare Ashton, editor. *The Documents of Twentieth Century Art: Picasso on Art, A Selection of Views* (New York: Viking Press, 1972) p. 8.
6 Eric White.

INTERVIEW
PETER COYOTE AND ERIC WHITE

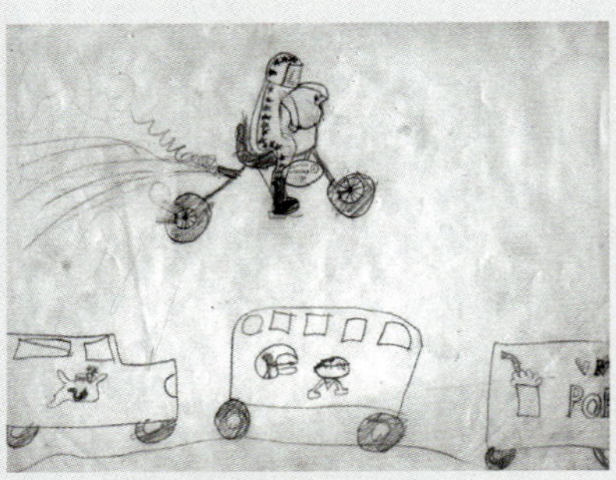

Eric White
Evel Knievel
1973
Graphite on paper

PC: Obviously craft is an abiding concern of yours (and a relief to see). Non-representational art has freed artists from what used to be the universal measure of skill—reproducing physical reality—and in reviewing contemporary work one often wonders, "Can he draw?" The great Italian portraitist Pietro Annigoni said, "Impulse alone does not make a work of art." And in a book of his collected works he stated that the abandonment of Nature as the model will turn out to be one of the great errors of the art world. Before asking you about that second statement, I'd like to get some idea of your thinking about craft. How much was studied? How much was innate? And why, as your work delves into the collective unconscious of America, you felt it necessary to harness rigorous craft to that exploration?

EW: There was a period as a kid where I would work from my imagination, albeit with cultural influences. I'd create little worlds populated by superheroes and Evel Knievel, and later couldn't help but rip off *Star Wars*. All through elementary school I had an amazing art teacher named Jo Miles Schuman, who incidentally published one of the first books on the teaching of multicultural art. She was incredibly kind and encouraging, and I think her influence was a significant factor in my interest in art at a young age. She showed us *Calder's Circus*, which completely astounded me. At some point early on I discovered the books of Ed Emberley, who had developed a brilliant and basic drawing method using geometric shapes. I became obsessed and collected all of his books. I could already draw pretty well, so it wasn't the instruction but rather his particular style that I was excited about. My burgeoning control freak tendencies compelled me to attempt to copy his drawings exactly. Years later my mom signed me up for a class on Betty Edwards's book *Drawing On The Right Side Of The Brain*, which was a huge turning point for me. Its various exercises help one to let go of preconceived notions and get closer to the way things actually look. The instructor, Kay Gould-Caskey, later became my private art teacher and good friend,

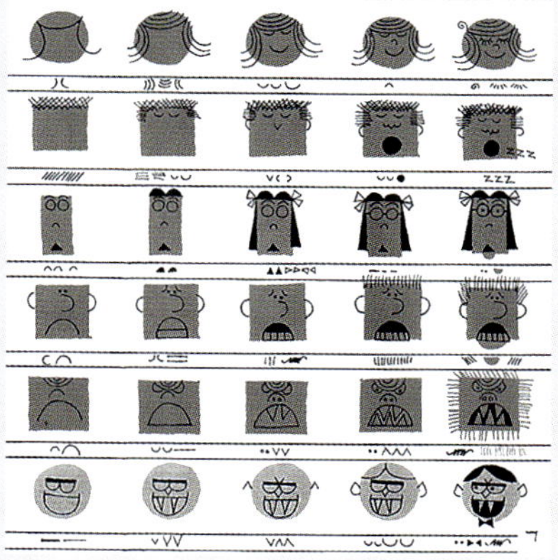

Ed Emberley (b. 1931)
Detail from *Ed Emberley's Drawing Book of Faces*

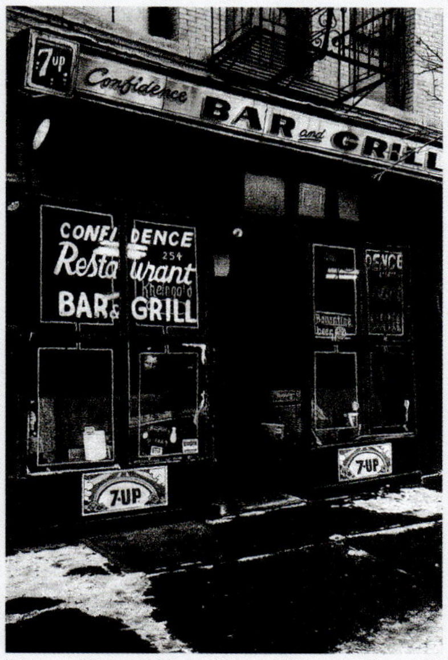

Eric White
Confidence Bar and Grill
1986
Graphite on board

and I worked closely with her for many years until I went off to college. In fact, she was instrumental in convincing my parents to let me go to art school. They were always incredibly supportive of my interest in art, but wanted me to get a more practical academic degree and minor in art. While working with Kay I realized I could draw from a photograph and get it pretty damn close. Once I had experienced the satisfaction of replicating reality I became determined to get better and better at it. By the time I got to RISD, I knew my major was either going to be painting or illustration. We had to make a decision after only one semester, and at that point I didn't really understand the implications of either choice. I remember someone saying that if I went with painting I would have to become a teacher to make a living, which sounded awful at the time. So I went the more practical, commercial route, and obviously there was a great deal of the study of craft. I Initially saw being a commercial artist as my long-term career path, but after doing it for a couple years I became bored and a lot of the work I was doing felt disposable. Most importantly I wasn't expressing the ideas that were in my head. But I was drawing and painting every day, so I look at that period as a sort of boot camp, a training that has benefitted me to this day. So there may be an aspect of craft that is innate, but for me I mostly think it's the thousands of hours of practice. I've only met a small handful of people in my life who do seem to have some kind of innate talent, and it's nauseating to see. My roommate at RISD had it, and everything he did seemed to be imbued with a sense of grace. He made drawing and painting look completely effortless. He was probably the most talented person I saw in my four years there, but I don't think he even realized he had it, and eventually he dropped out. I certainly don't think I have the natural flow of ability that the few folks I'm thinking of possess. I've really had to work at it, and I think that's true for most artists.

In terms of working with a high level of craft, for me it's a satisfying way of making art and always has been. I don't know if it's done out of necessity or if it's even a choice. Perhaps it's my way of asserting control in a chaotic reality.

I think it helps the viewer identify with something immediately, allowing them to enter into the reality of the picture and be affected by the things going on there. If they're engaging in a visually familiar world it's easier to take them to the next level conceptually.

As for Annigoni's statement, I do get his point, and we're certainly on the same team, but I don't entirely agree with him. It is true in many cases, but I think there is plenty of art that is devoid of highly skilled craft yet does have power and stands on its own. I don't see the revolutionary moves that Duchamp made or abstract expressionism or conceptual art being dismissed in the future because of a reliance on idea, impulse, or action. I think art would be incredibly boring if everyone depicted only aspects of nature, and as it is I find a lot of representational work pretty uninteresting. As I get older, I find myself more excited by work that is further afield from mine. I am thoroughly impressed when I see a successful abstract work, since I know how hard it is to do. There is certainly a lot of garbage abstraction, but then again, there's a lot of garbage everything. My mind was blown by the Sigmar Polke show at MoMA. That guy could do anything. John Baldessari is one of my favorite artists, and he relies heavily on idea and has made a huge body of compelling and groundbreaking (and often hilarious) work.

PC: Back to Annigoni. It is obvious that imitation of nature is not your concern, and I would hazard that your work is kind of a modern extension of early Picasso's where he intended to show the multiplicity of views of even a single person or event.

EW: In that respect there is a connection to Cubism. I'm interested in the complexity of the various facets of personality

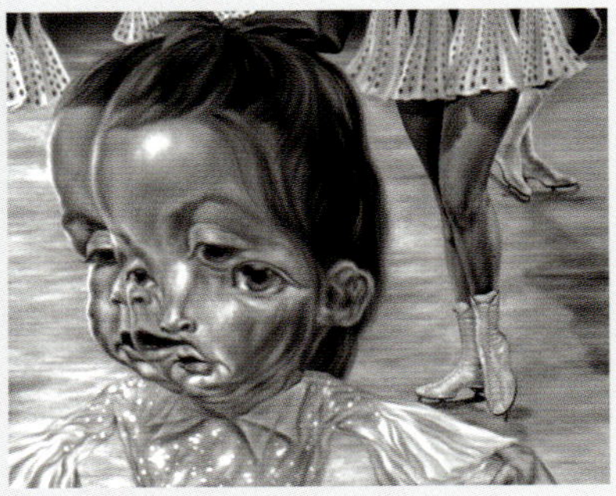

Eric White
Production Number **(detail)**
1999
Oil on canvas

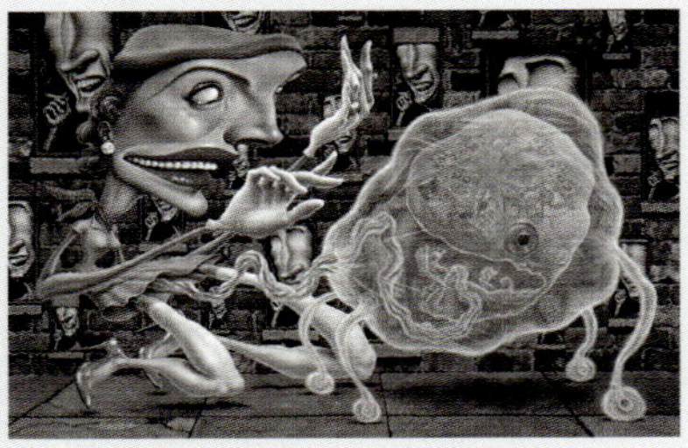

Eric White
You Add Fresh Eggs
1996
Acrylic on board

and psychology, and I like thinking about the possibility of multidimensional existence. I also like the challenge of trying to create the sense of a temporal progression in a static image. I'm using repetition and superimposition as a means to convey the passage of time, and in the compression of a sequence of events into a single instant. I think that's why I was so excited about the multiple exposure portraits, because I was able to represent different aspects of a personality and of time in one picture. That came about by accident (if there is such a thing) when I was sketching *Production Number*. I was just learning photoshop and didn't know what the hell I was doing, and I inadvertently superimposed one version of a face over another. The result was startling and exciting, and fit within my own "conceptual continuity," as Frank Zappa calls it. Imitation of nature in the traditional sense is not what I'm up to. We don't think about it because it's all we've ever known, but until just a couple hundred years ago, all people had to look at (aside from each other) was the natural world—the countryside and it's flora and fauna. We are now living in a synthetic ecosystem, a landscape of media and images and advertising, which does constitute the "natural" environment for most of us. So in a sense by drawing on this relatively new cultural landscape, I do consider myself to be imitating nature.

PC: Your works incorporate celebrity, films, and iconic images (which often have cheap and ready-made associations) that you break up and distort in a way which, to my eye, does two things: First, it allows us to regard the original without the attachment of superficial cultural "semiotics," and second, by exaggerating and distorting certain aspects of the image and conflating it with overlays from science, religion, etc., you create a tension that liberates the image and lets it float in a wholly new reality. Do you think I'm correct about this observation? If so, please expand on it and describe the degree to which this process is both rigorously intellectual, and also completely impulsive.

EW: Yes, I think you're correct. Often I'm appropriating specific imagery that has it's own existing context and I'm placing it into a new frame of reference. I try to free up the existing narrative so that it's open to broader interpretation. I like to keep things anchored in a familiar reality, but then upend it with a distortion or an incongruity. That seems intellectual to me. But there is definitely randomness and intuitiveness associated with my process and with the conception and composition of the work. The desire to make the type of work that I make was not intellectual at first; rather, it developed naturally over time without awareness of where it was coming from or where it was going. Now that I work this way it does tend to get intellectualized and I sometimes have to step out of my own way to let the impulsiveness back in.

I often think, "How can I bring more of myself into these paintings?" Not to have it more about me in a narcissistic way, but in order to be open and explore my own psychology in my work. I once had a therapist say "Oh, another mommy painting." This was kind of striking at the time—I hadn't really thought of it that directly before then. Baldessari said: "I'm just interested in fucking people up when they're looking at my work. I think the artist should make things difficult for the viewer." For me it isn't about being weird for weird's sake, or to be sensational or shocking for no reason. I've always found normal life to be pretty frightening, and a lot of my work is an expression of that fear. We're living in a schizophrenic world, and we're also half asleep, so things need to be amplified a bit in order to communicate the message to our over-stimulated and desensitized brains. William Gibson said: "I'm not trying to predict the future, I am trying to use science fiction to somewhat understand an unthinkable present." I think I'm doing something similar with my work, by attempting to manifest a parallel but skewed reality to remind people that our

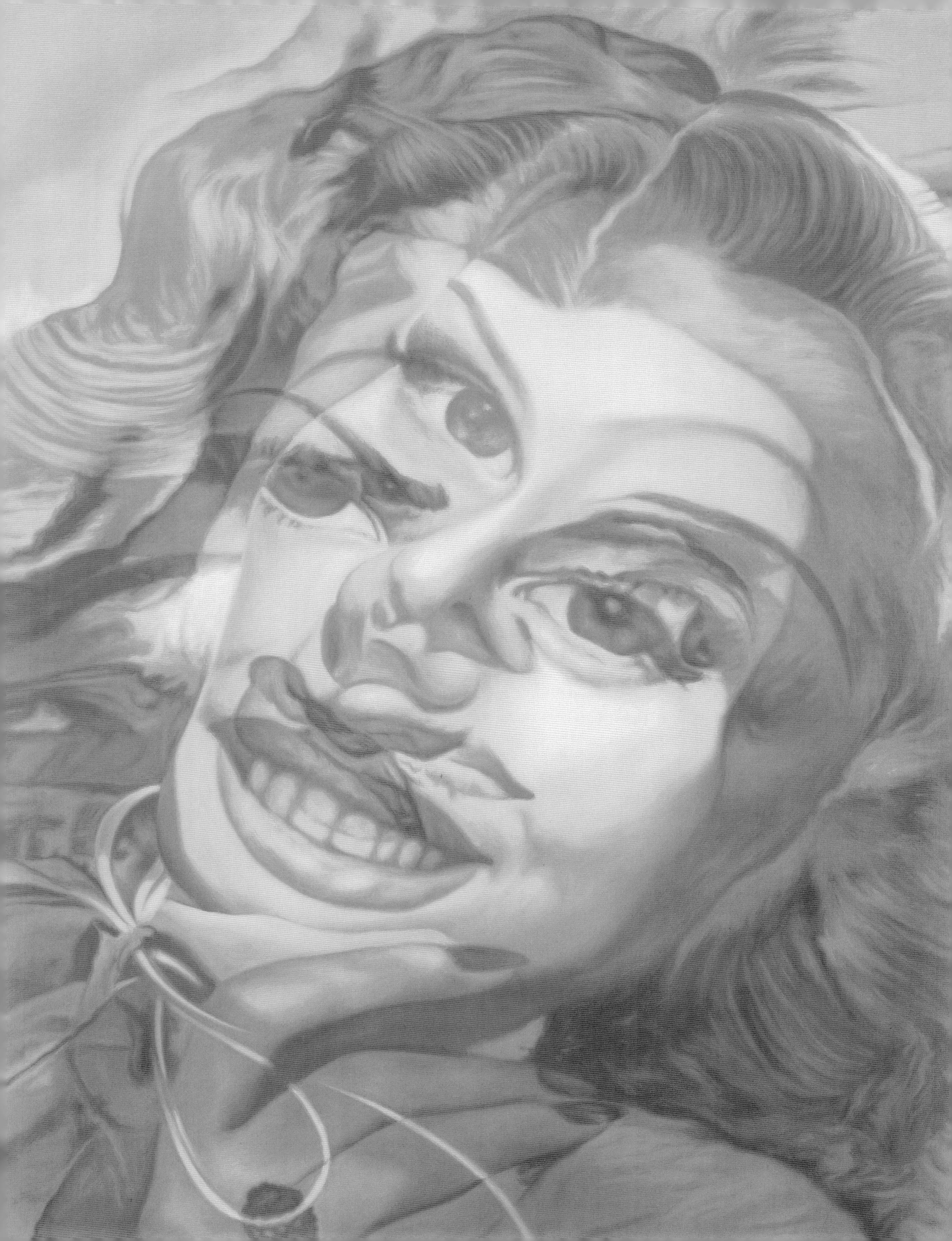

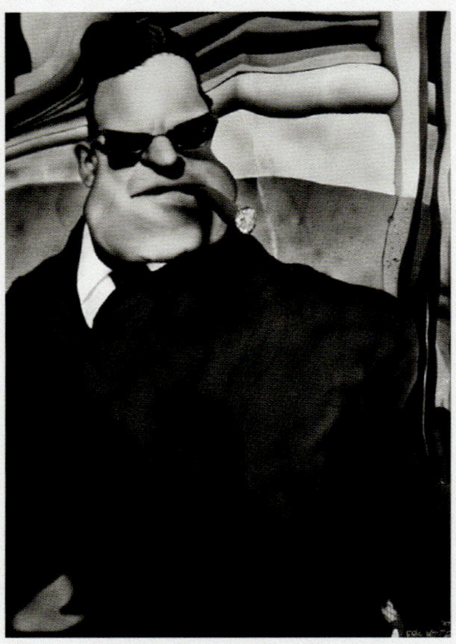

Eric White
Cigar Man
1987
Gouache on board

perception of reality is not reality itself. I'm fascinated by the way we confuse our subjective view of the world with objective facts. It's a concept fundamental to my work. We generally operate as if our *perception* of reality is the way it *is*. Unless you can step outside of that and realize that it's only your interpretation of it, not the way it actually is, everything you're experiencing will be colored by your perception, and you won't even know it. What if there are things which exist beyond our senses that are impossible for us to perceive or comprehend. For example, time may not progress in a linear way at all, but our brains are only capable of comprehending it that way. Quantum physics has shown that matter can actually exist in multiple places simultaneously. Neither of these concepts make any sense to a rational mind. I love the idea that our underlying concepts about reality may be completely wrong.

PC: One of the most provocative and specific impacts of visual imagery is that one can conflate them (as Eisenstein discovered) in ways where one image affects the other, altering its original associations and creating something "unspeakable"—something that cannot be described in language because it was not born of language. There's a shadow side to this, especially in this world of easy and facile reproductions, where "artists" conflate different images and the viewer simply likes them or doesn't, but the artist rests immune from criticism. I think that your work directs such meticulous attention to the surface and the impeccable representation (even of distorted perception) that you sidestep the question of skill. However, do you create these paintings (particularly—*Czechsicle*, *Golden Moments*, or *Holy Matron of Ridicule*) from an "idea," an impulse that leads to another impulse, or one or the other, which, by stepping back and evaluating what you've placed on the canvas, you become drawn to the next piece of it?

EW: It's a subtle distinction, but I'd say the answer is both, depending on the piece. Hopefully the visual reality of the picture is sufficiently grounded and the technical aspects become secondary, allowing the concept to come forward. In the case of both *Czechsicle* and *Golden Moments*, the initial inspiration came from found photographs. I bought a bunch of old class pictures when I was in Prague, and *Czechsicle* developed from there. The deer image is from a publicity still I found in a film book. I cropped it with a circular motif that I had developed for *Spores Of Today*, and superimposed it over a found '70s family portrait. *Holy Matron of Ridicule* was a further exploration of the idea of a multidimensional portrait. Sometimes there is an idea before there is any reference imagery at all. I then look for and/or take photographs to flesh out the idea, which was the case with *Mommie Issues 2: The Reckoning*. Day after day I would work in a sketchbook trying to envision what the show would be about and what the paintings would look like, and I kept drawing this image of people watching a movie about a guy defacing a magazine. I just couldn't get it out of my head and I don't know where it came from. In the painting a man is drawing cartoon faces on photographs in a magazine, while a woman talking on the phone stands naked in front of him. There is some bizarre kind of sexual tension going on, and the guy is consciously making himself oblivious to what's directly in front of him by engaging in a childish activity. Psychologically I think it's about being unwilling to really engage and be vulnerable to another person in a real relationship. It was yet another case where the entire concept was just kind of there, I didn't really have to work at it very hard and I could not escape it. There are times when something seems to open up and ideas suddenly come pouring through. I don't really understand it, but I tend to think it is coming from some level beyond consciousness. Mondrian said, "The position of the artist is humble. He is essentially a channel." I wish inspiration was something that I could generate on a consistent basis, but it doesn't often happen like that. When it does it's pretty remarkable. But I'm running a business and I have to eat. I don't have a trust fund to fall back on, so most of the time I just have to force it and work like hell and hope for the best. As Chuck Close says, "Inspiration is for amateurs; the rest of us just show up and get to work."

PC: Do you have any conscious connections to the work of Gerhard Richter?

EW: I respect him and like a lot of his work, but I don't think I draw a line to him consciously. I love his painting *Betty*, and I like his early smeared black and white stuff. I'm not a big fan of his abstraction. It seems a bit too calculated. Apparently I do have an unconscious connection to his work, however. Years ago I made a painting called *Swims*, which is a beach scene from a normal perspective, with another beach upside down in the sky. A few years later I went to a Richter retrospective at SF MoMA, and saw a painting that was basically the same concept—an ocean on the bottom and top, with a band of sky in between. I'd never seen it before that moment and I wanted to throw up. It was so upsetting because I thought I had come up with something really unique. Speaking of that painting, a strange thing happened with the title. Generally titles either seem to come out of nowhere and are exactly right, or they require a lot of work. With *Swims*, the perfect title suddenly materialized with zero effort while I was still working on the painting. I didn't realize until much later that it fit even more perfectly than I'd thought—it was pointed out to me that the word spells the same thing when flipped upside down. I couldn't believe it. It was not at all intentional, but how could it have been merely a coincidence? Some might say it was my unconscious mind at work, which in itself would be pretty remarkable, but I tend to believe that it came from somewhere else, though I don't pretend to understand how.

PC: How do you judge the success or failure of your own works?

EW: Because my work is often so labor-intensive and complex, I sometimes simply run out of time, in which case it's pretty easy to consider a piece a failure. I could probably continue to work indefinitely on just about every piece I've ever made. It's impossible to ever be objective about one's work, but with some physical distance and time, I'm more capable of judging it fairly. I can be a pretty harsh critic of my work and I'm definitely a perfectionist, but sometimes I'm pleasantly surprised when I see something I haven't seen in a while. There are a lot of pieces that I wish had never been released into the world, but one day I will be dead and won't have anxiety about that anymore. And before that day comes I'll have another bonfire to destroy a few ugly things I still have in my inventory . . .

SELECTED WORKS

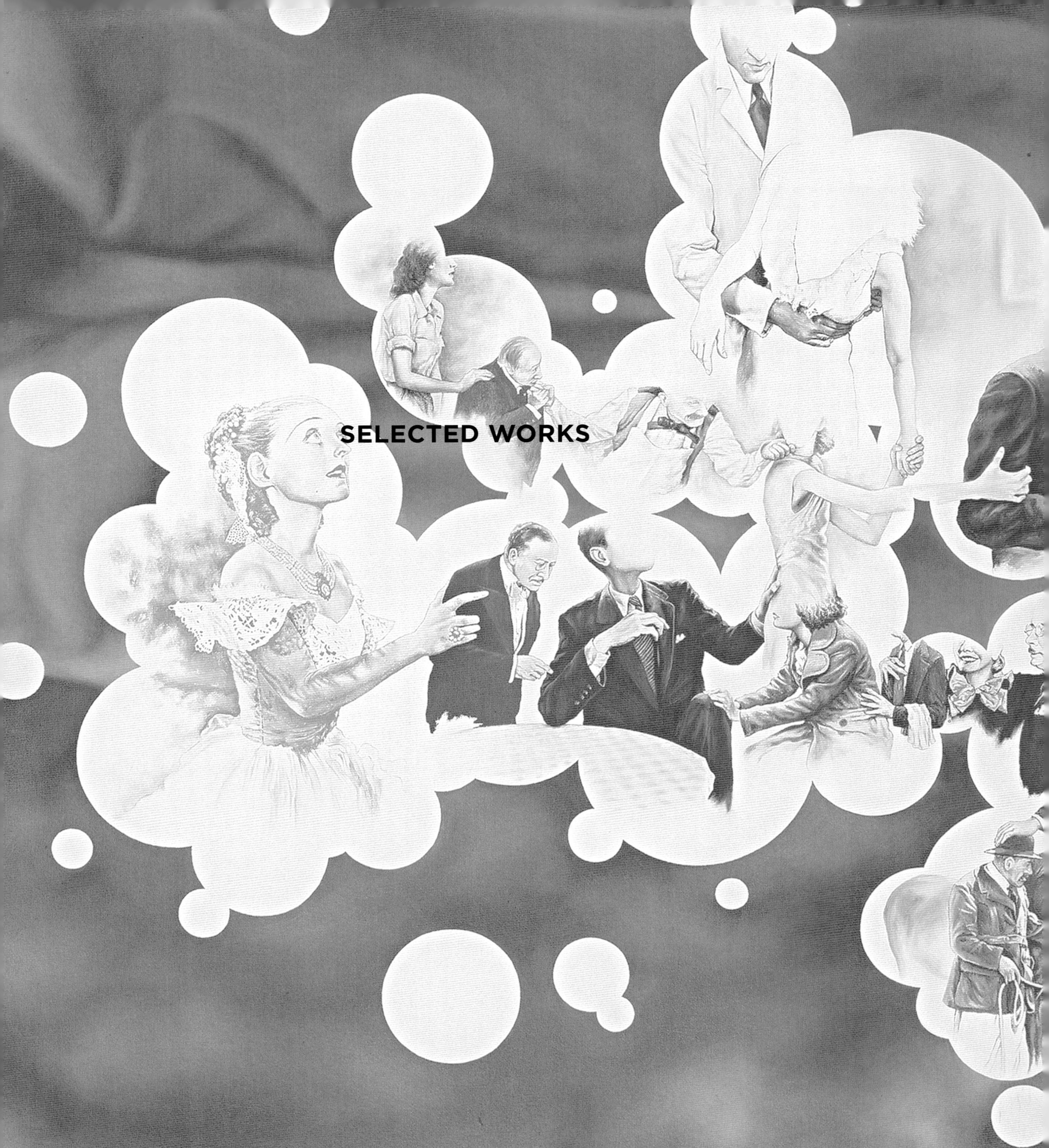

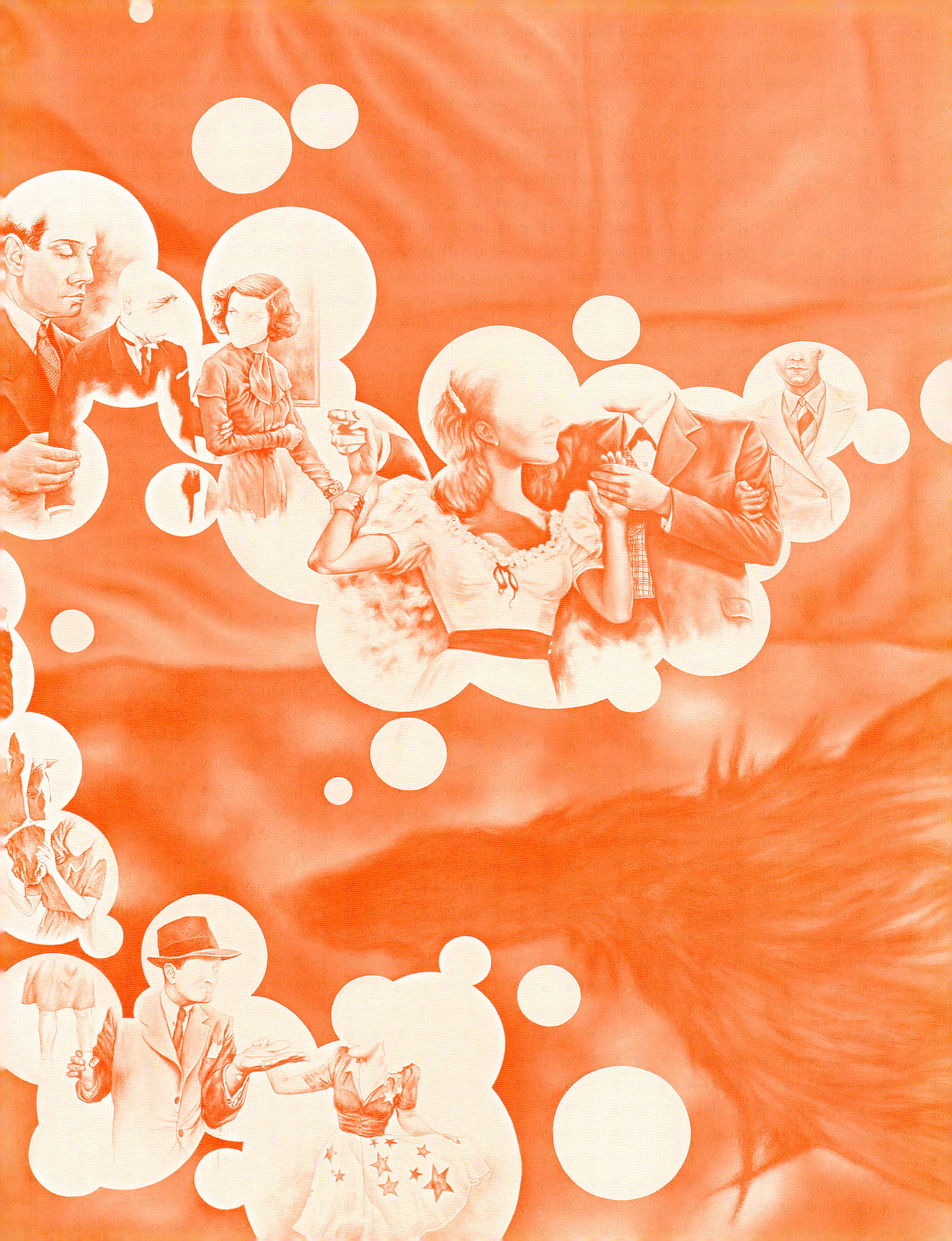

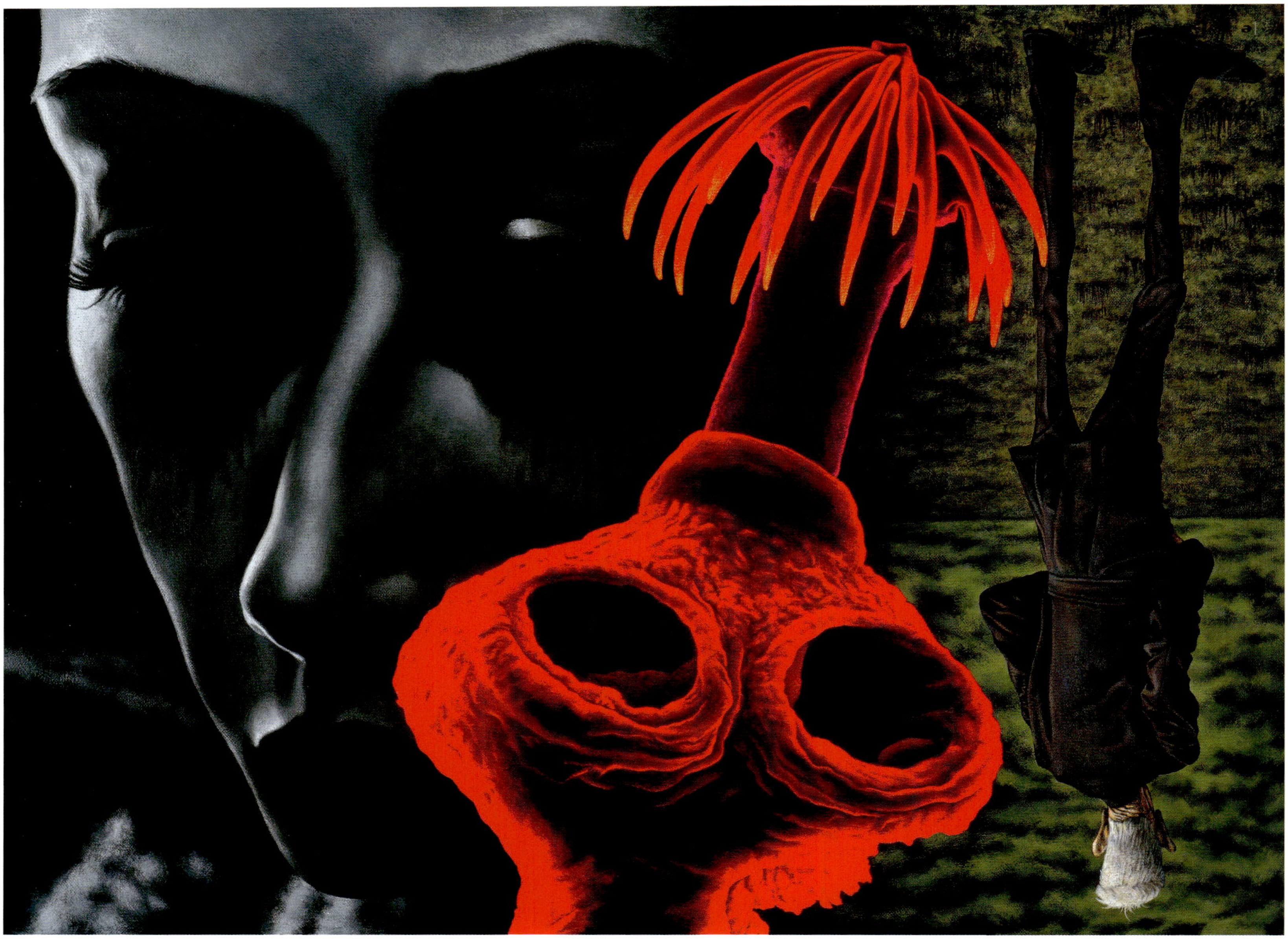

Preceding page:
Spores of Today (Anima Rising)
(detail)
2003
Oil on canvas
35 x 72 in.

Expulsion From Paradise
1996
Acrylic on canvas
18 x 24 in.

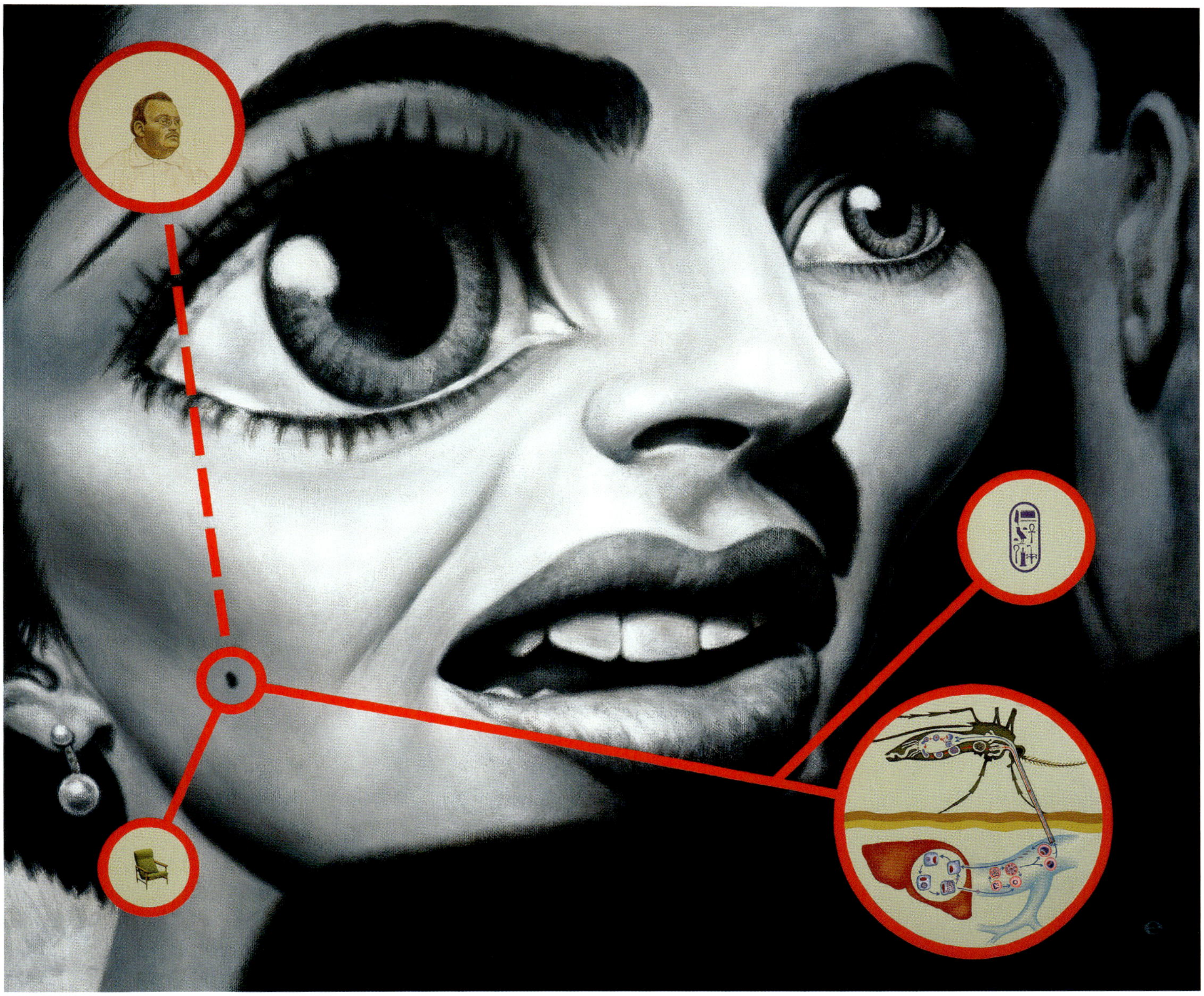

A Place In The Sun (explained)
1996
Acrylic on canvas
20 x 24 in.

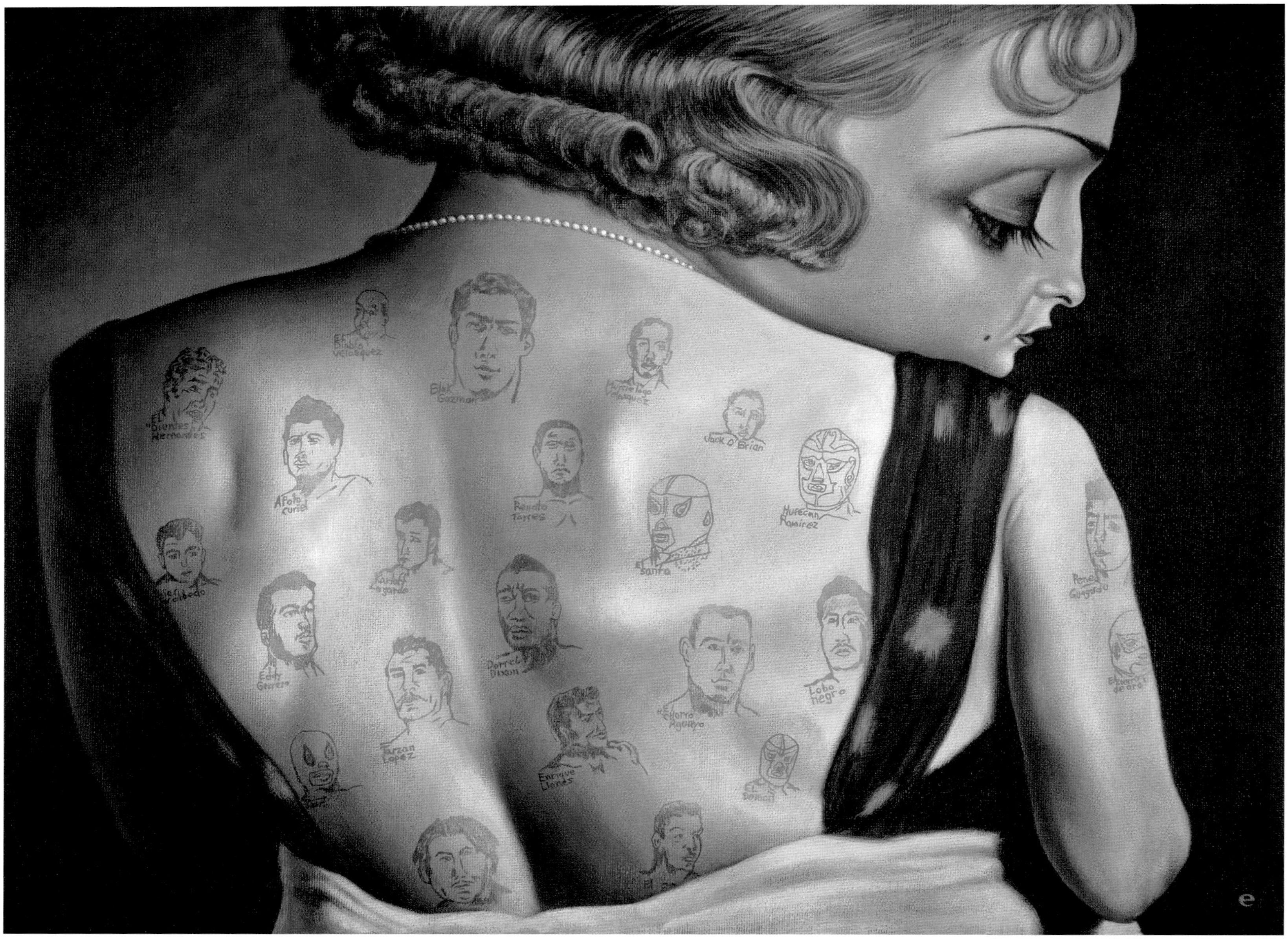

Pursuit Of Happiness
1996
Acrylic on canvas
12 x 16 in.

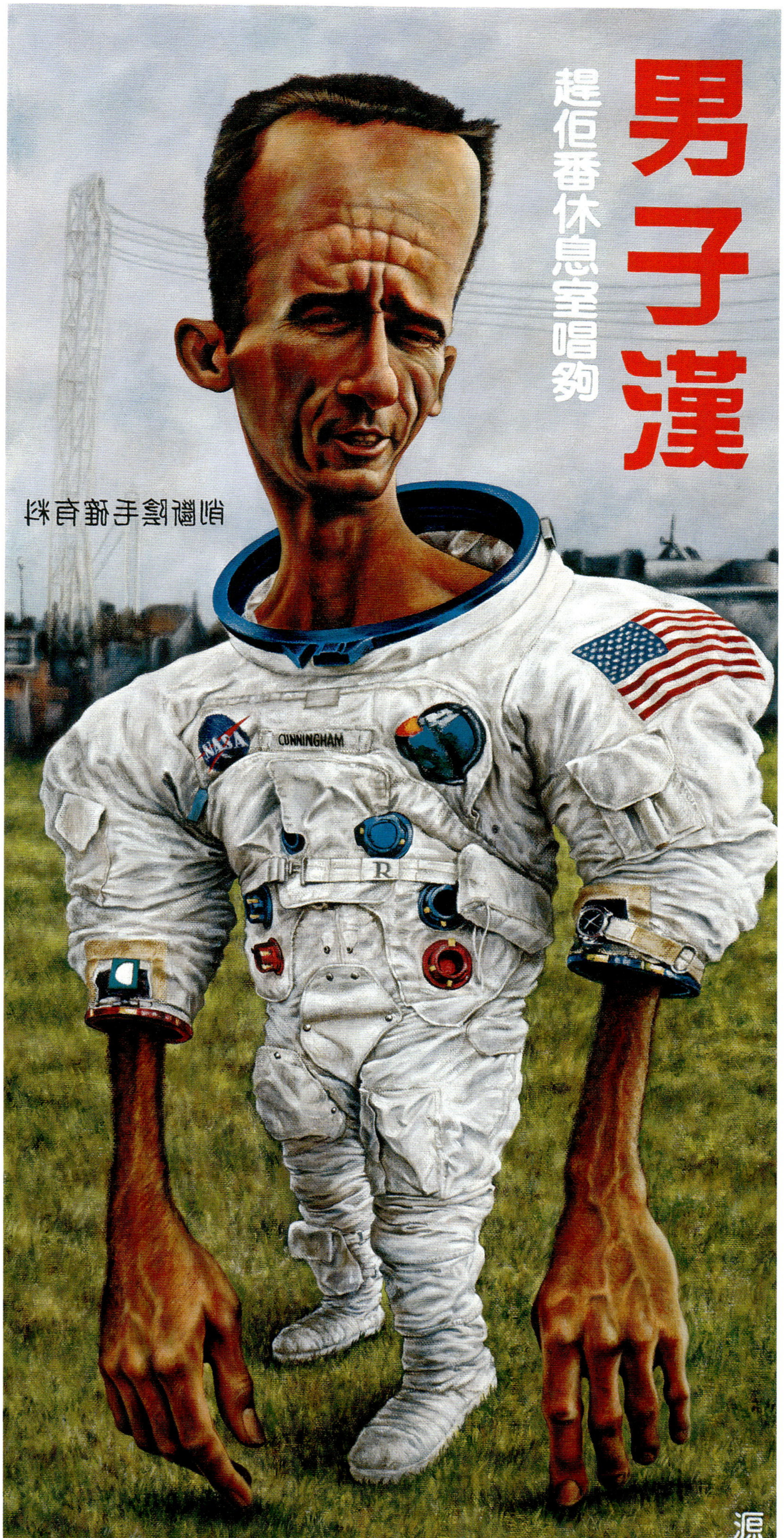

Apollo 7
1996
Acrylic on canvas
30 x 15 in.

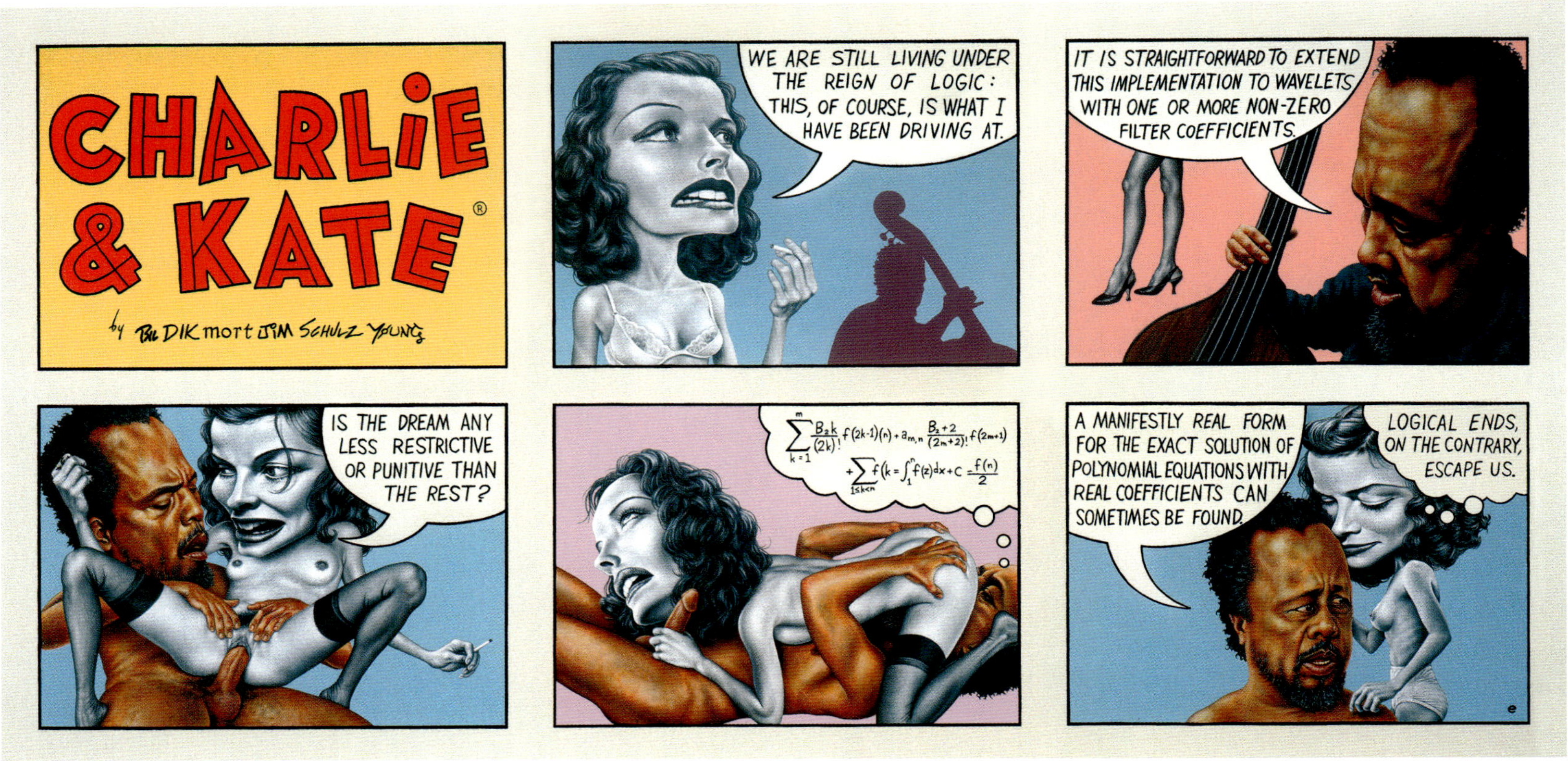

The Sunday Funnies No. 1
1996
Acrylic on canvas
18 x 36 in.

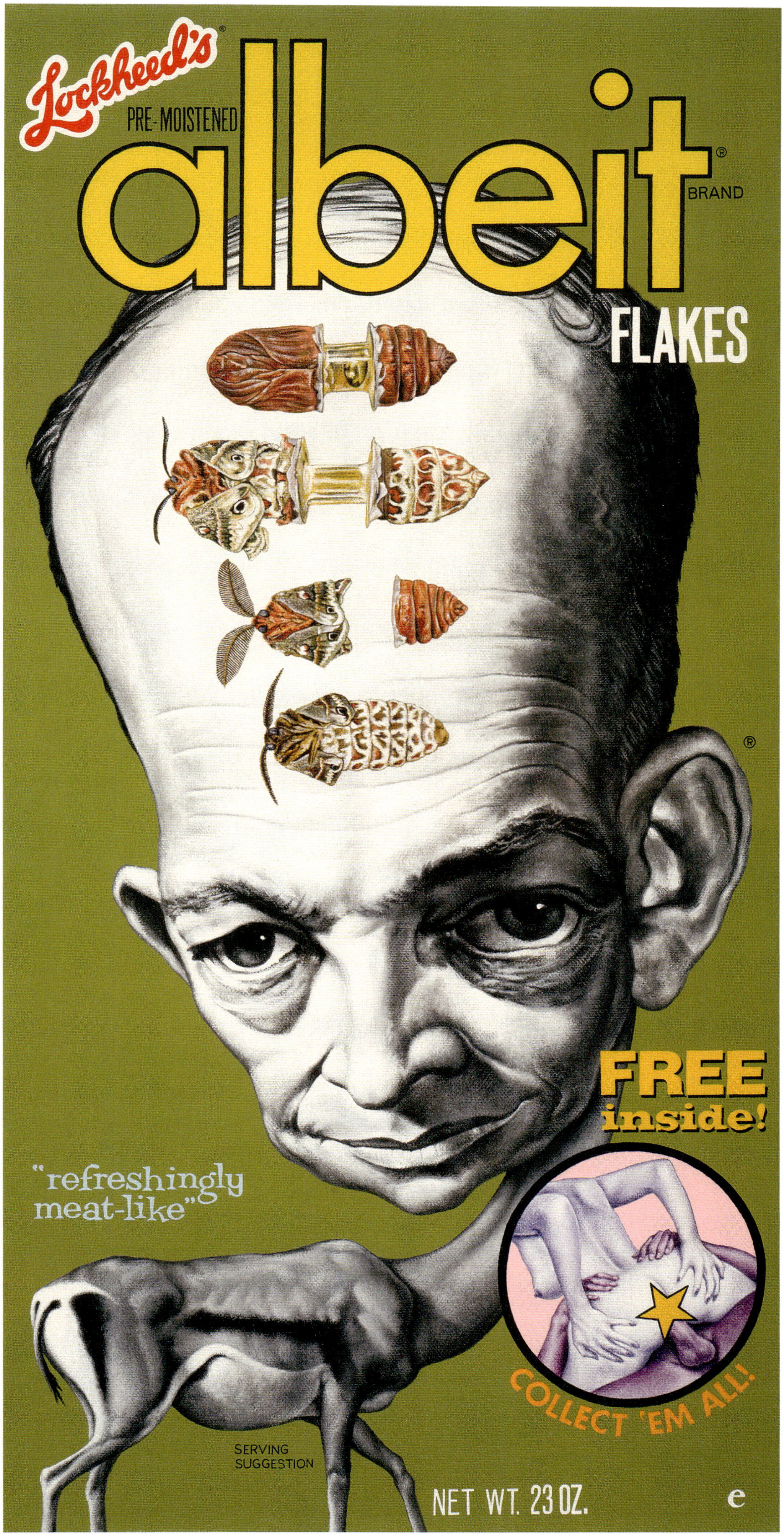

Product (Anti-Love Expurgated)
1997
Acrylic on canvas
24 x 12 in.

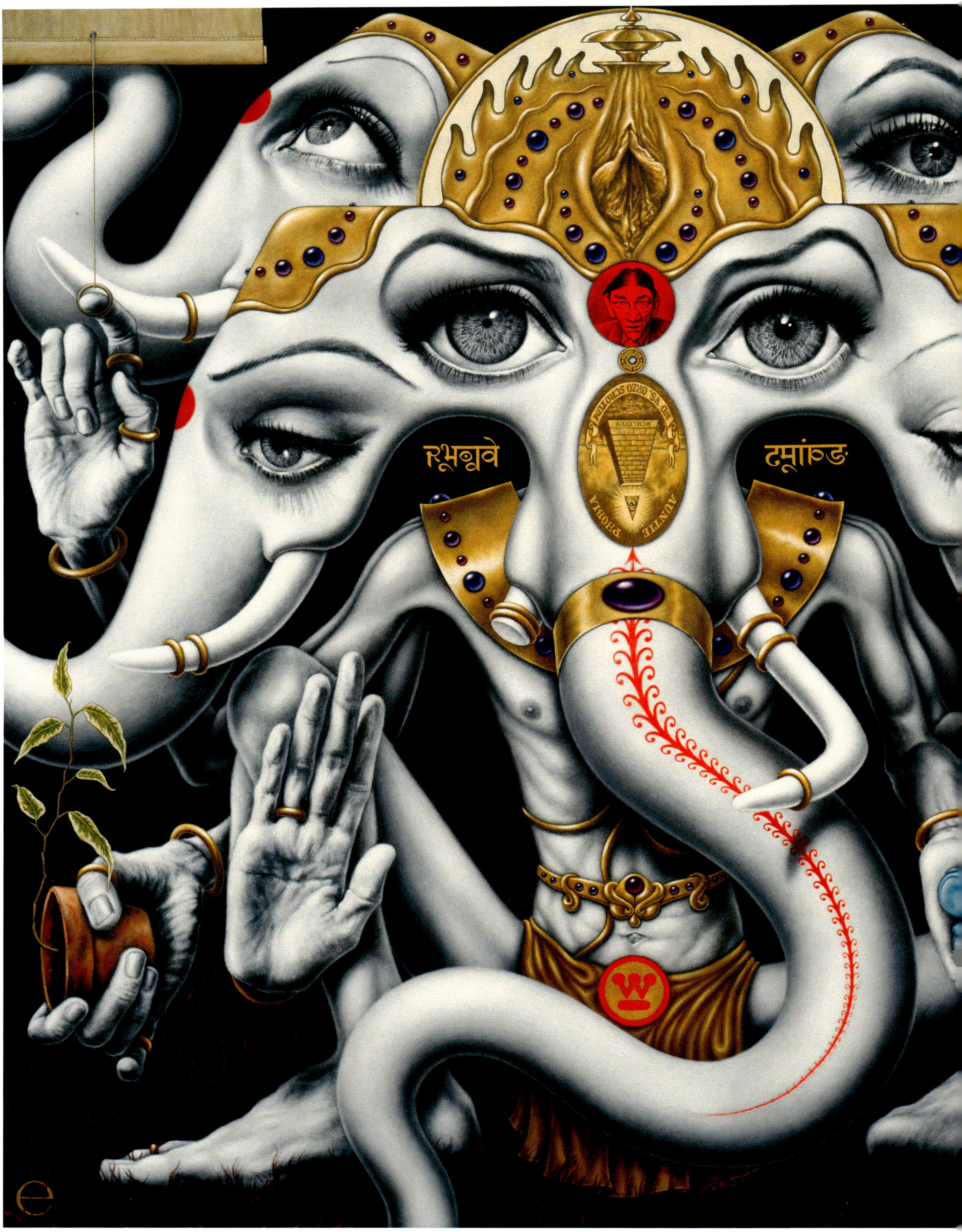

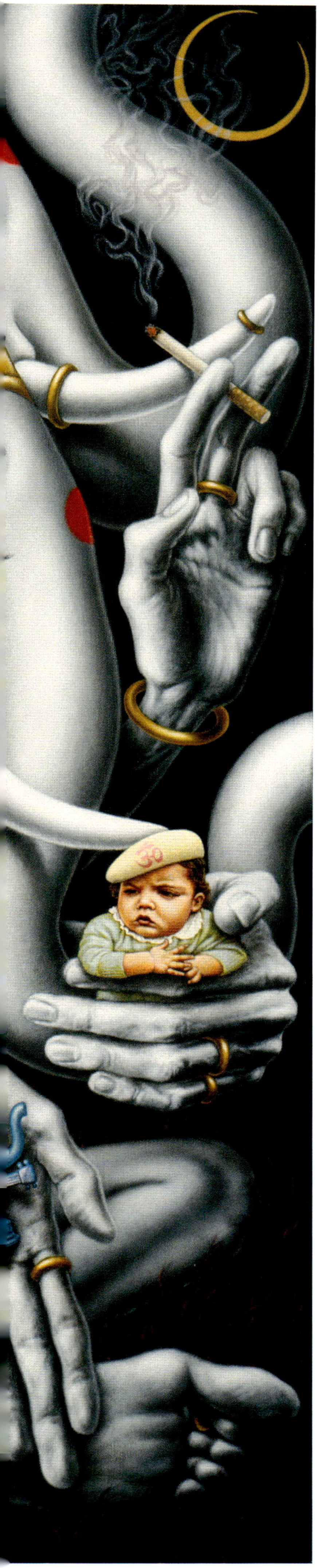

Our Beloved Ganesa
1998
Acrylic on canvas
36 x 36 in.

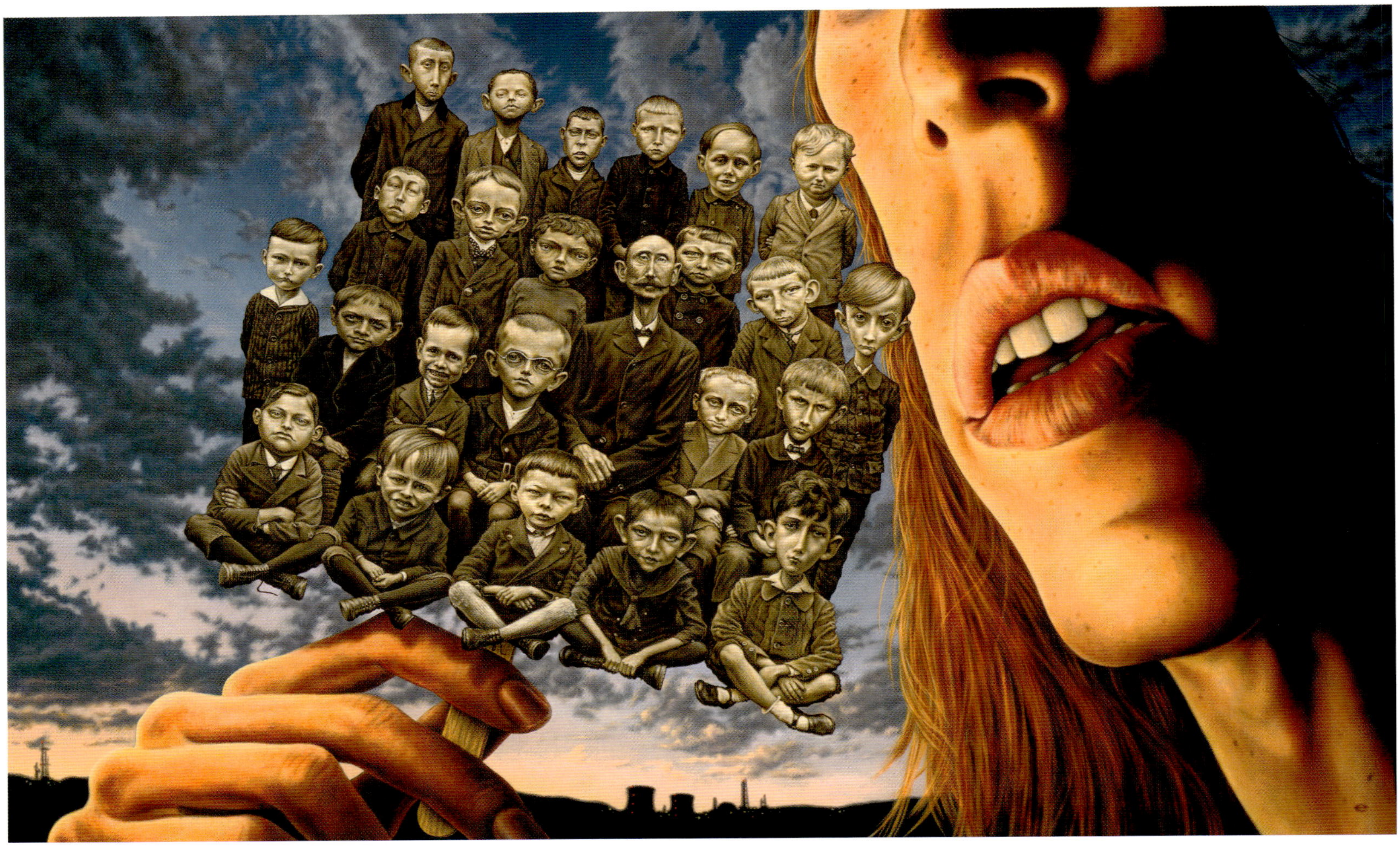

Czechsicle
1998
Acrylic on canvas
30 x 48 in.

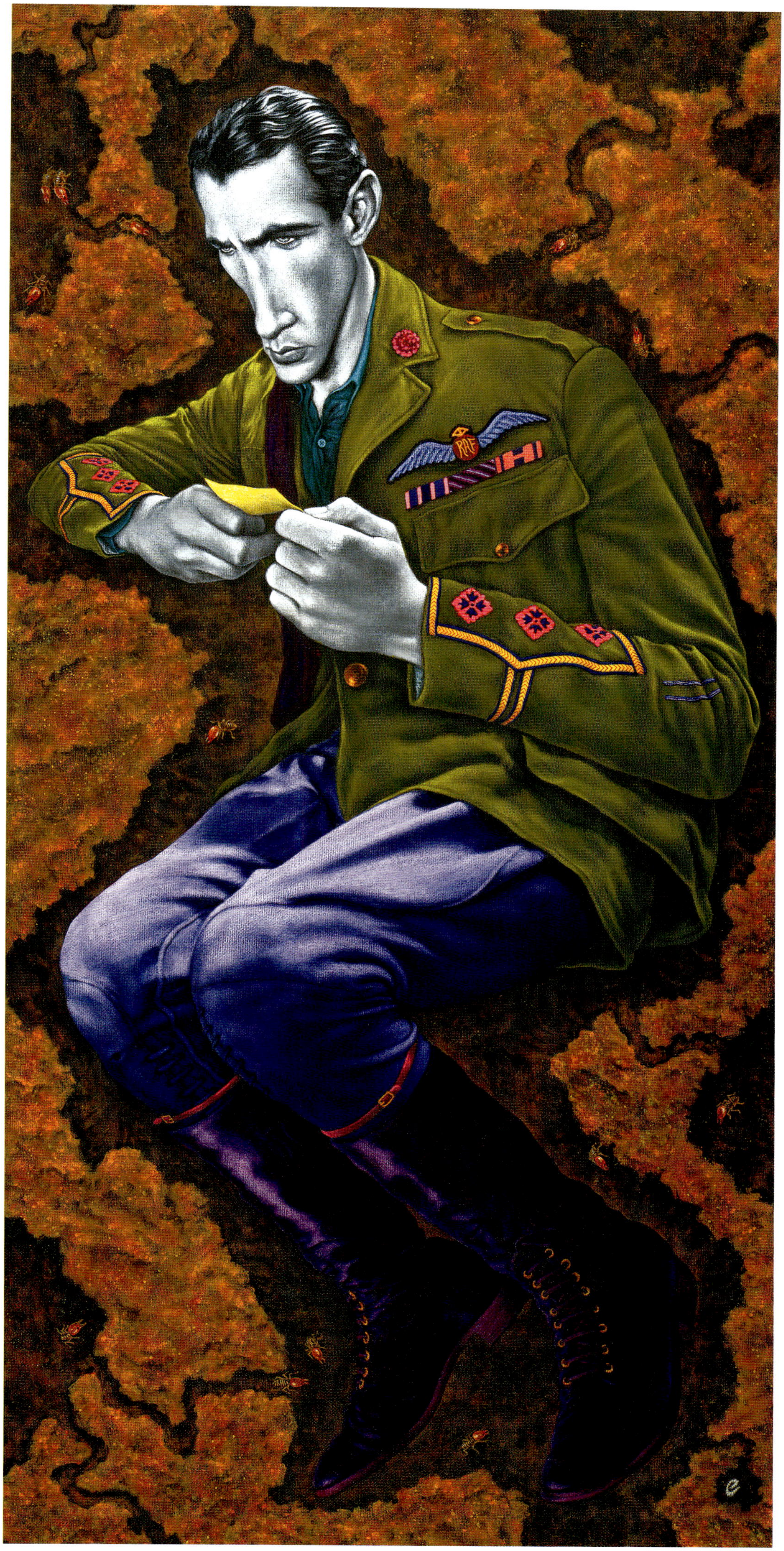

Young Gary Cooper in Termite Mound with Post-It™
1998
Acrylic on canvas
30 x 15 in.

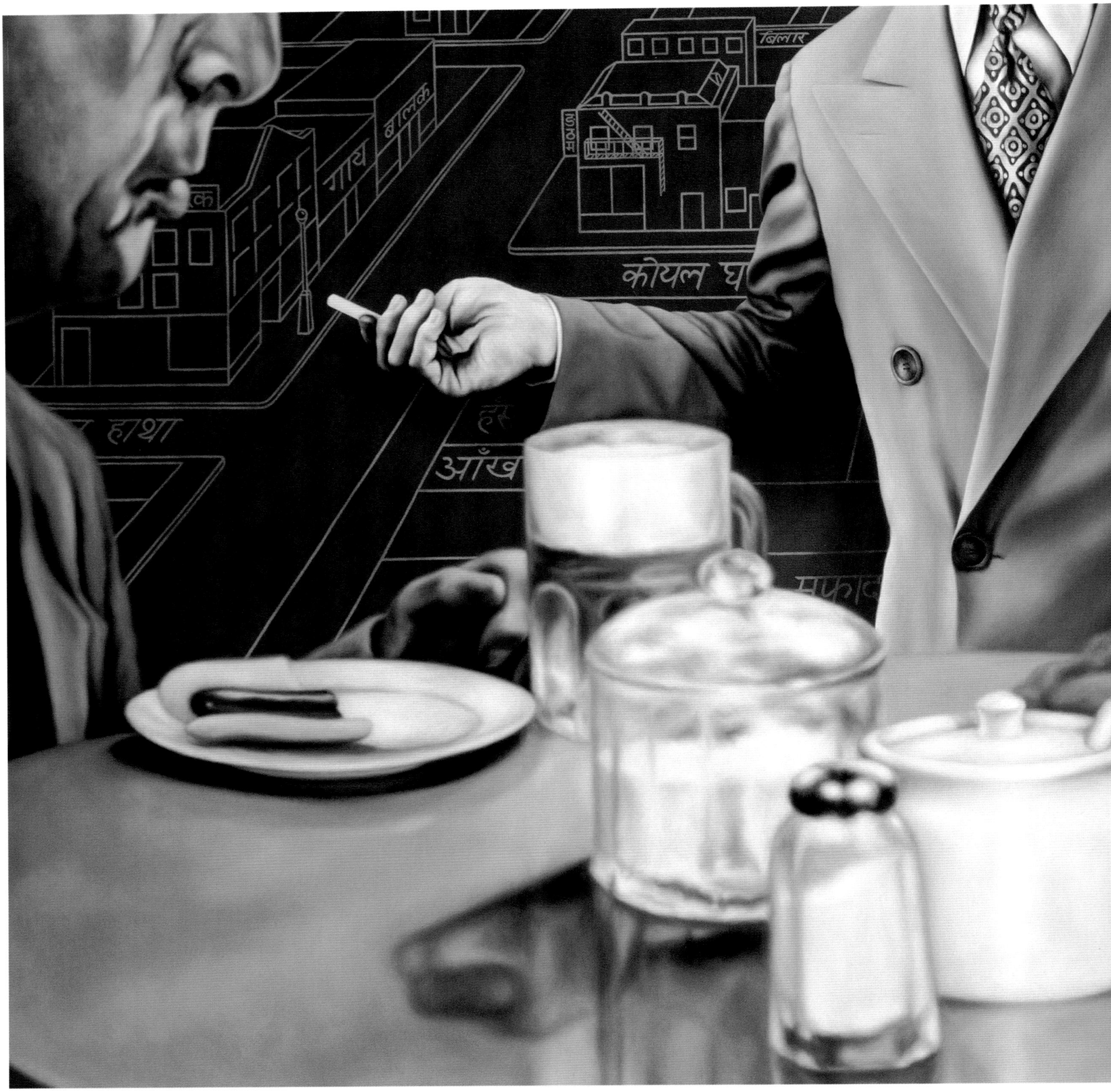

Intermezzo
1999
Oil on canvas
36 x 72 in.

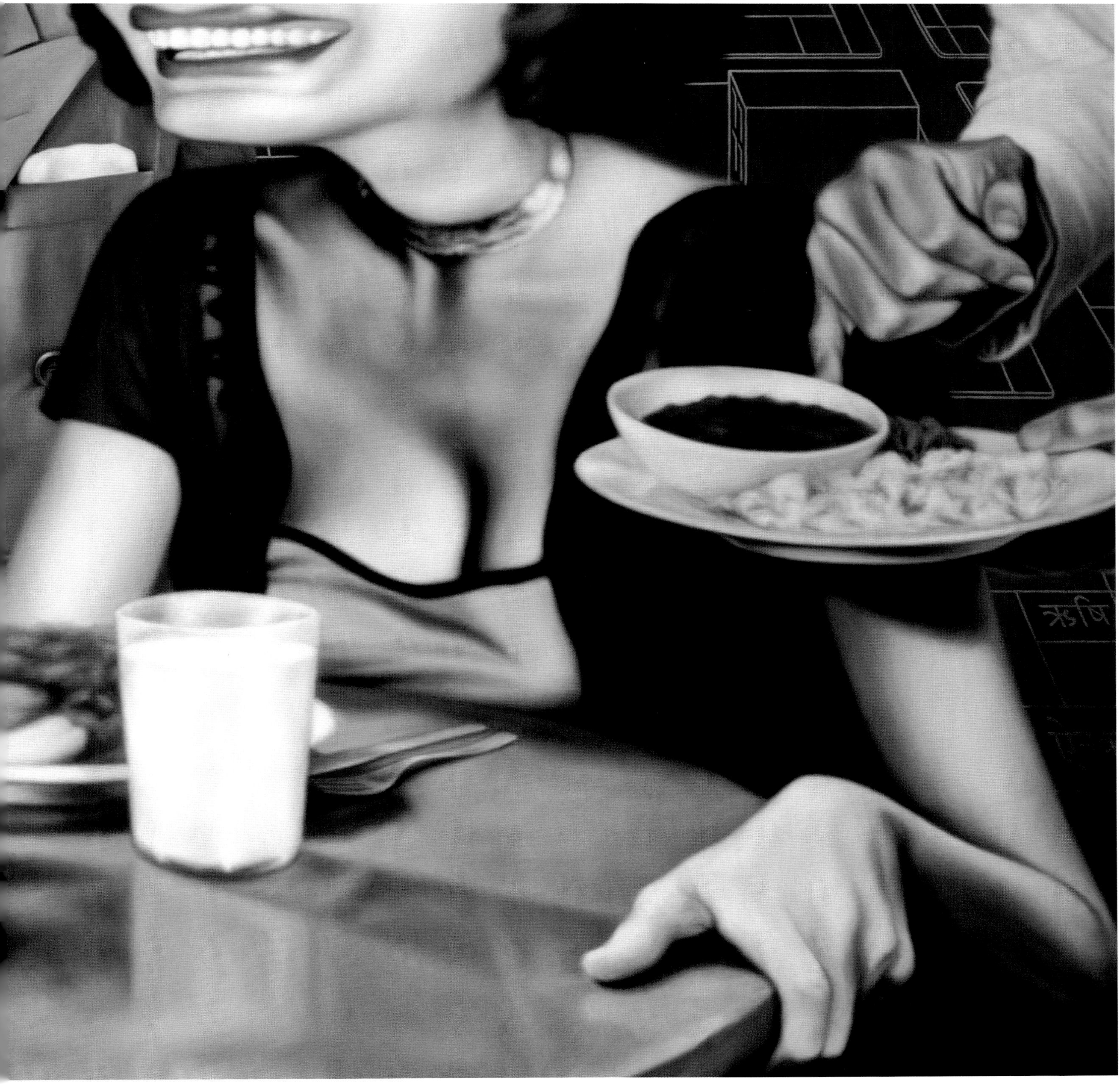

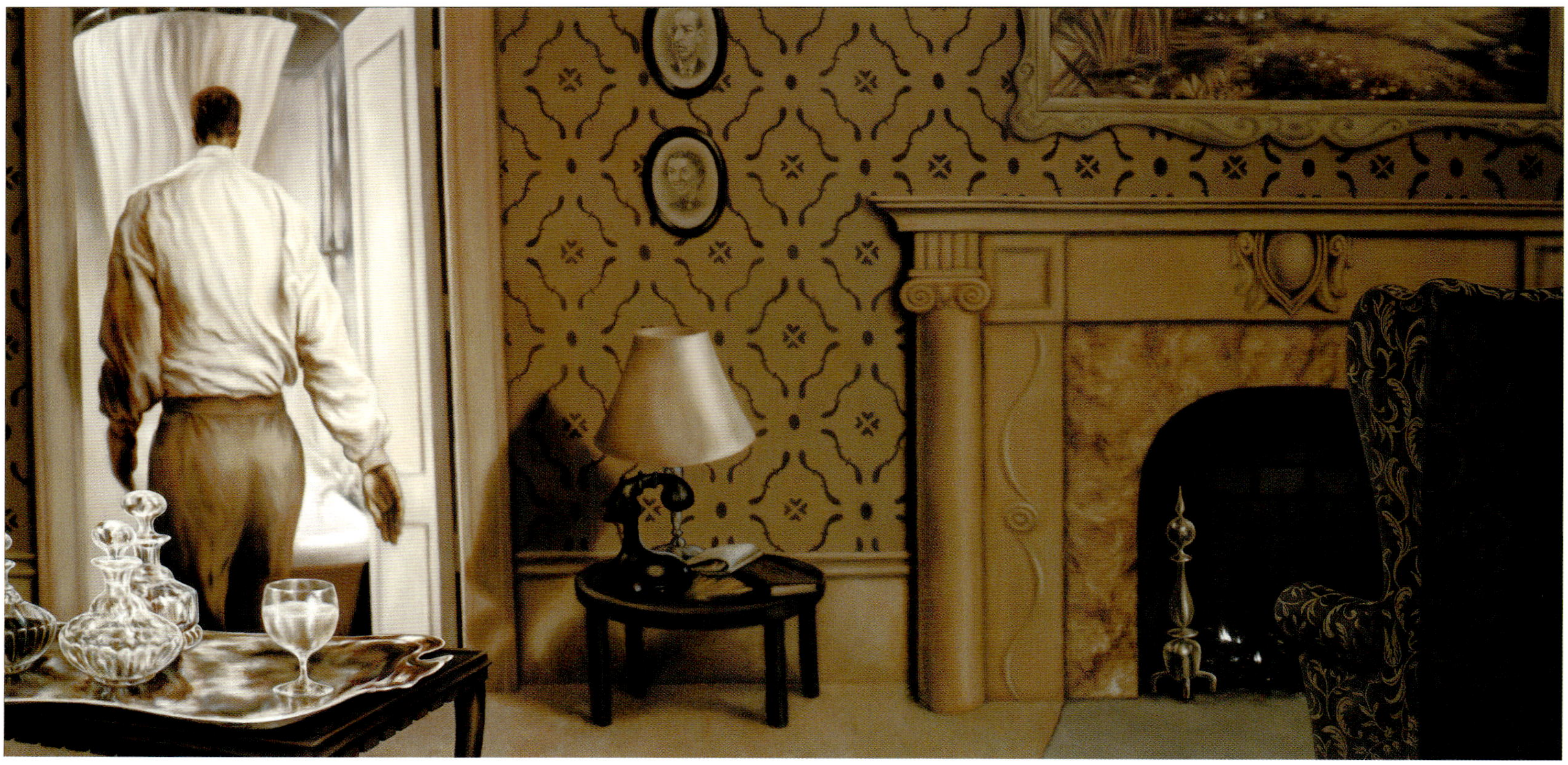

Untitled
1999
Oil on canvas
36 x 72 in.

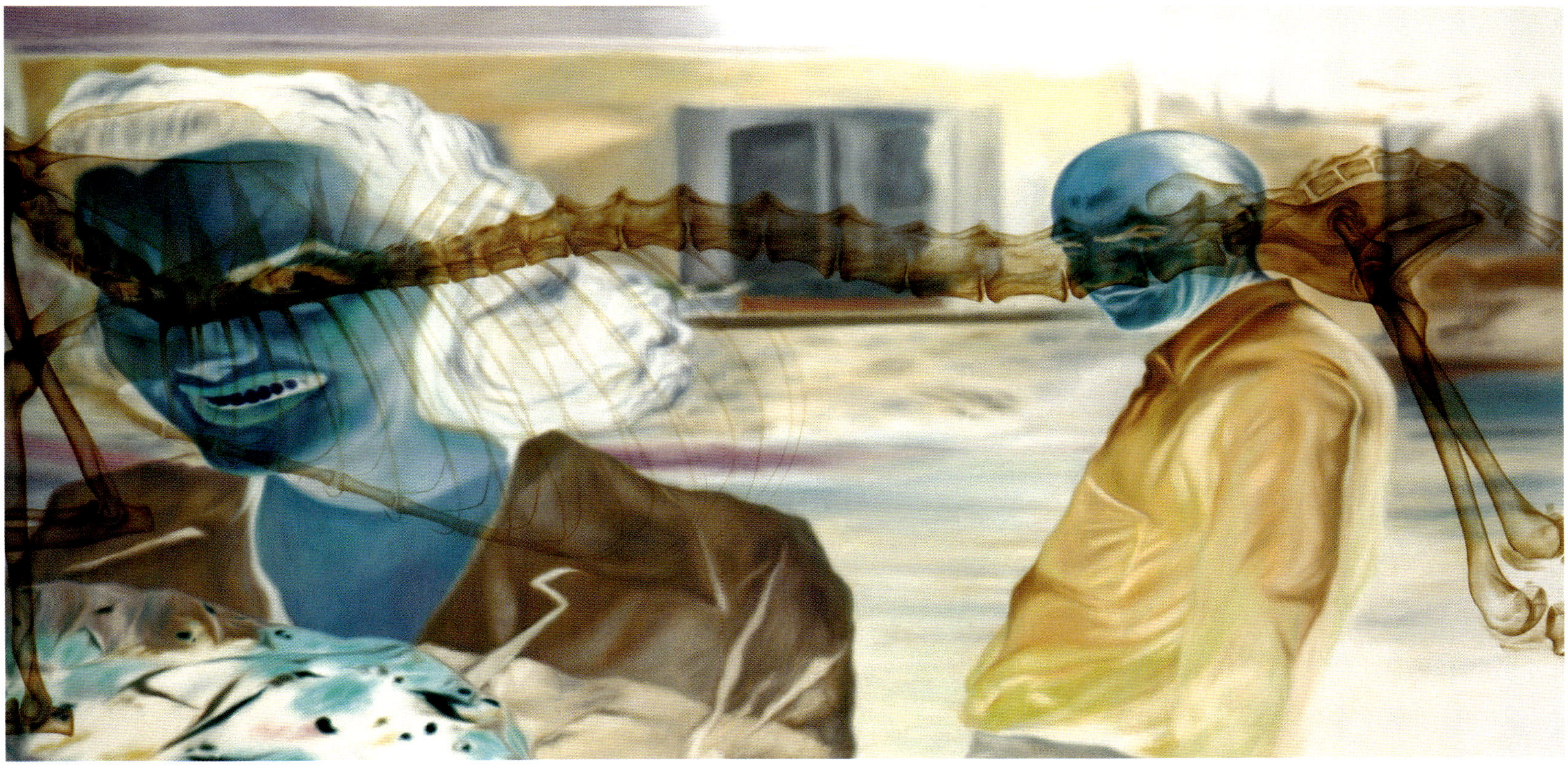

Death Isn't
1999
Oil on canvas
36 x 72 in.

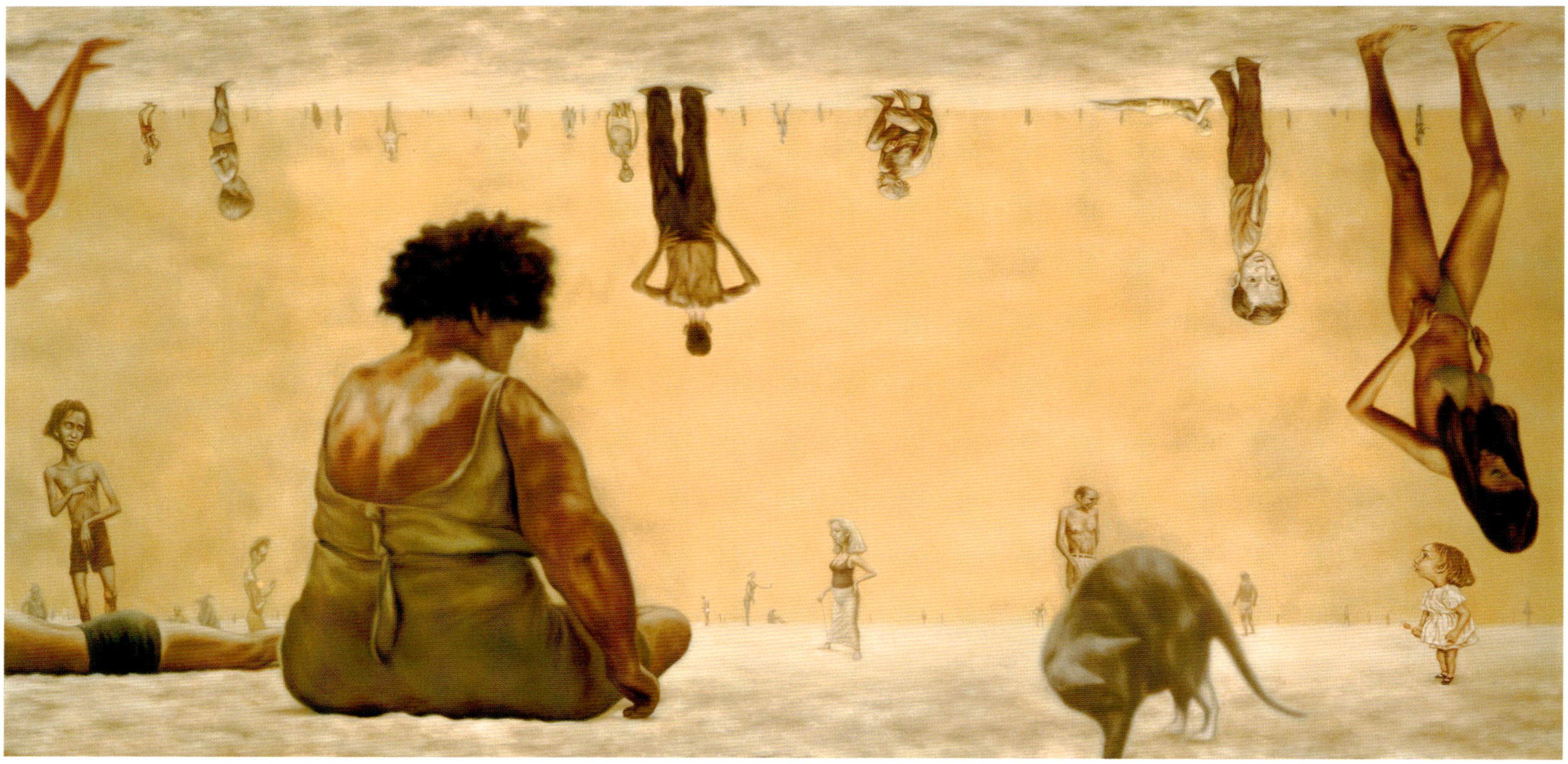

Swims
1999
Oil on canvas
36 x 72 in.

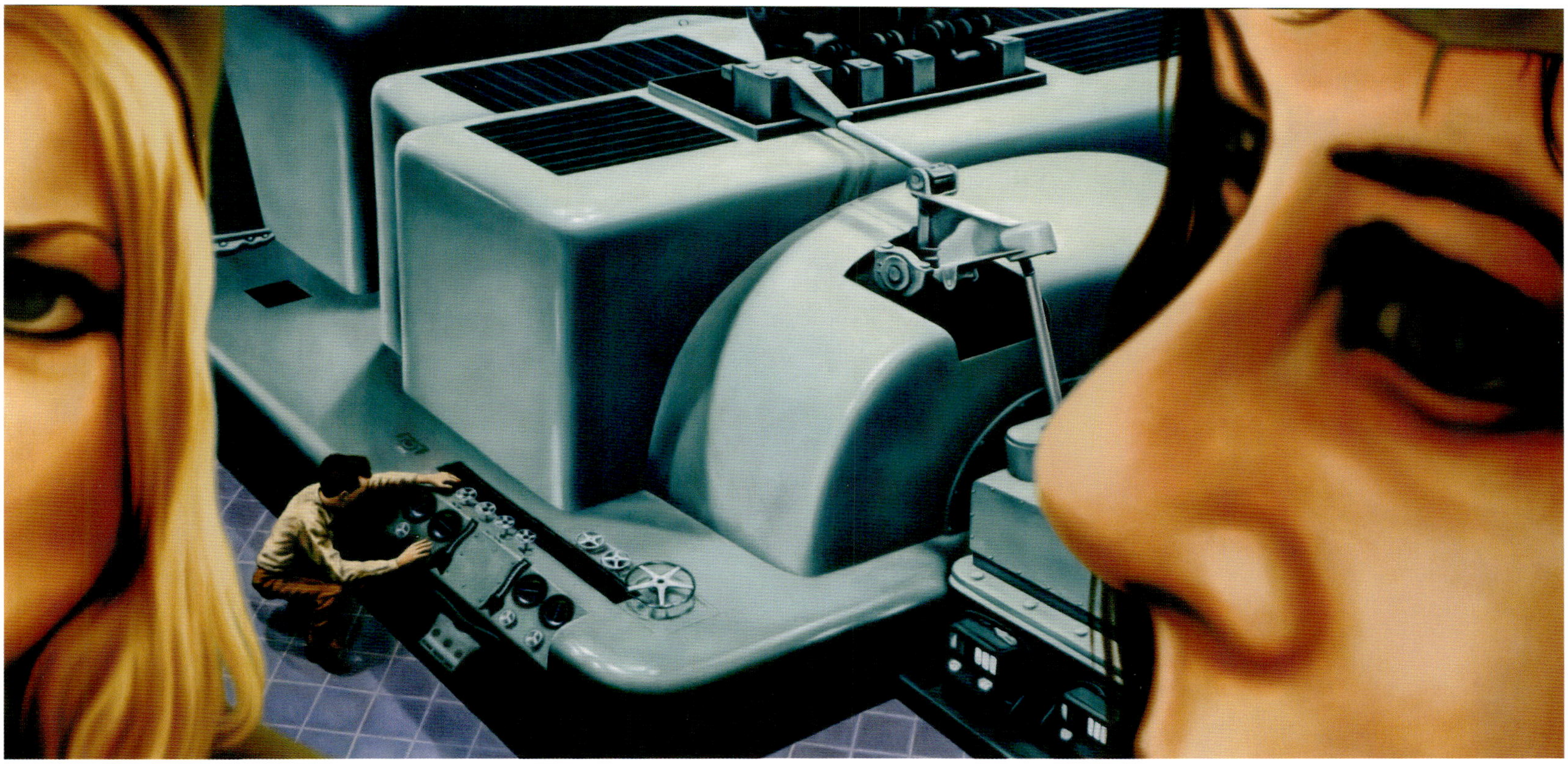

The Orientation
1999
Oil on canvas
36 x 72 in.

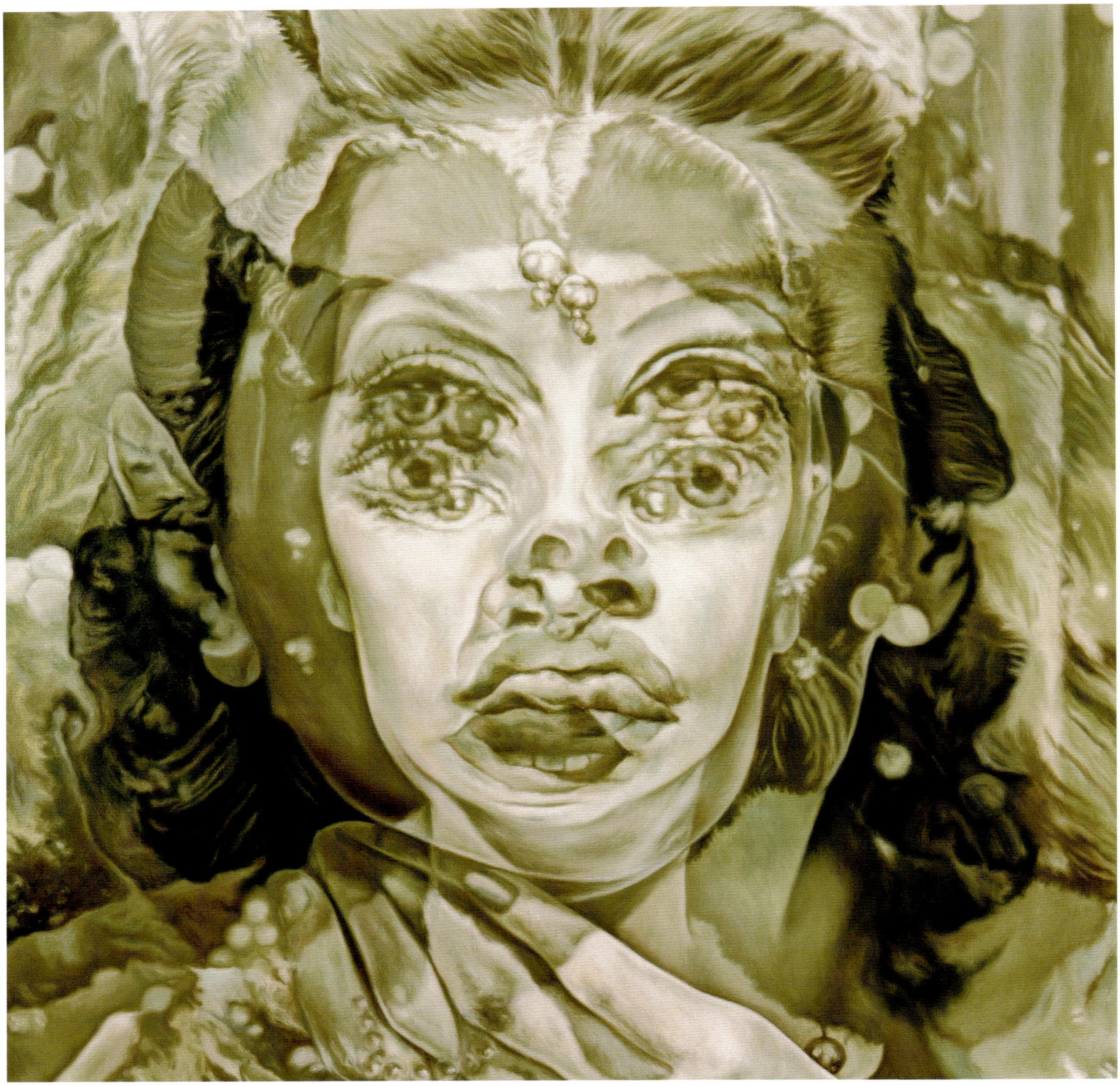

Divine Mother of Guilt
2002
Oil on canvas
36 x 36 in.

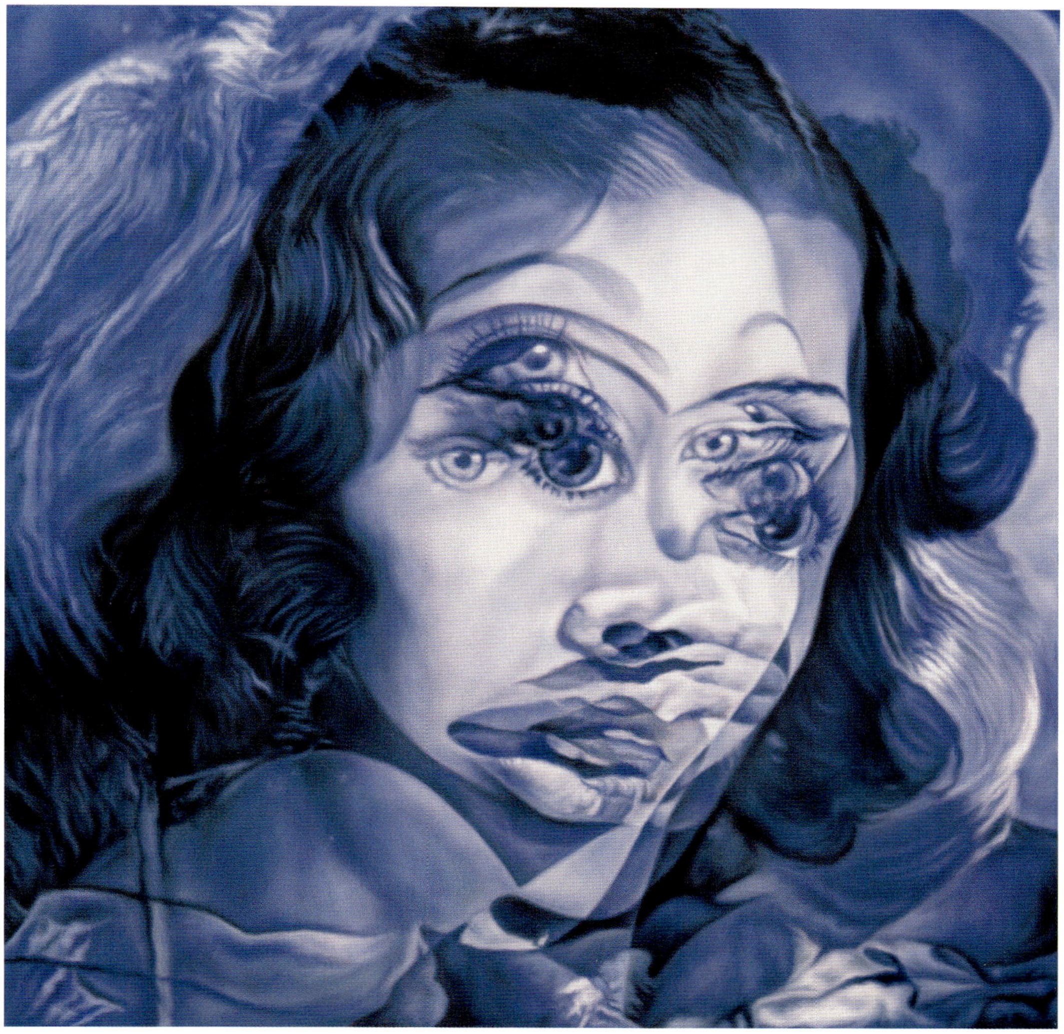

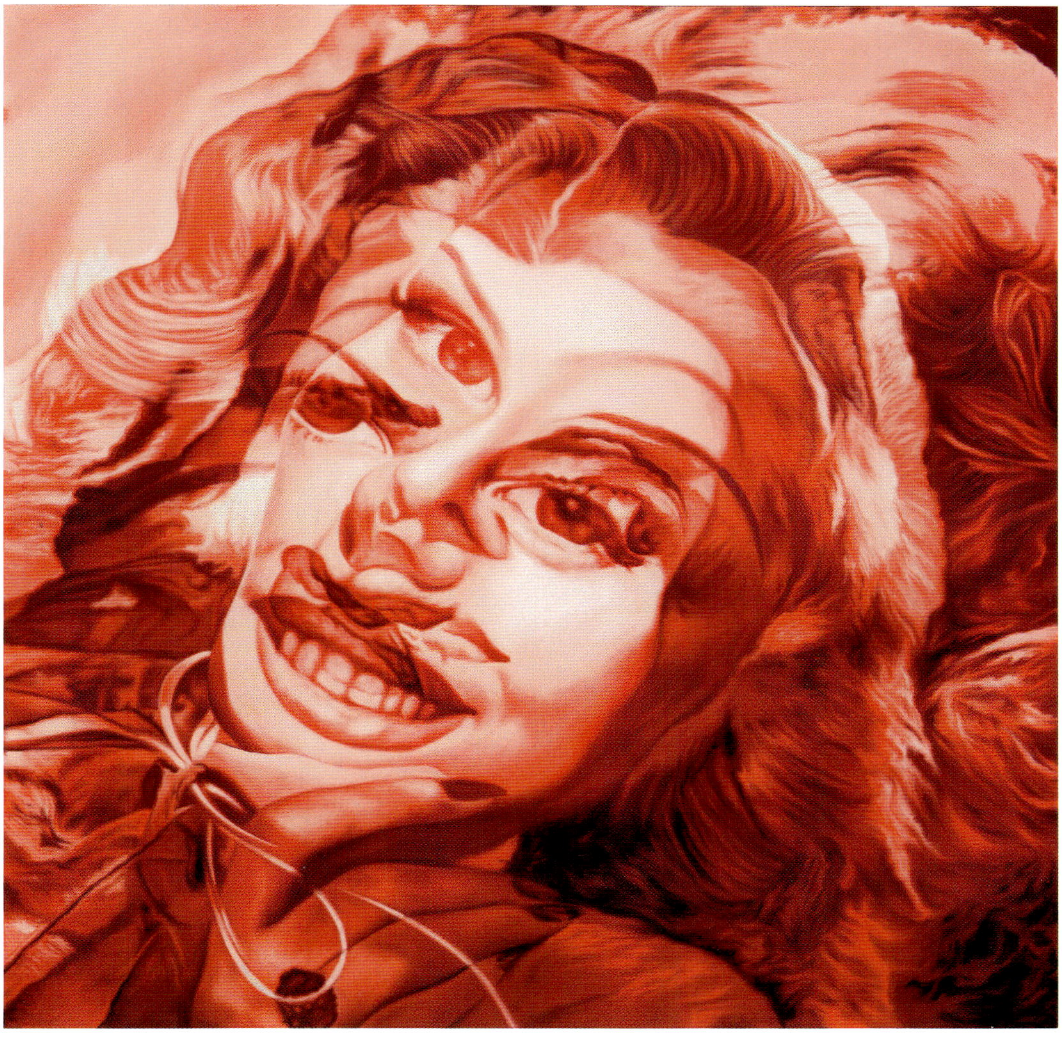

Sacred Lady of Bias
2002
Oil on canvas
36 x 36 in.

Holy Matron of Ridicule
2003
Oil on canvas
36 x 36 in.

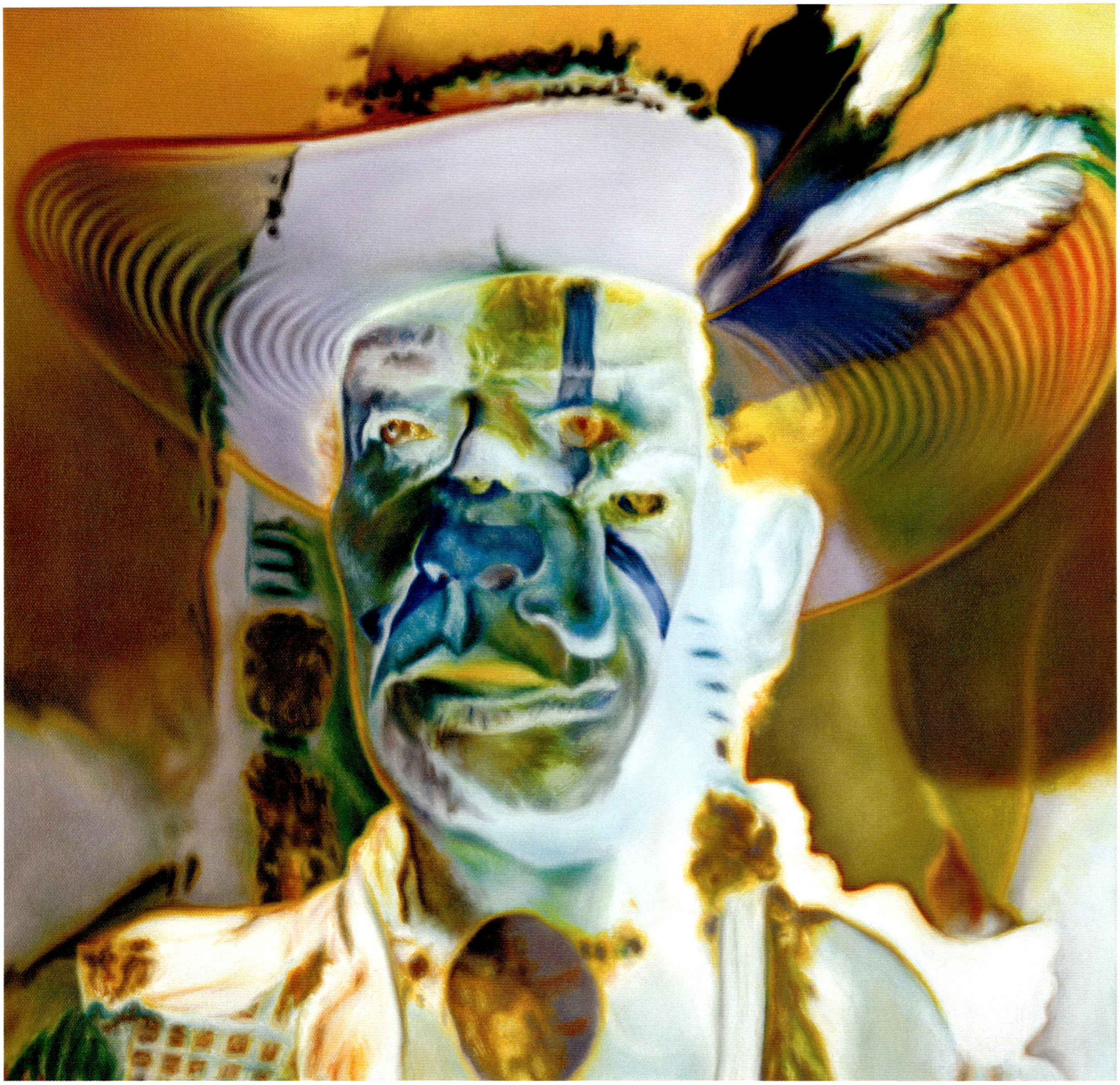

Them Or Us
2003
Oil on canvas
18 x 18 in.

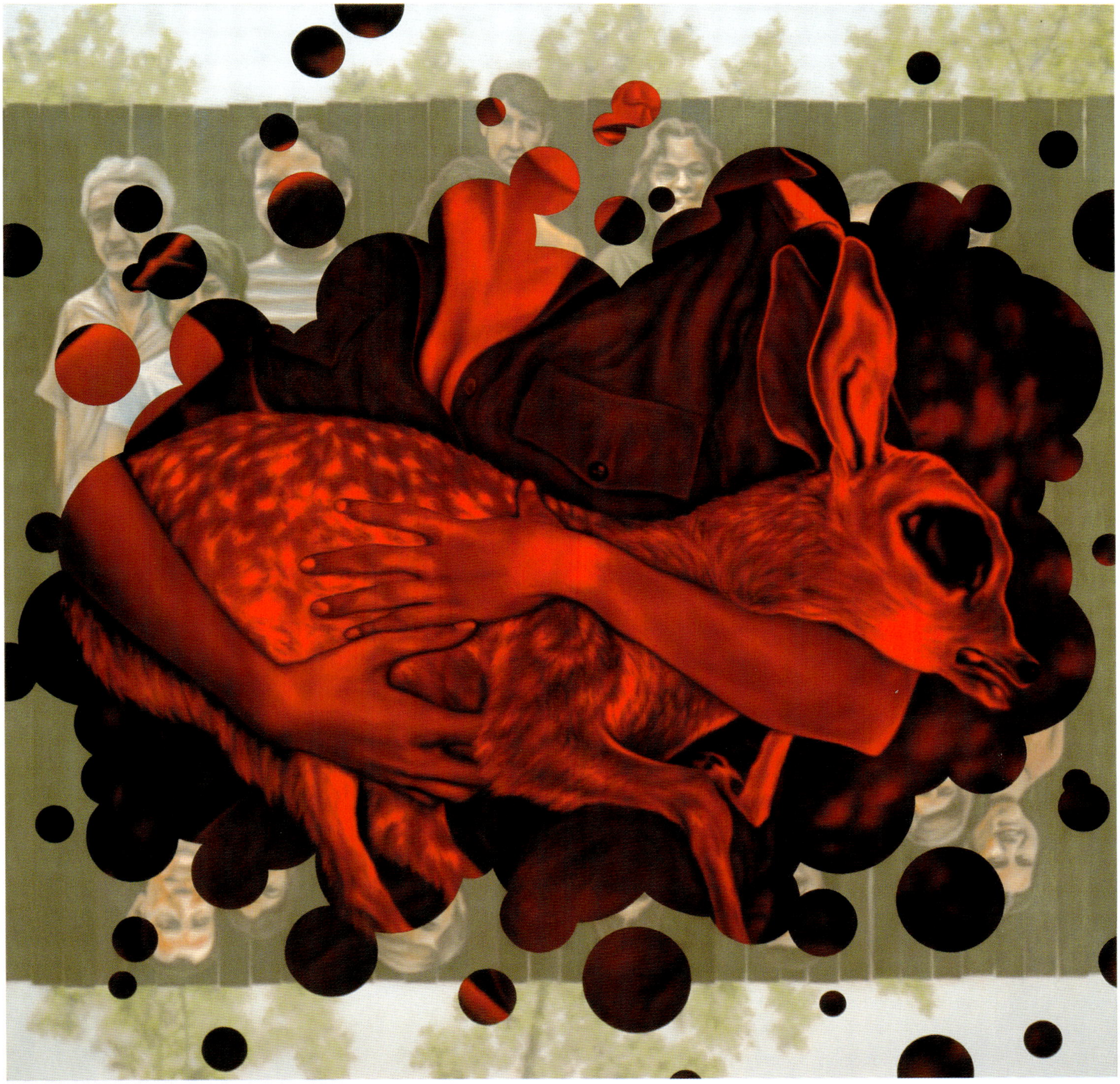

Golden Moments
2001
Oil on canvas
36 x 36 in.

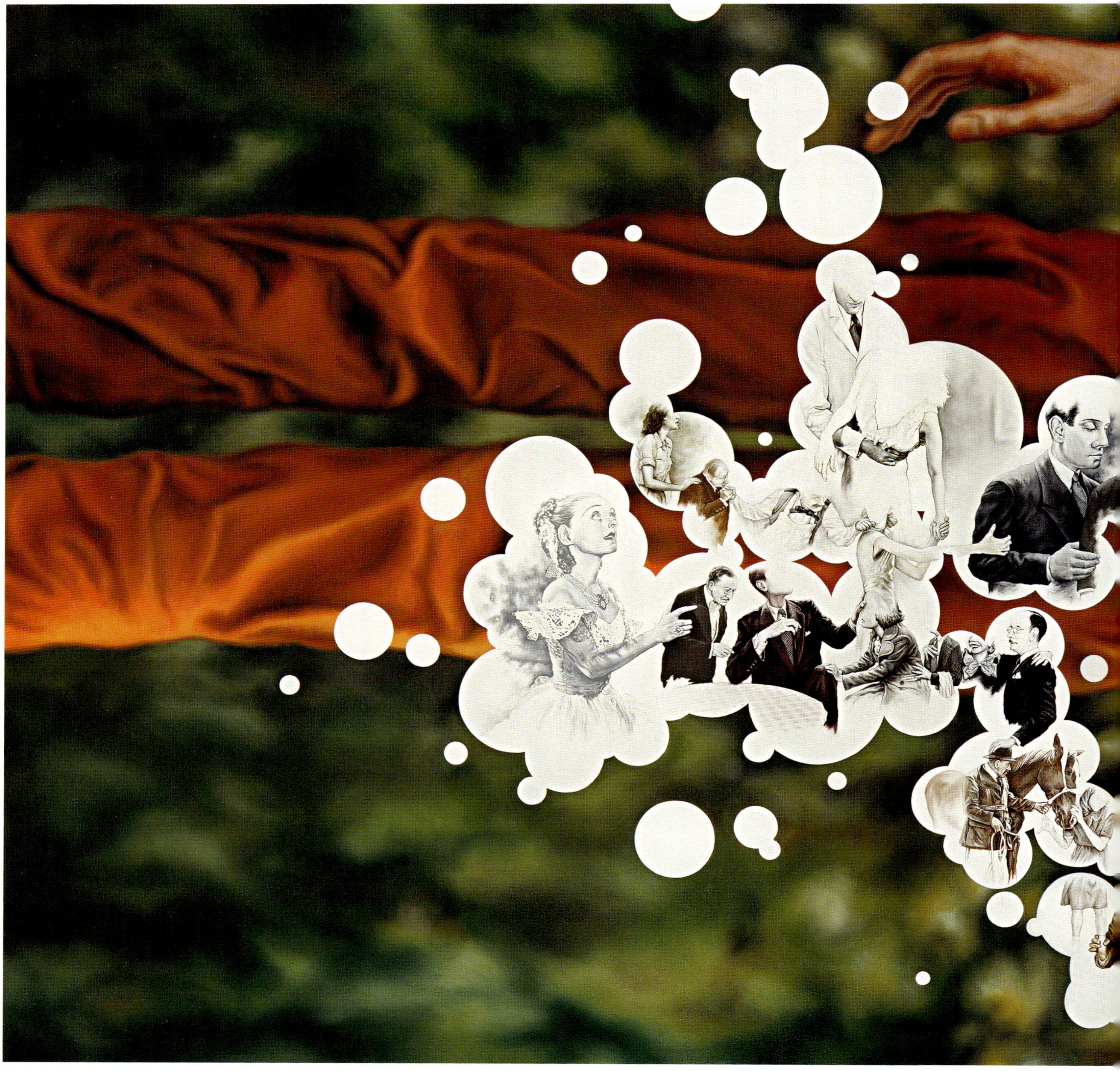

Spores of Today (Anima Rising)
2003
Oil on canvas
35 x 72 in.

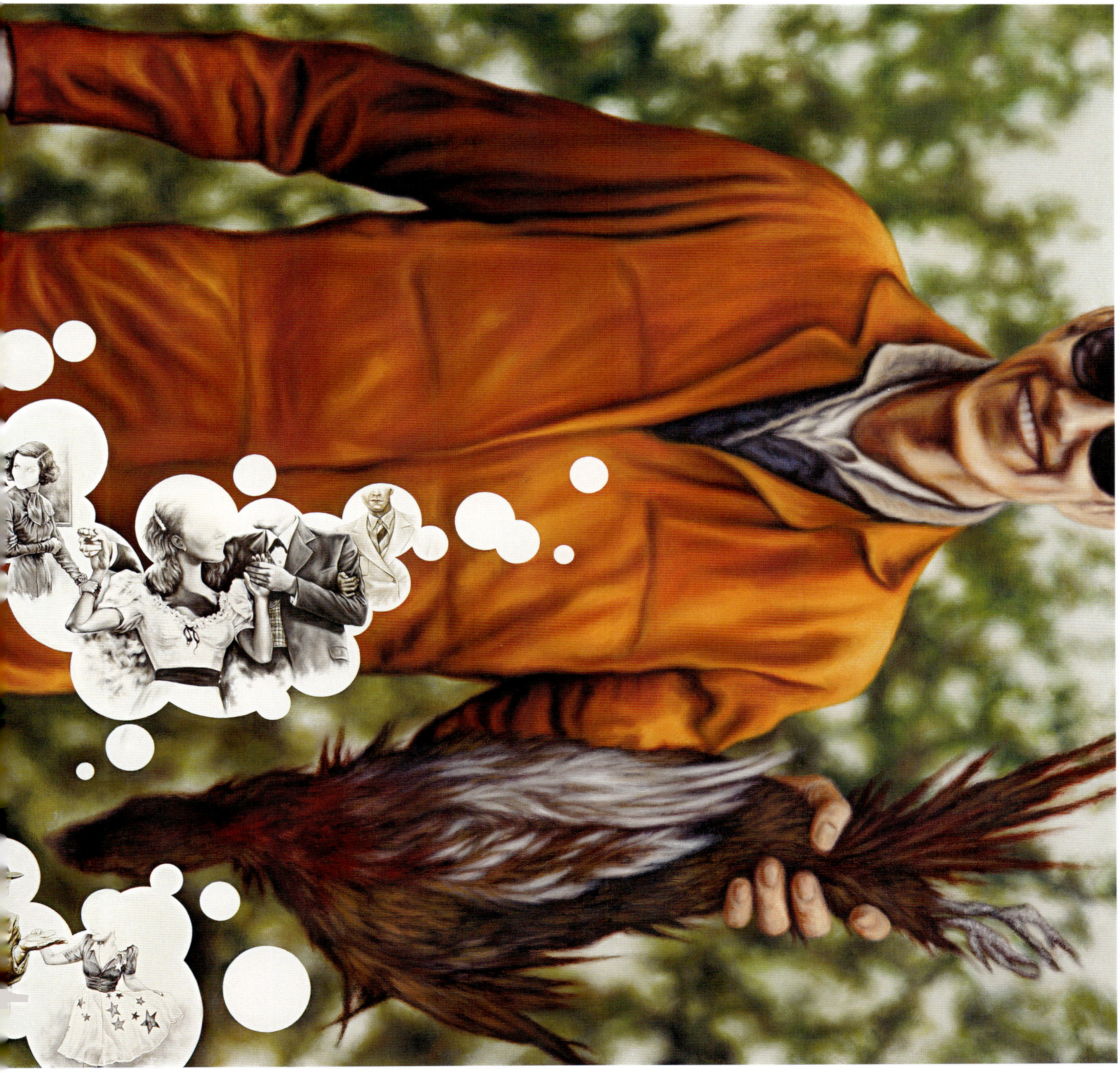

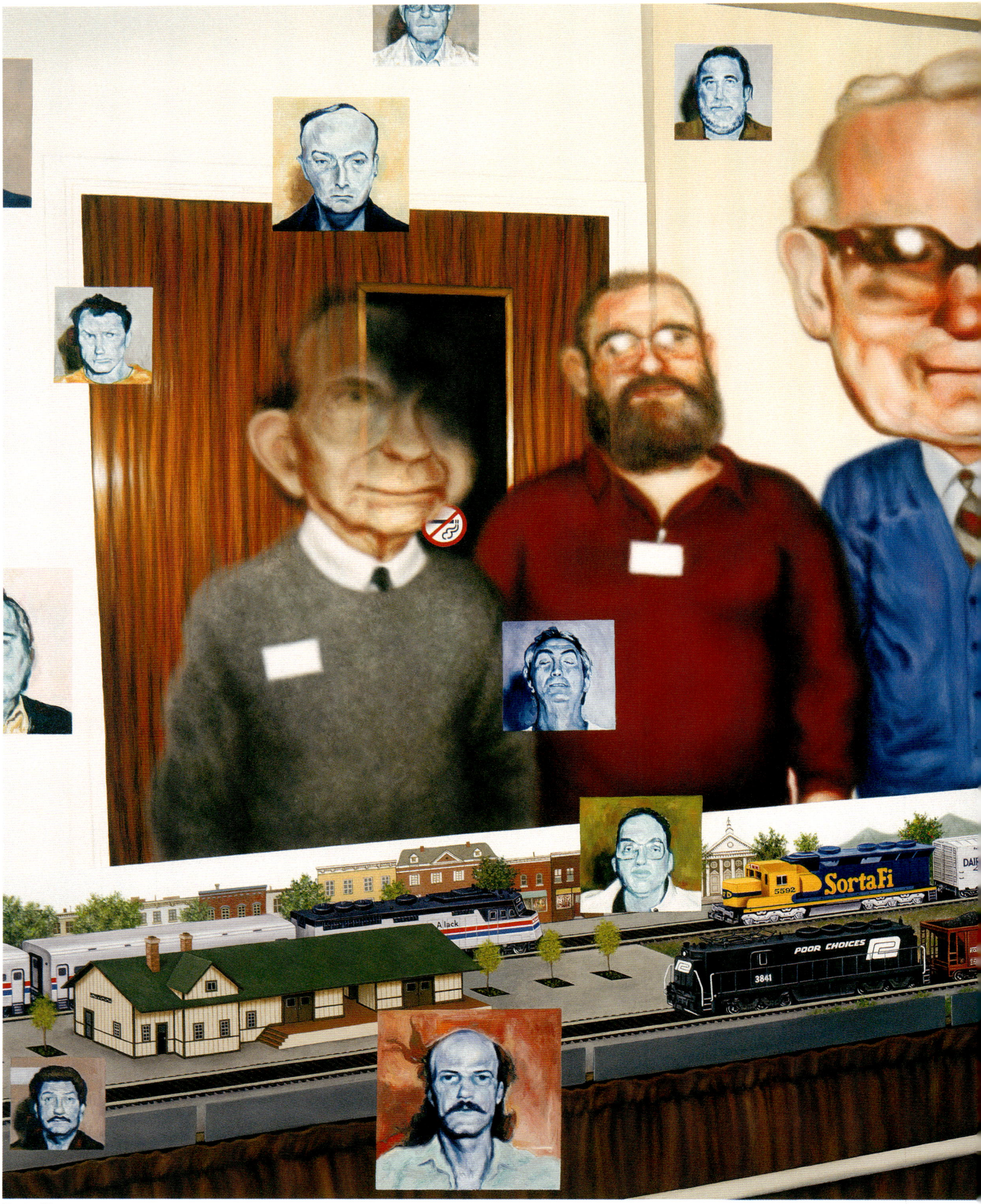

Dadsville
(detail on following page)
2003
Oil on canvas
36 x 60 in.

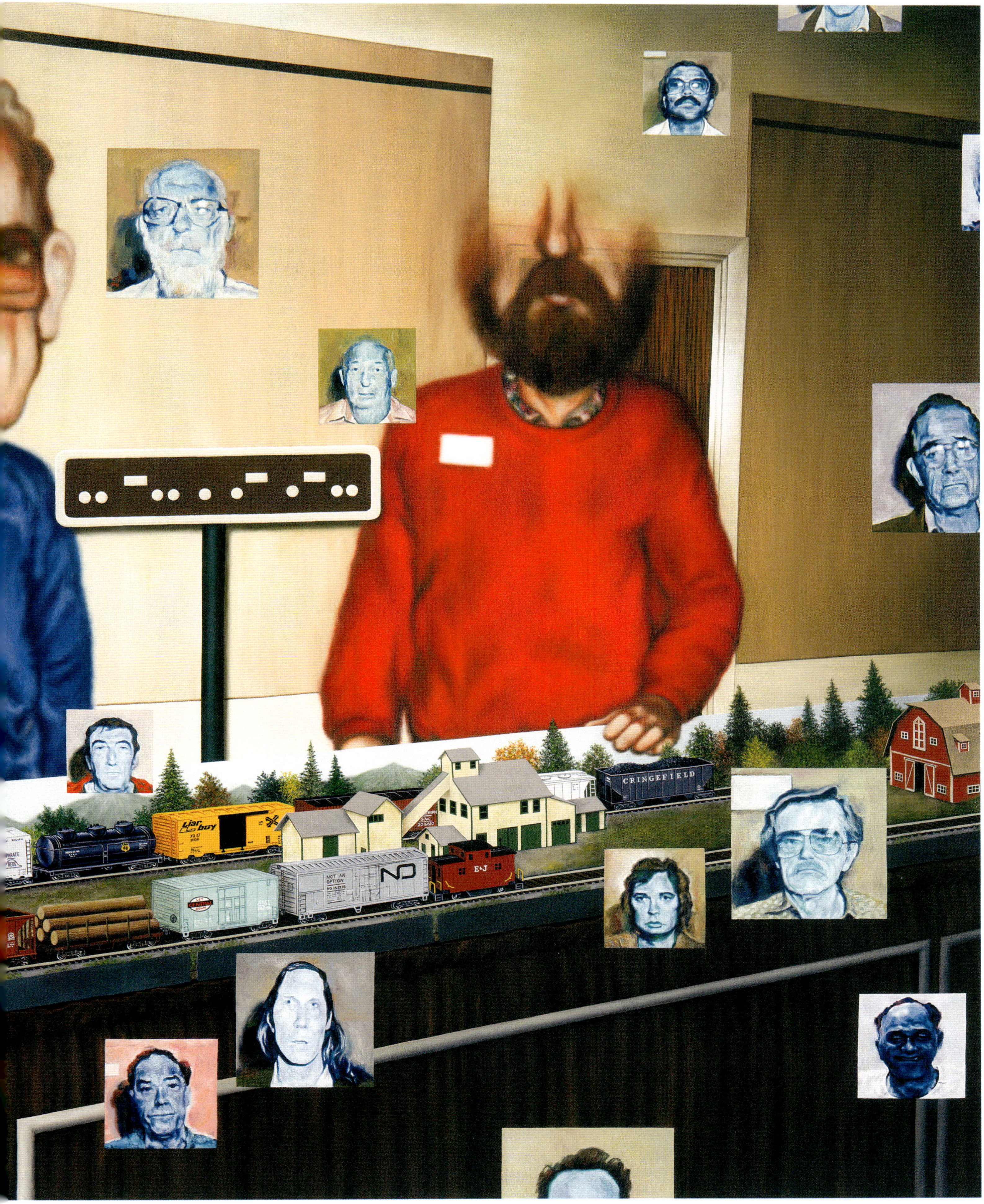
CRINGEFIELD
NOT AN
OPTION

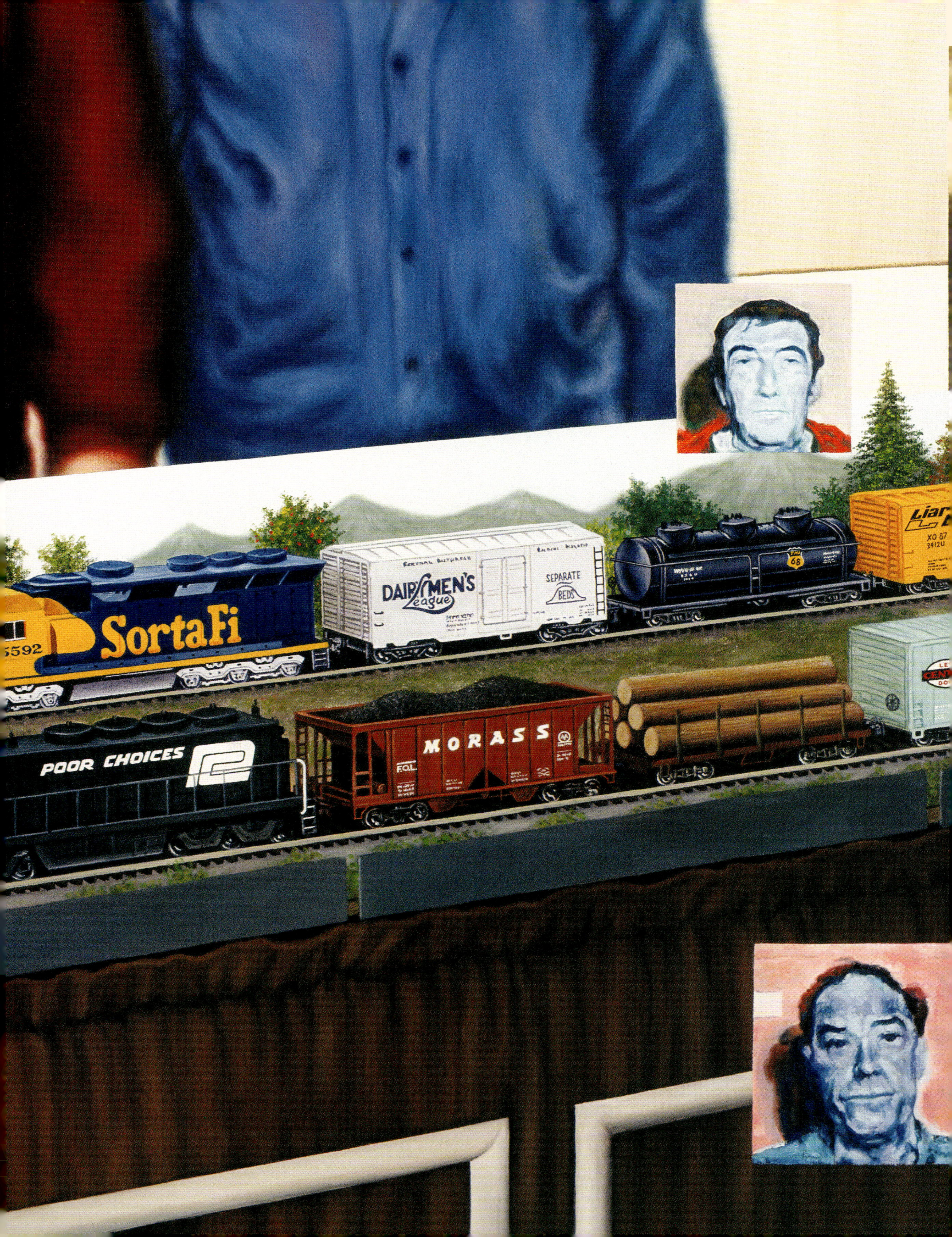
SortaFi
DAIRYMEN'S League
SEPARATE BEDS
POOR CHOICES
MORASS

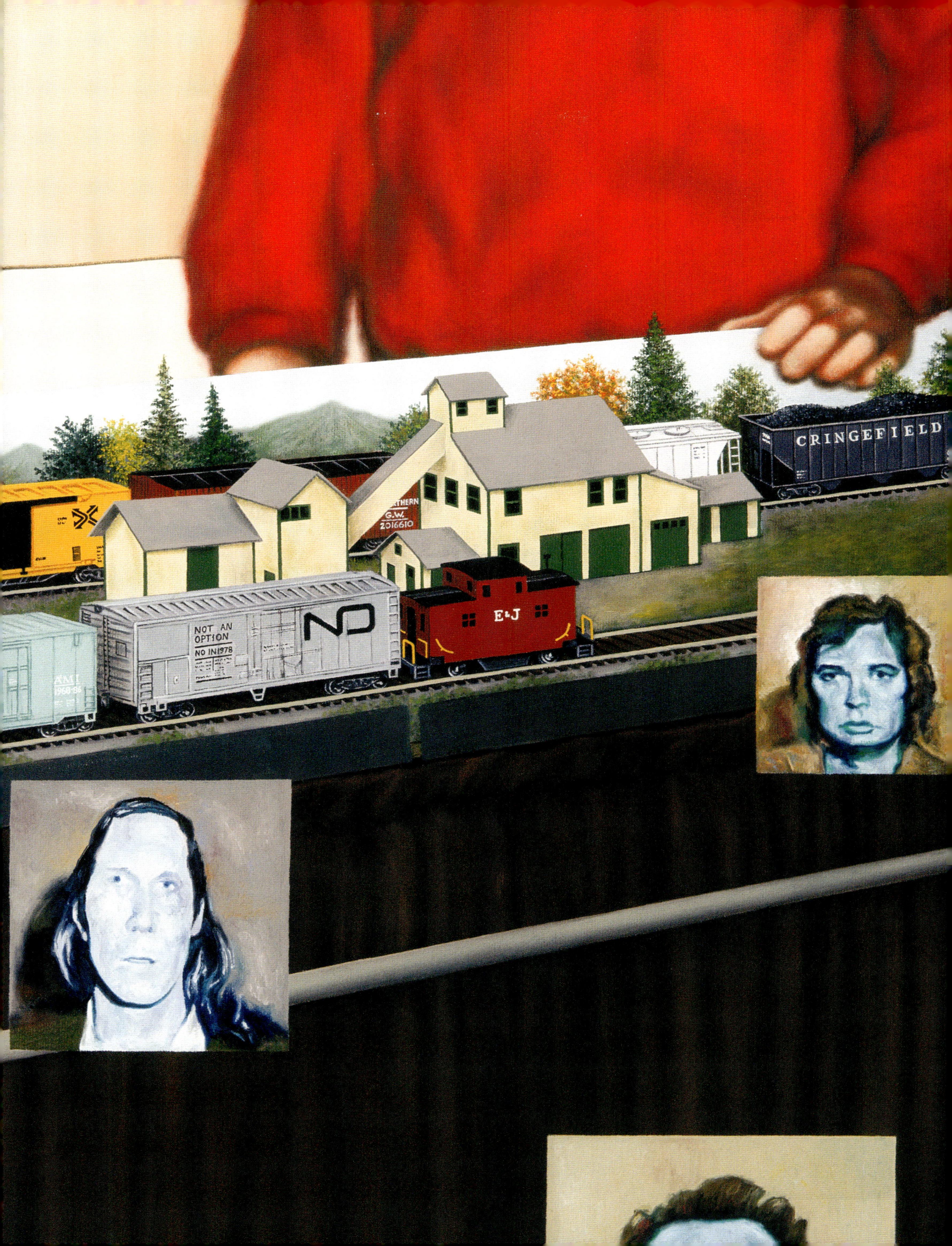
CRINGEFIELD
G.W.
2016610
NOT AN
OPTION
NO IN1978
E&J

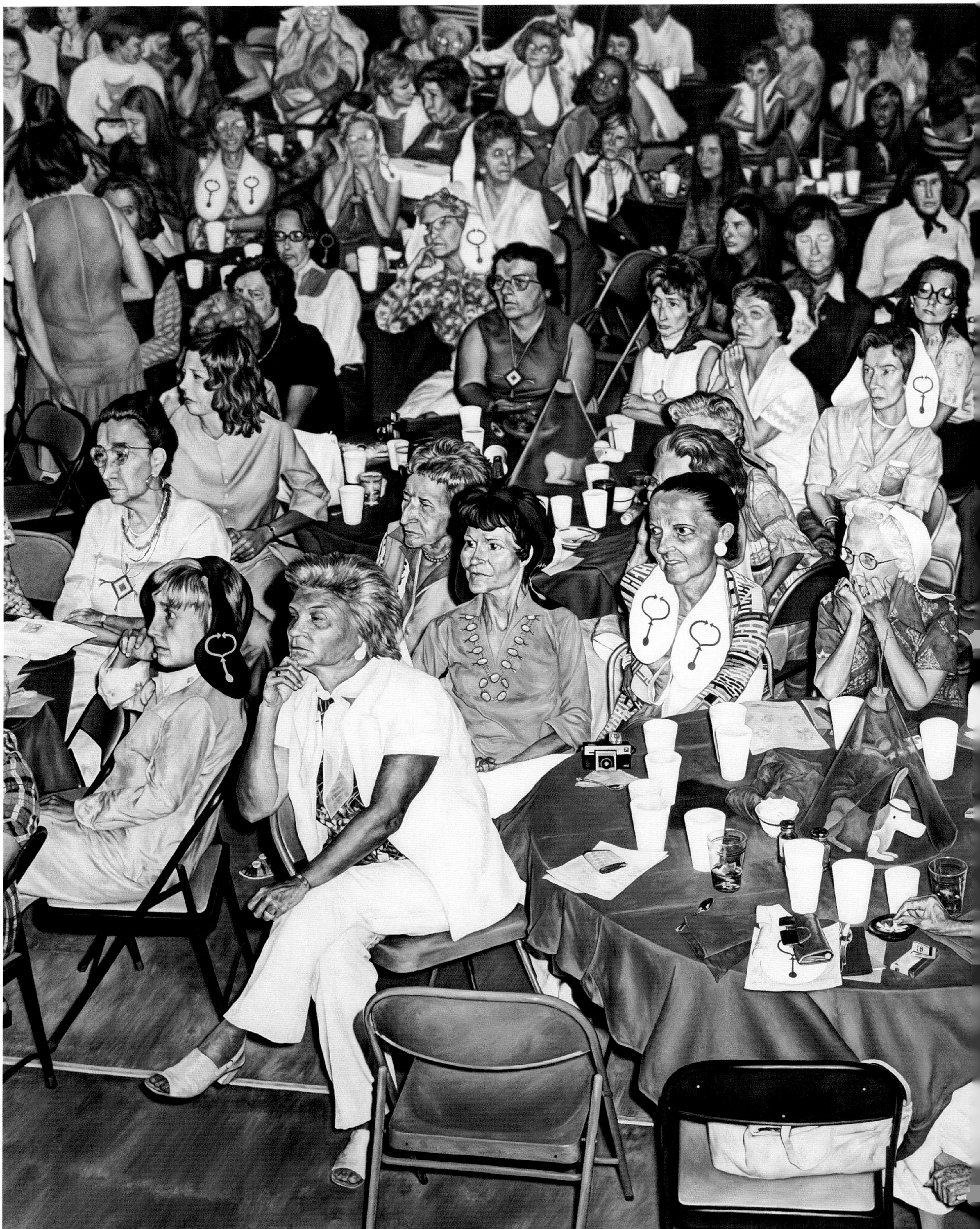

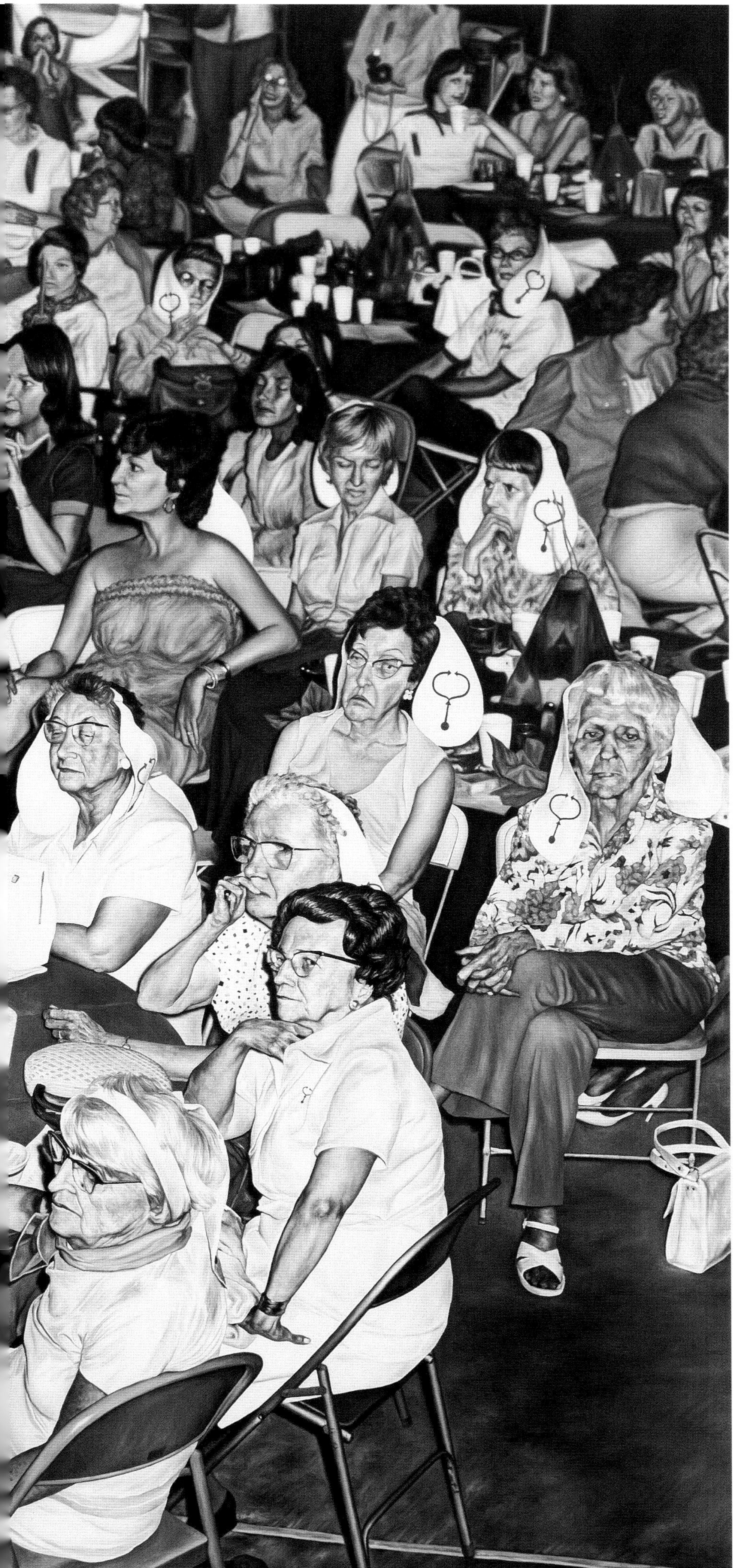

Orgonomic Functionalism Conference, 1973
2003
Oil on canvas
48 x 60 in.

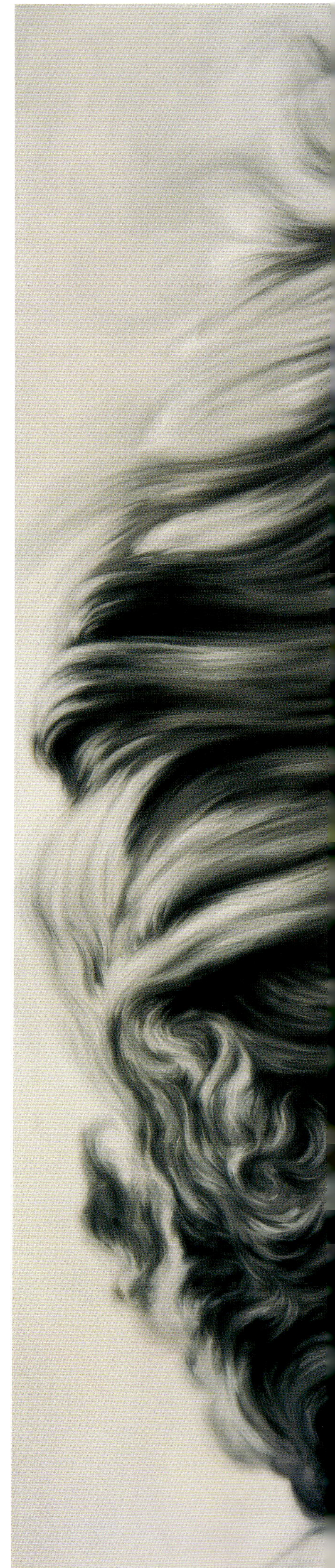

The One
2004
Oil on canvas
36 x 36 in.

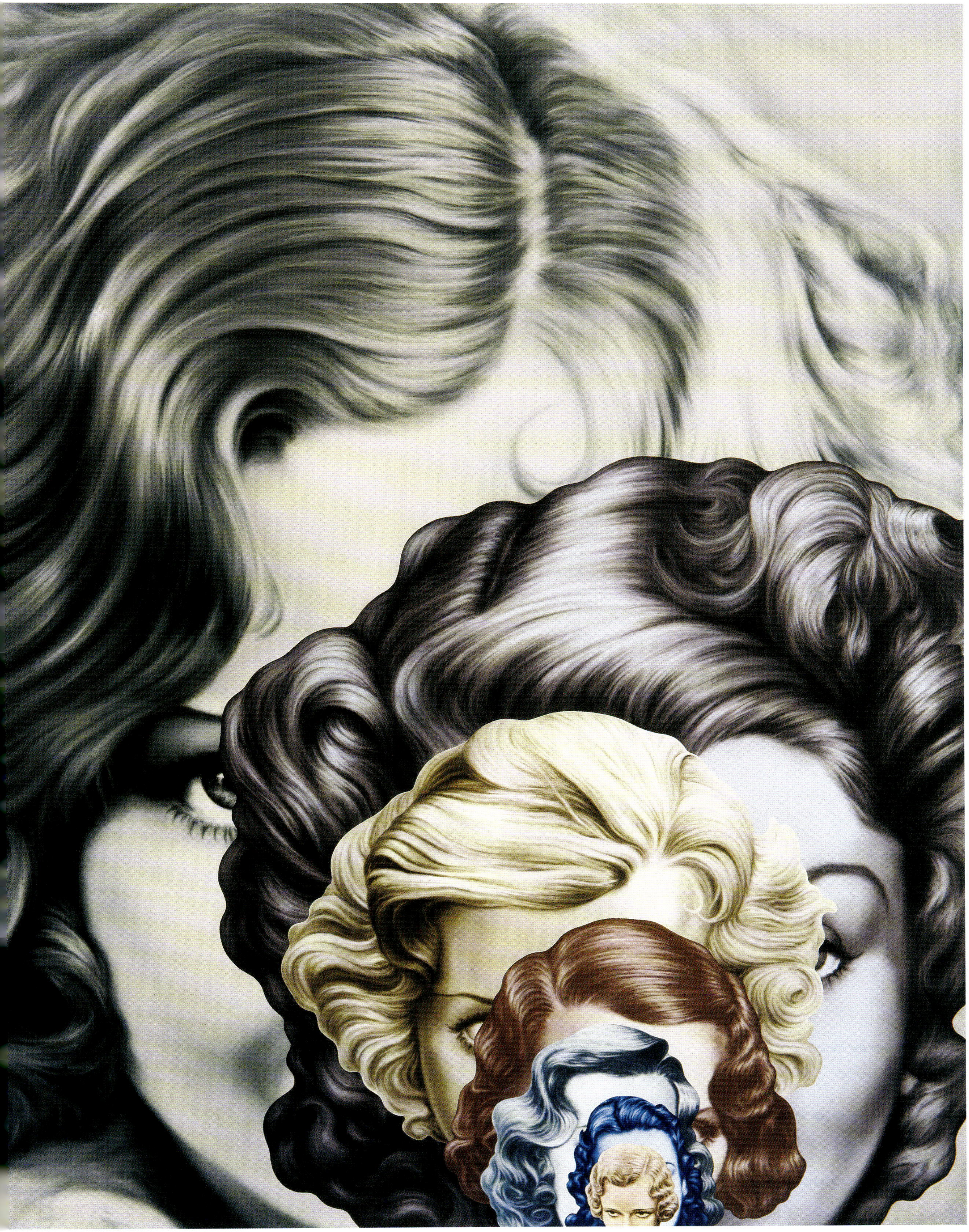

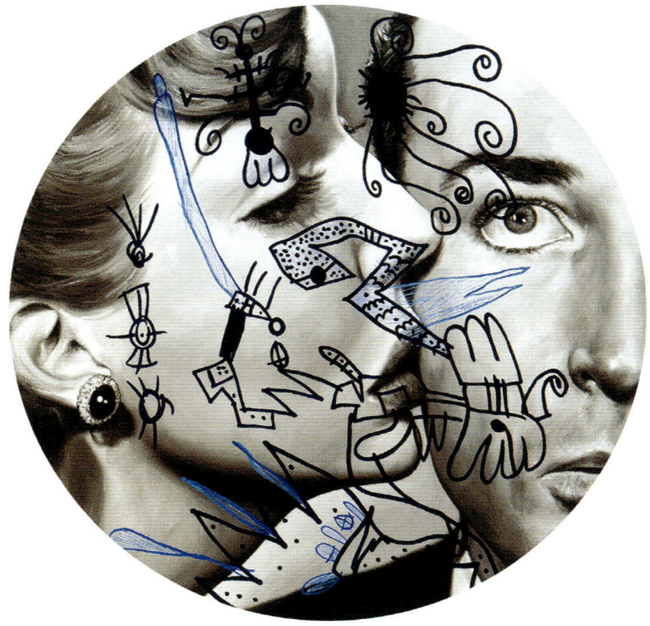

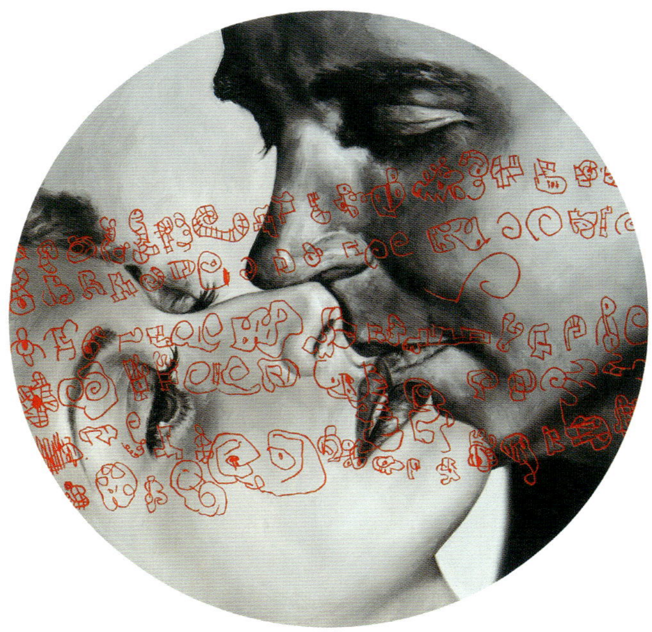

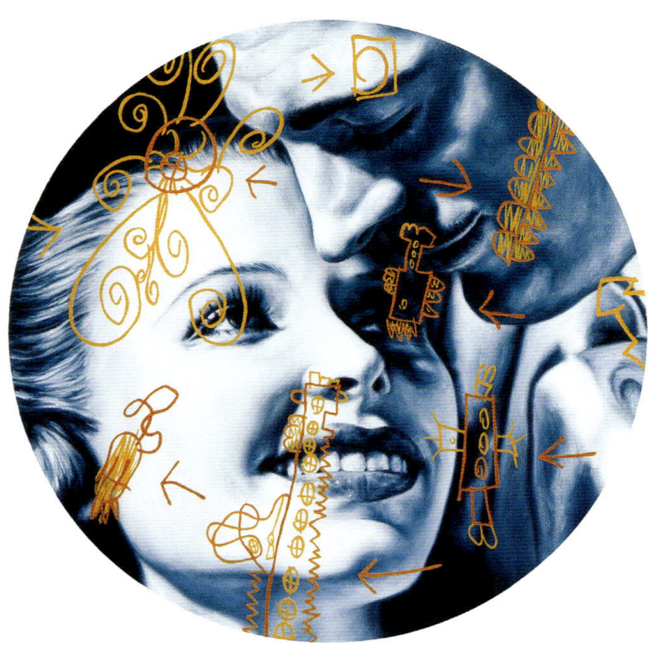

Divorce (w/ Casey Gallagher)
2004
Oil on canvas
12 in. diameter

Divorce (w/ Casey Gallagher)
2004
Oil on canvas
12 in. diameter

Divorce (w/ Casey Gallagher)
2004
Oil on canvas
12 in. diameter

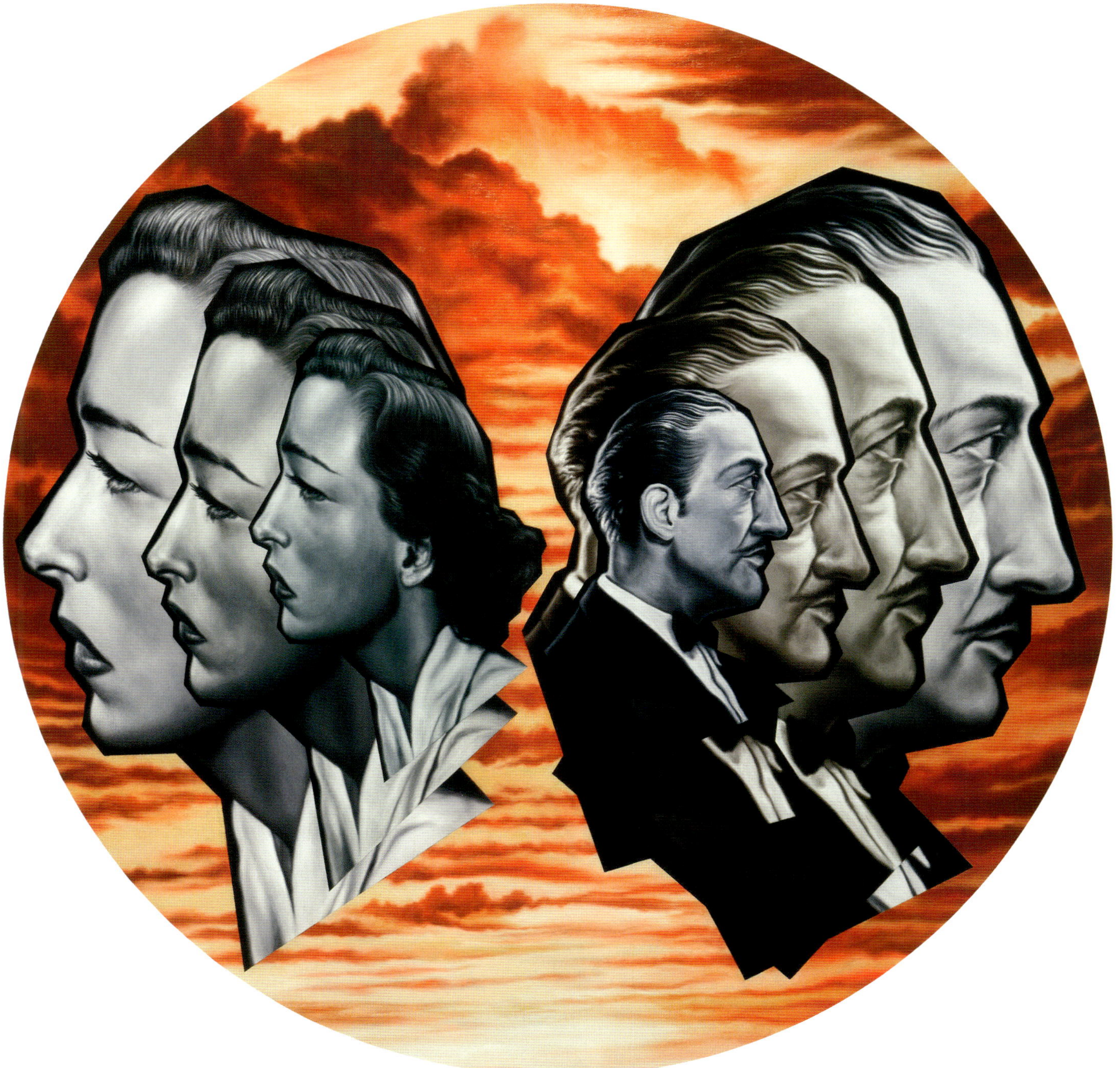

Divorced
2004
Oil on panel
26 in. diameter

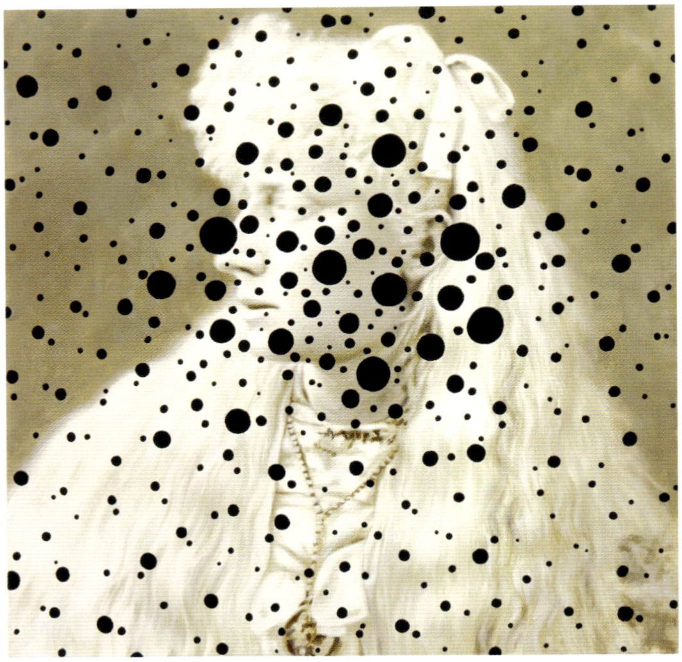

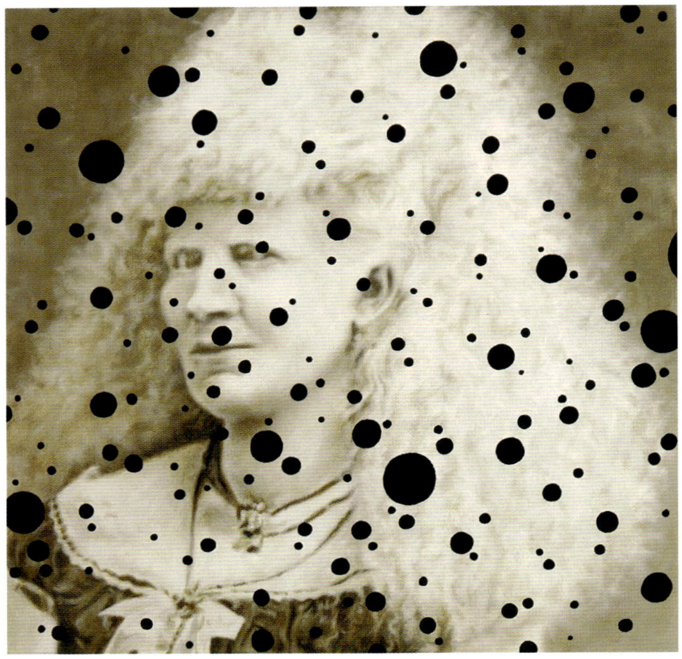

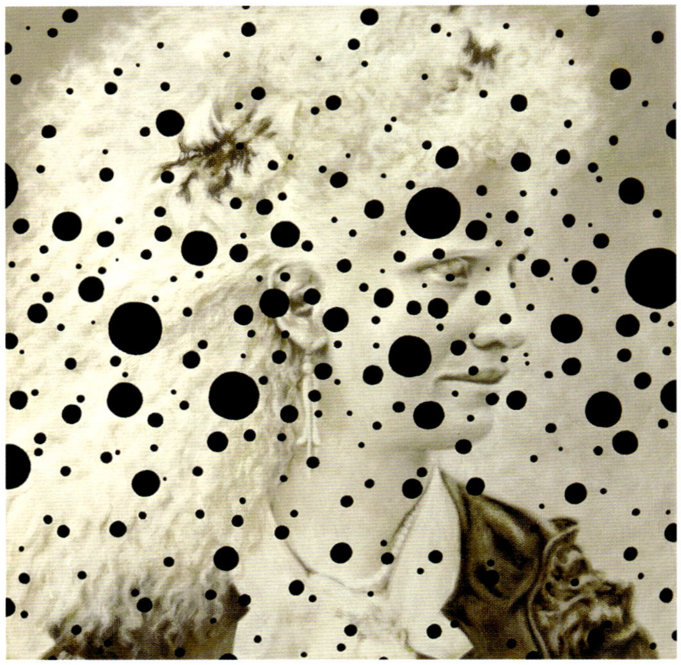

Albina et Pois Noirs
2005
Glow-in-the-dark acrylic on canvas
12 x 12 in.

Albina et Pois Noirs
2005
Glow-in-the-dark acrylic on canvas
12 x 12 in.

Albina et Pois Noirs
2005
Glow-in-the-dark acrylic on canvas
12 x 12 in.

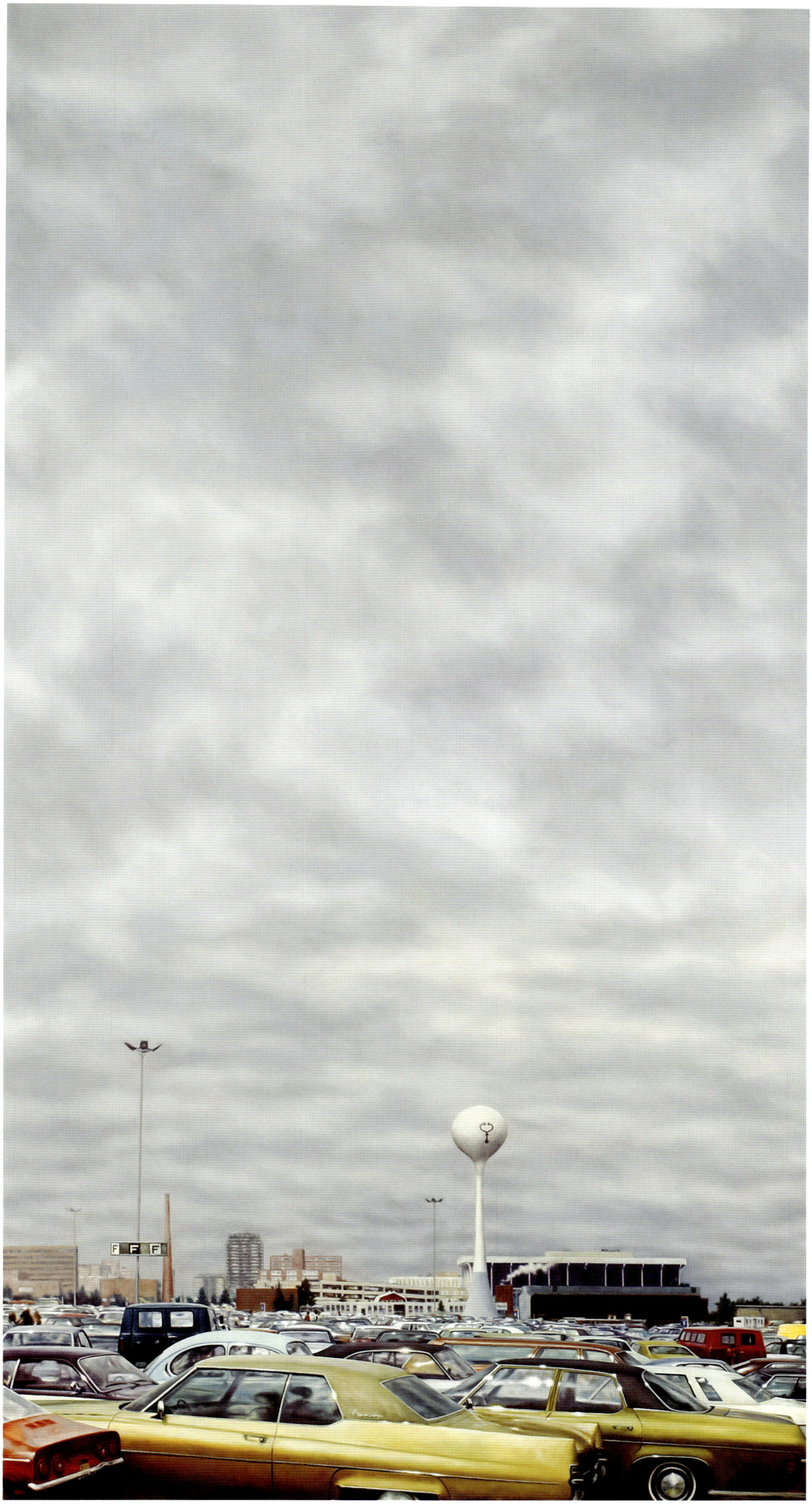

Northland
2004
Oil on canvas
72 x 36 in.

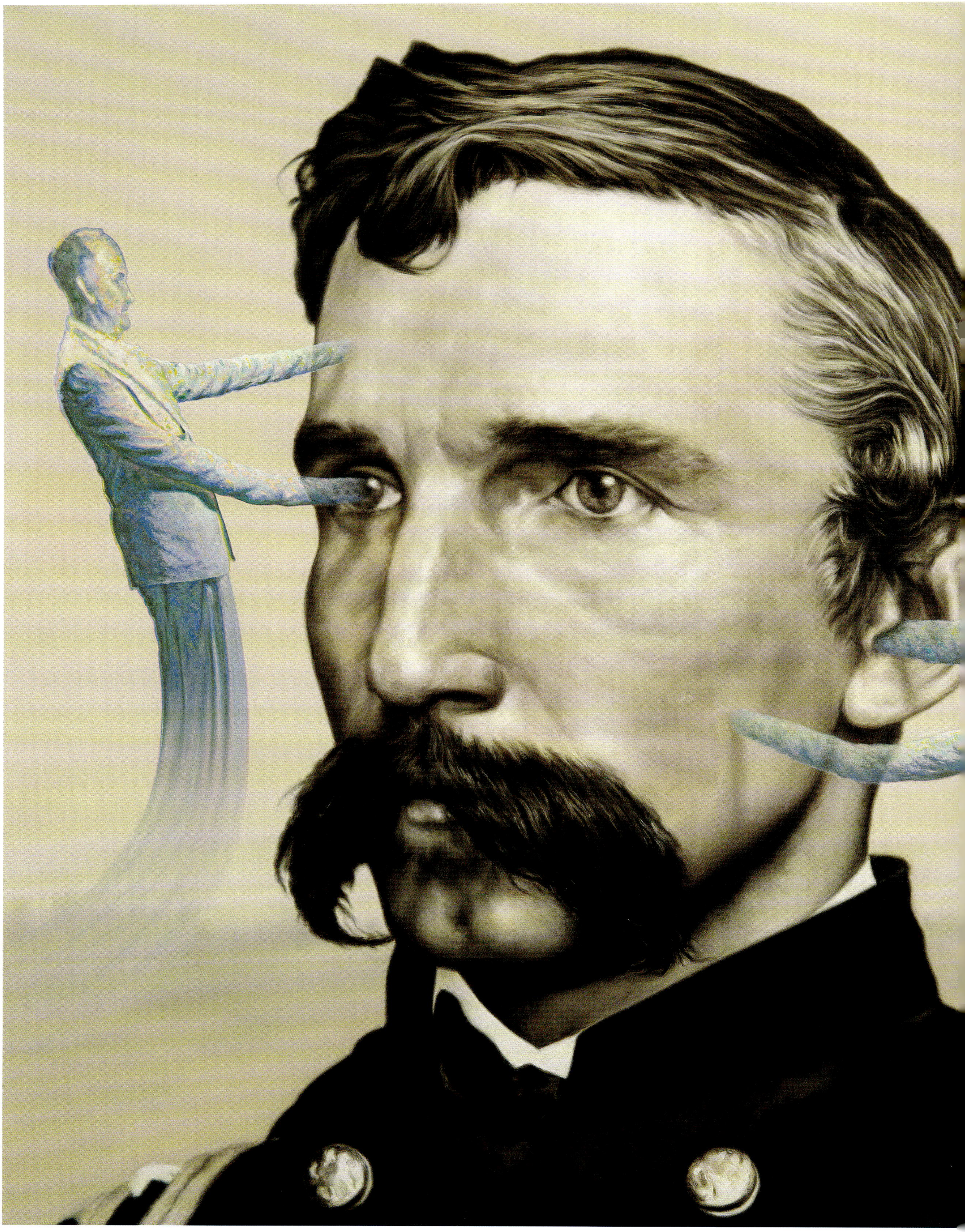

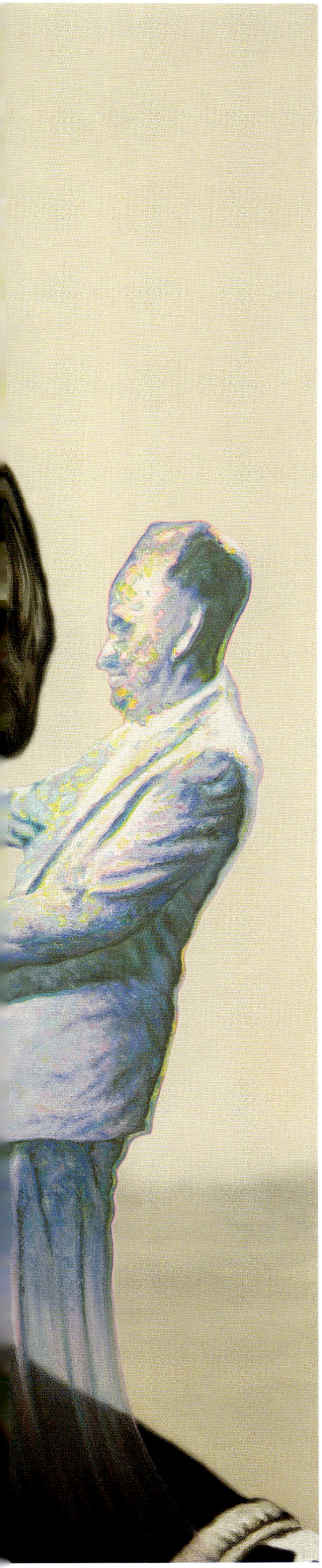

Joshua L. Chamberlain and The Angels of _________
2006
Oil on canvas
24 x 24 in.

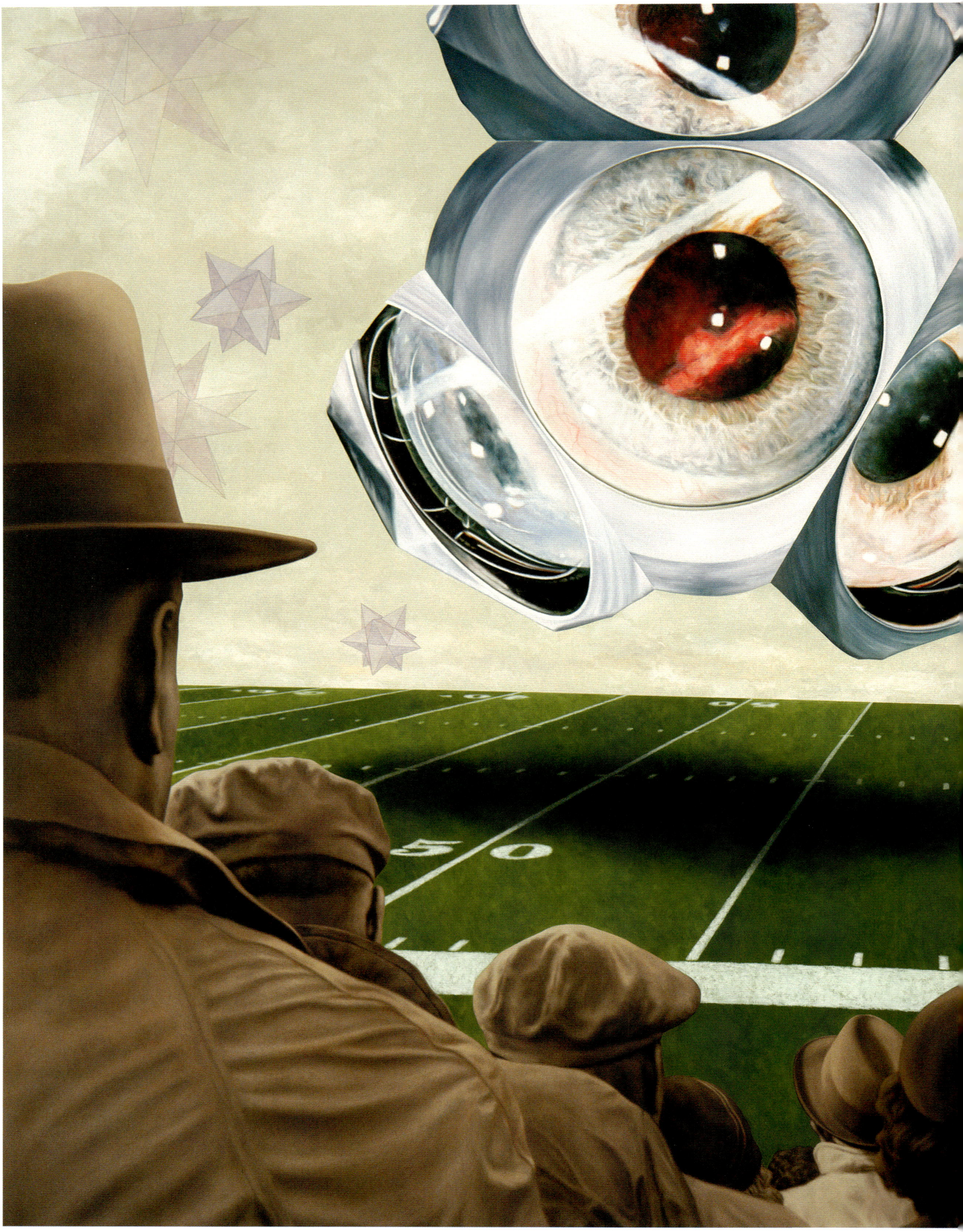
50

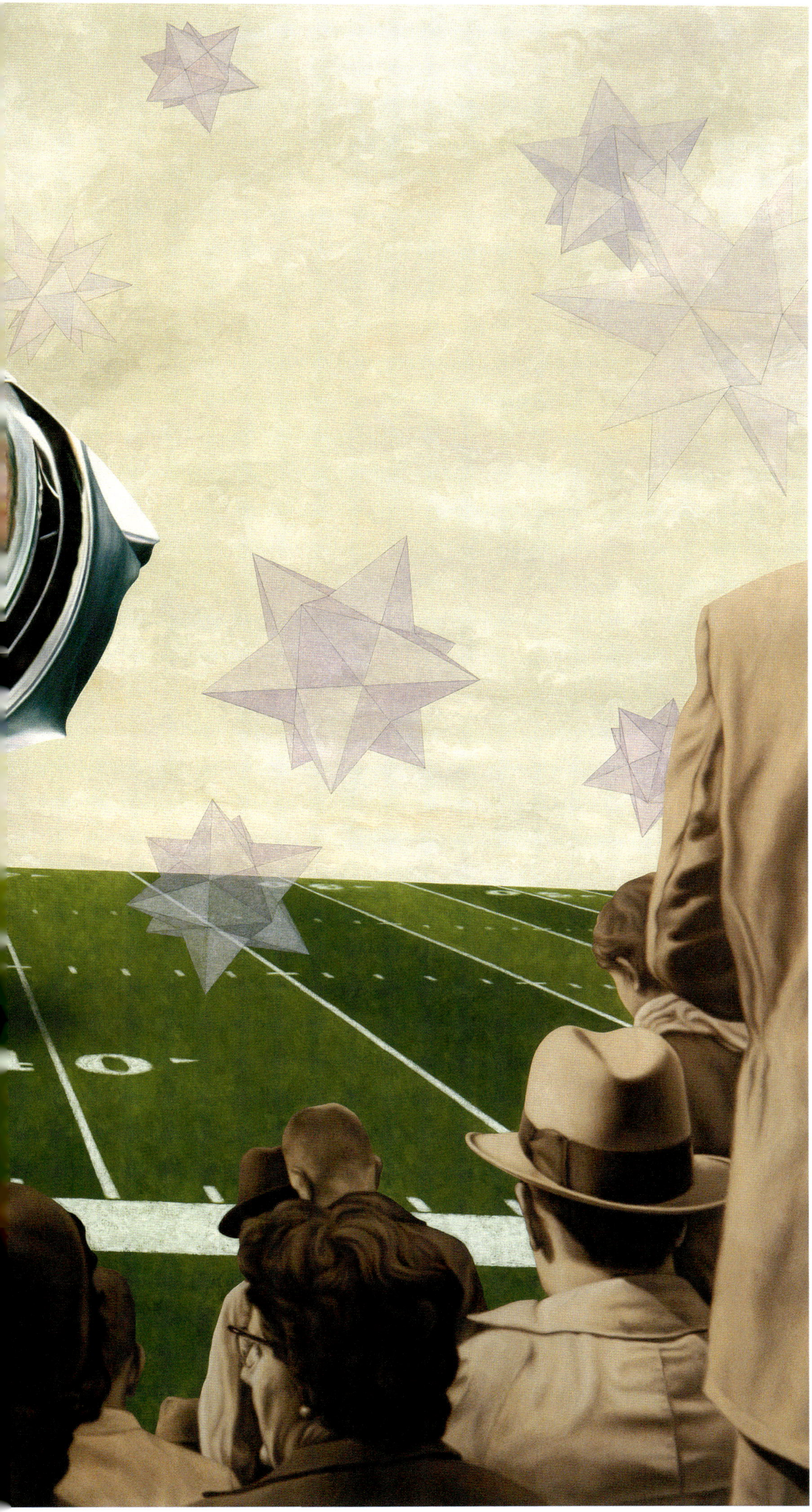

The Ascension
2005
Oil on canvas
67 x 89 in.

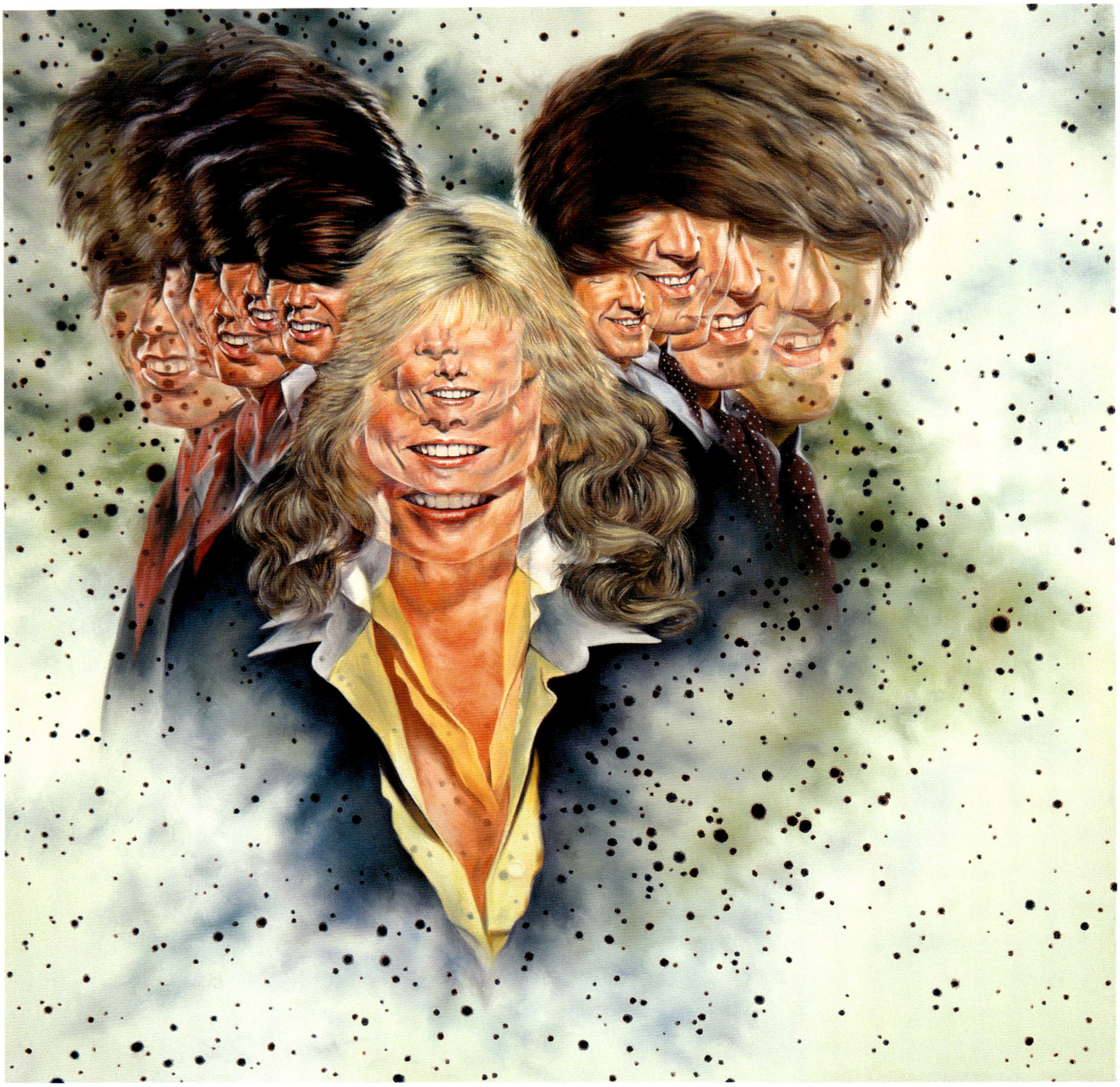

The Truth Emerges From Beyond The Crab Nebula and Finds You Very, Very Attractive
2005
Oil on canvas
24 x 24 in.

The Truth Yet Again Asserts Itself in Obdurate Reprisal, And in So Doing Belies the Fact That You, No Longer Besieged by Doubt, Have Come to the Conclusion That Maybe Things Aren't Really All That Bad After All
(Opposite; detail on following page)
2006
Oil on canvas
60 x 36 in.

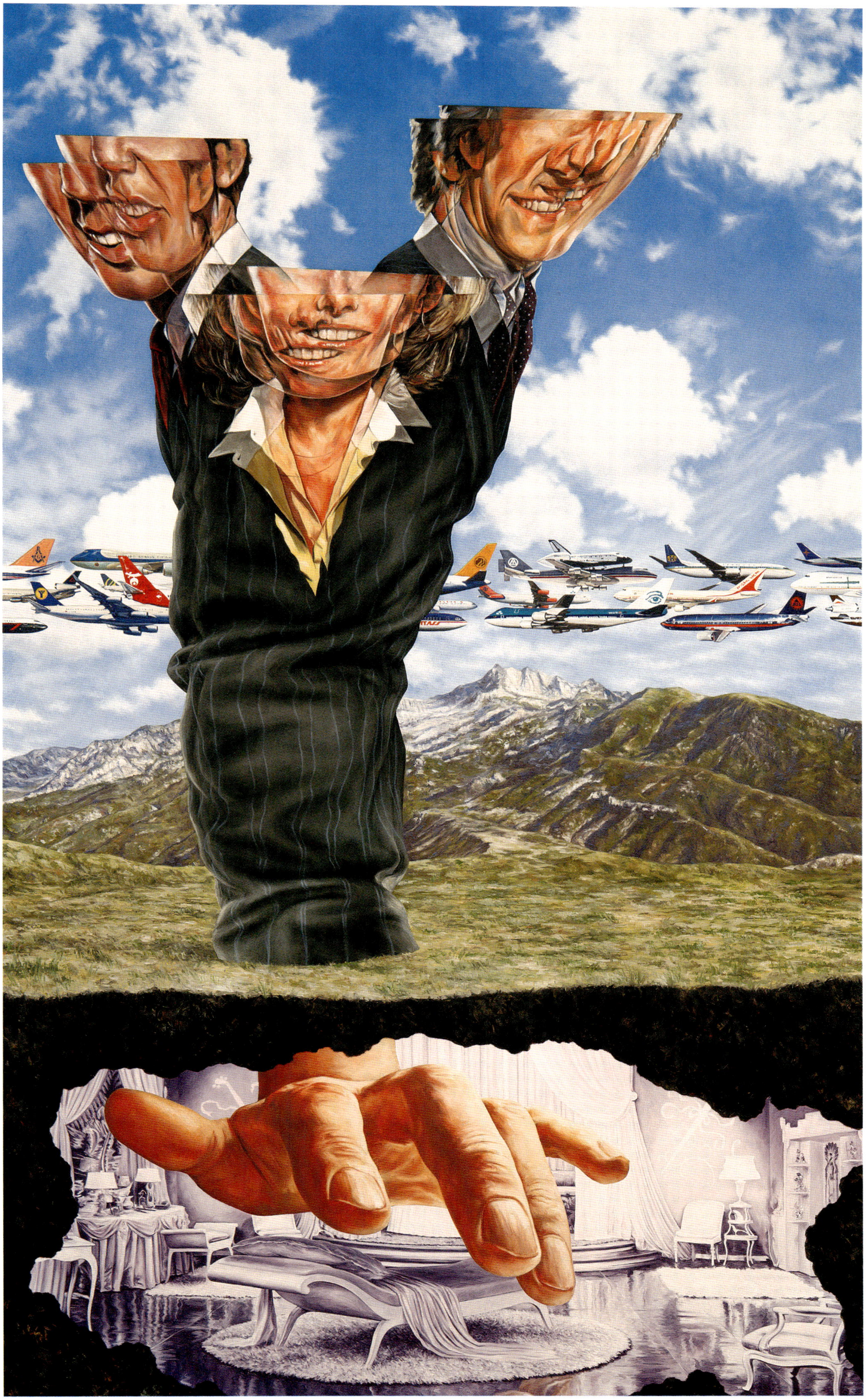

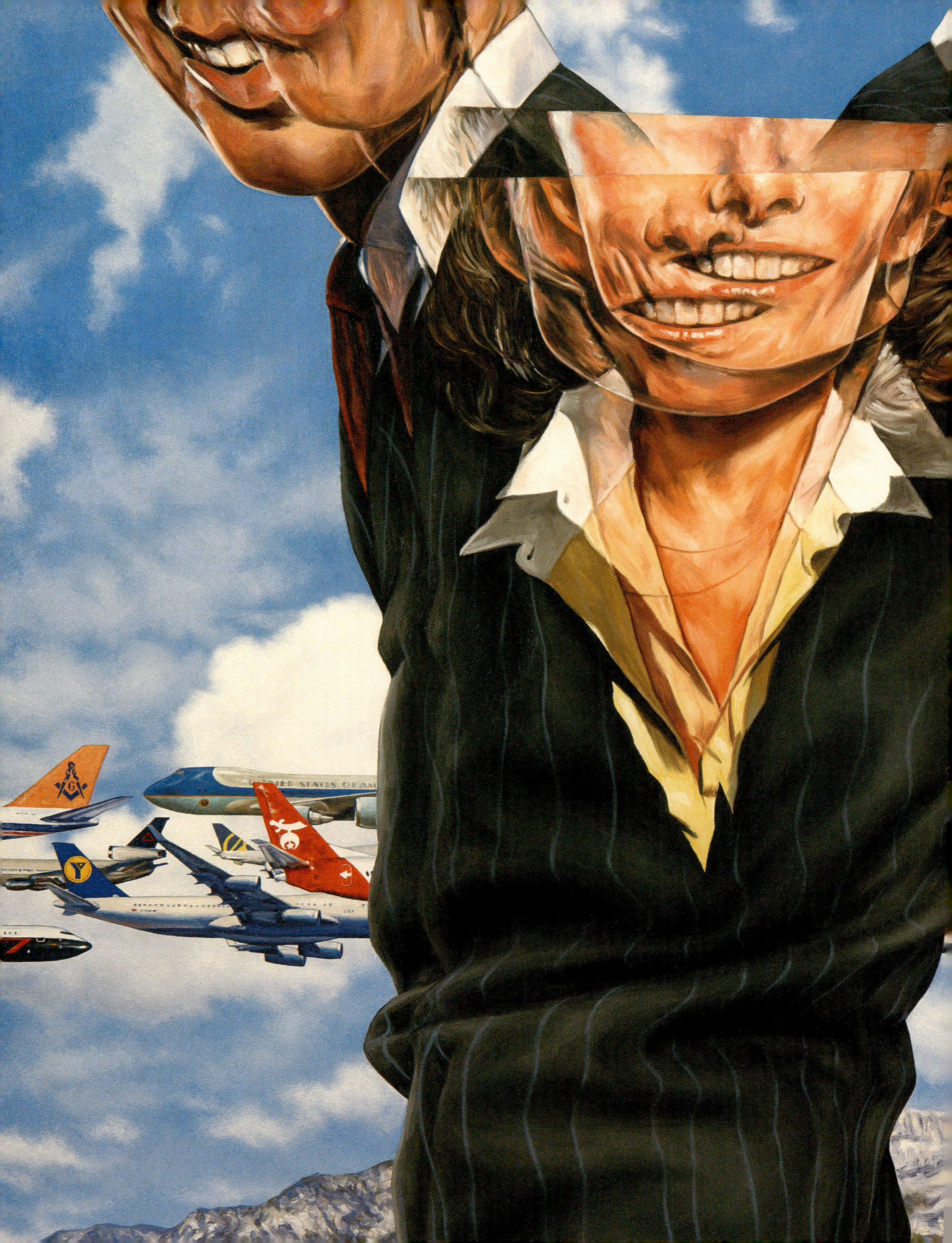

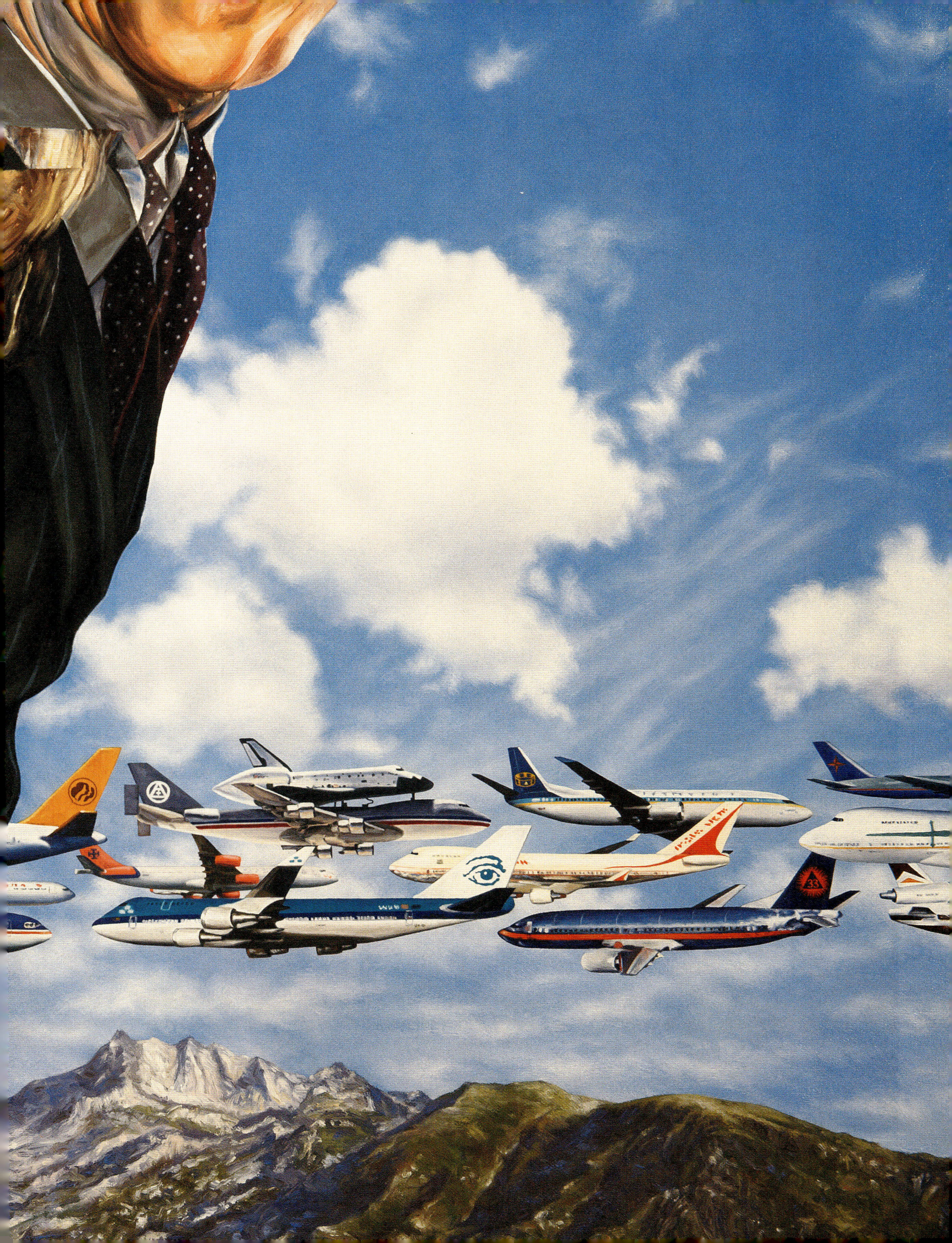

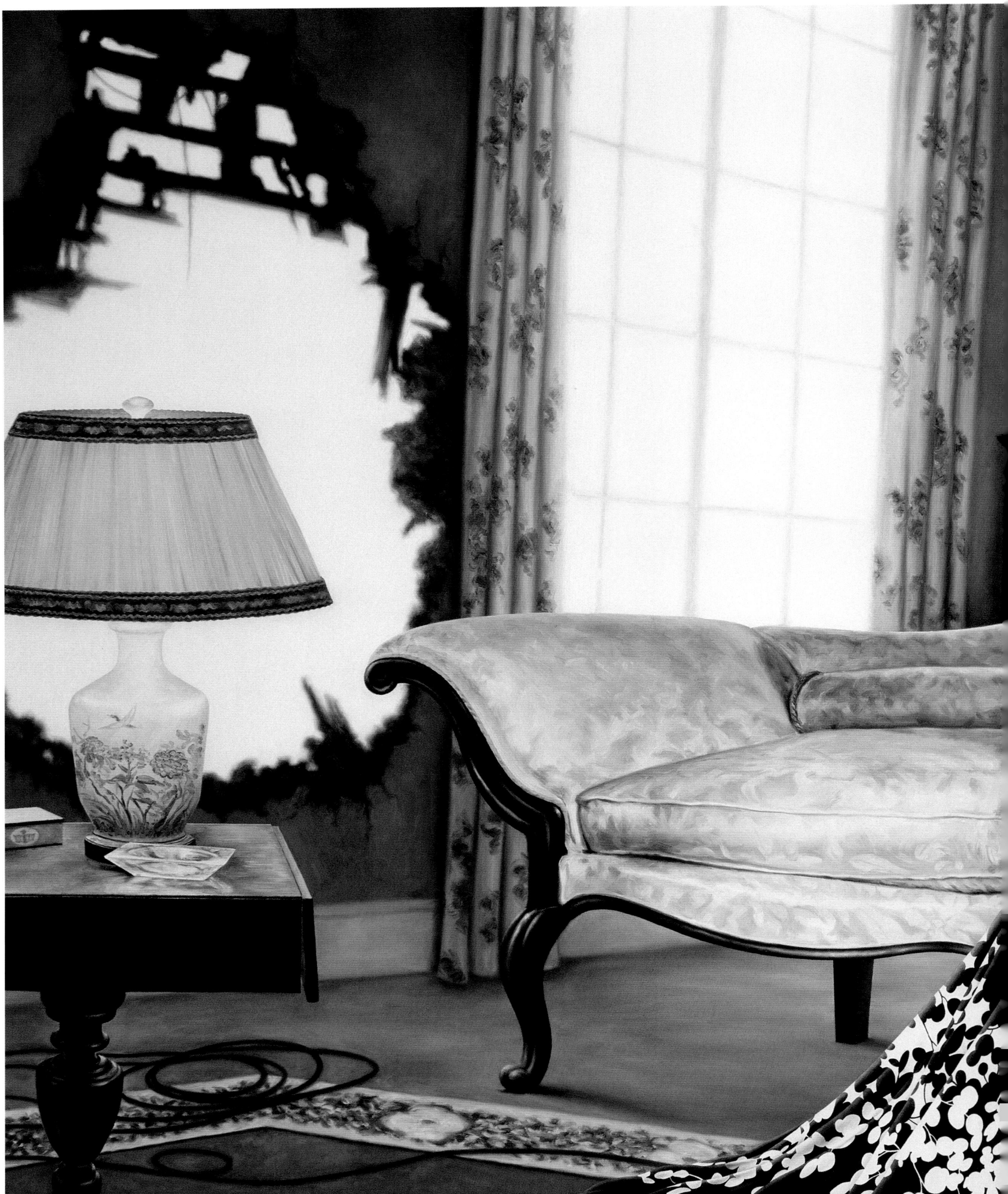

House & Home
2006
Oil on canvas
36 x 60 in.

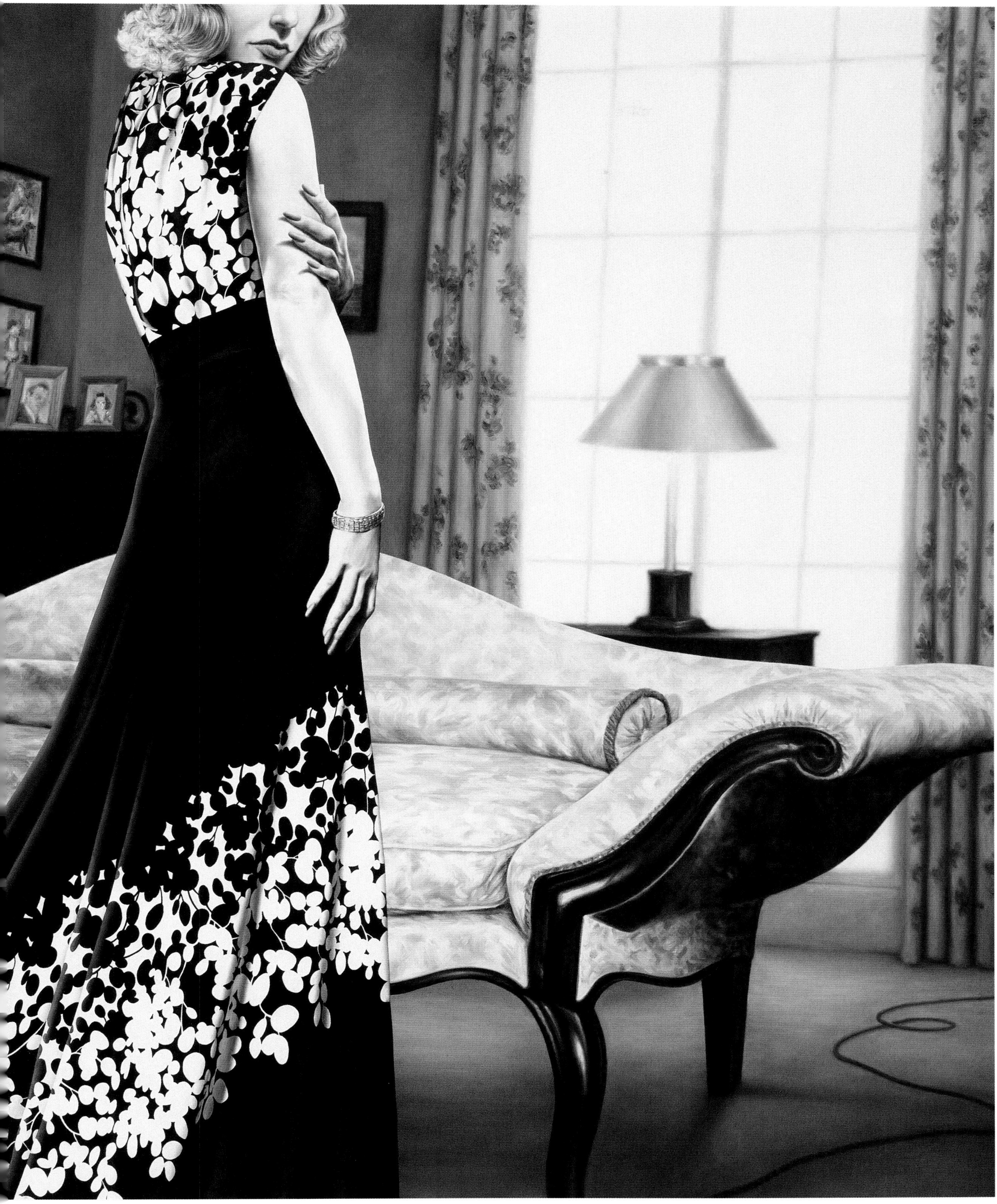

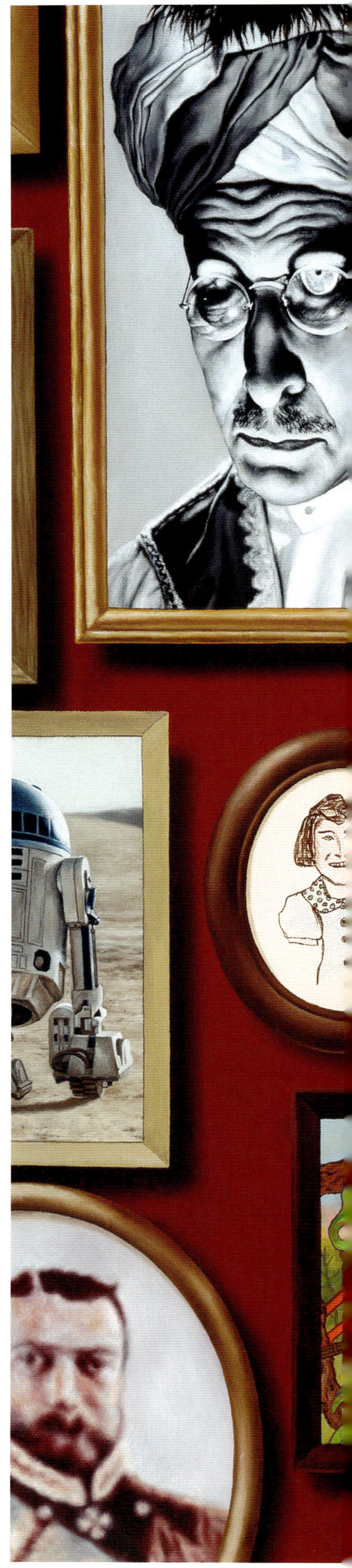

Collusion
2002
Oil on canvas
24 x 24 in.

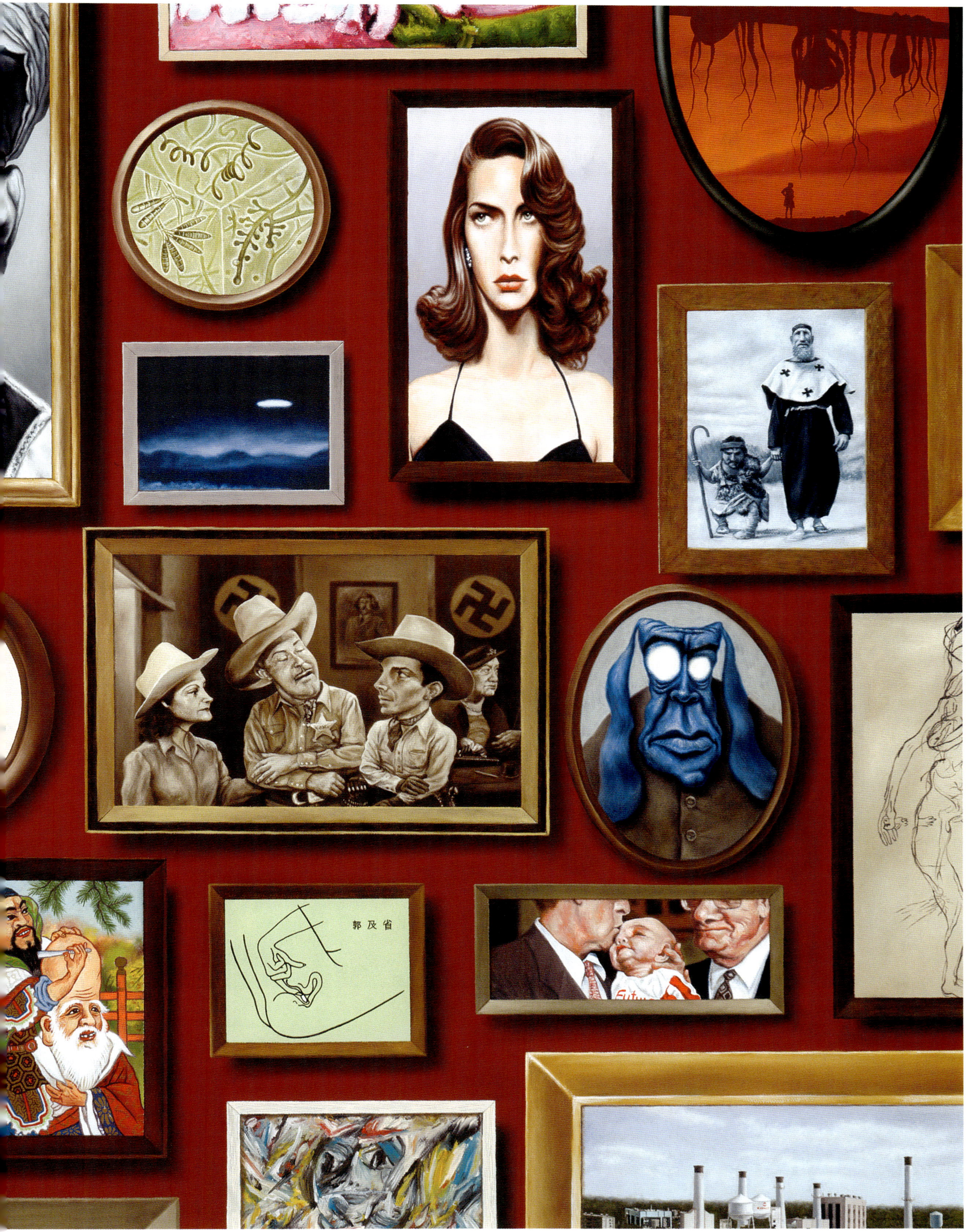
郭及省

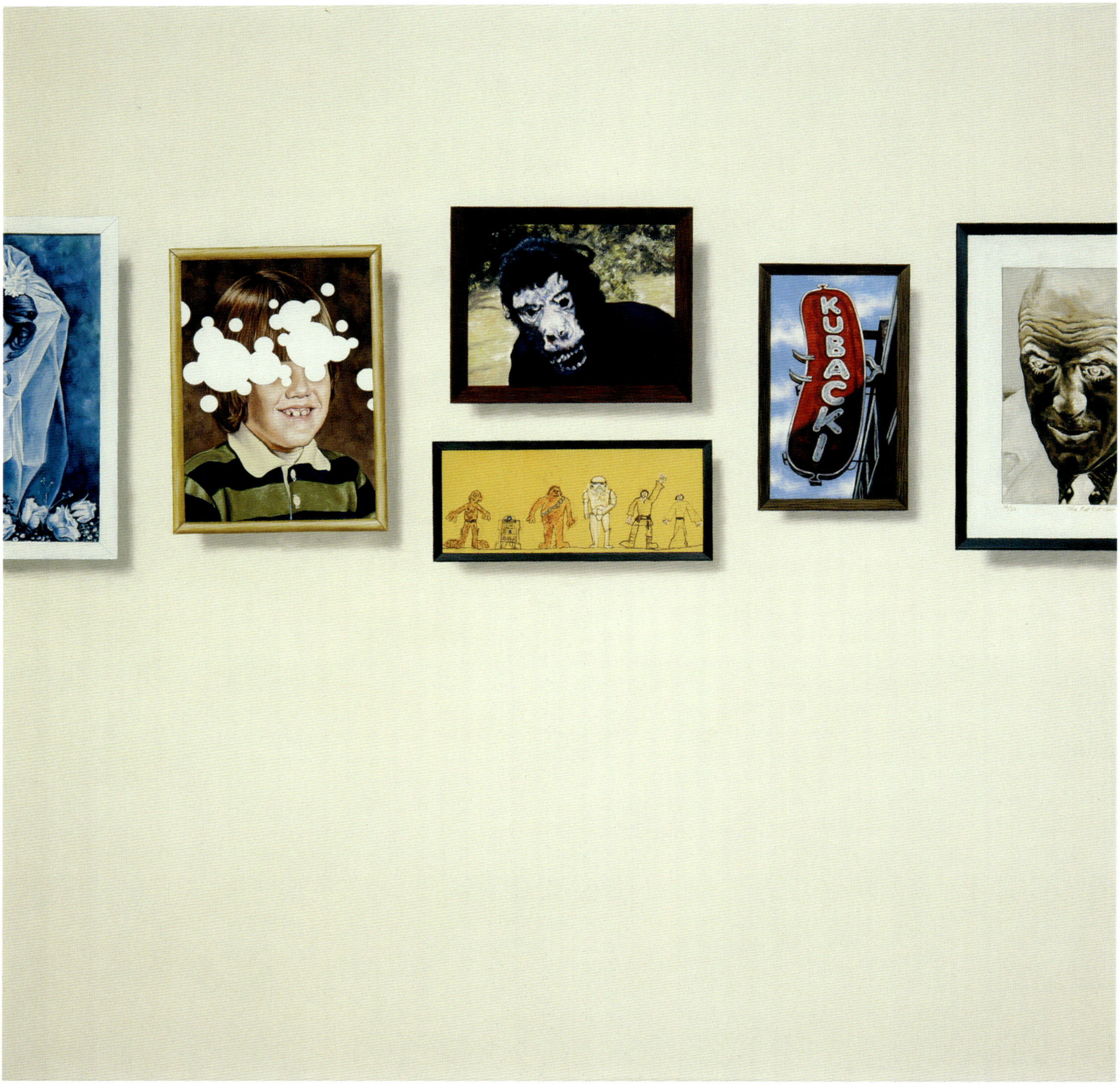

Collusion: Angst
2003
oil on canvas
24 x 24 in.

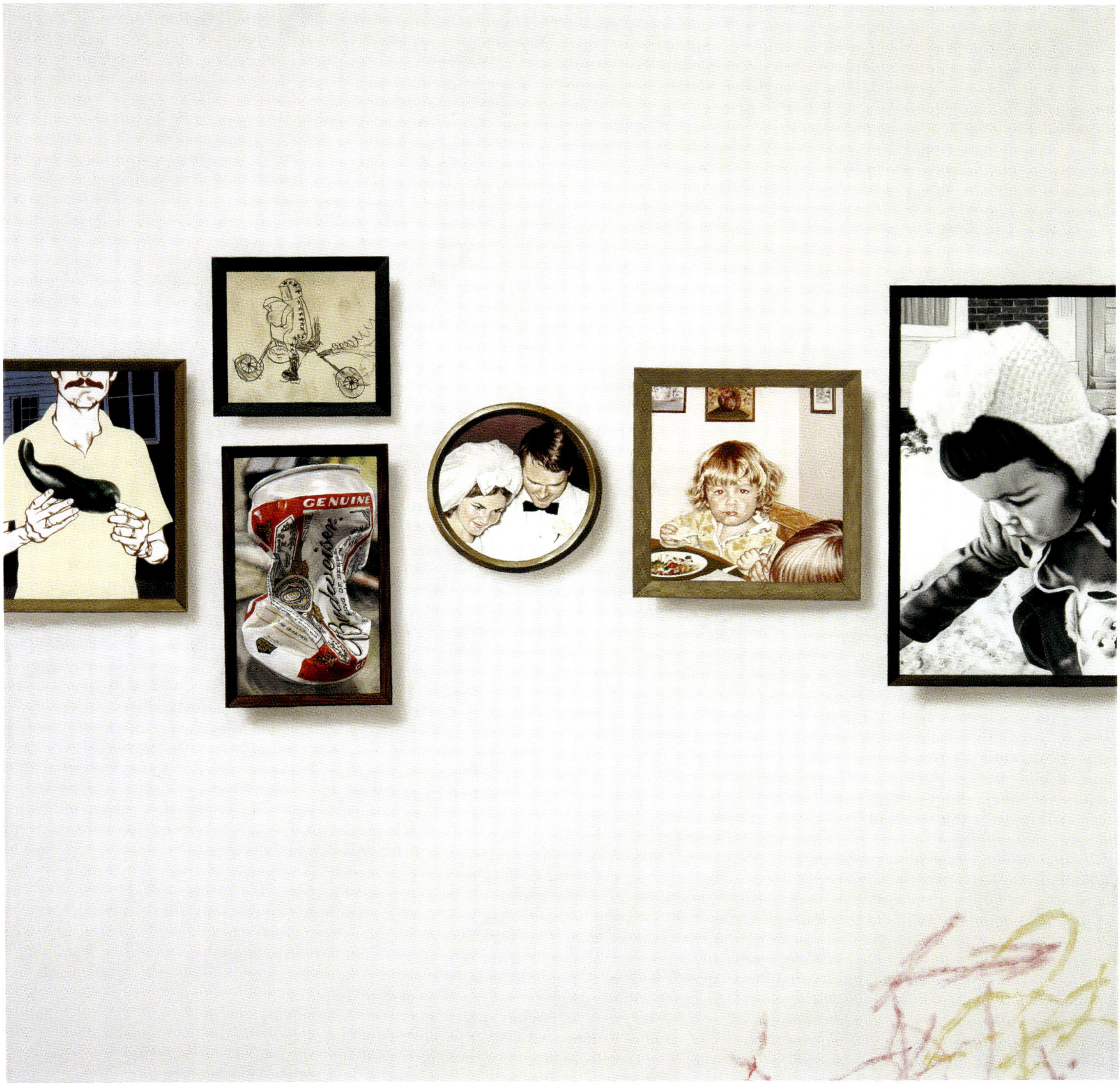

Collusion: Knievel
2003
Oil on canvas
24 x 24 in.

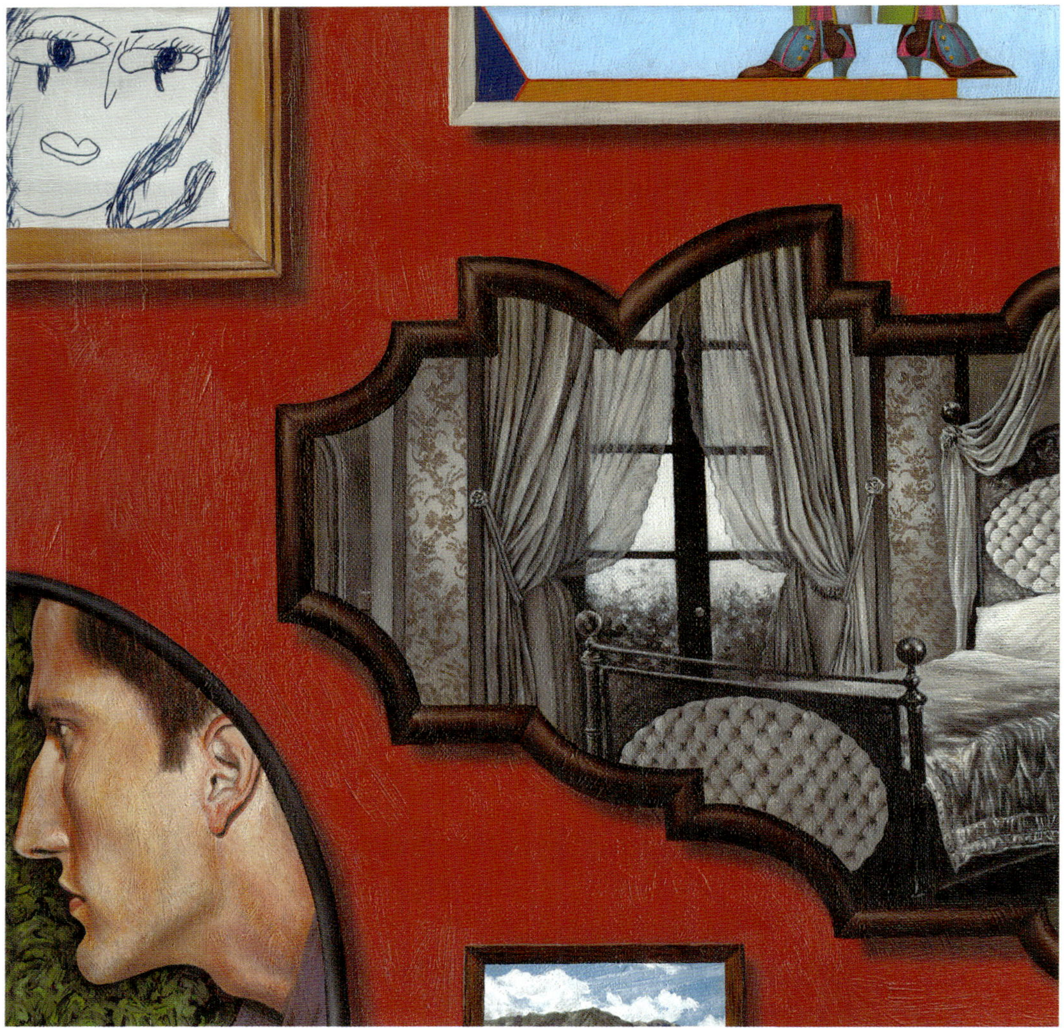

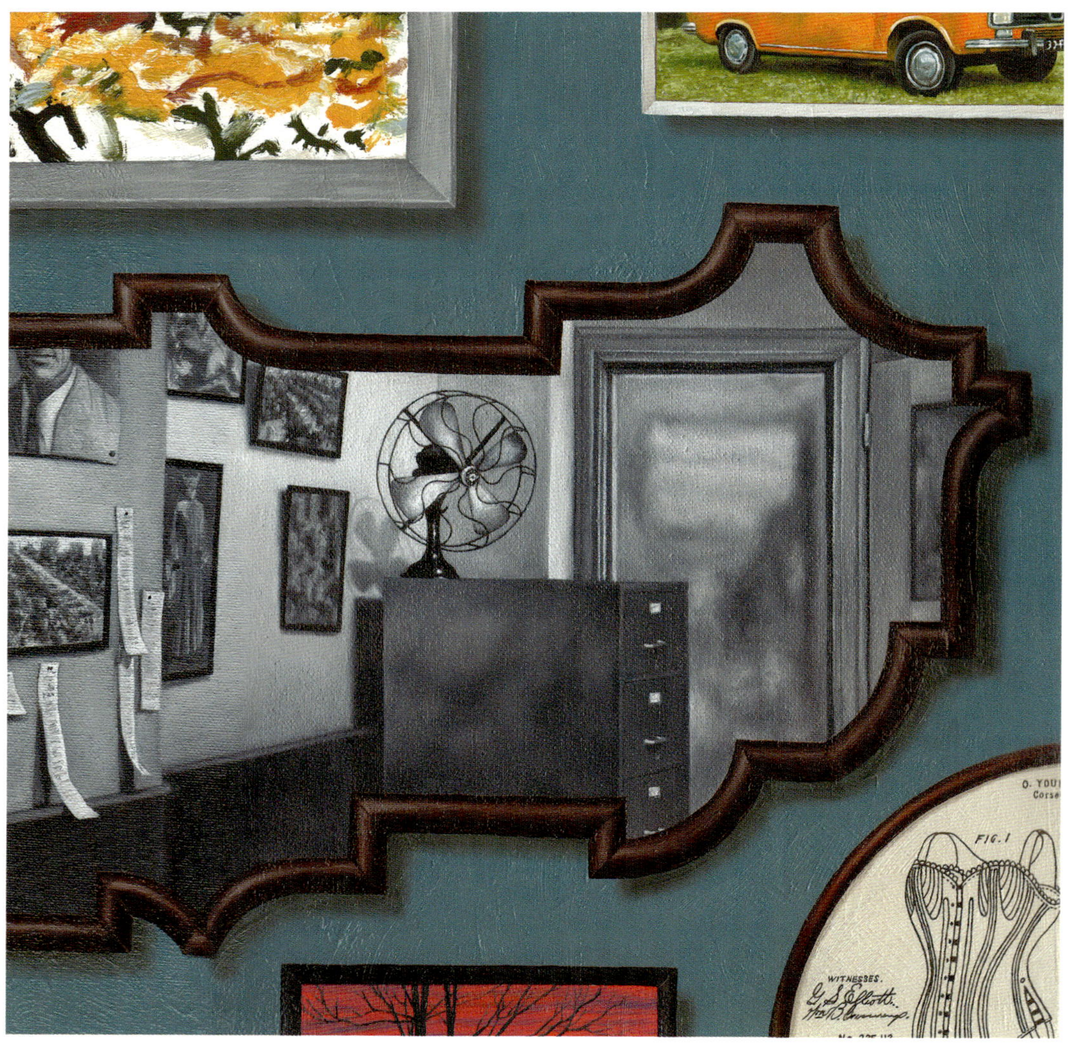

Collusion: Fragment 1
2006
Oil on canvas
12 x 12 in.

Collusion: Fragment 2
2006
Oil on canvas
12 x 12 in.

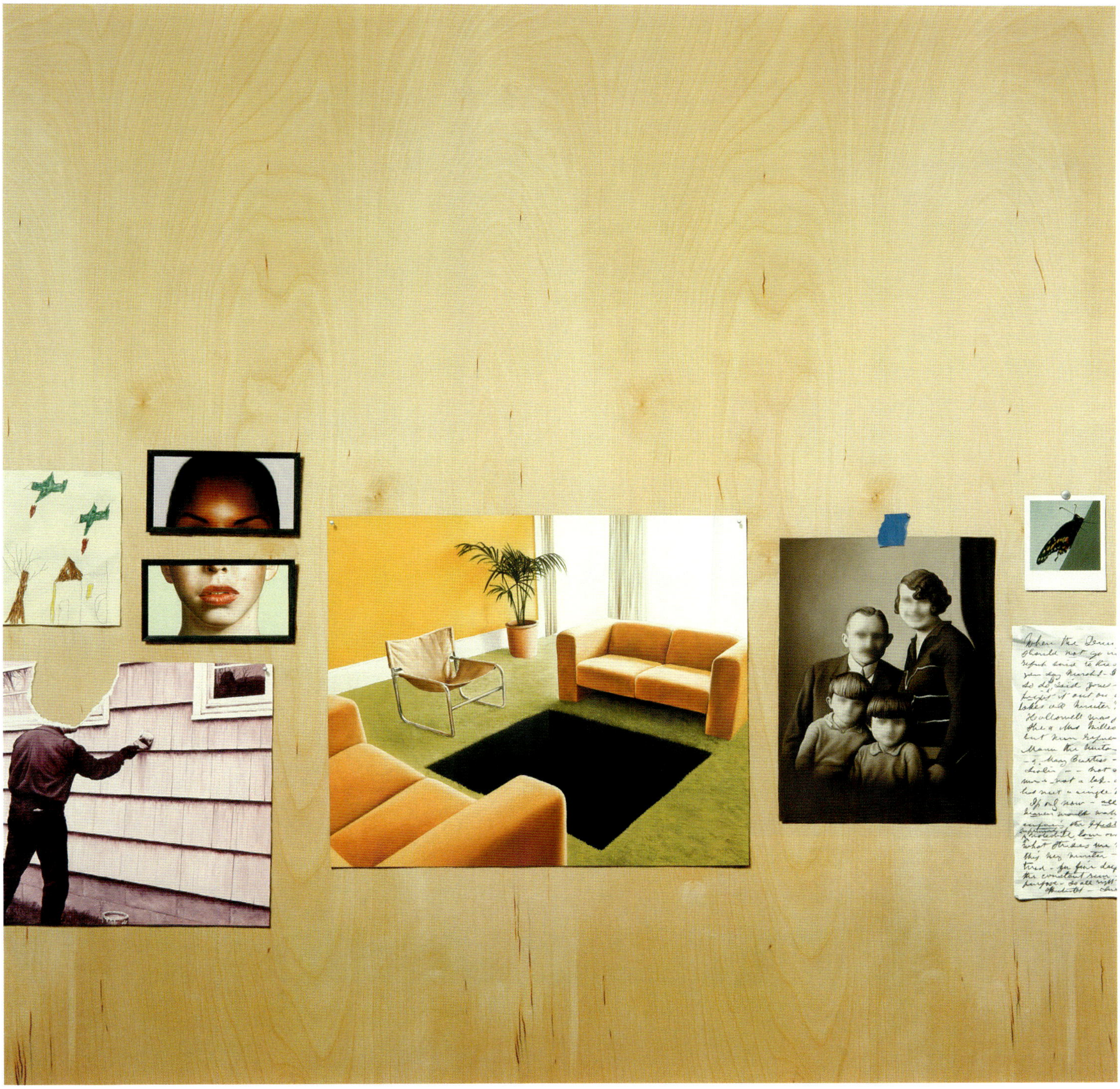

Collusion: The Risk
2006
Oil on wood
48 x 48 in.

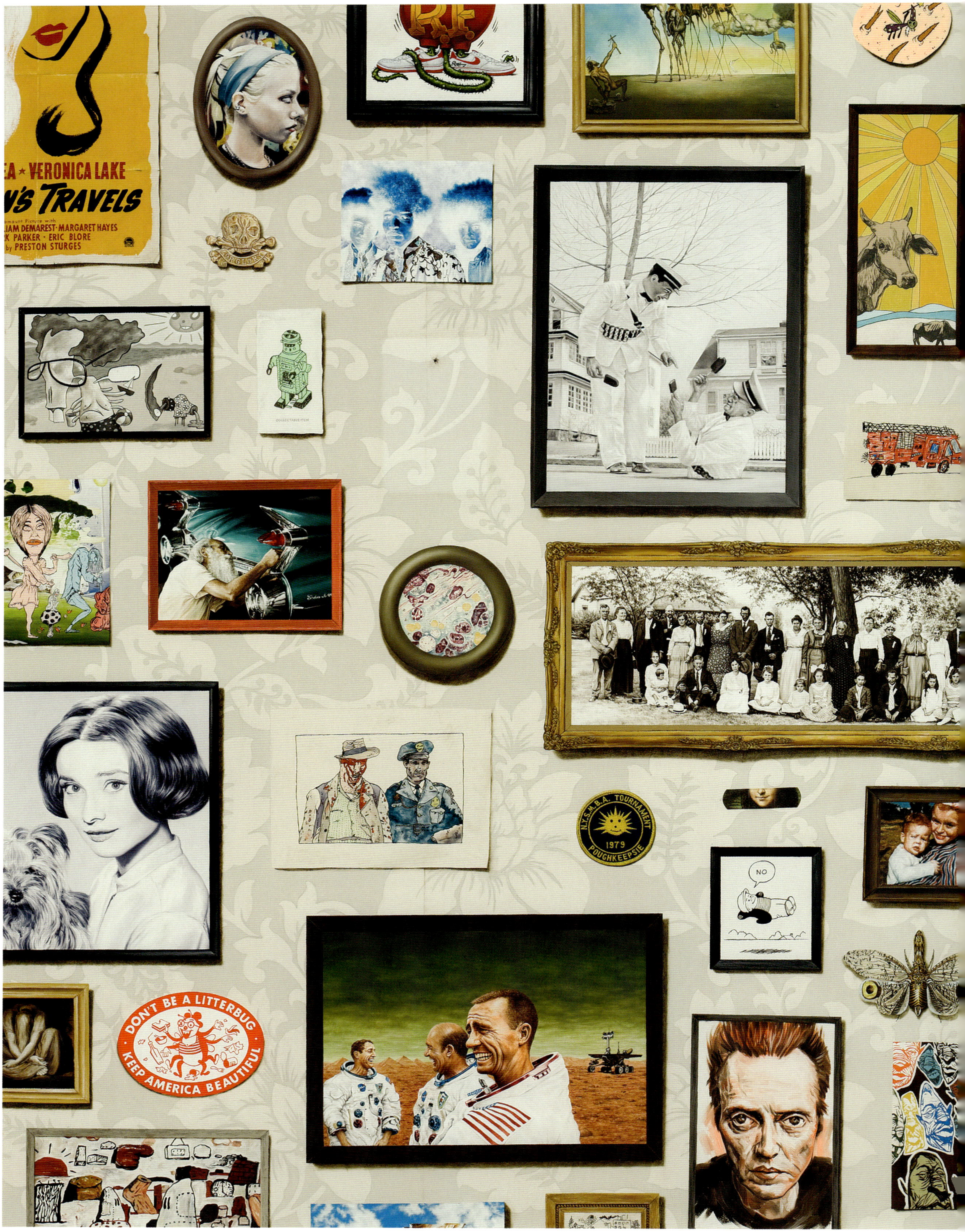
VERONICA LAKE
MARGARET HAYES
ERIC BLORE
by PRESTON STURGES
DON'T BE A LITTERBUG
KEEP AMERICA BEAUTIFUL
N.Y.S.M.B.A. TOURNAMENT
1979
POUGHKEEPSIE
NO

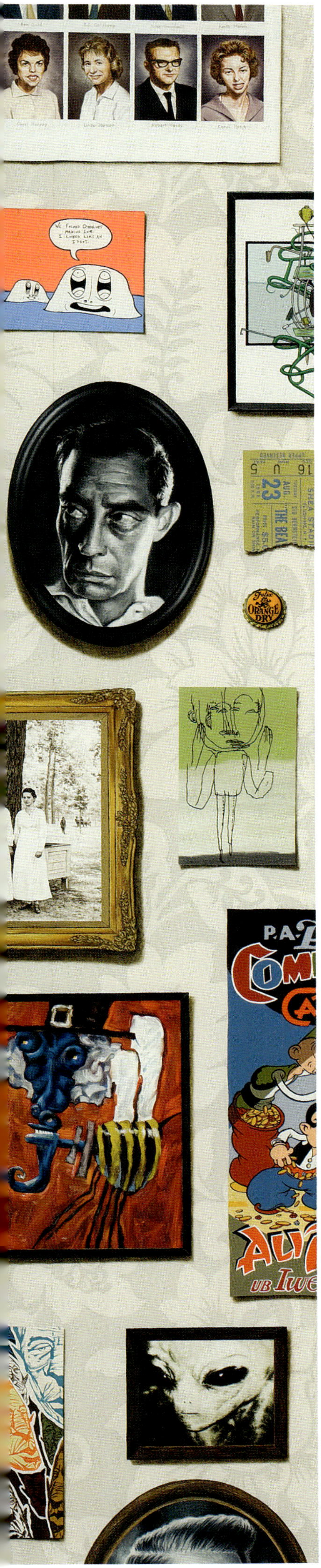

Collusion: Behemoth
(detail on following page)
2007
Oil on canvas
48 x 48 in.

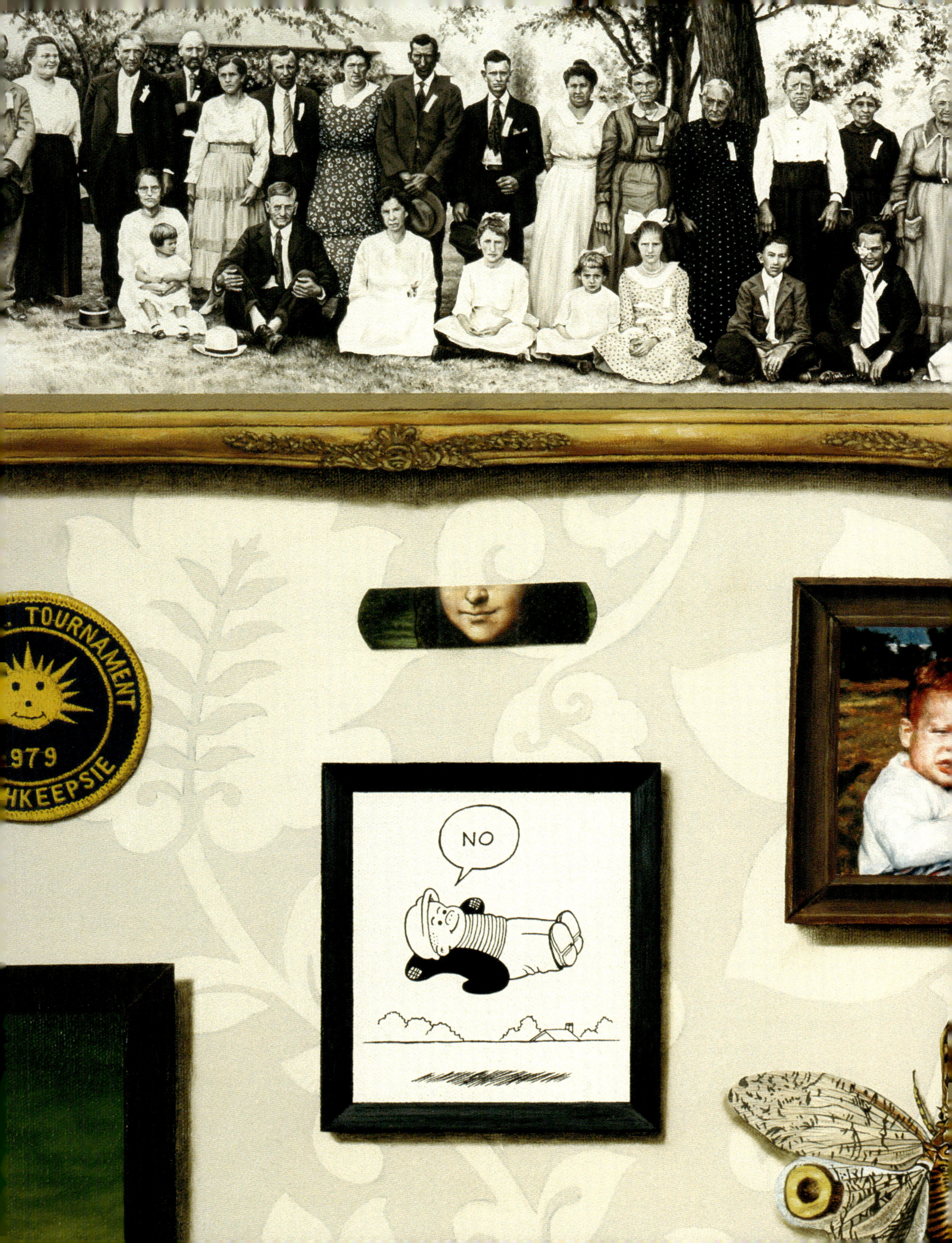
TOURNAMENT
NO

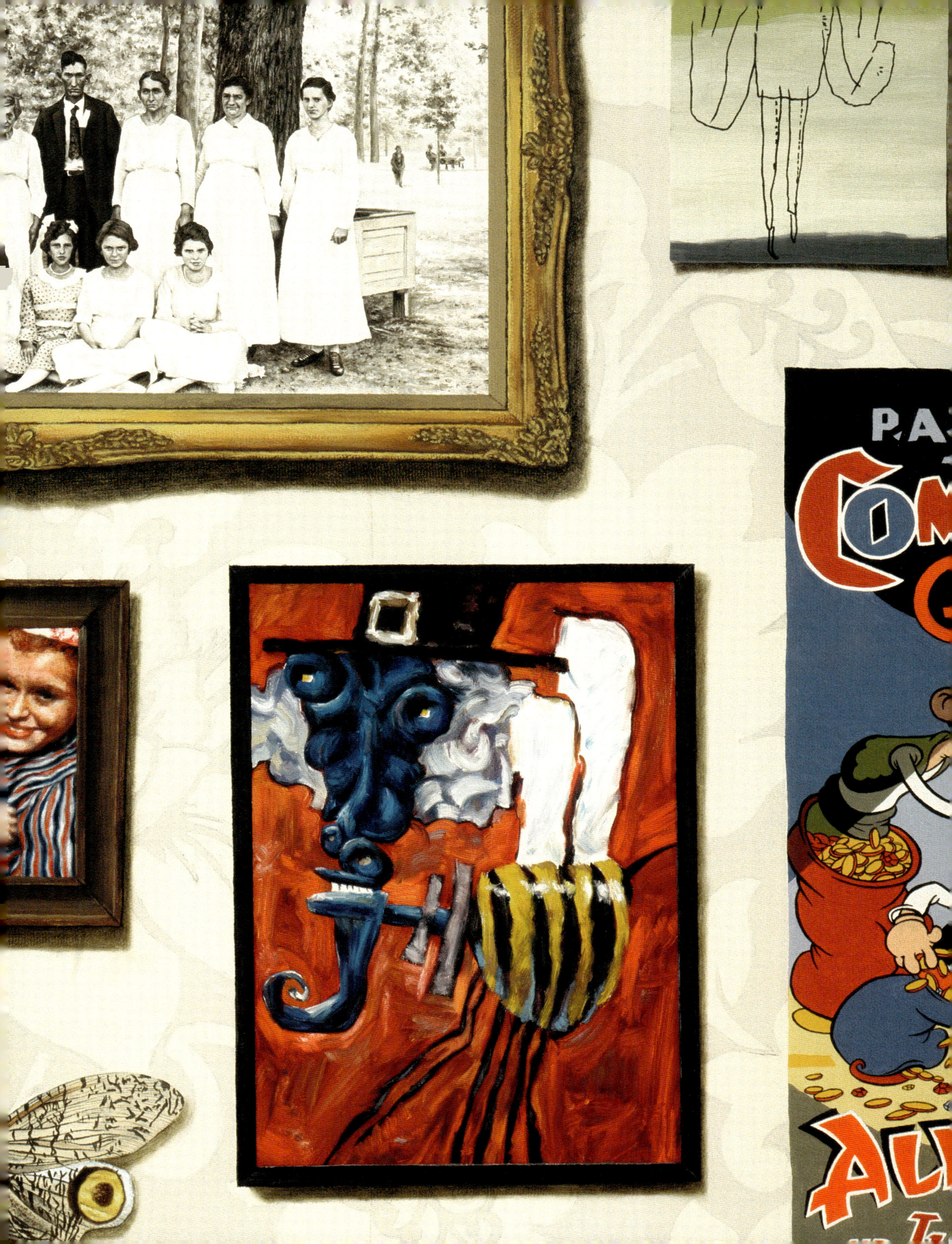

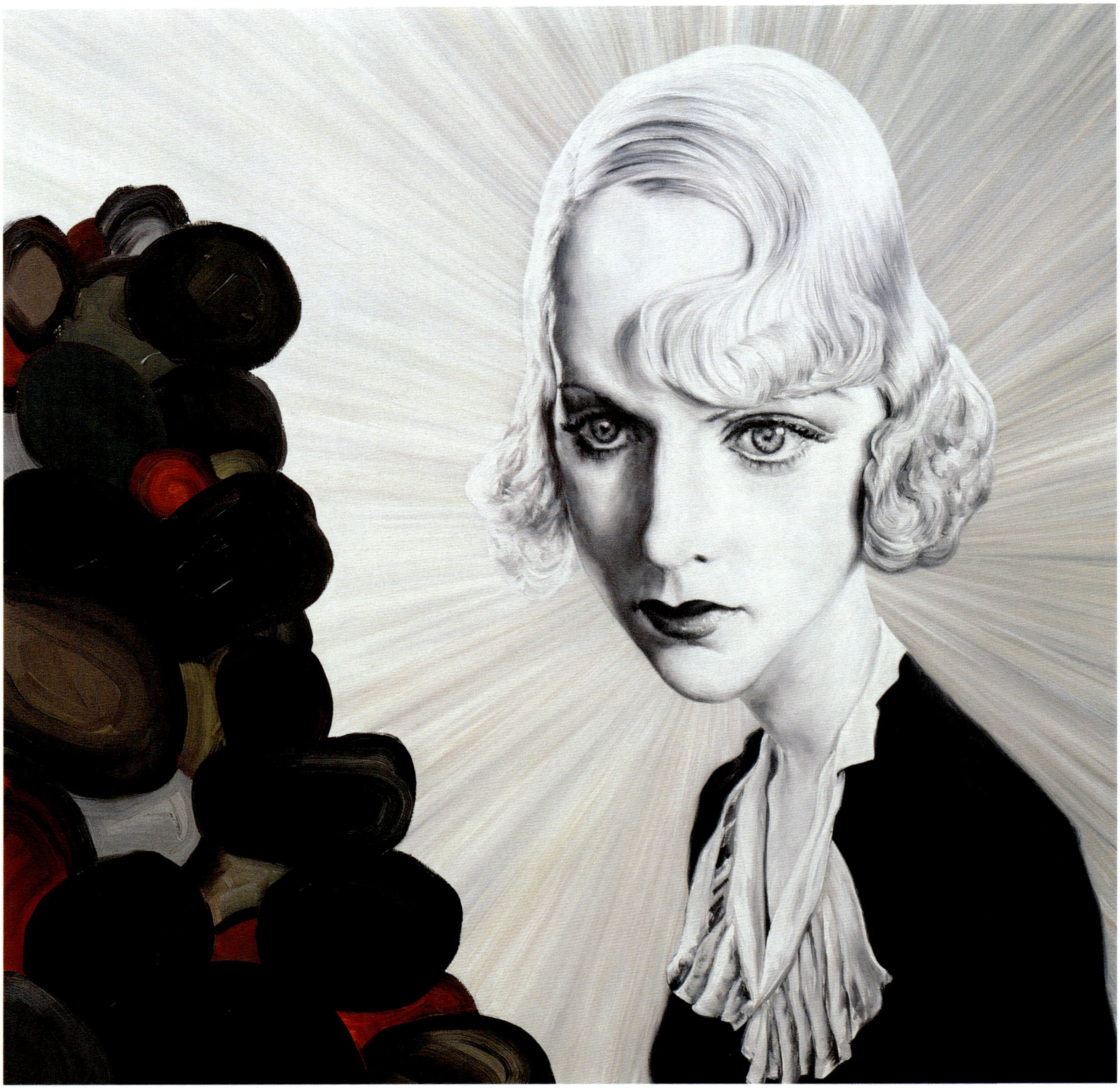

Encuentro
2007
Oil on panel
18 x 18 in.

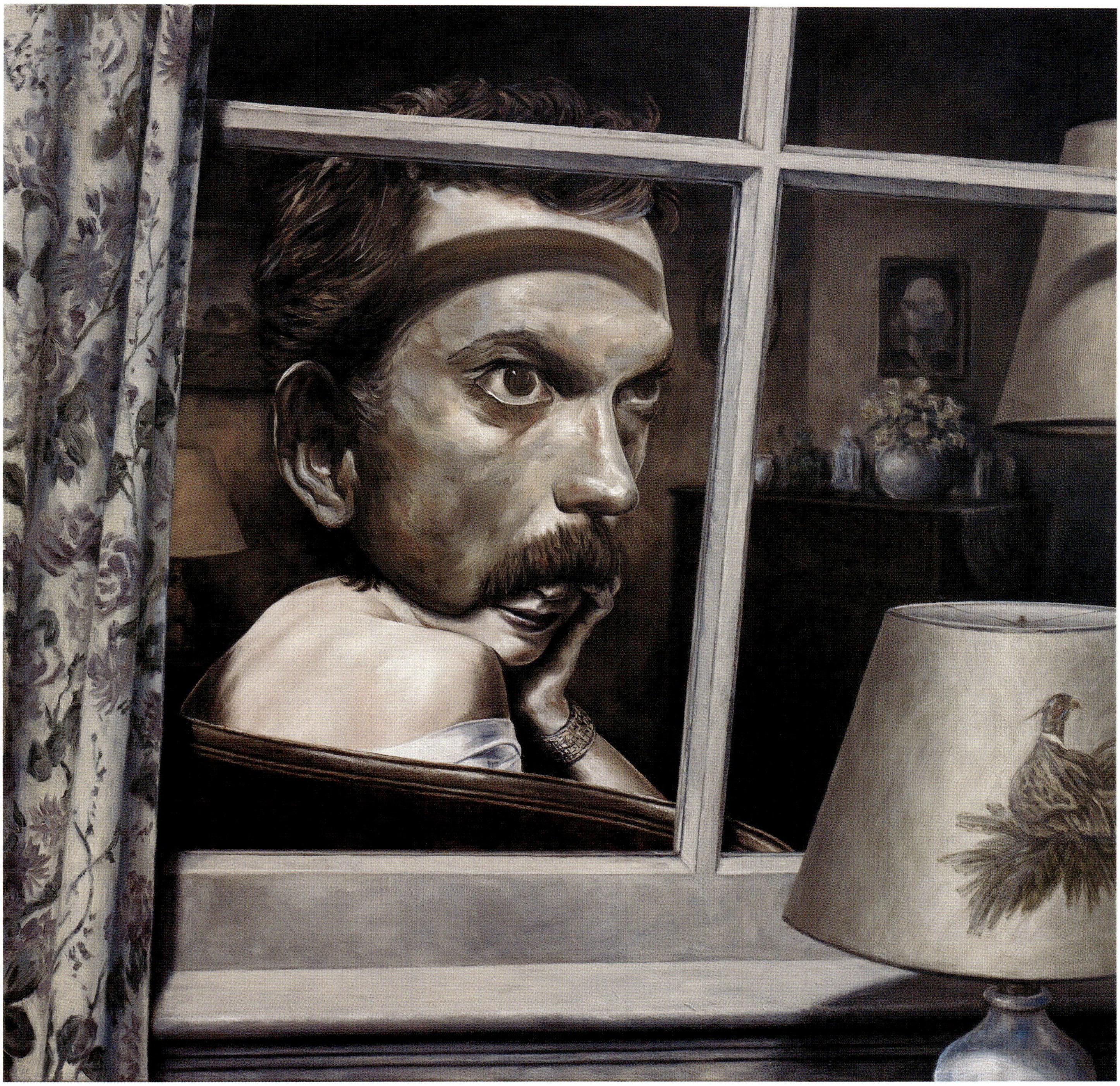

Untitled (Jason's Painting)
2006
Oil on canvas
24 x 24 in.

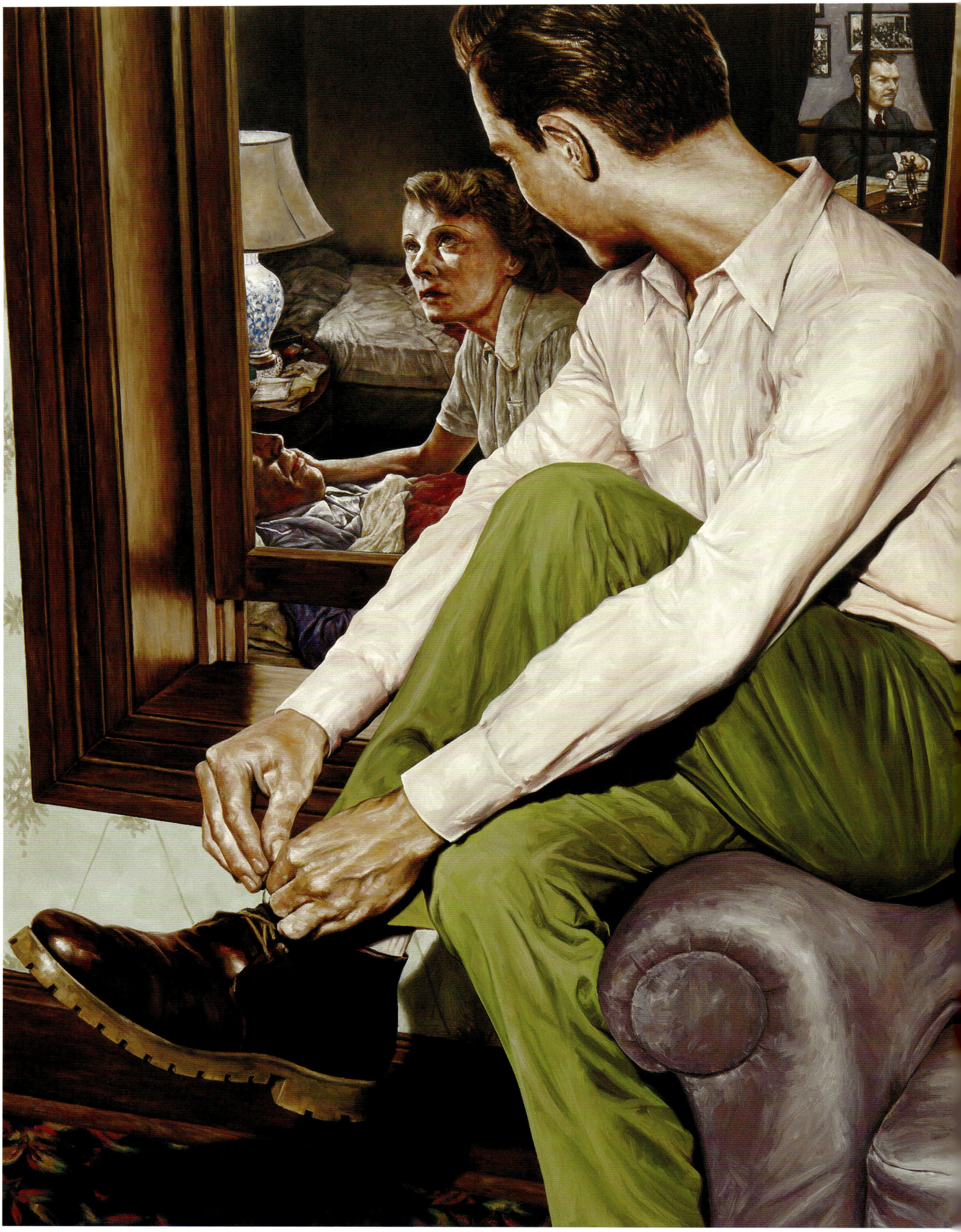

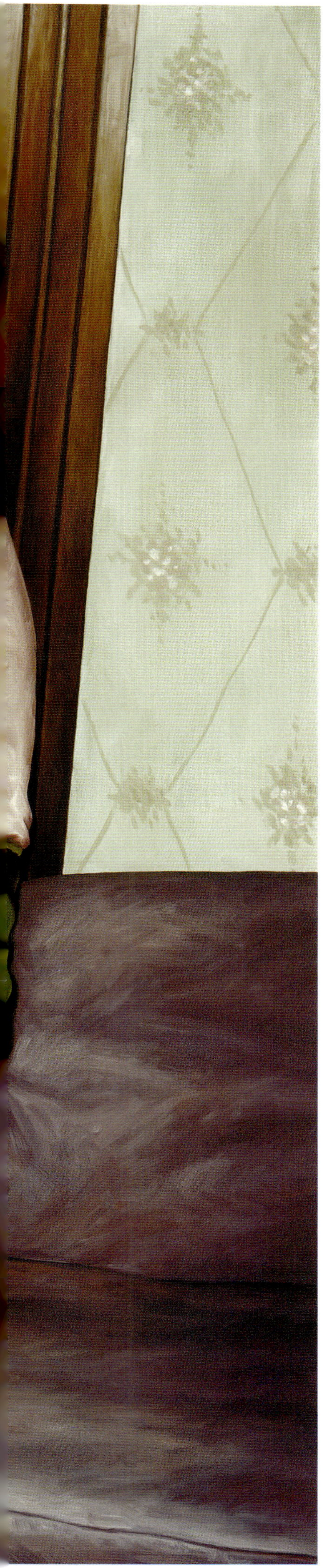

Fortify
(detail on following page)
2007
Oil on canvas
36 x 36 in.

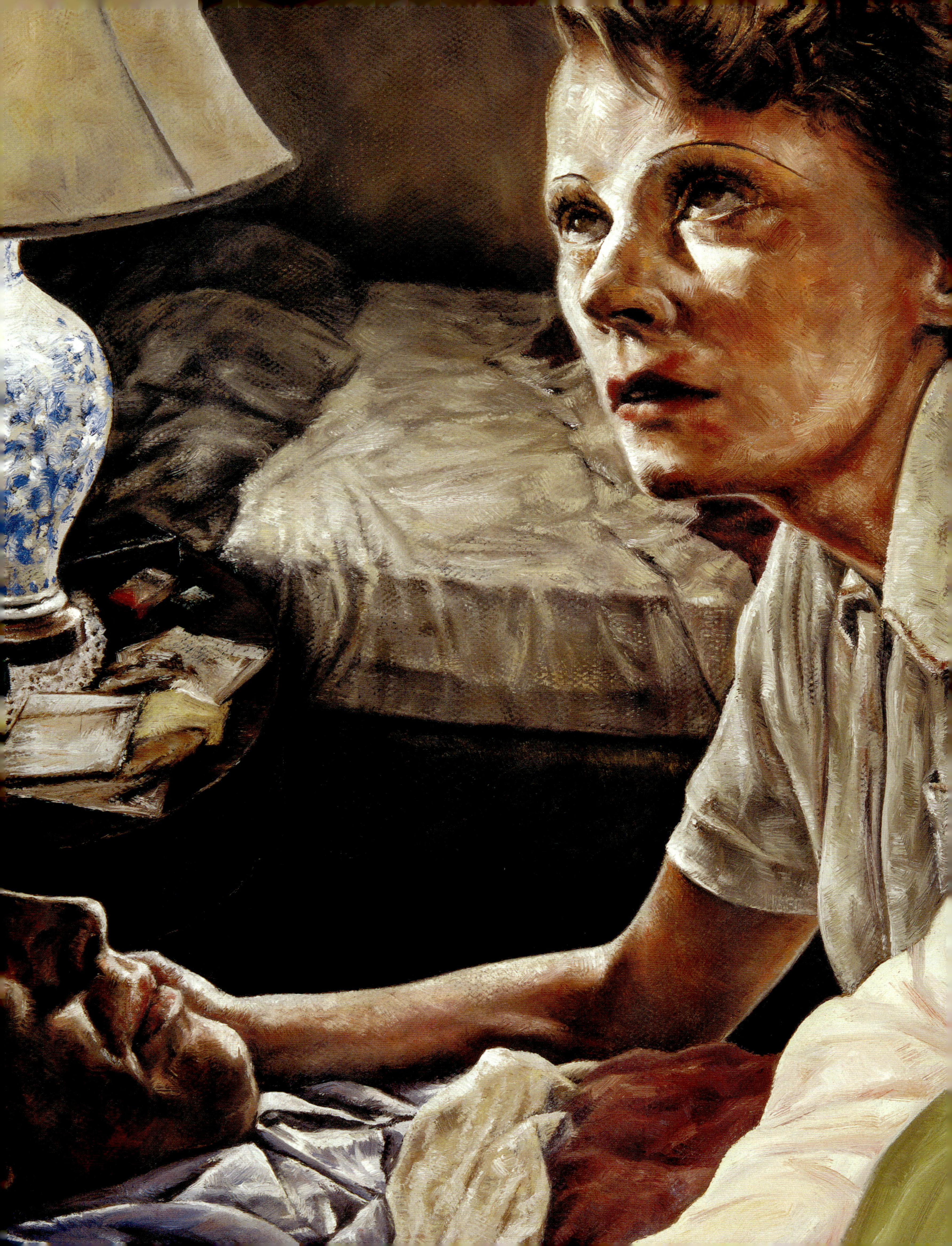

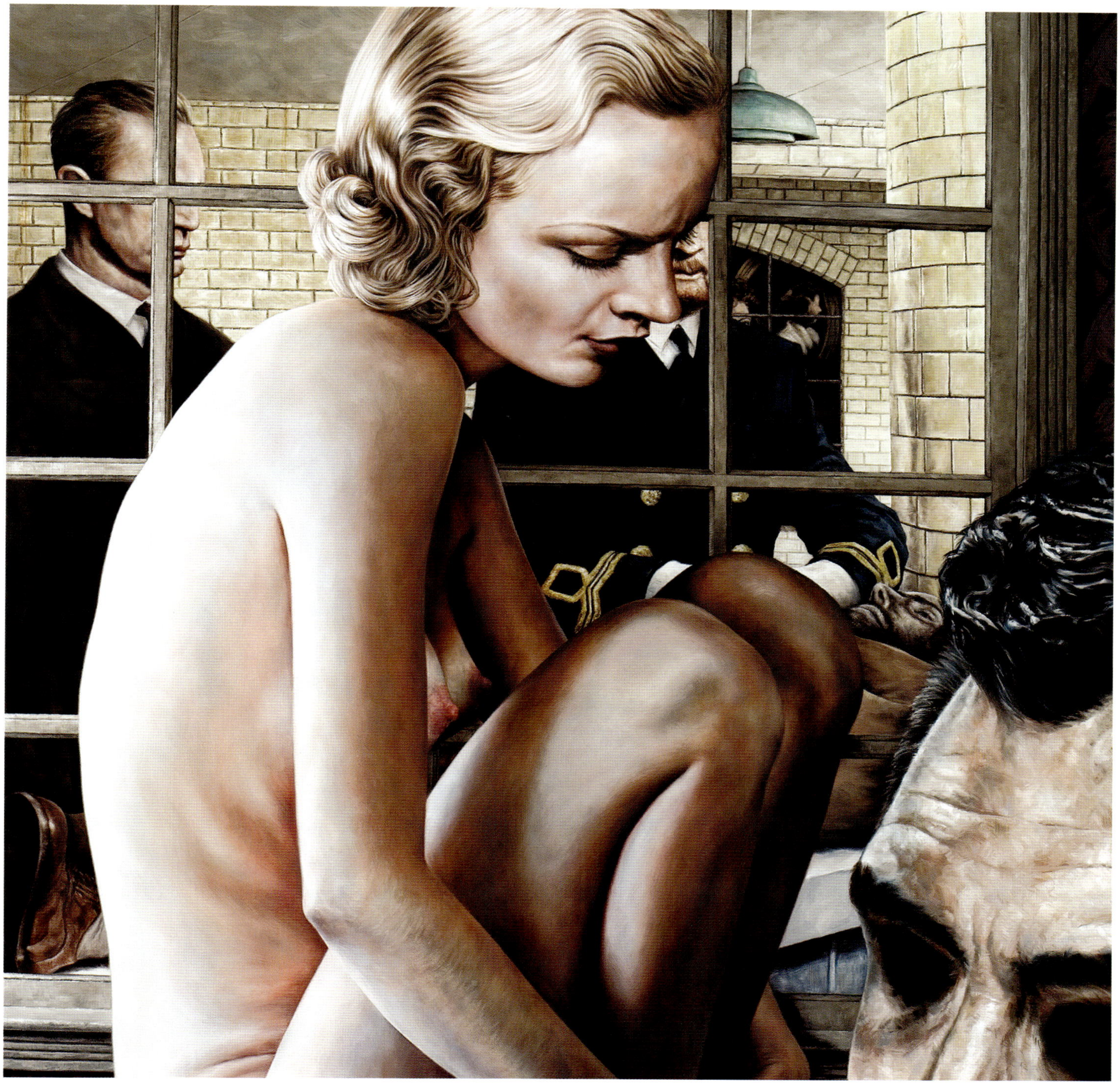

A Gentleman's Mistake
2008
Oil on canvas
36 x 36 in.

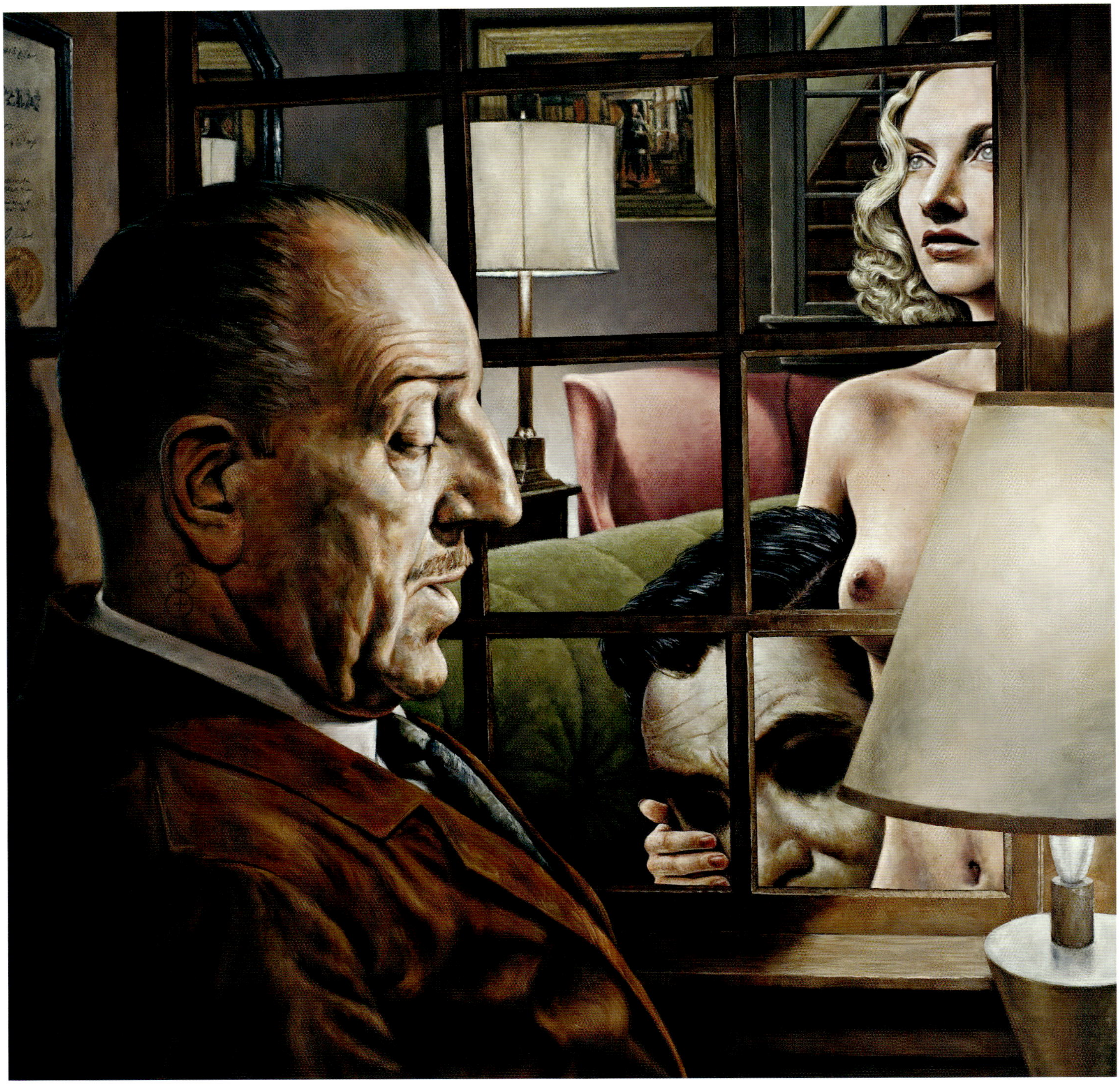

The Settle-Down
2008
Oil on canvas
36 x 36 in.

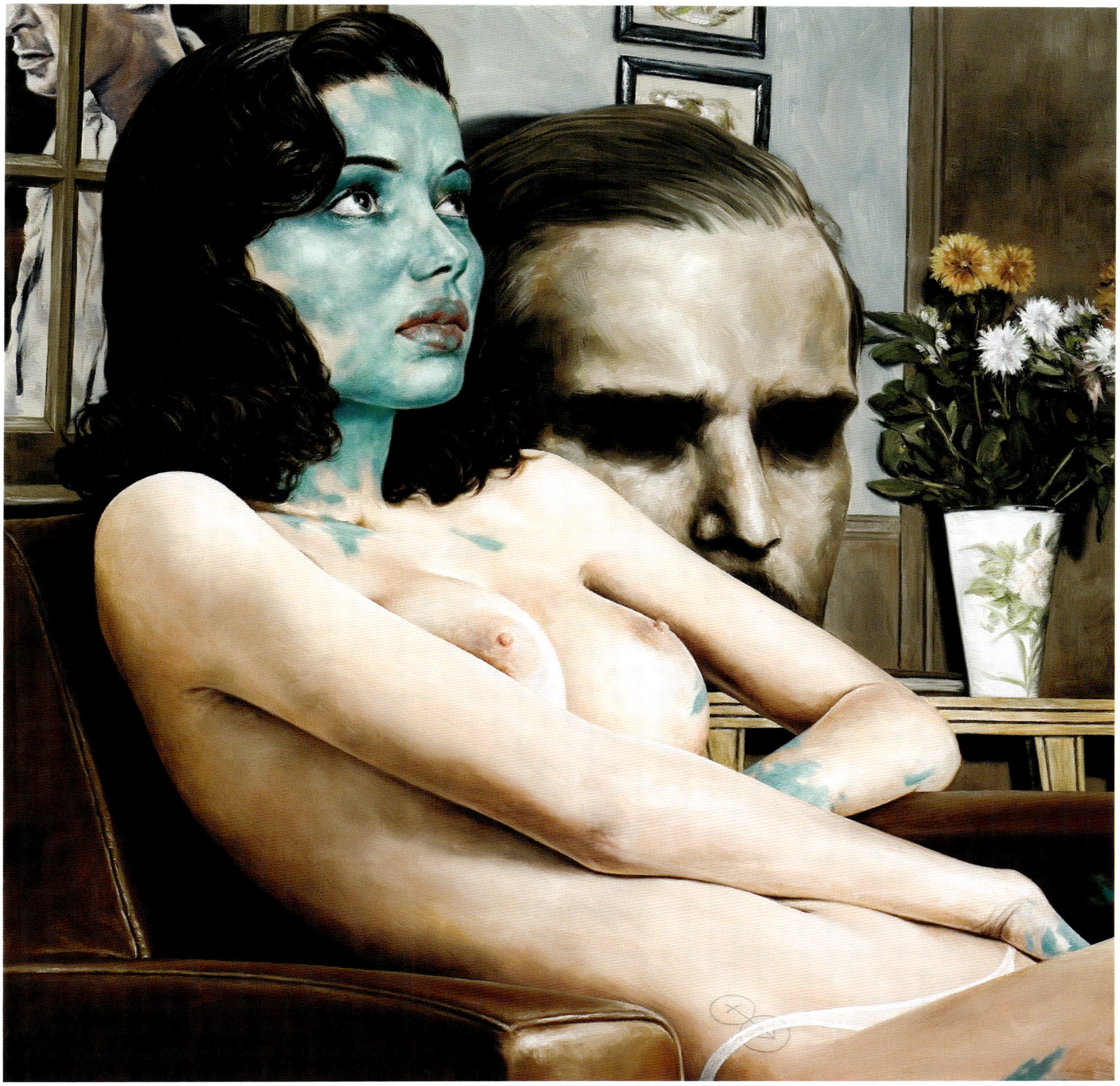

No Neutral Thoughts
2008
Oil on canvas
24 x 24 in.

Following page:
On The Air
2008
Oil on canvas
48 x 72 in.

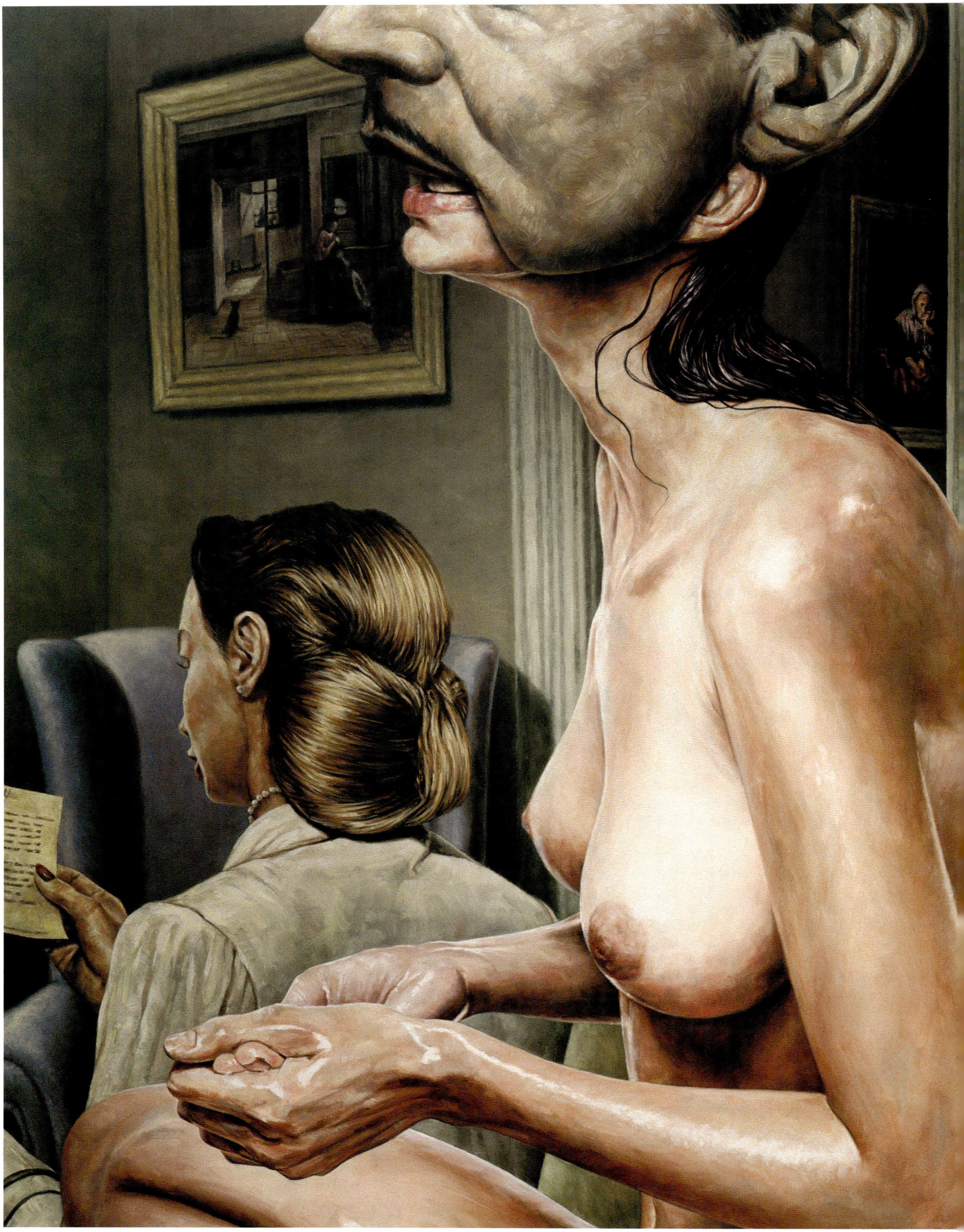

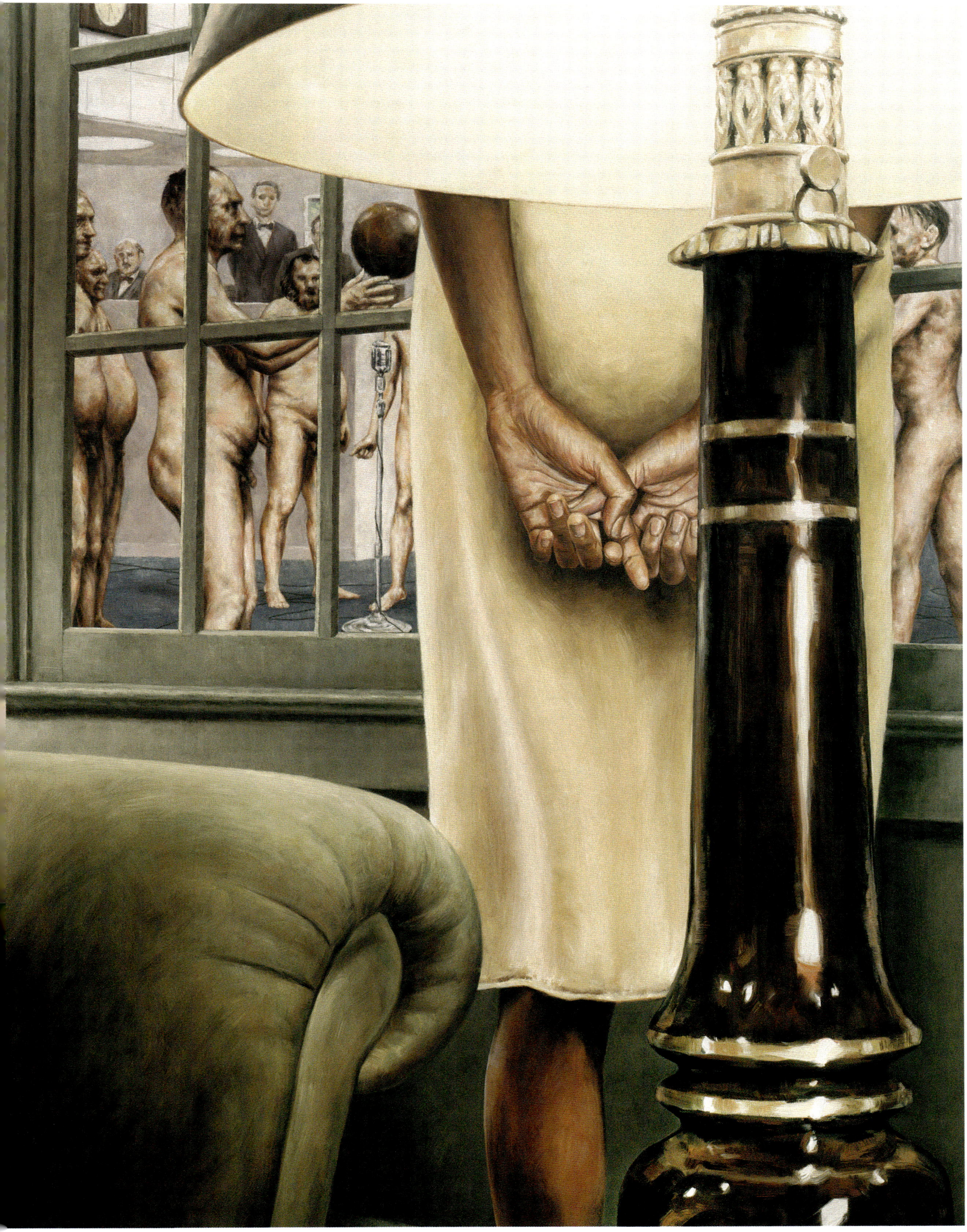

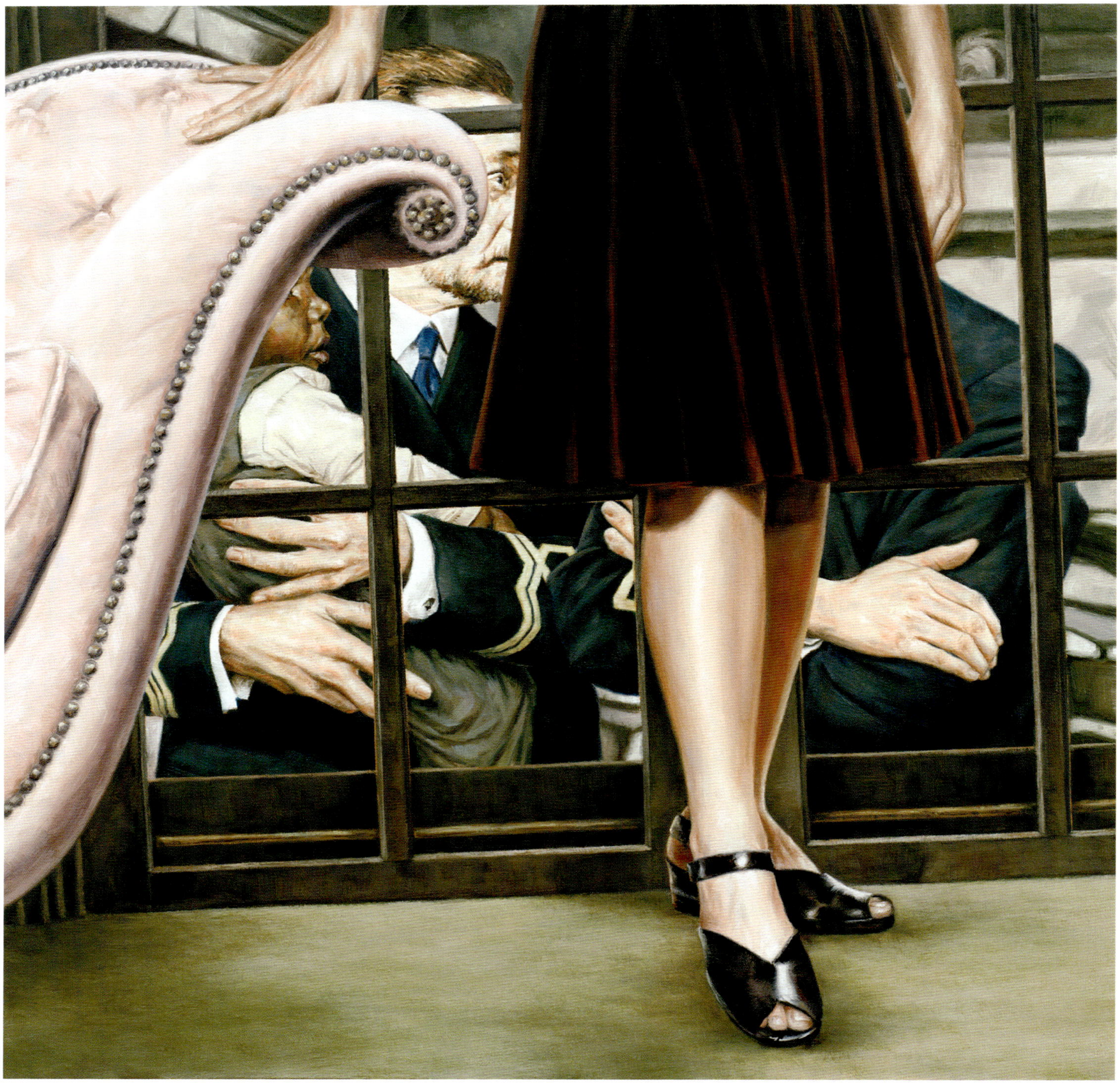

Outsourced
2008
Oil on canvas
24 x 24 in.

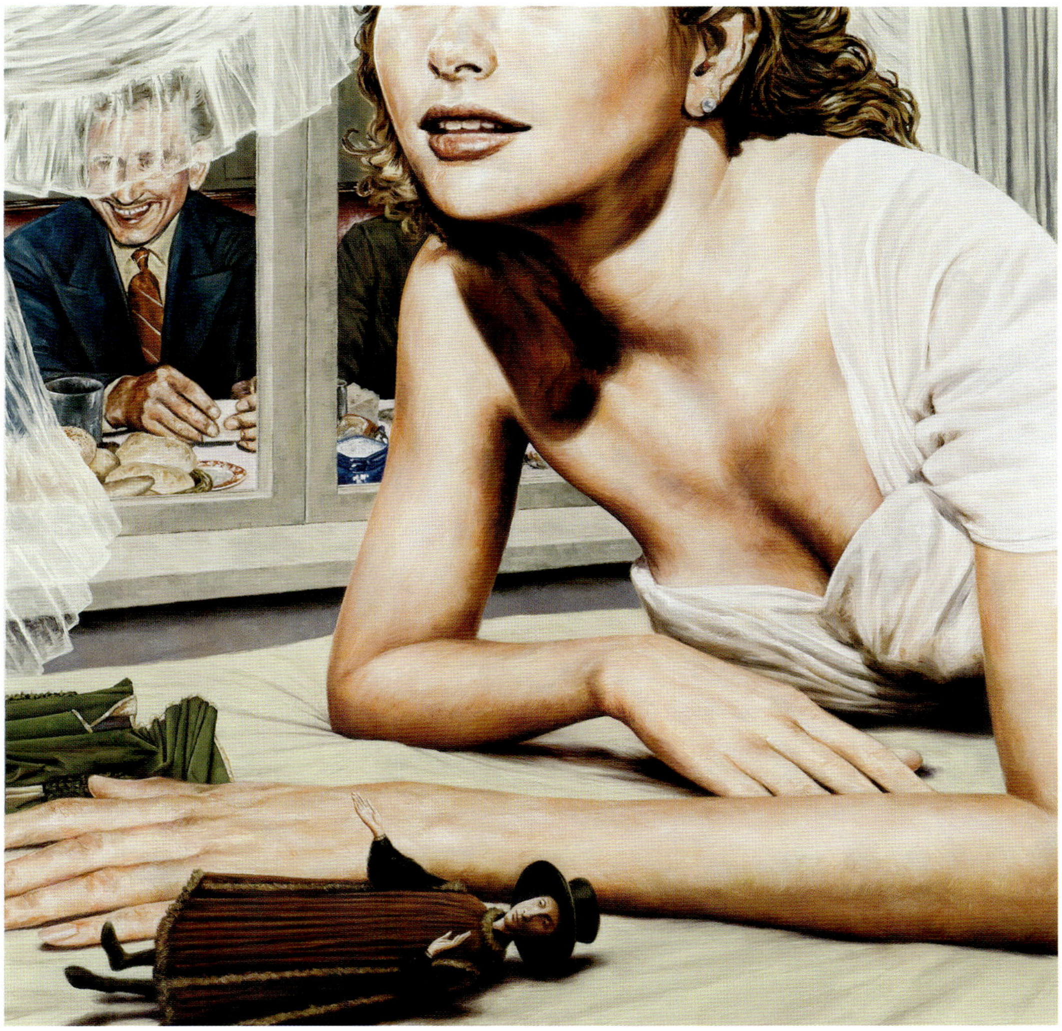

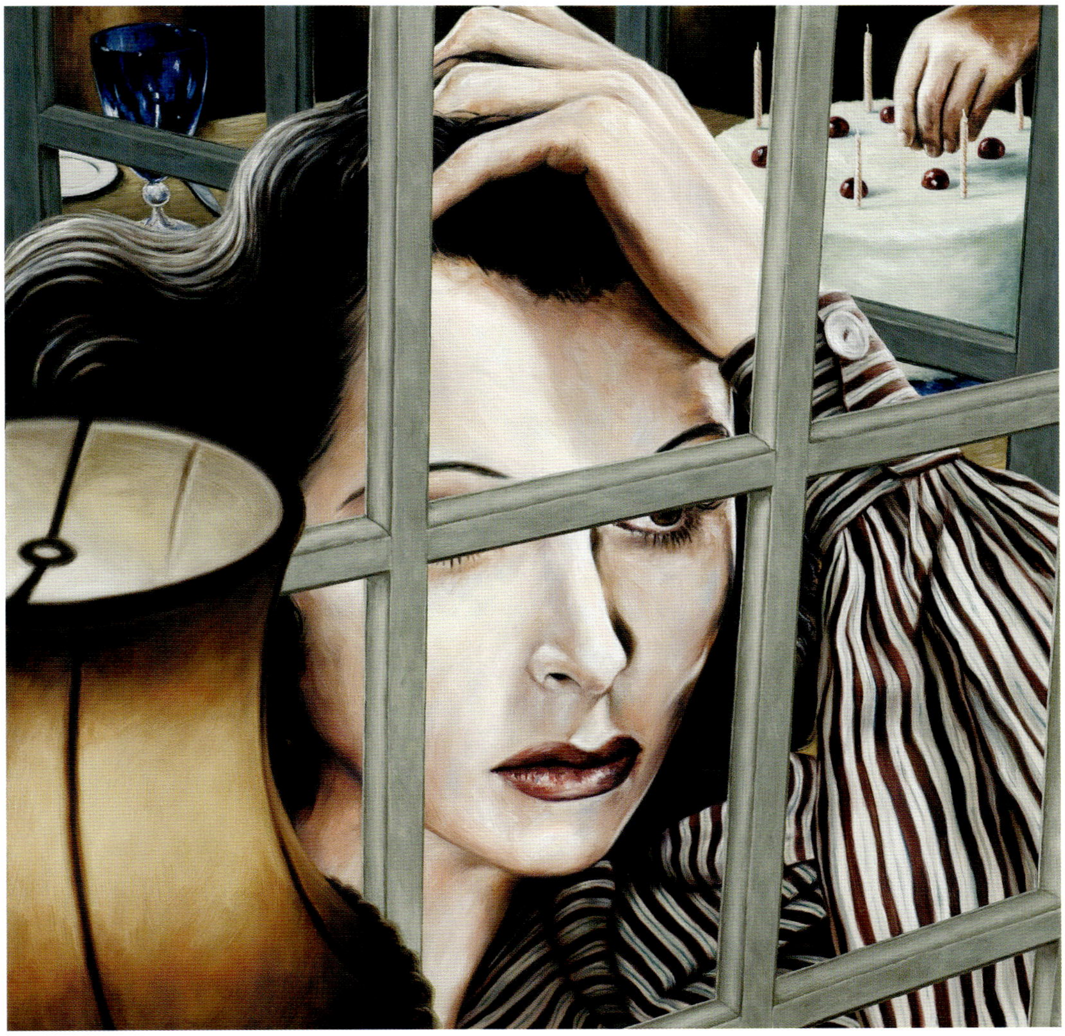

Adjustments
2008
Oil on canvas
24 x 24 in.

The Crunge
2009
Oil on canvas
24 x 24 in.

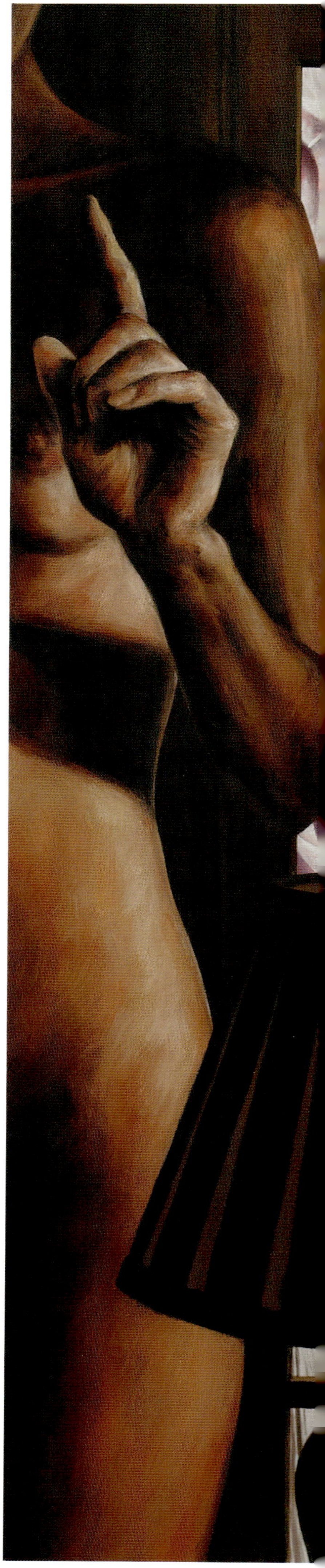

The Big Foist
2010
Oil on canvas
36 x 36 in.

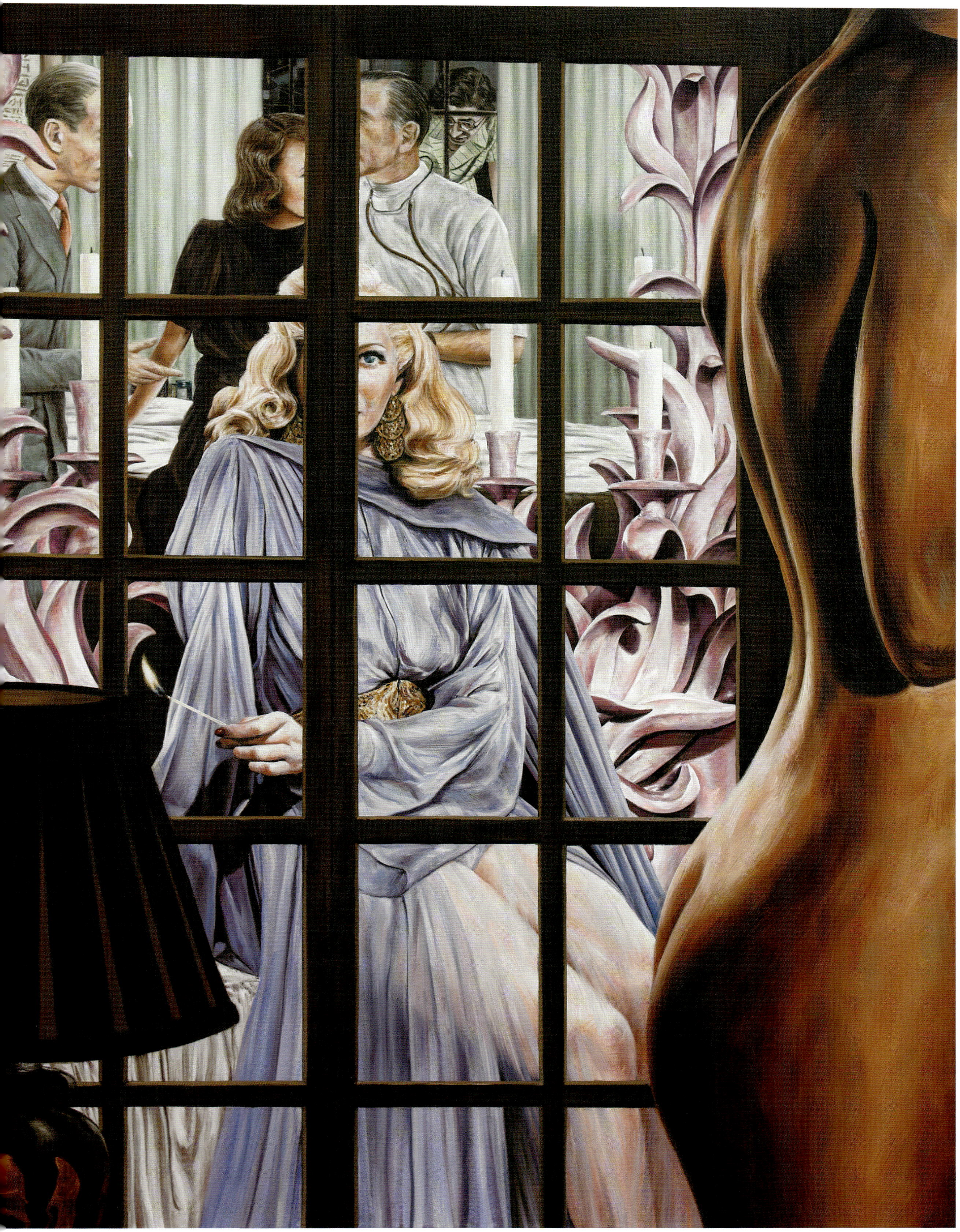

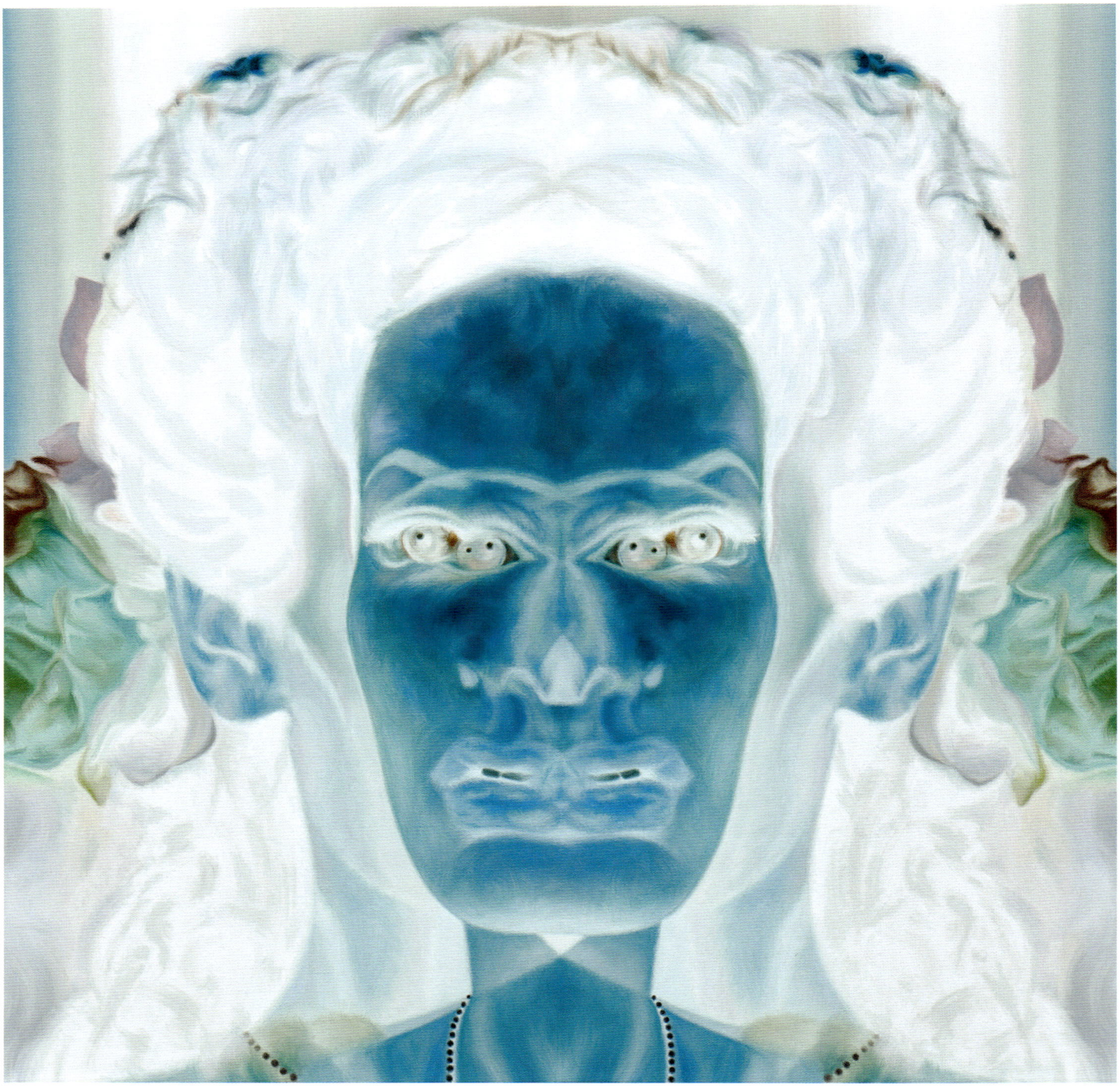

Heaven Can Wait
2008
Oil on canvas
24 x 24 in.

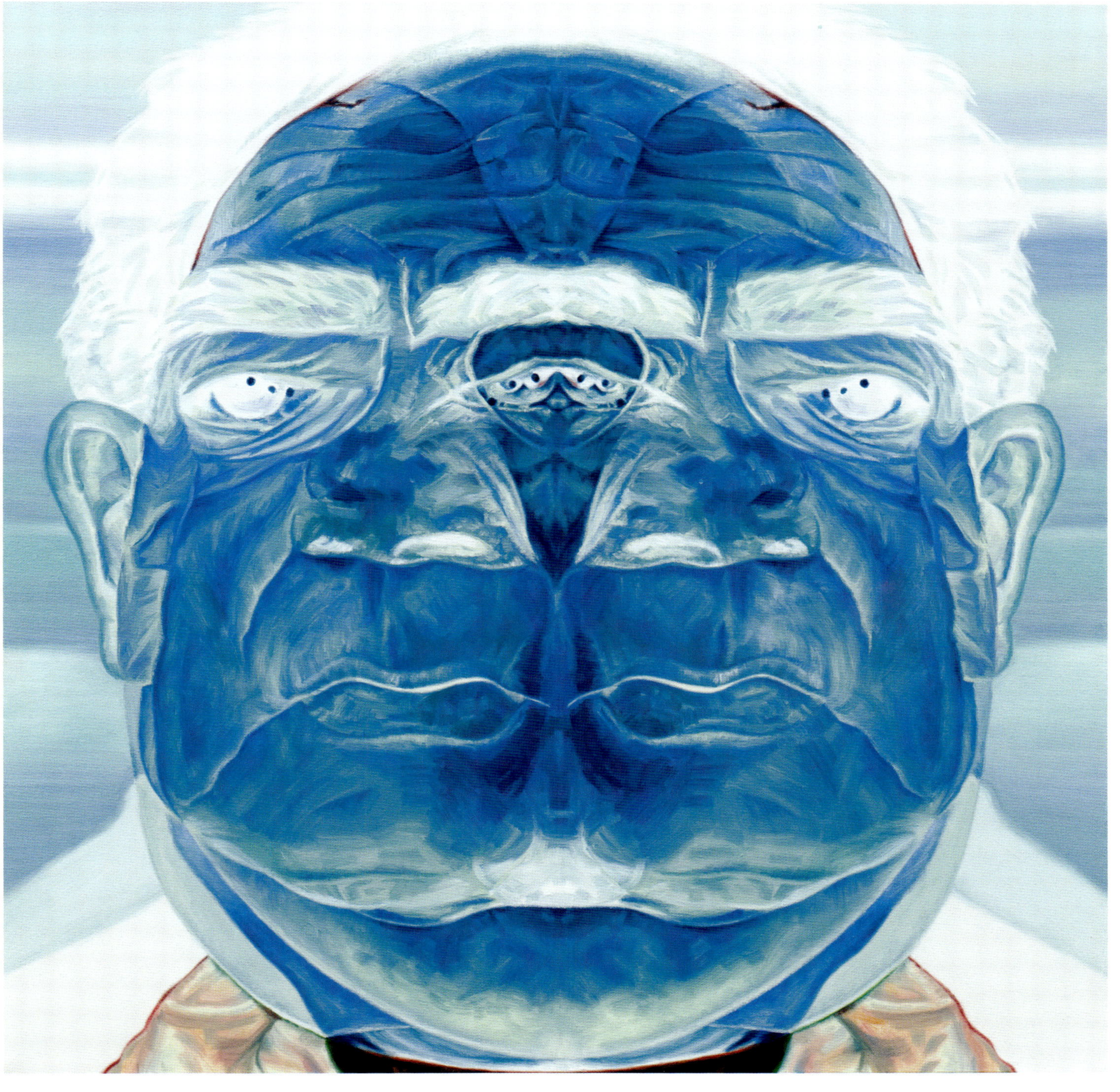

Heaven Can Wait
2008
Oil on canvas
24 x 24 in.

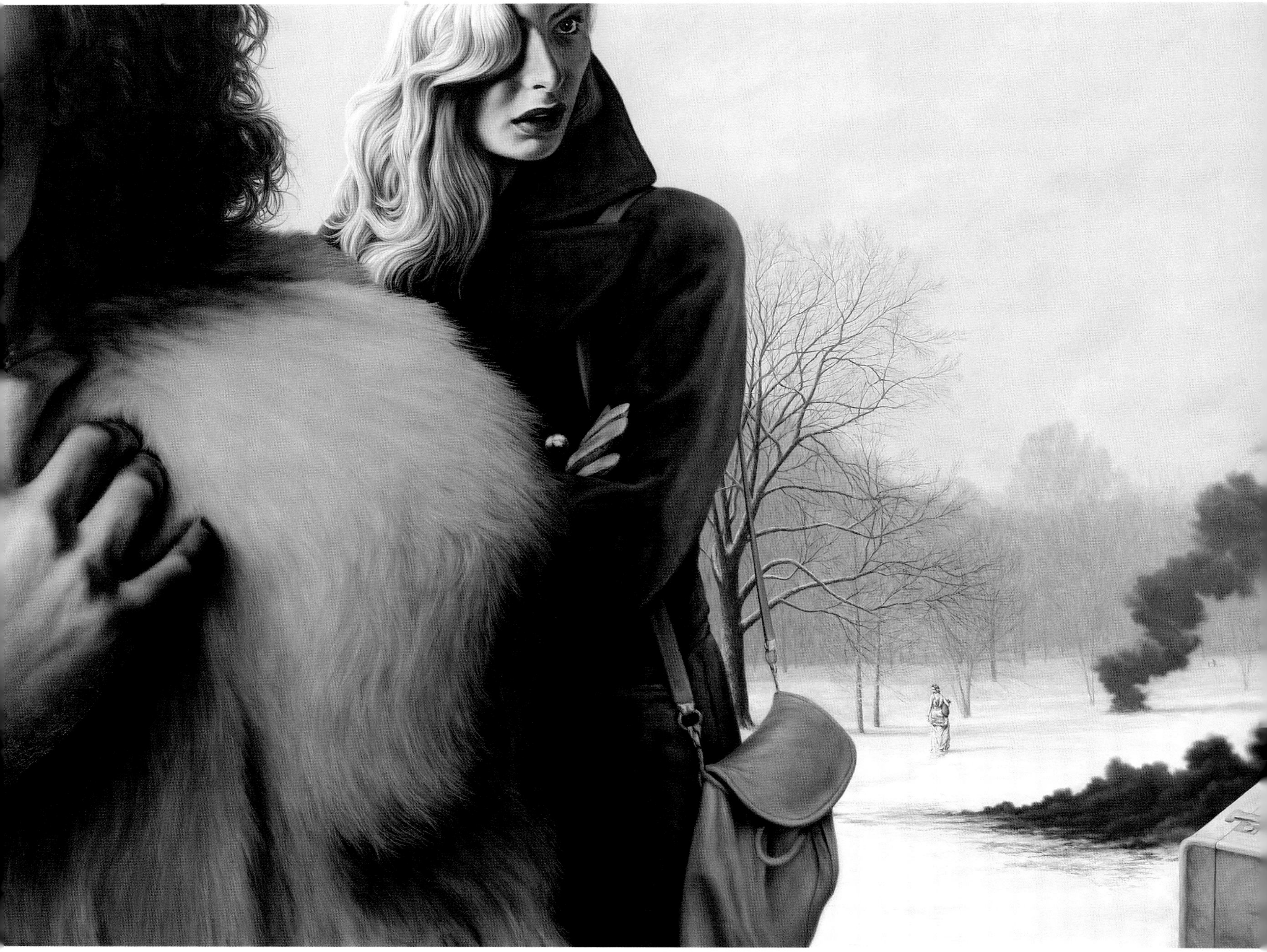

Massacre Of The Innocents
(detail on following page)
2010
Oil on canvas
48 x 192 in.

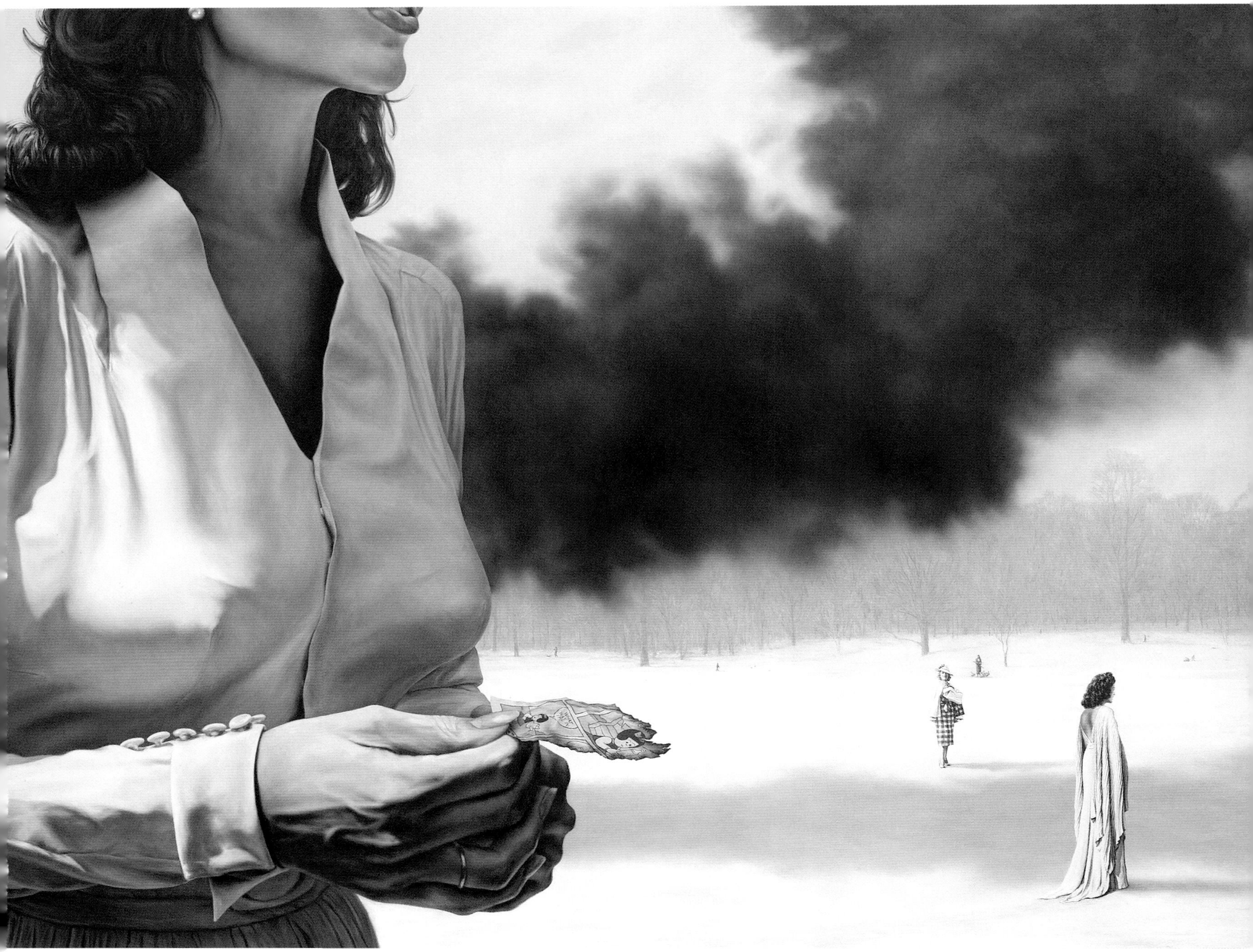

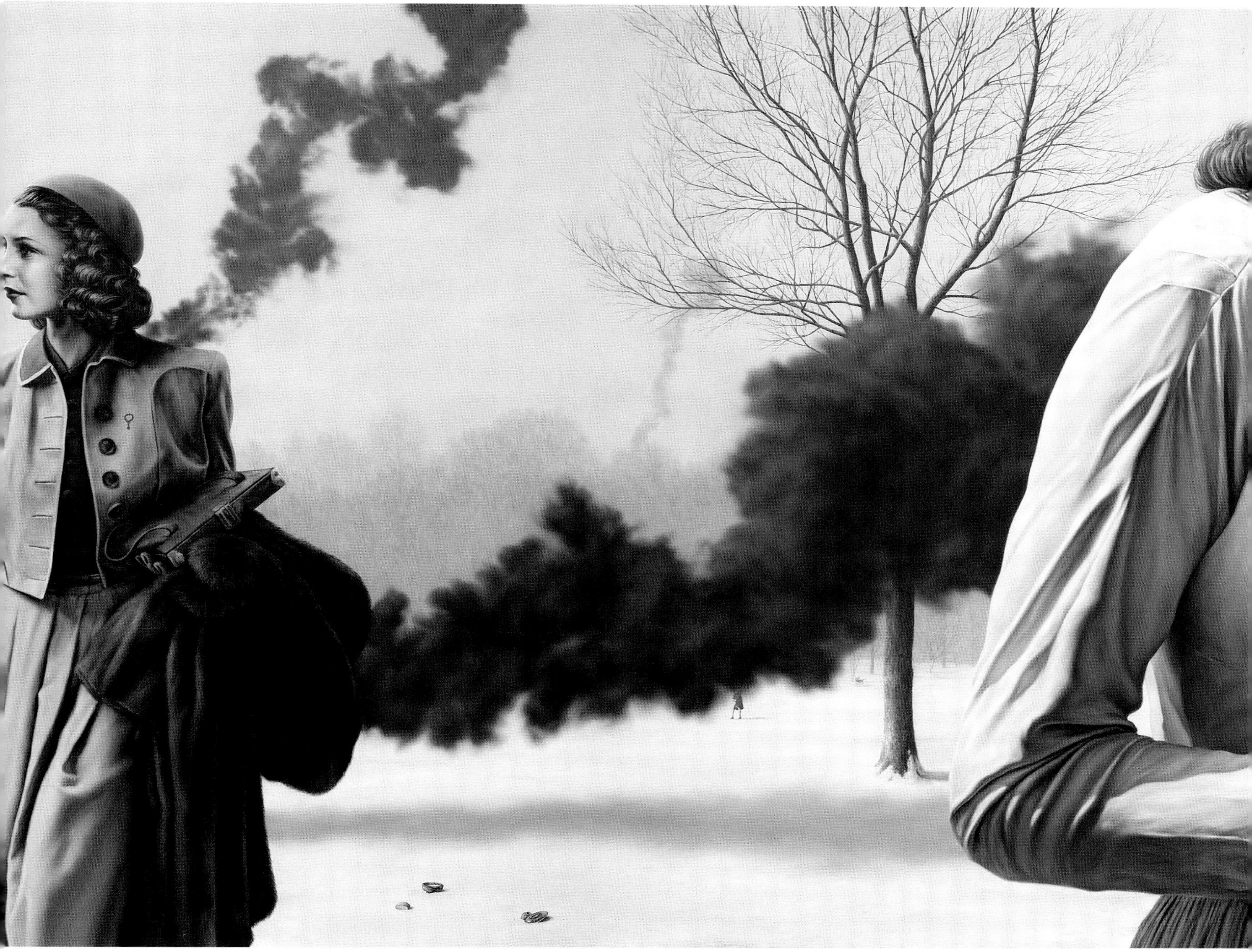

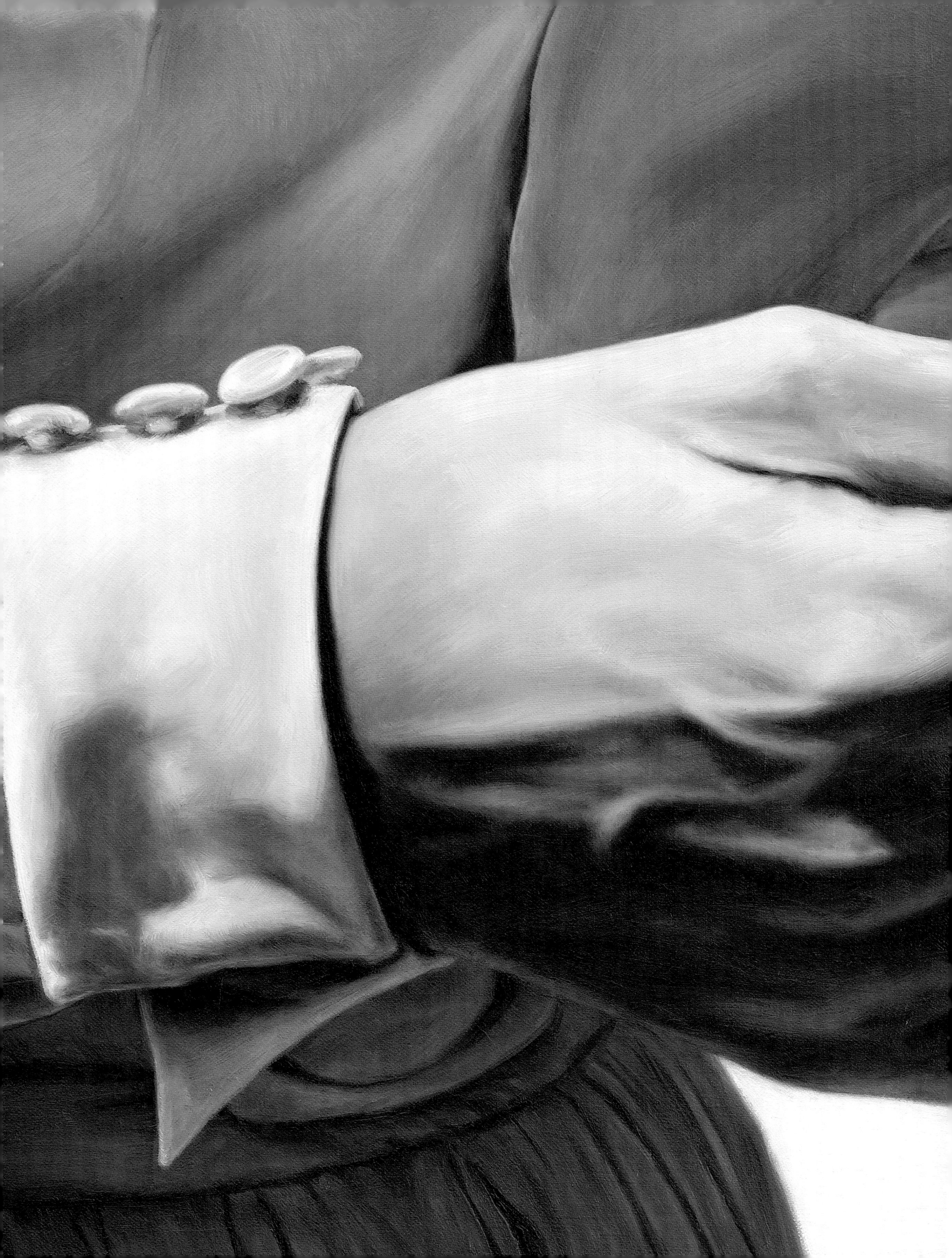

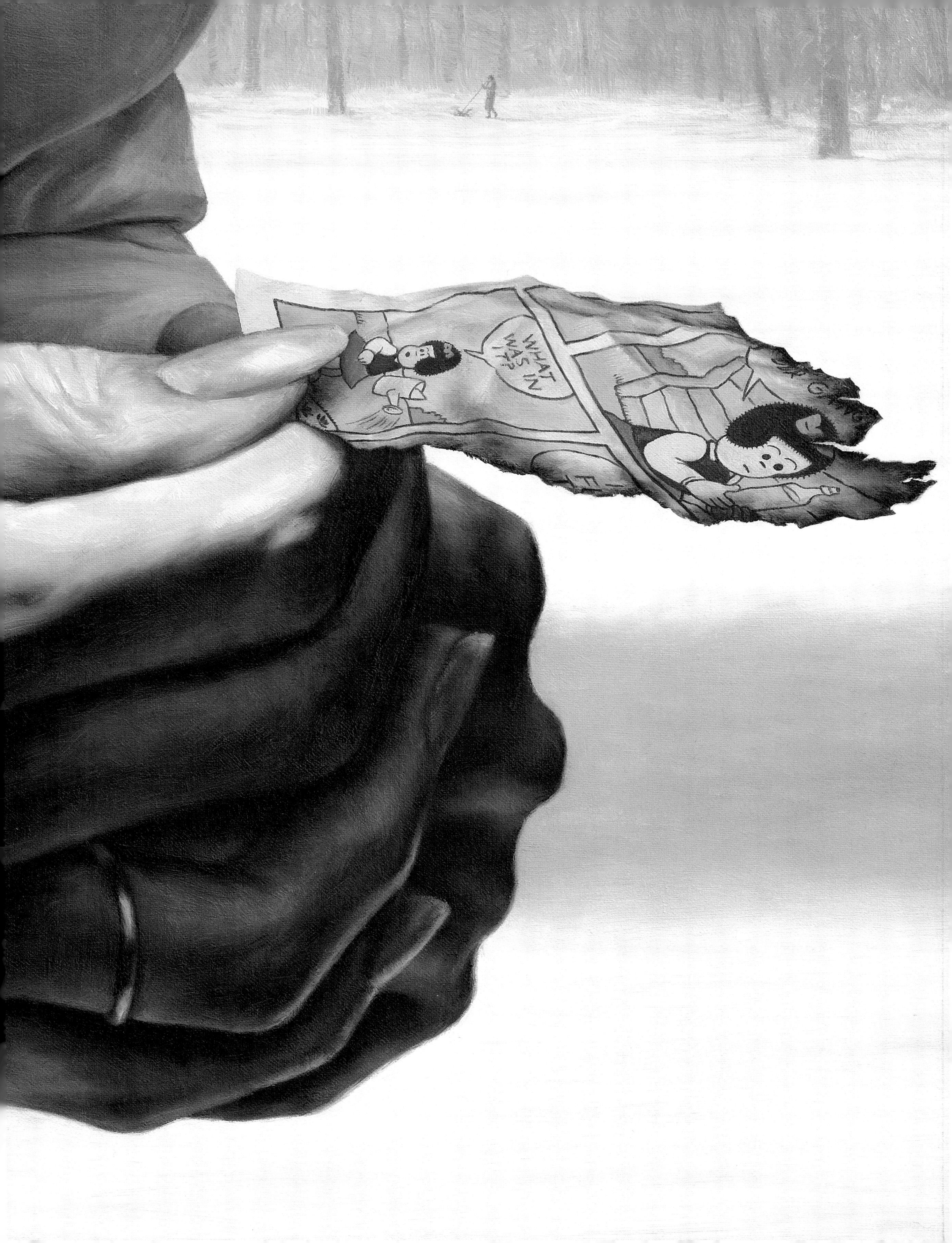
WHAT WAS IN IT?

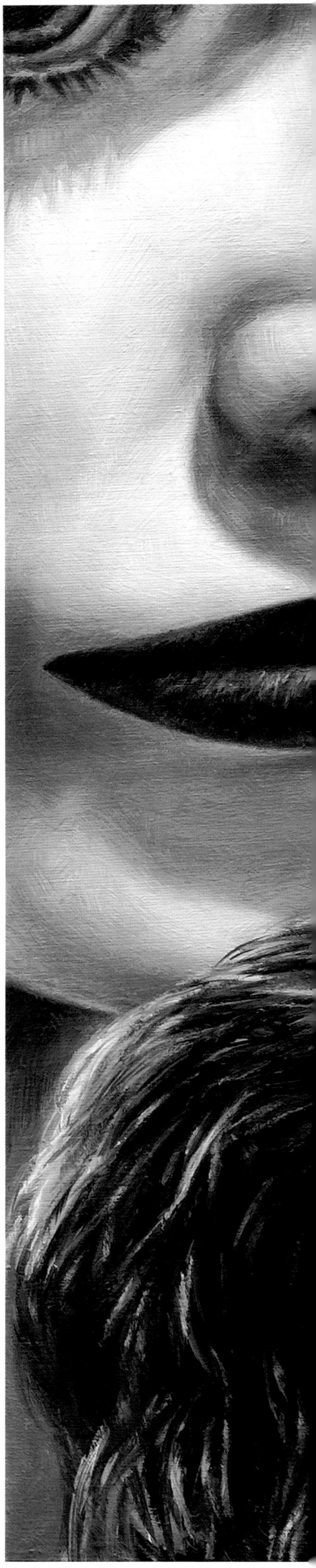

Dualism N' Such
2009
Oil on panel
10 x 10 in.

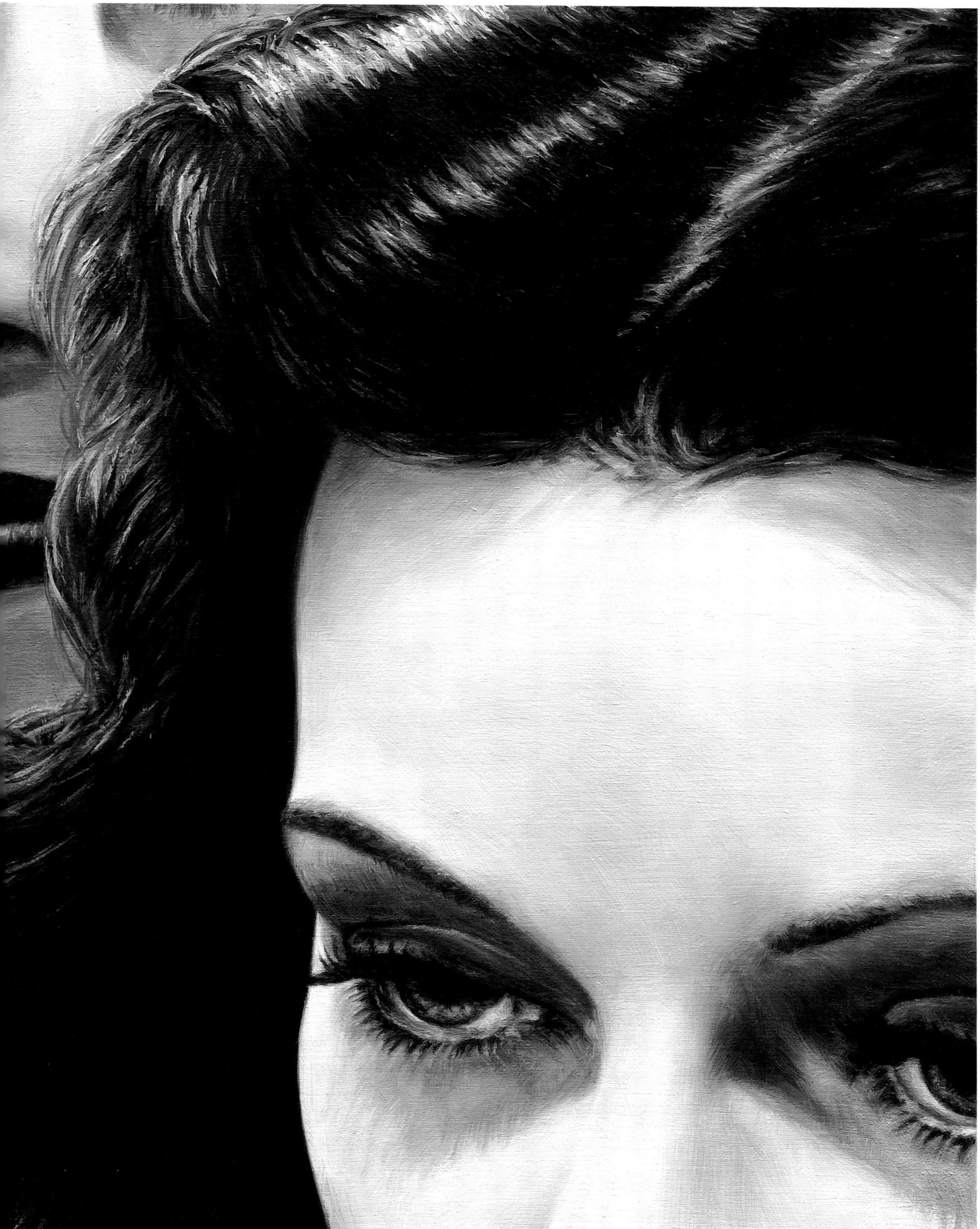

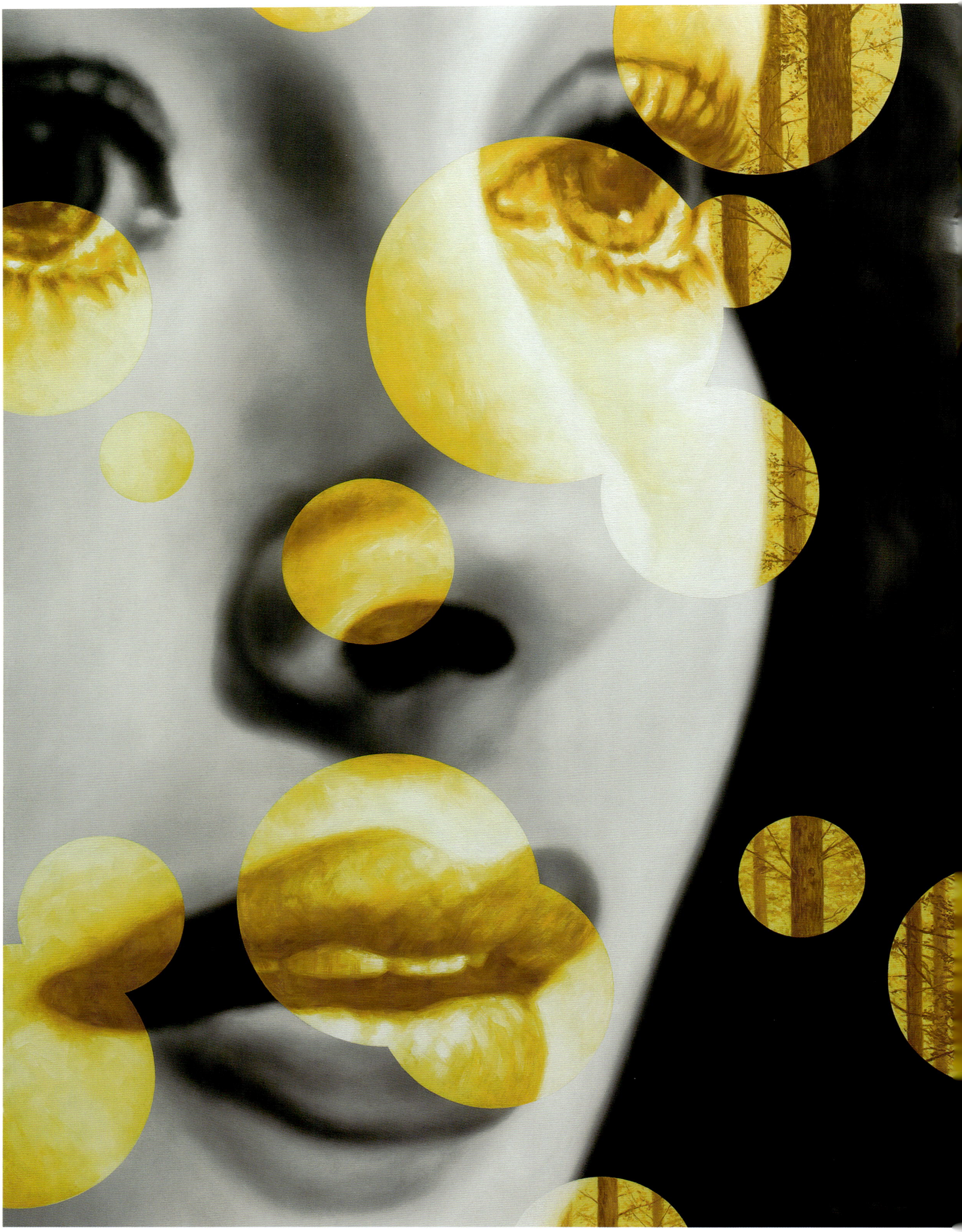

Foyer
2009
Oil on canvas
48 x 72 in.

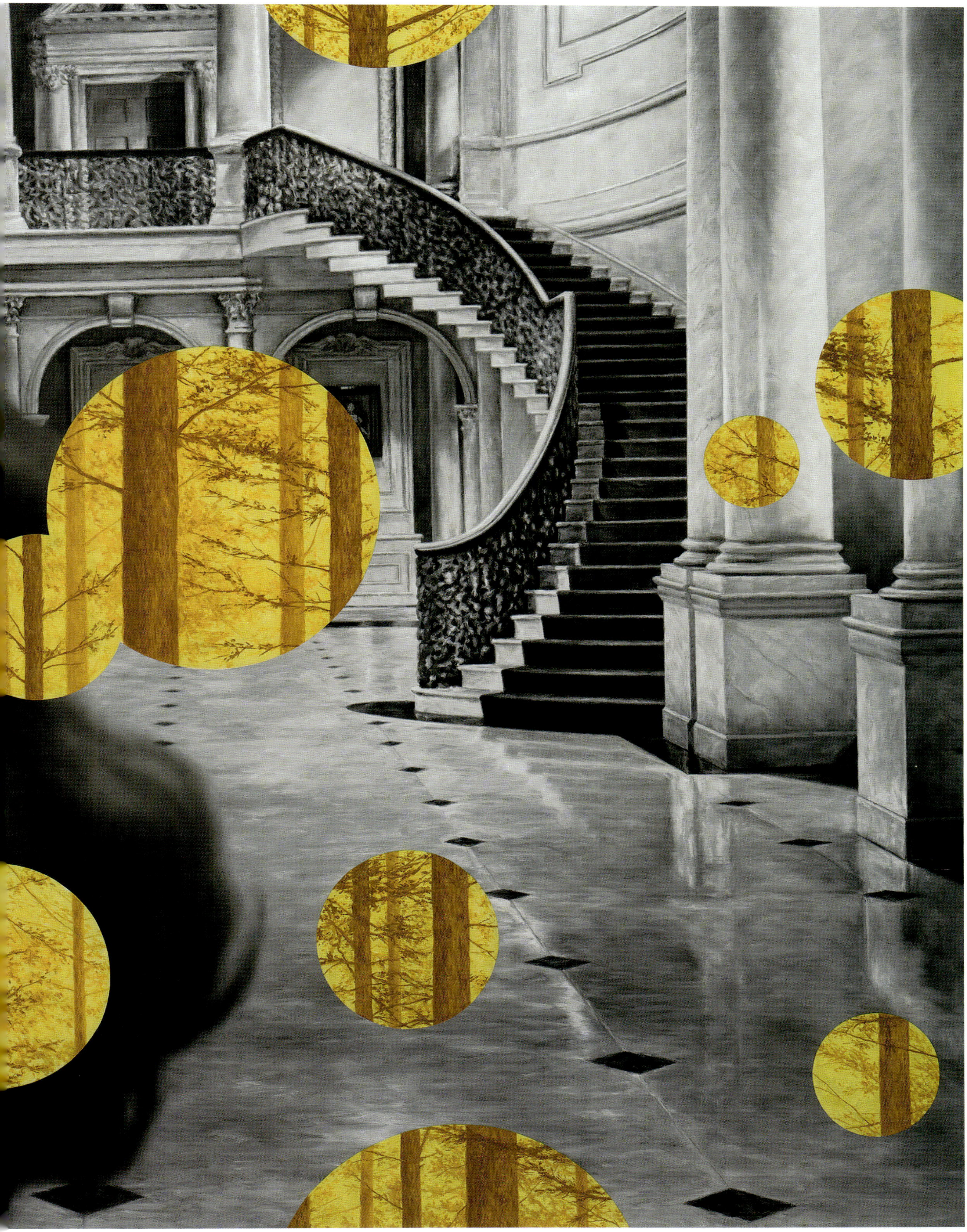

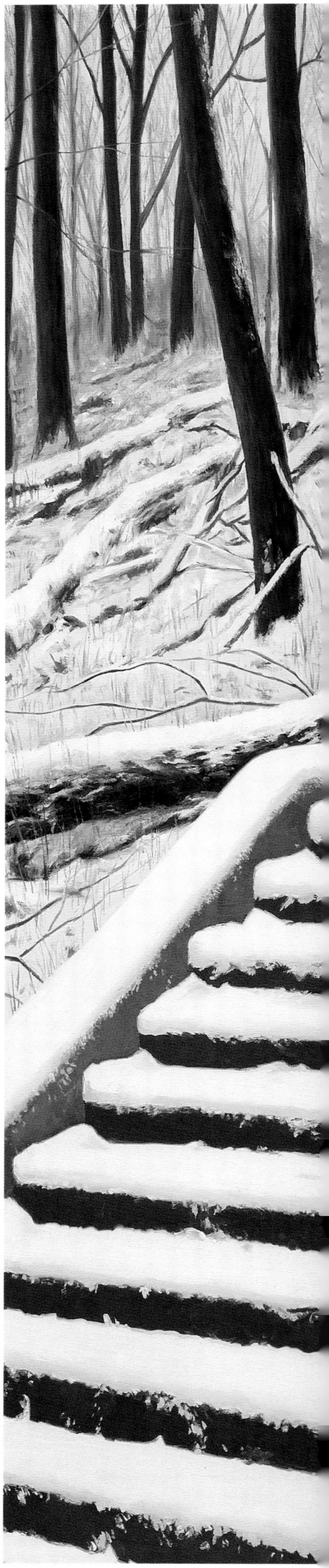

Portal
2010
Oil on canvas
36 x 36 in.

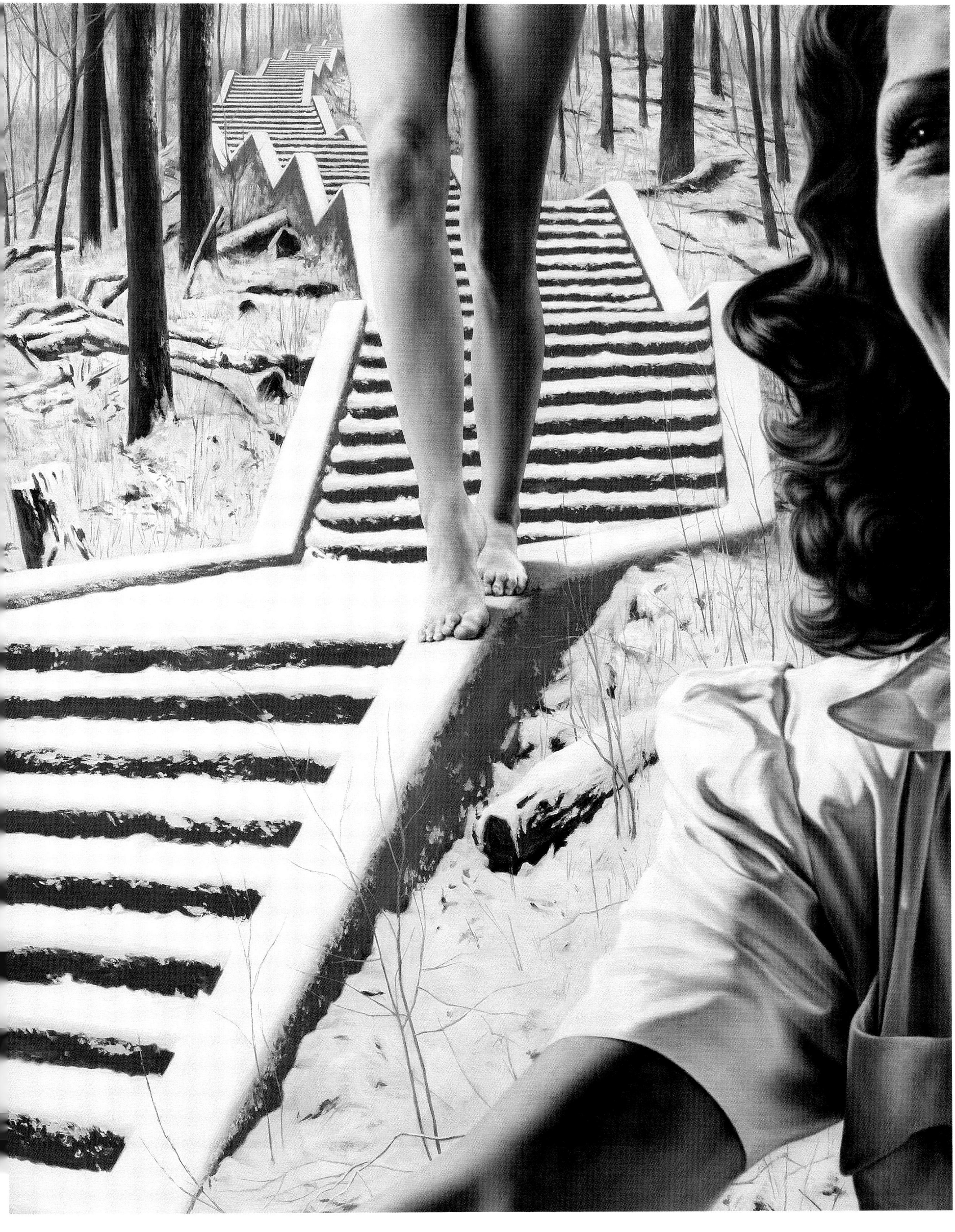

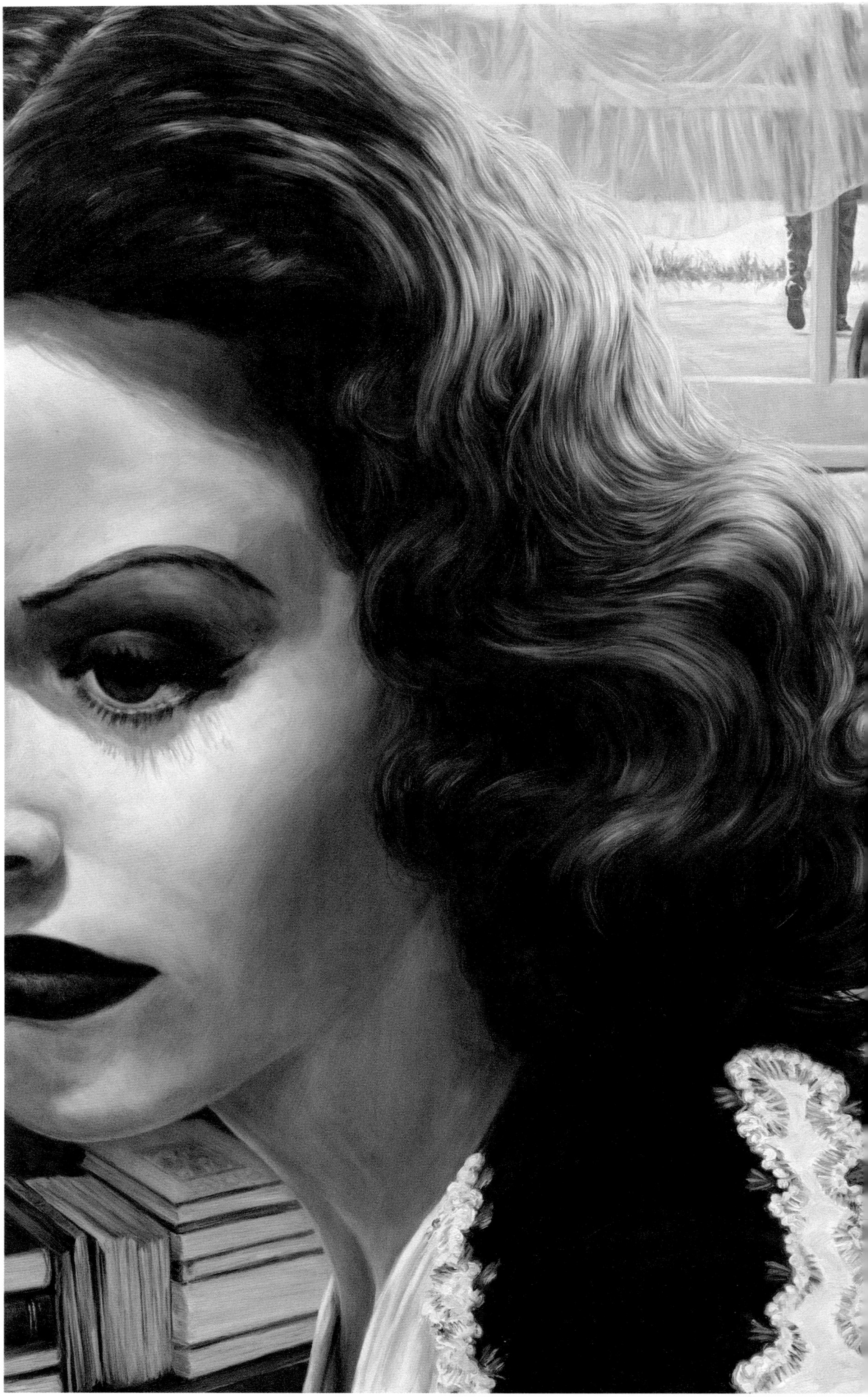

The Drifter
2010
Oil on canvas
40 x 60 in.

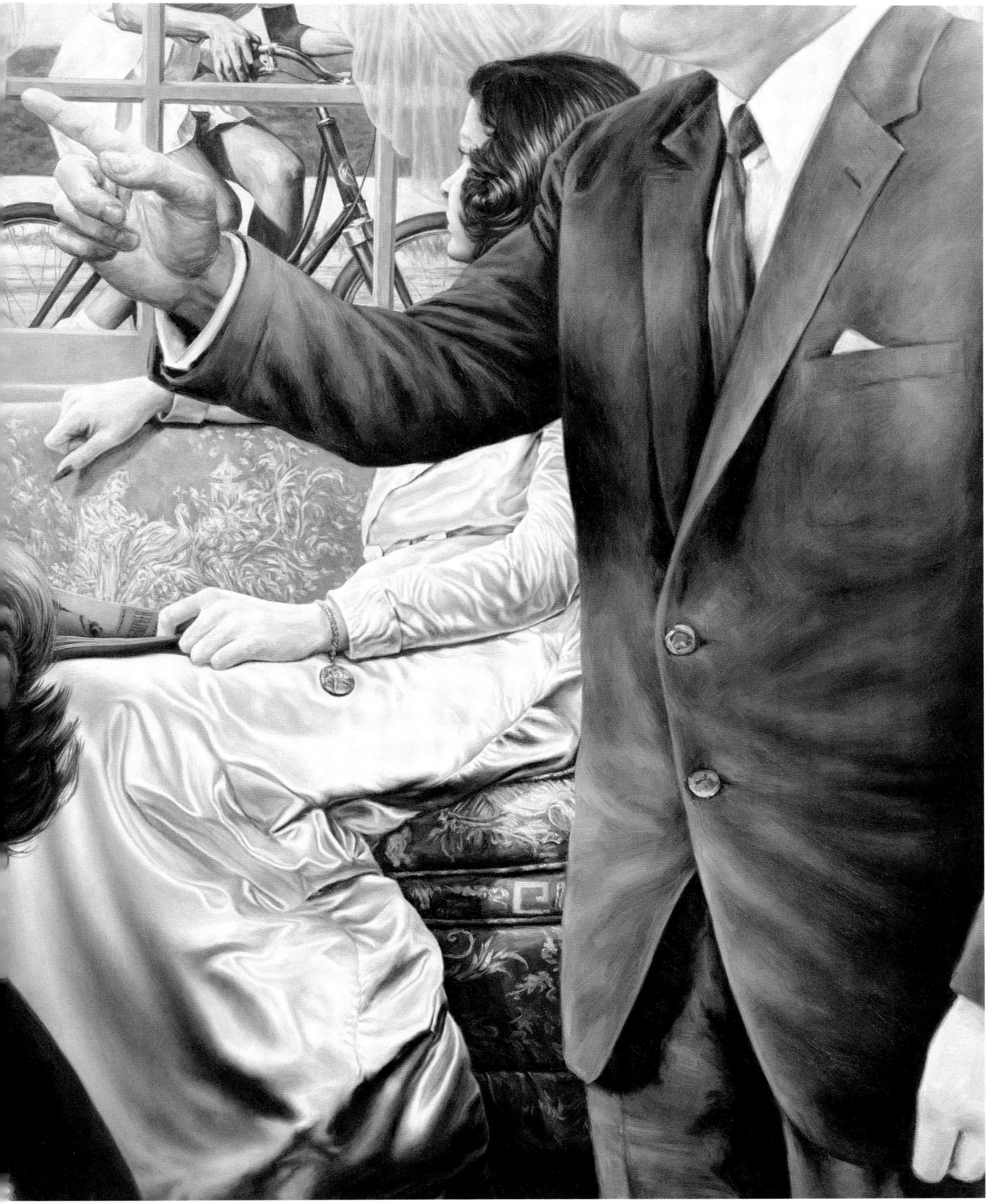

LP PAINTINGS
MIKE NEWTON

Eric White's *LP* series feels like something out of a dream—indeed, White began it after having a strange dream about a record store—but not just his personal dream, rather a joint or collective dream. After all, this is the stuff everyone likes, the stuff you'd find in any decent, American record store. Or at least, you used to be able to. Records have power, and album covers—the sales-floor inducements to partake, the distinct visual-cultural marks made by musical artists—share in that power. It's a strange and particular mix of sociality, historical resonance, movement, and pleasure. These paintings draw on the significance of famous album covers, a recognition shared by so many of us on some unspoken, visceral level. They take on the size and shape of actual records, appearing as finds from the dollar bin of a decadent parallel universe. The yearning, pink-skinned children from Led Zeppelin's 1973 hard-rock landmark *Houses of the Holy* become, in White's version, gobsmacked albino animals. *The Pink Flag* from Wire's 1977 art-punk classic is rendered as big as a bed sheet. The ringed, flowery vortex from Stevie Wonder's 1976 opus *Songs in the Key of Life* is still recognizably there, but Wonder's face has been removed and the orange wormhole just continues infinitely, his name now replaced with the words "Sit and Worry." These are exercises in both loving fidelity to their widely revered sources and cheeky impertinence in the face of fading cultural legacies.

Greatest Hits
2009
Oil on panel
12 x 12 in.

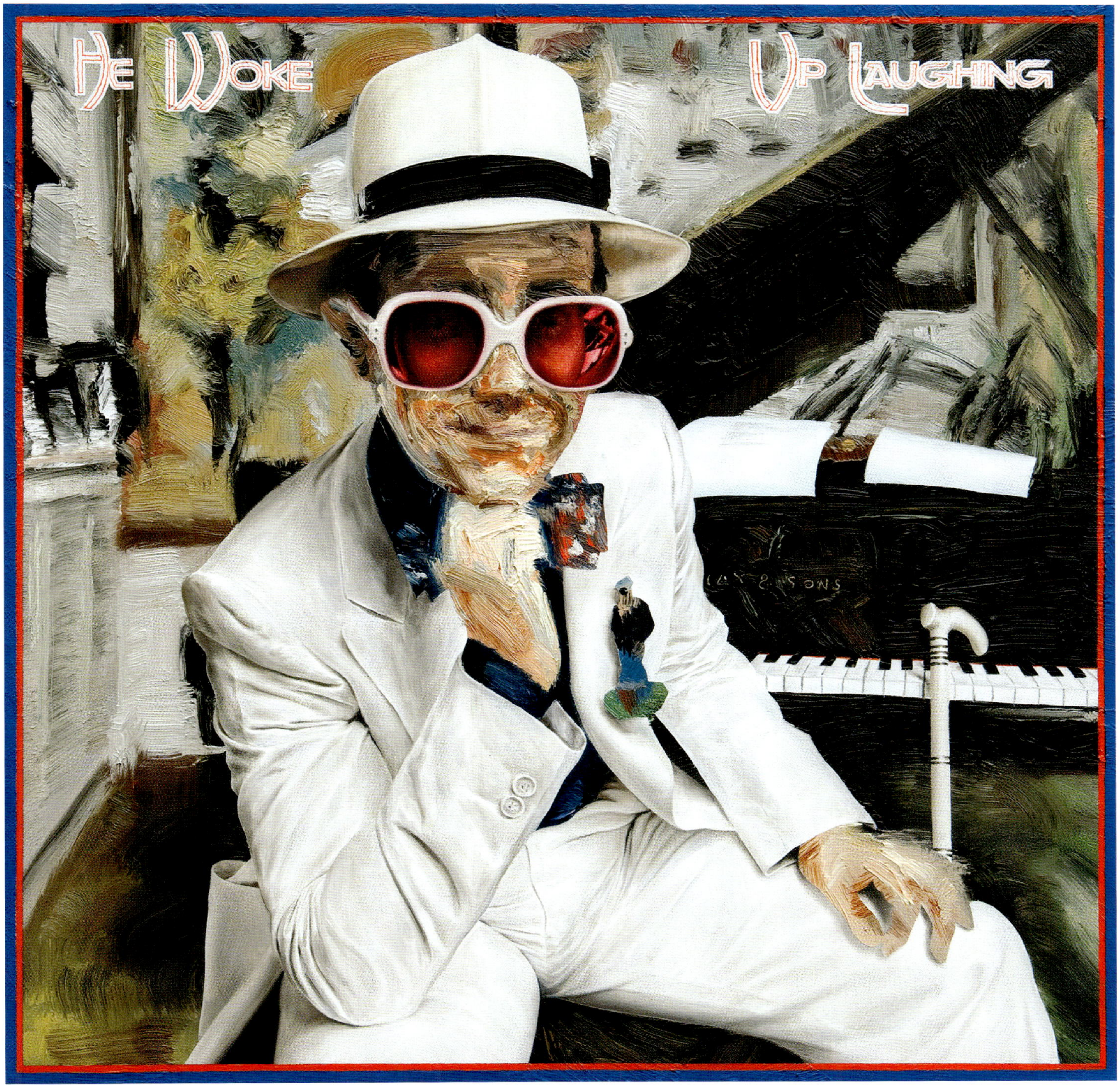

Belafonte
2009
Oil on panel
12 x 12 in.

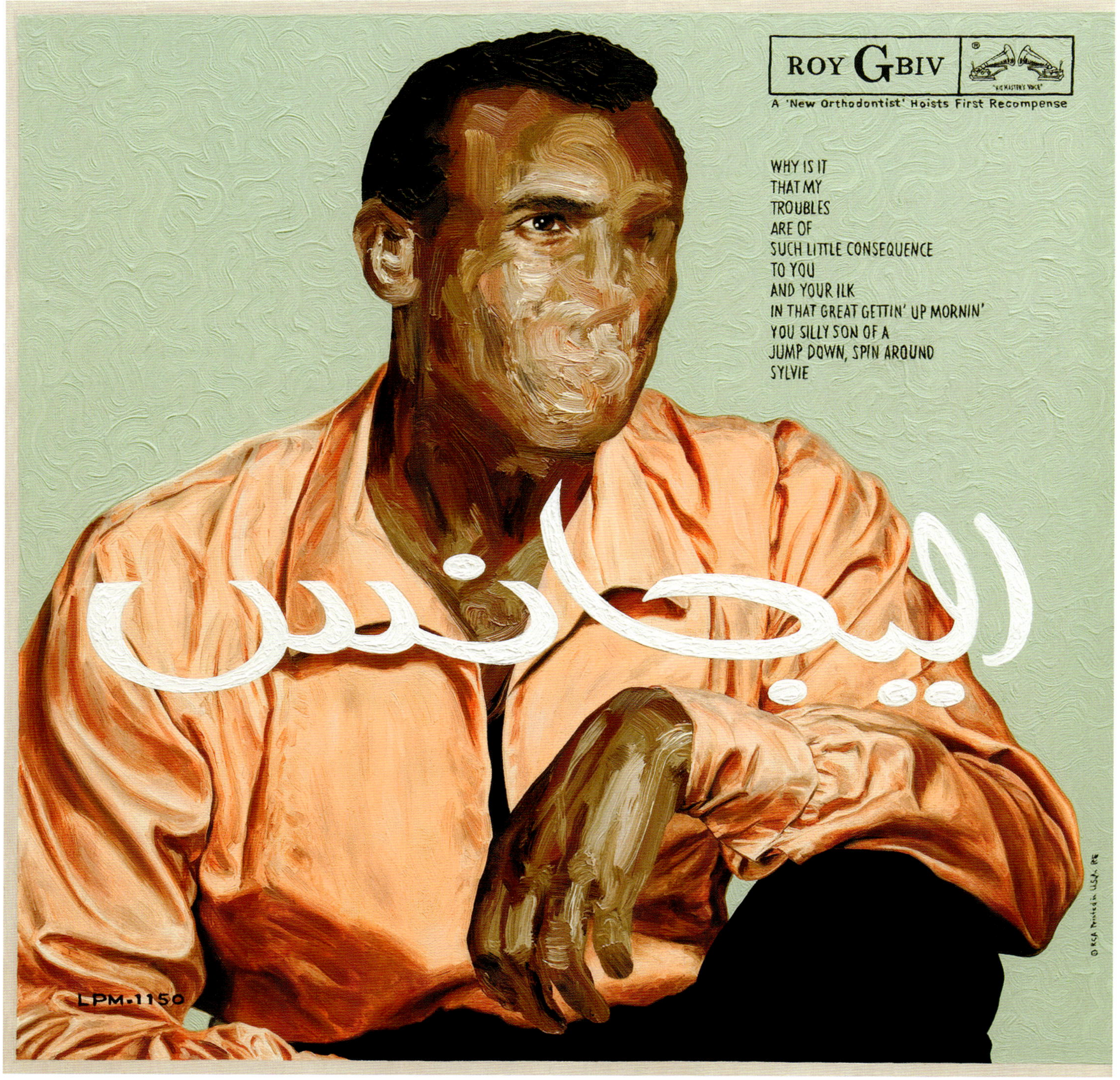

For Members Only
2011
Oil on panel
12 x 12 in.

Rumours
2009
Oil on panel
12 x 12 in.

Françoise Hardy
2011
Oil on panel
12 x 12 in.

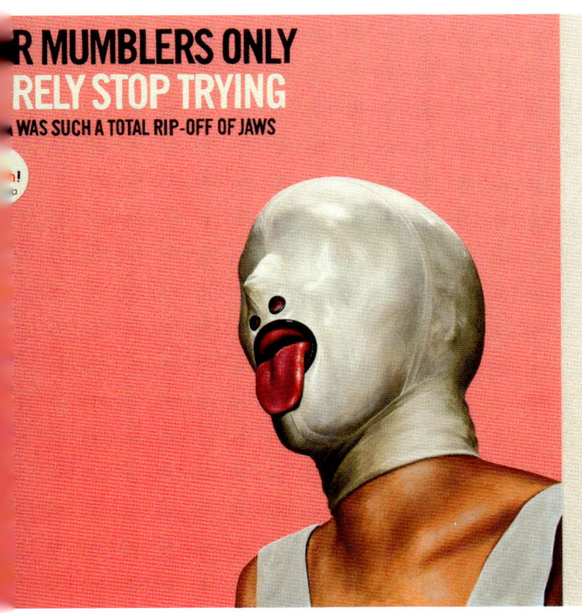

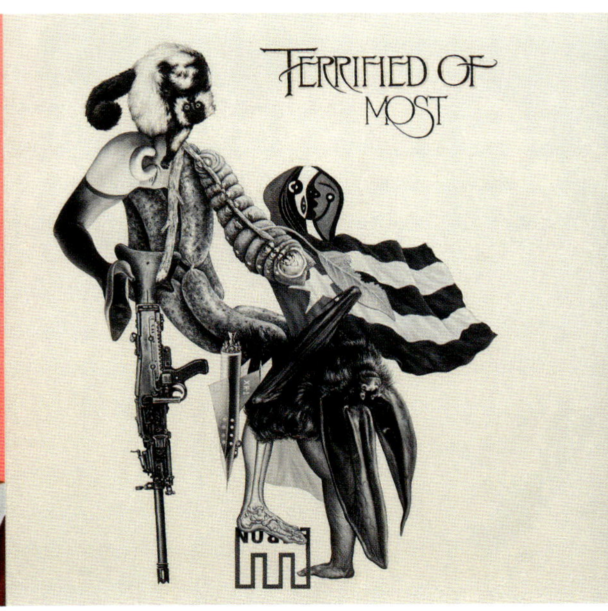

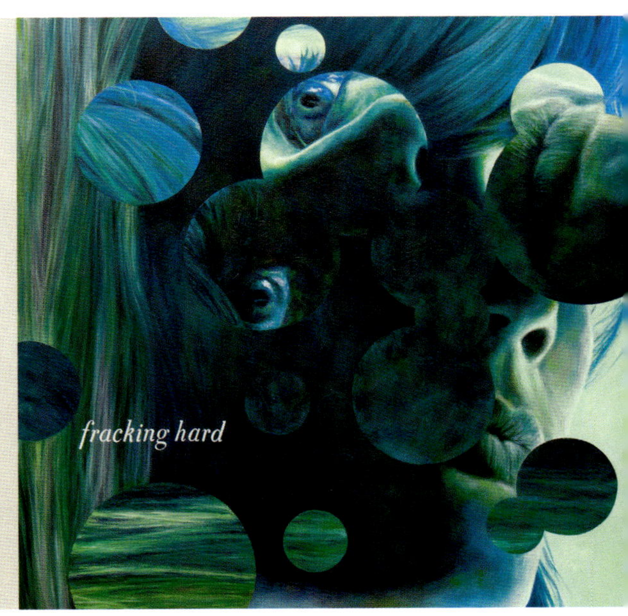

Songs In The Key Of Life
2009
Oil on panel
12 x 12 in.

Andy
2009
Oil on panel
12 x 12 in.

Adolescents
2011
Oil on panel
12 x 12 in.

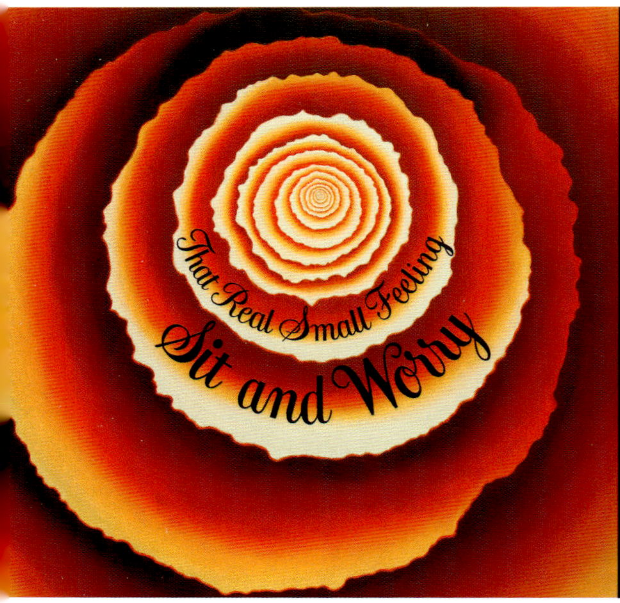

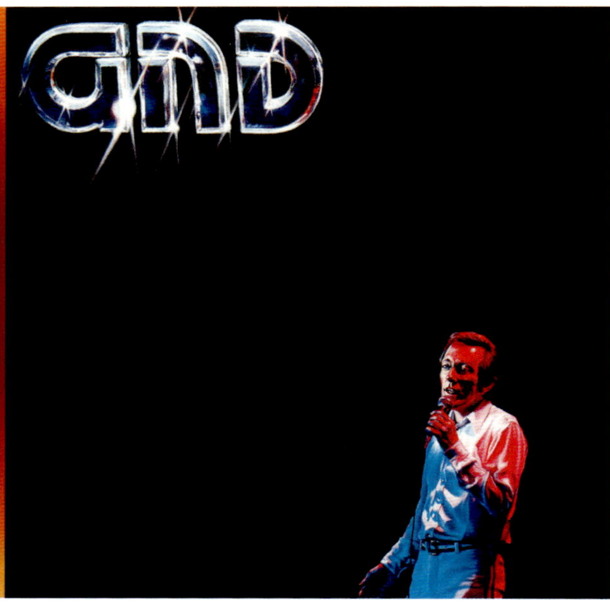

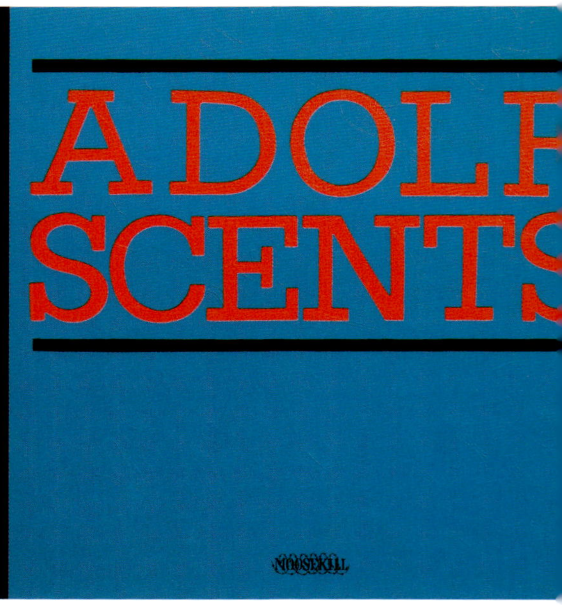

Who's Next
2009
Oil on panel
12 x 12 in.

Hot Rats
2009
Oil on panel
12 x 12 in.

I'm Still In Love With You
2009
Oil on panel
12 x 12 in.

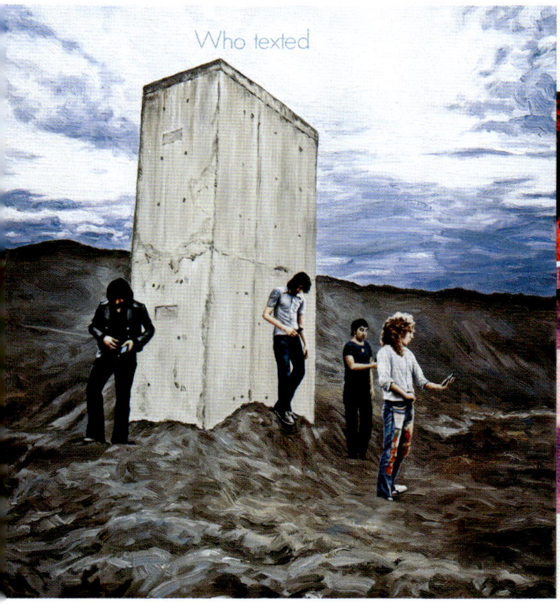

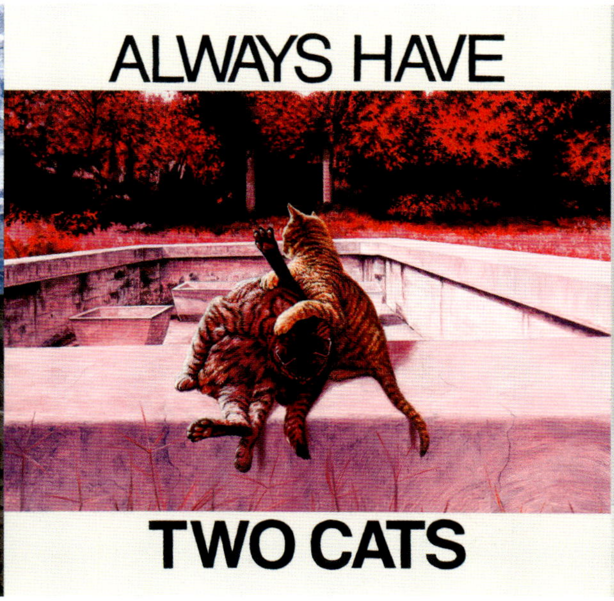

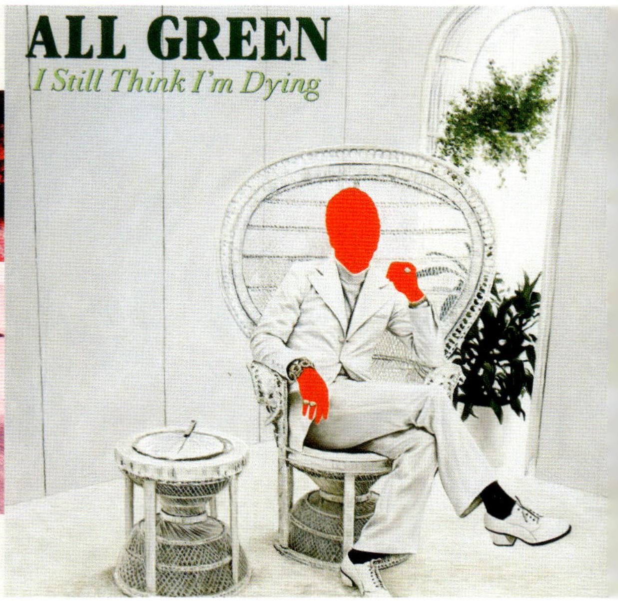

Yes
2009
Oil on panel
12 x 12 in.

Faces
2009
Oil on panel
12 x 12 in.

Their Greatest Hits 1971–1975
2009
Oil on panel
12 x 12 in.

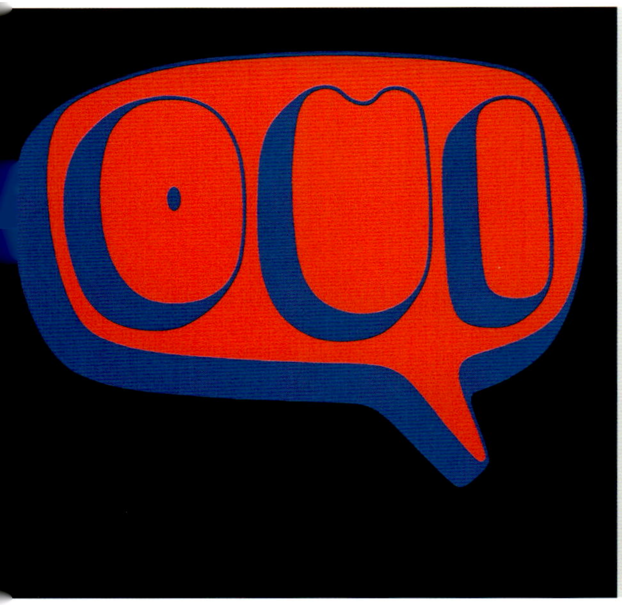

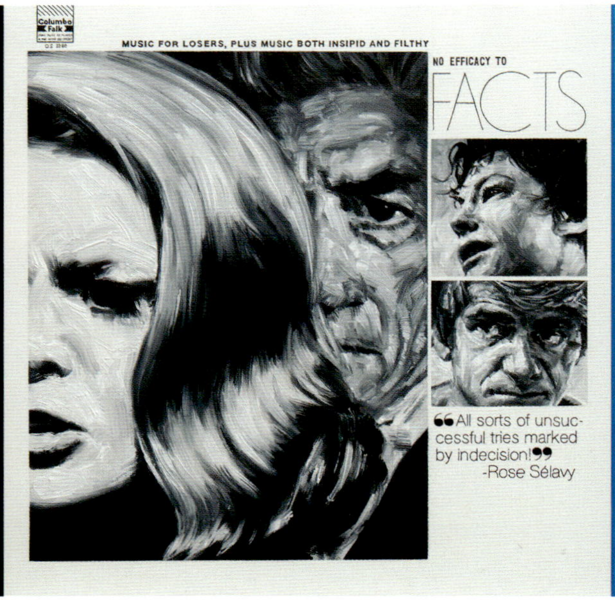

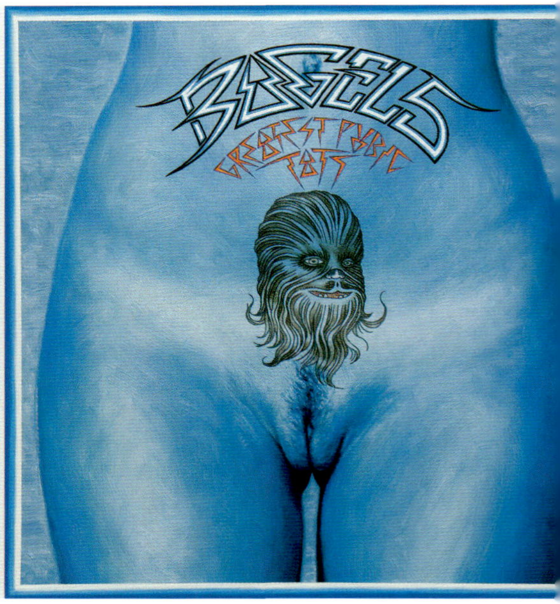

Houses Of The Holy
2009
Oil on panel
12 x 12 in.

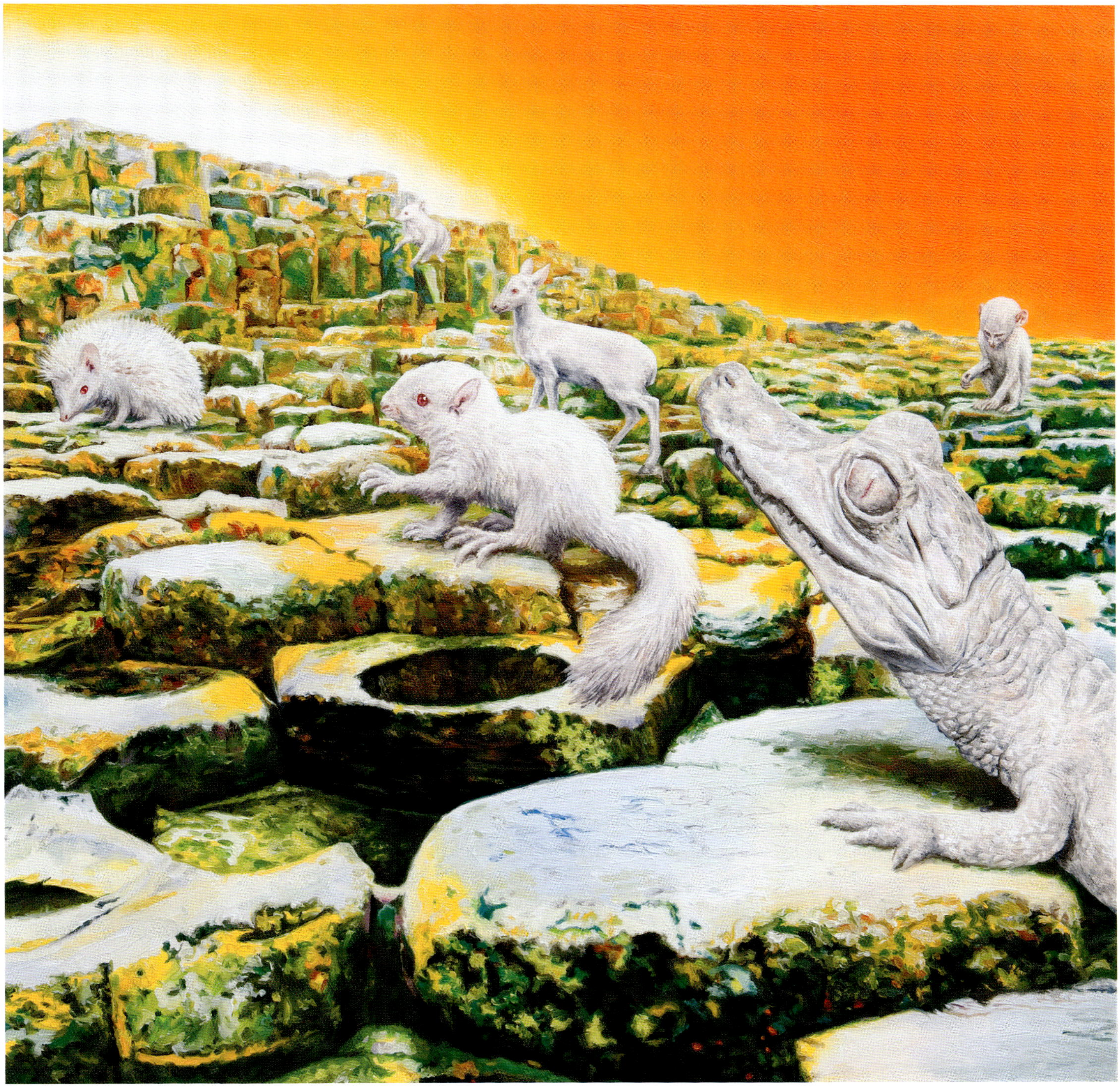

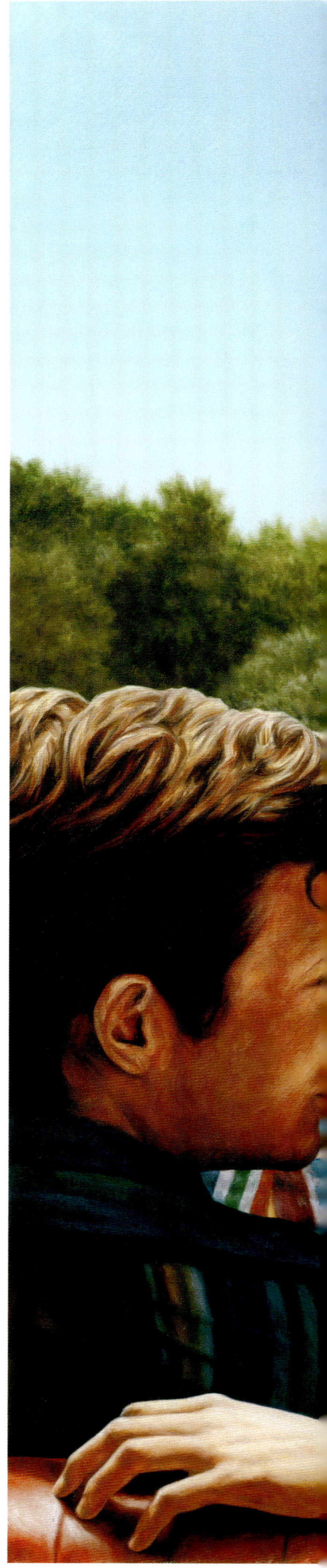

1961 Ford Galaxie 500 Sunliner (Pierrot Le Fou)
2010
Oil on canvas
48 x 48 in.

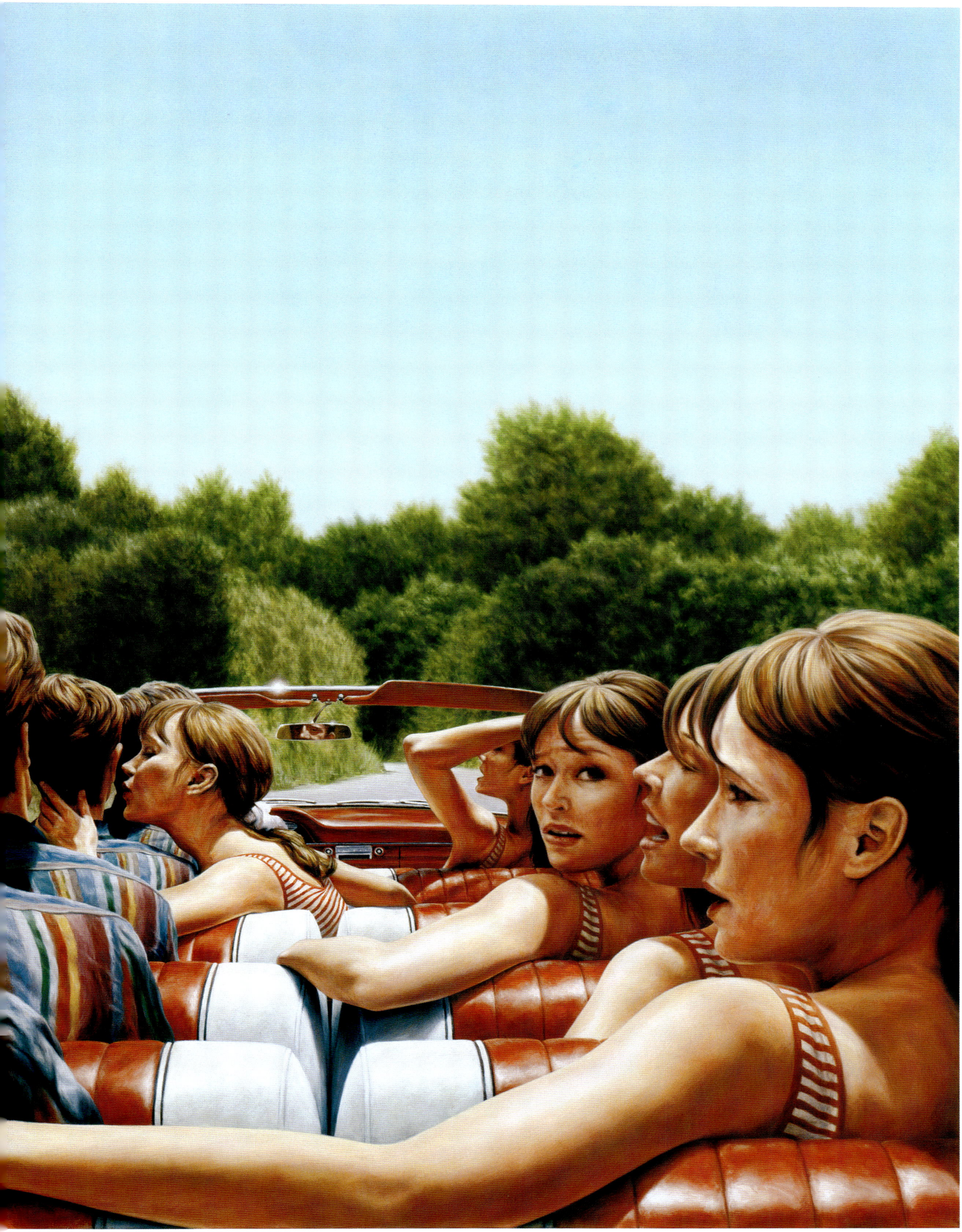

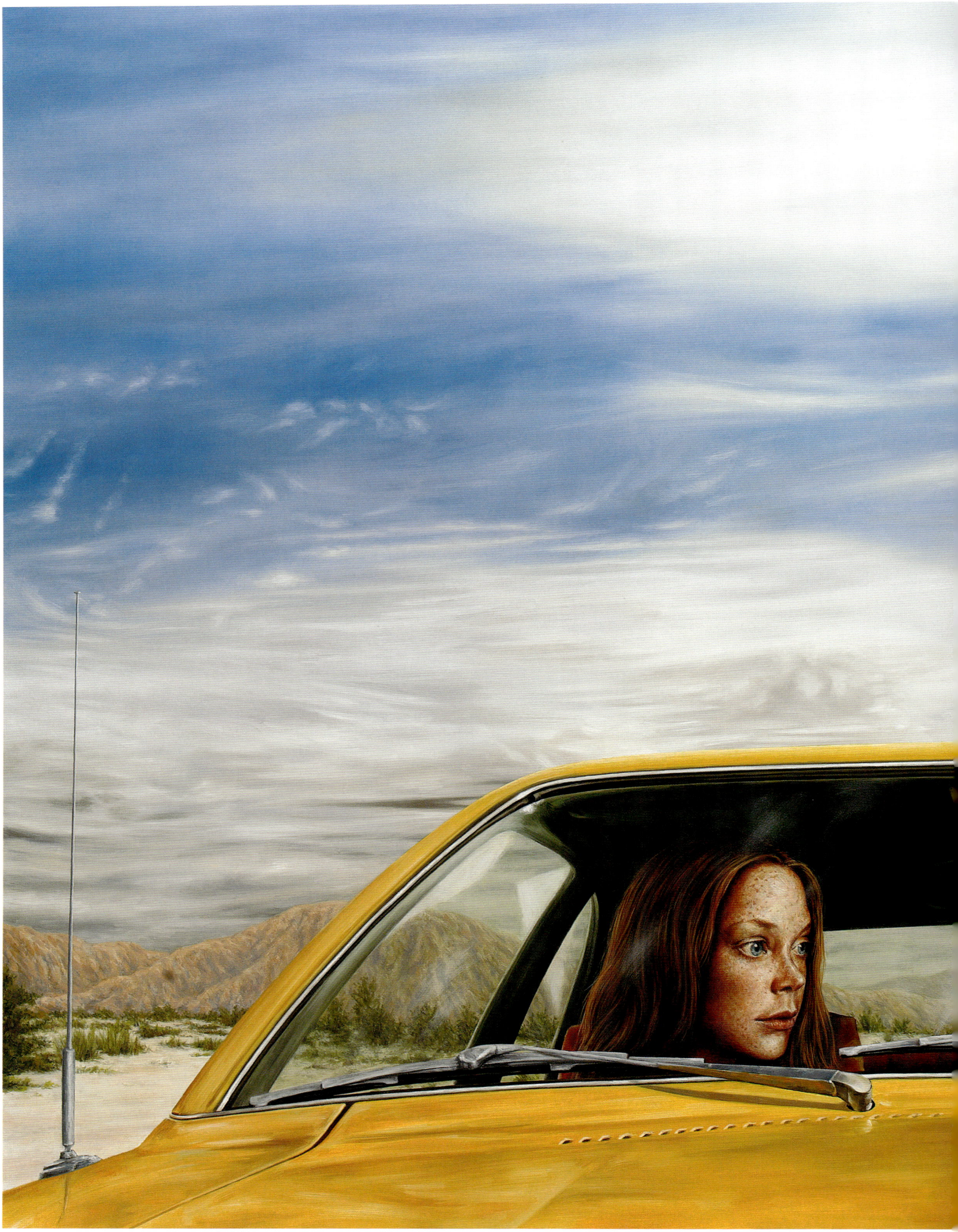

1973 Ford Pinto with Tanguy Sky (3 Women)
2011
Oil on canvas
40 x 60 in.

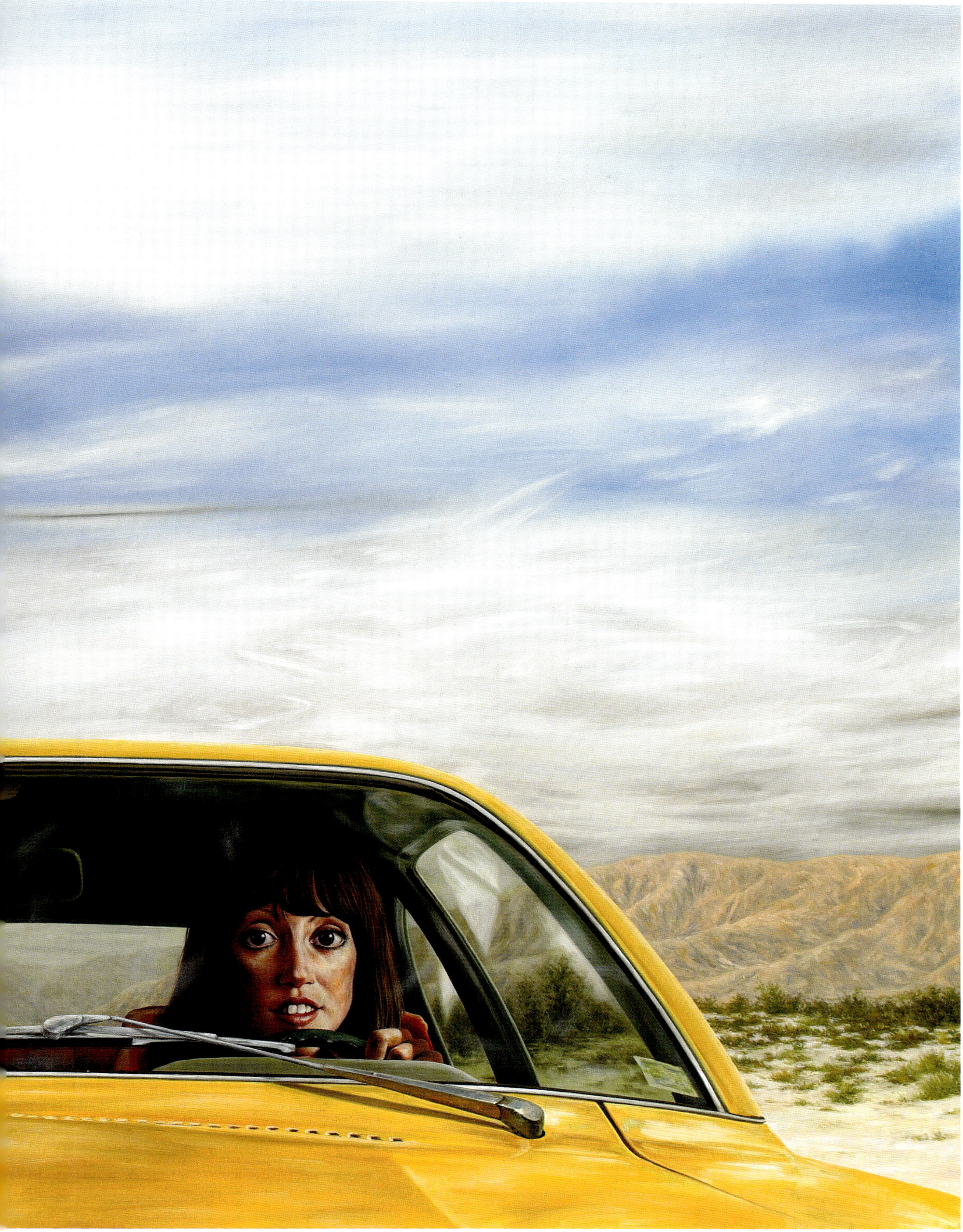

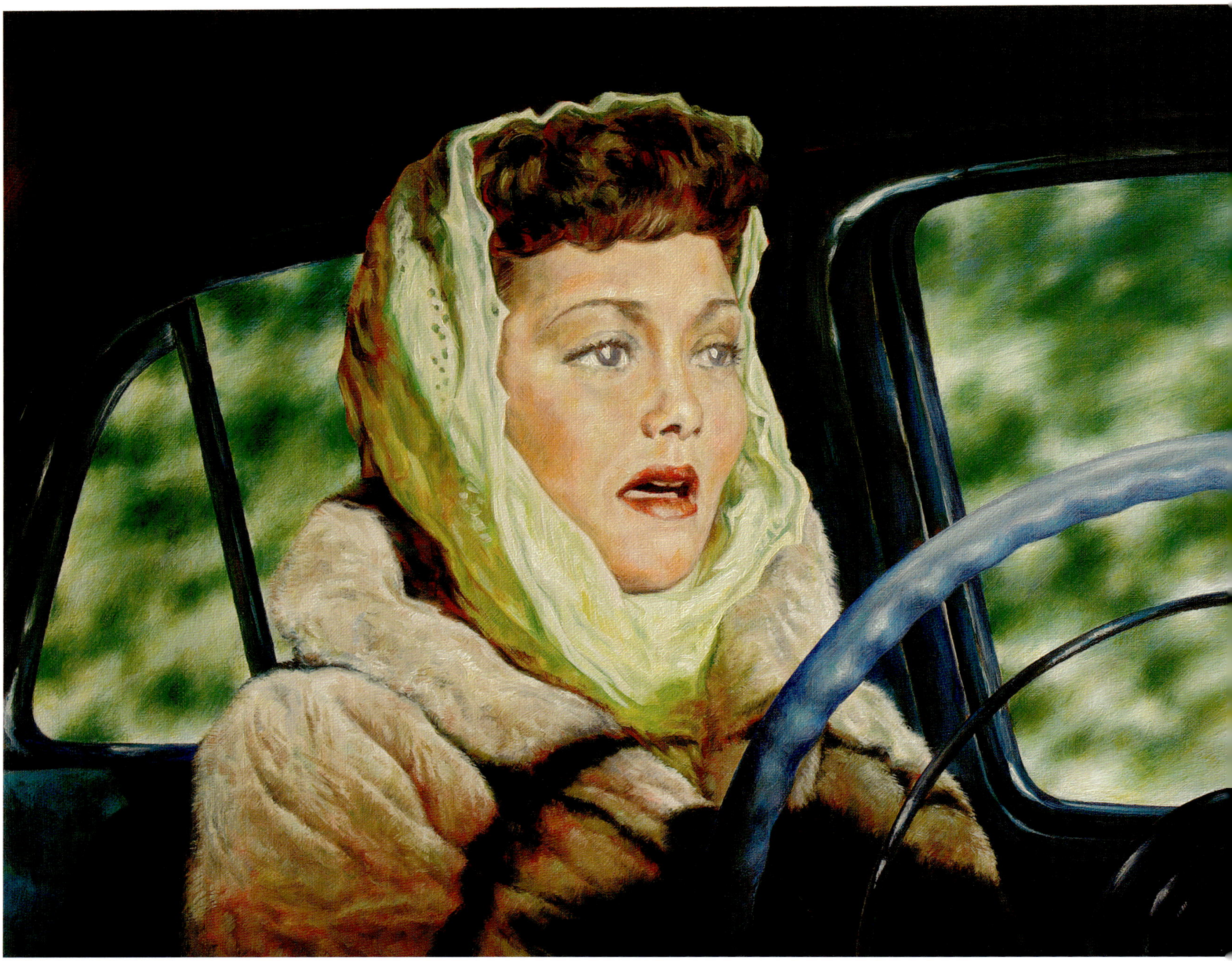

1954 Lincoln Capri (All That Heaven Allows)
2011
Oil on linen
18 x 46 in.

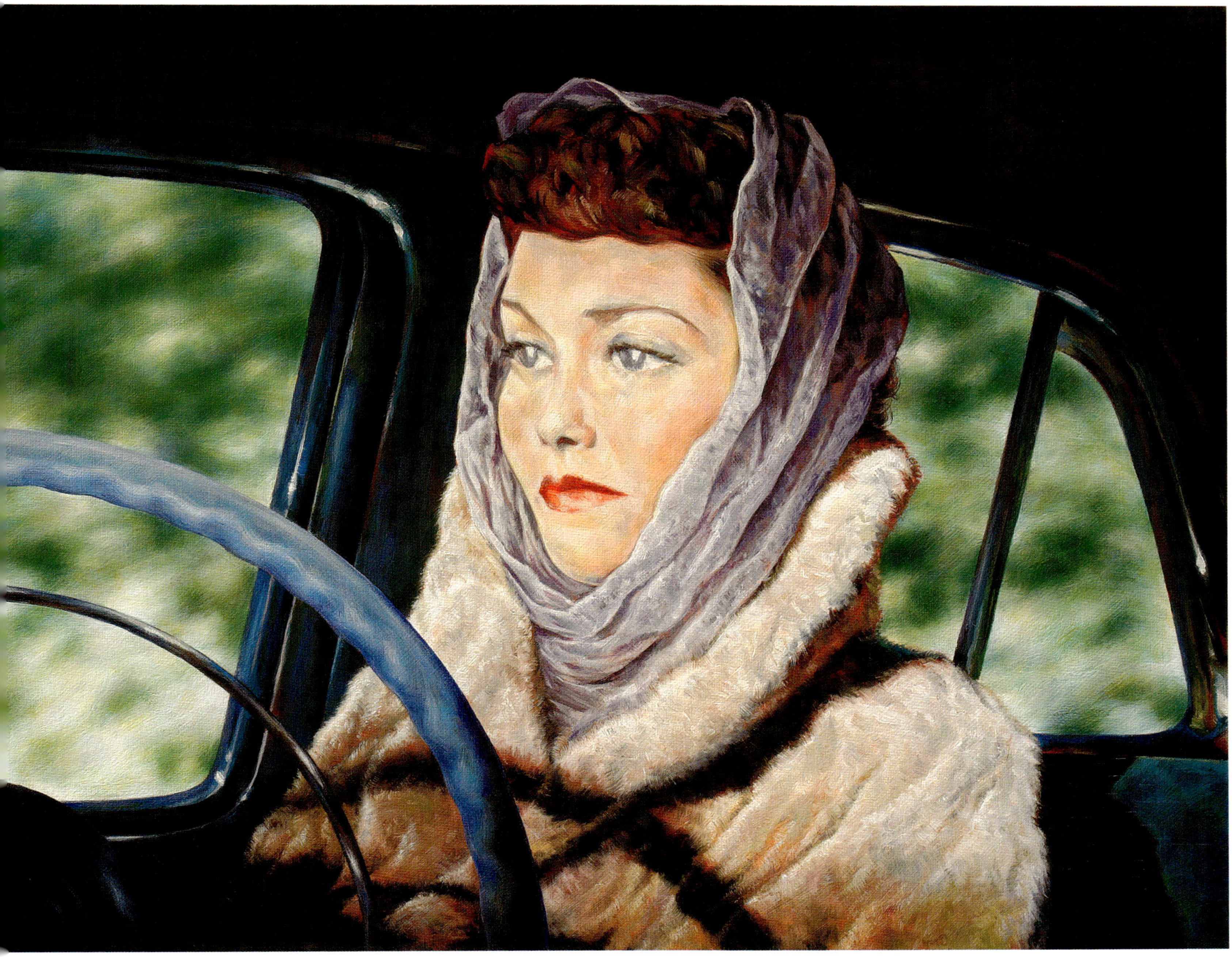

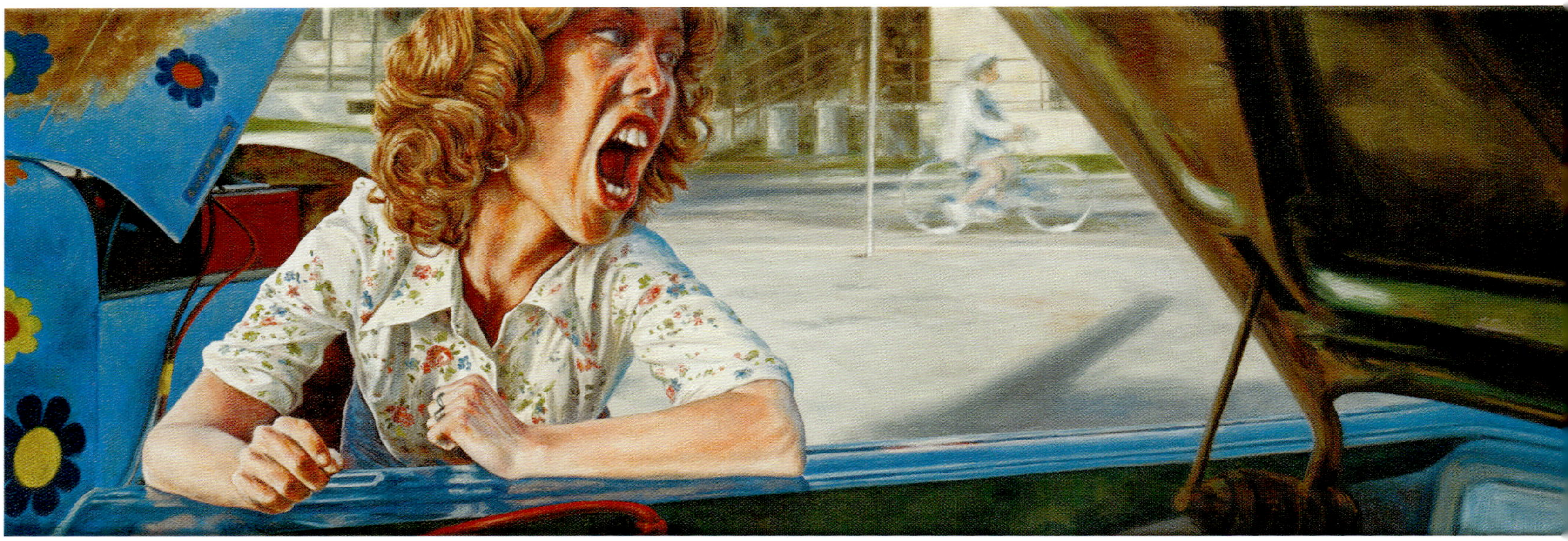

1967 Ford Ranchero (Coming Home)
2011
Oil on canvas
8 x 46 in.

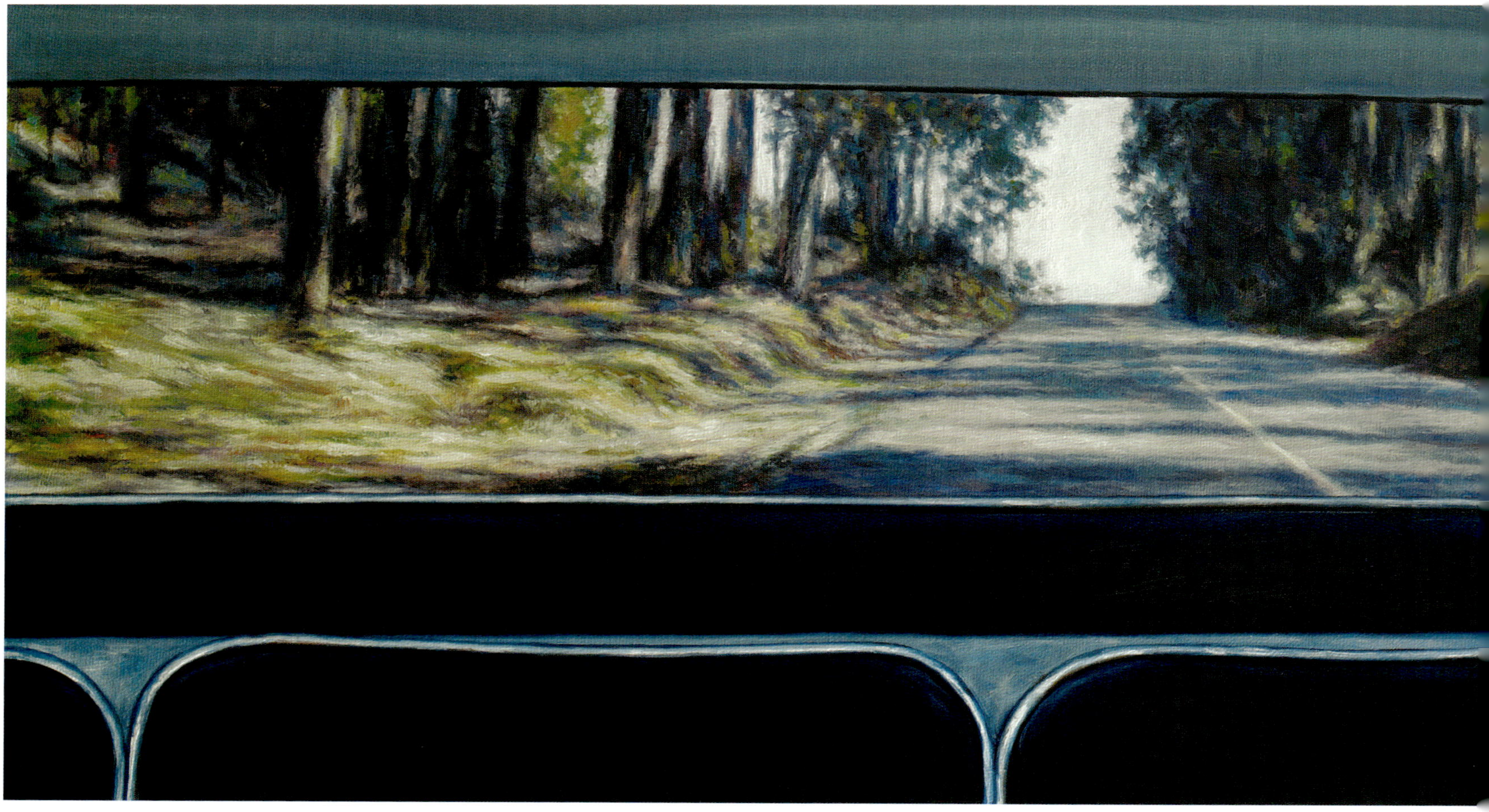

1956 De Soto Firedome Sportsman (Vertigo)
2011
Oil on canvas
10 x 36 in.

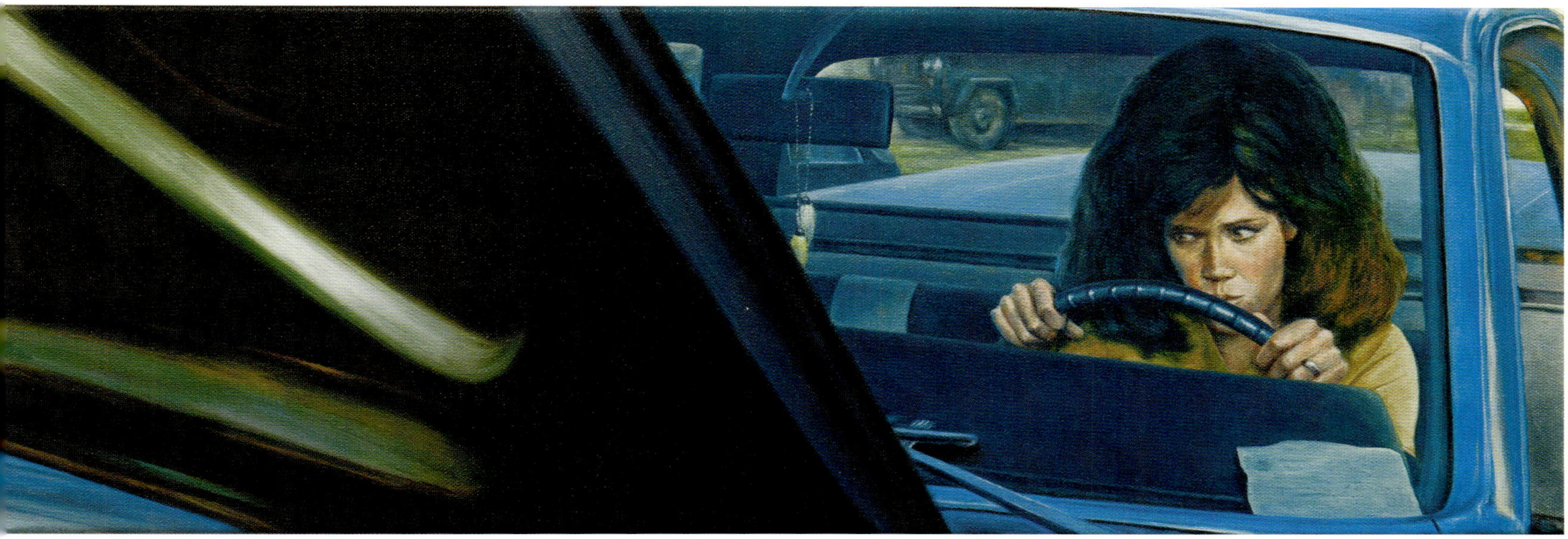

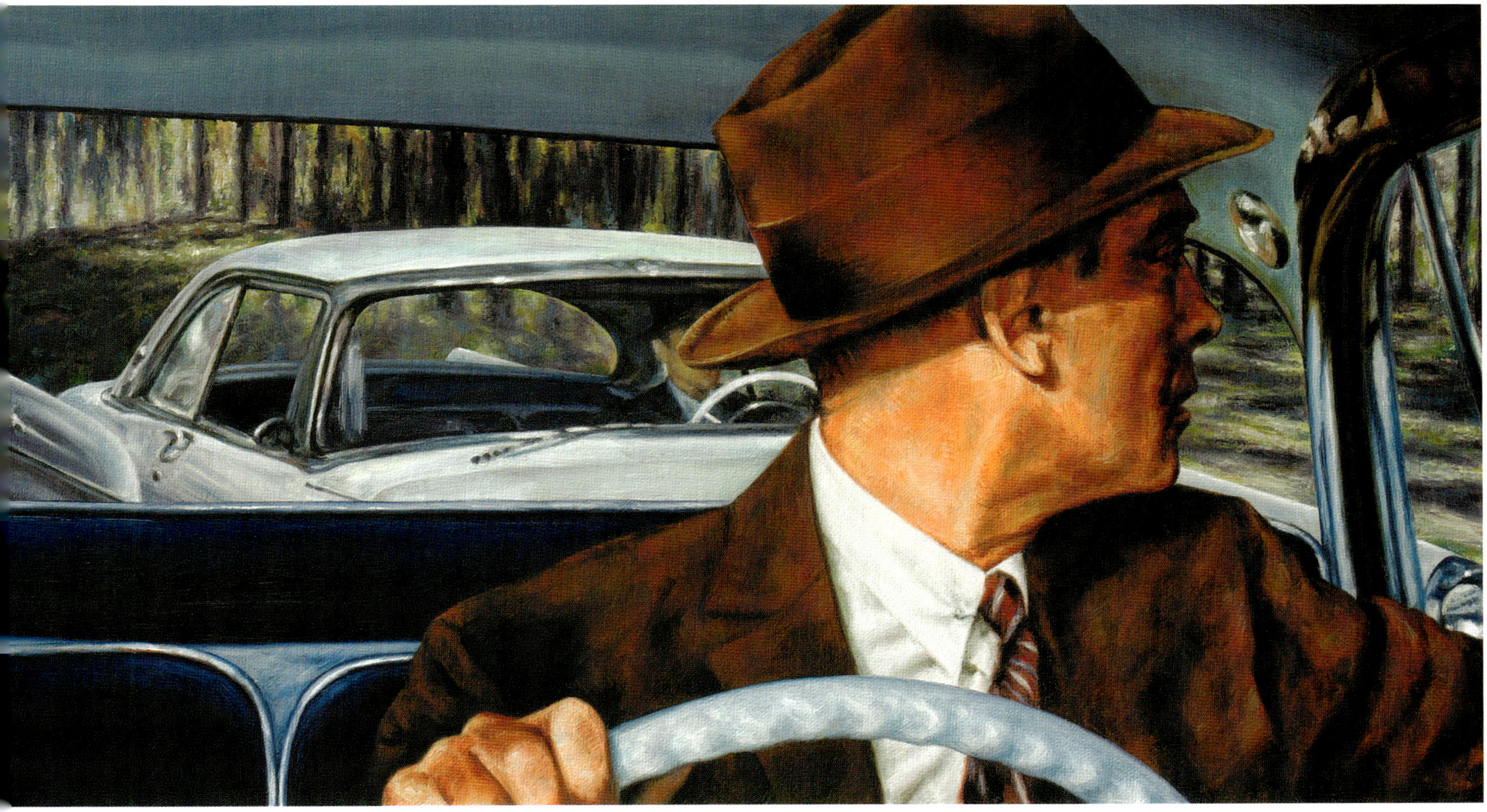

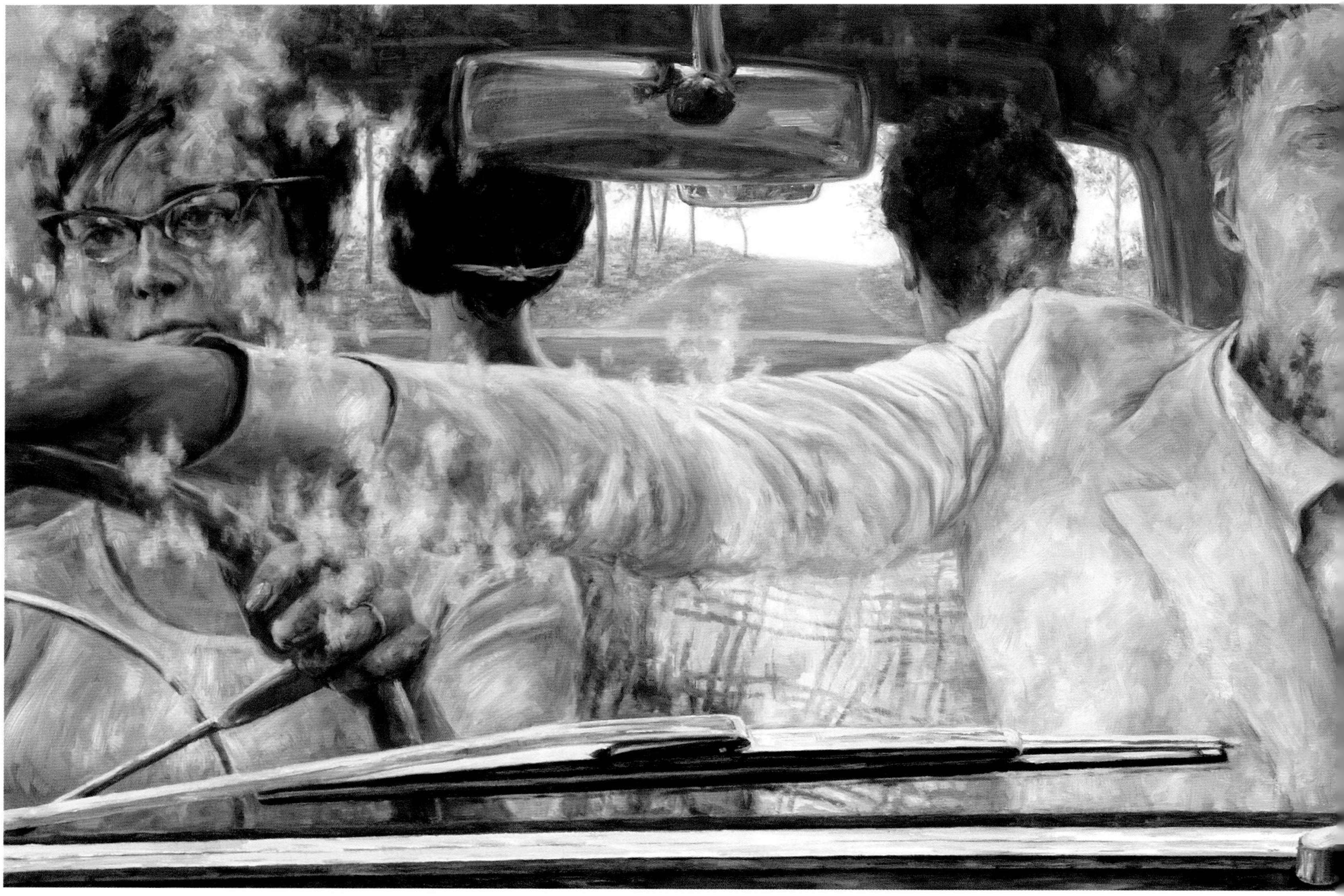

1957 Peugeot 403 (Nóz W Wodzie)
2011
Oil on canvas
26 x 78 in.

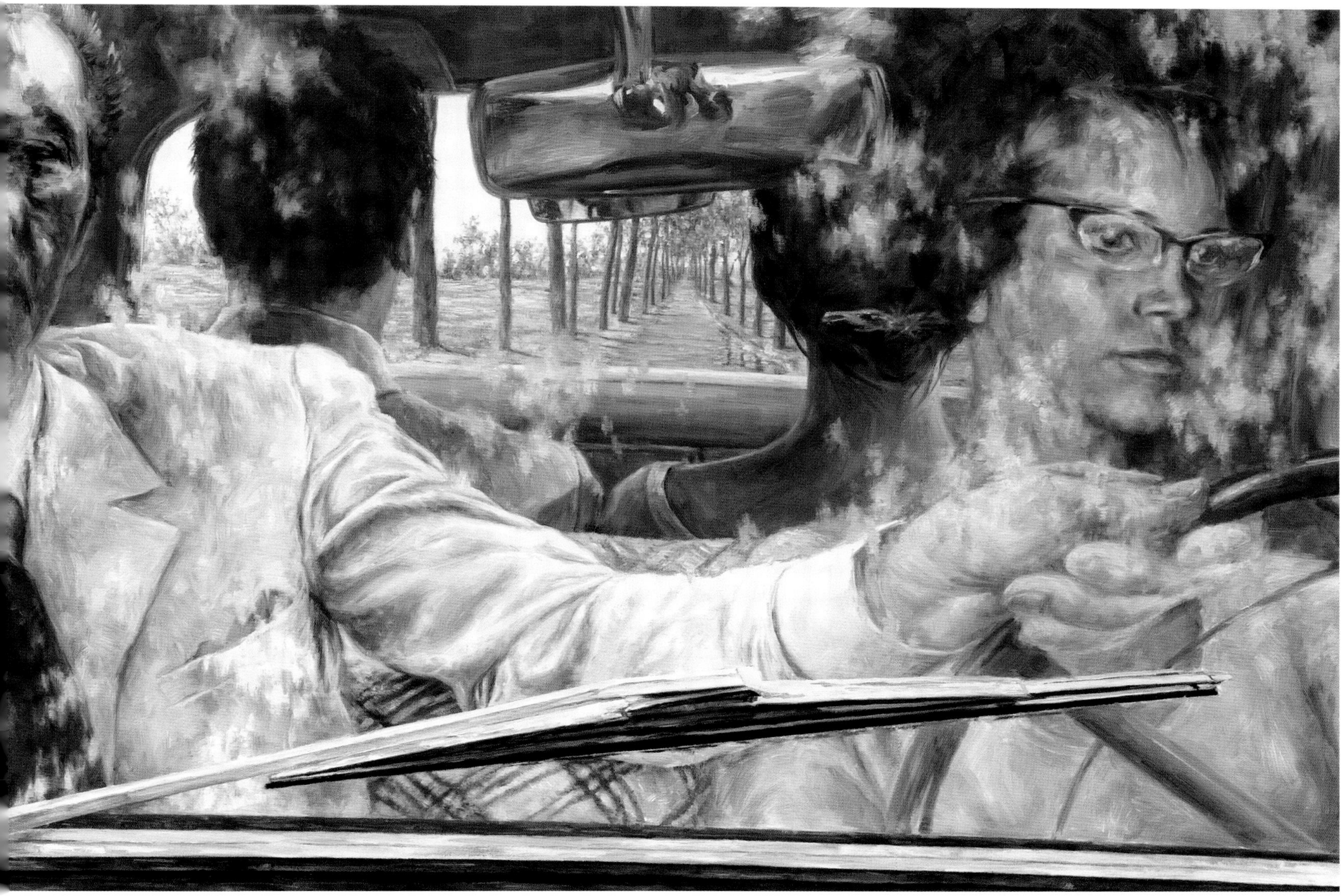

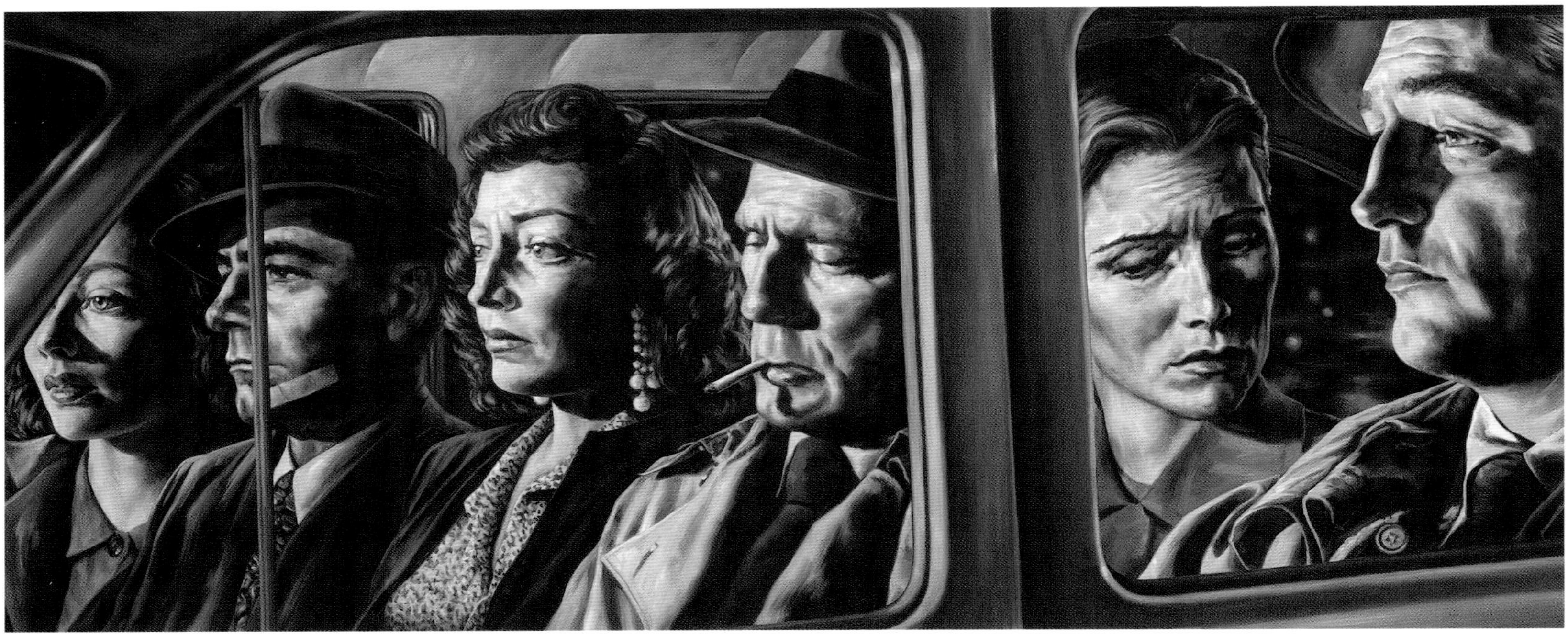

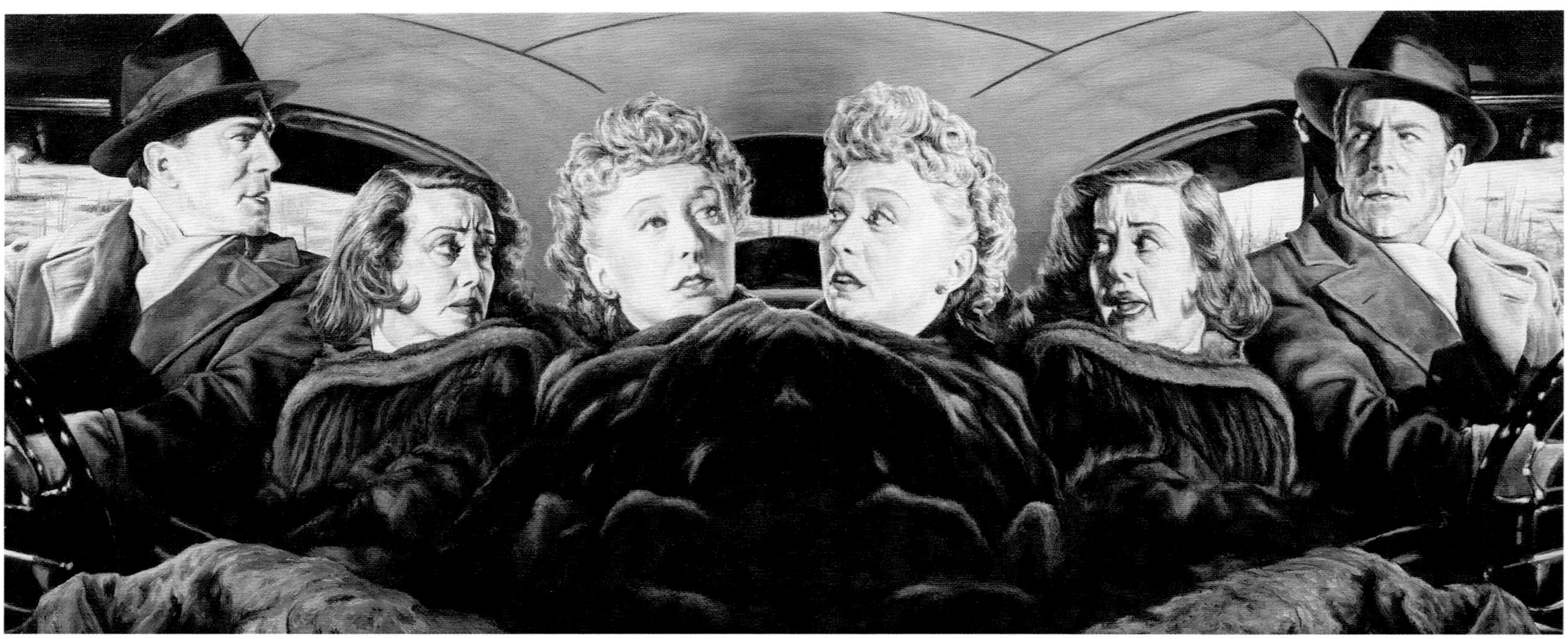

1940 Dodge De Luxe (Noirpool)
2011
Oil on canvas
20 x 50 in.

1950 Mercury Coupé (All About Eve)
2011
Oil on linen
13 x 32 in.

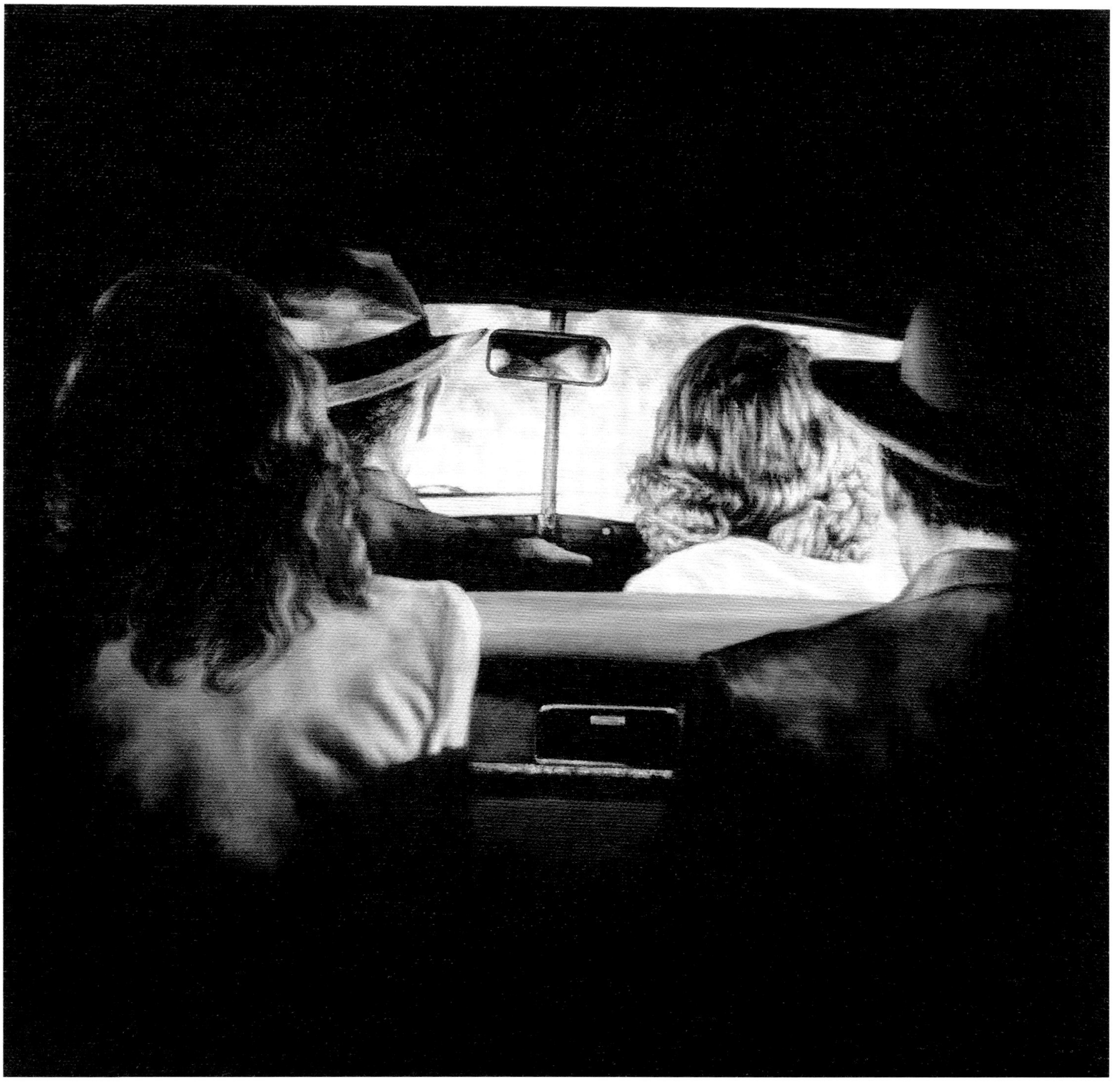

1941 Plymouth Special DeLuxe Sedan (Fear In The Night)
2011
Oil on canvas
12 x 12 in.

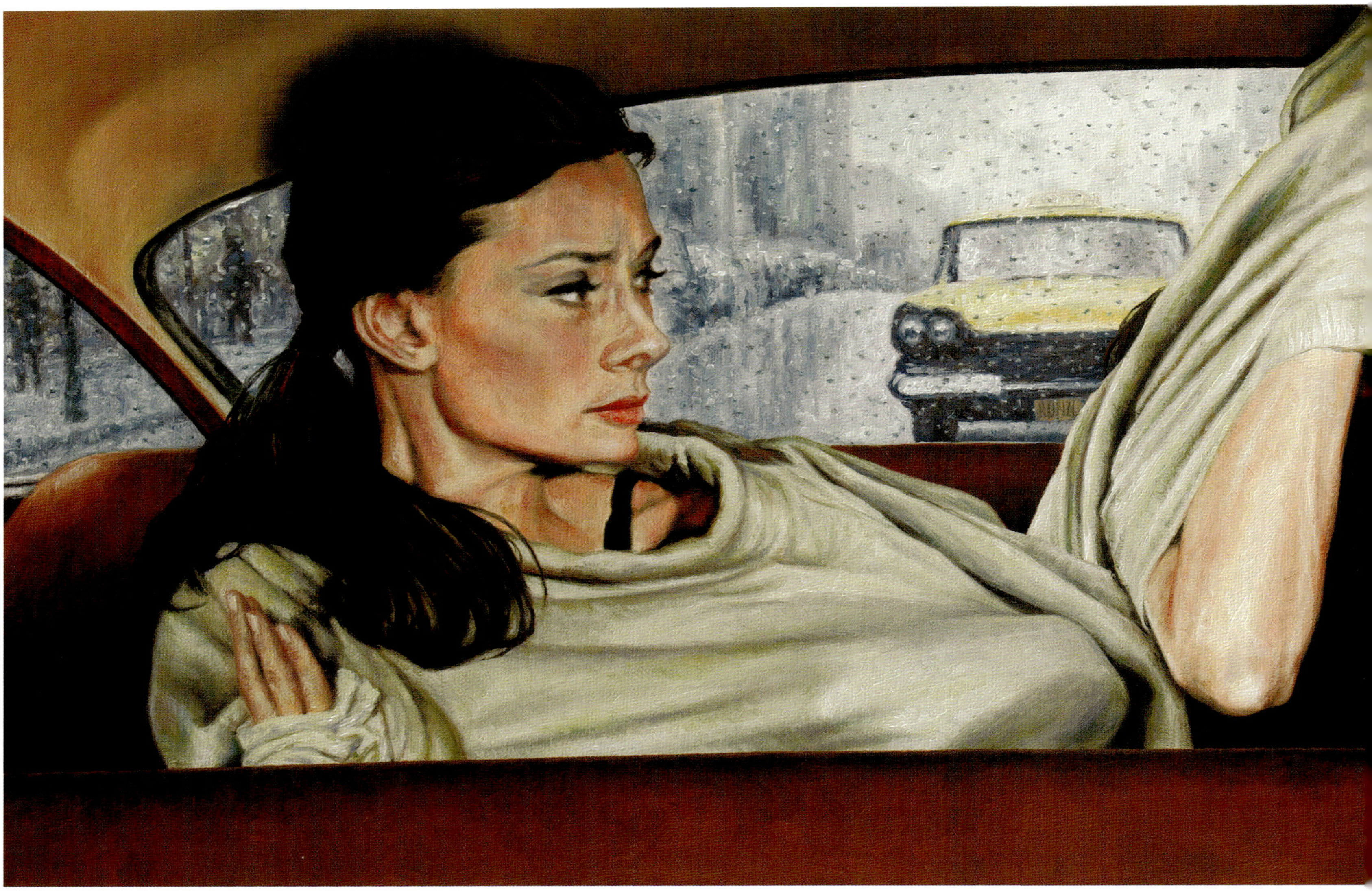

1957 Plymouth Plaza Sedan (Breakfast at Tiffany's)
2011
Oil on canvas
10 x 30 in.

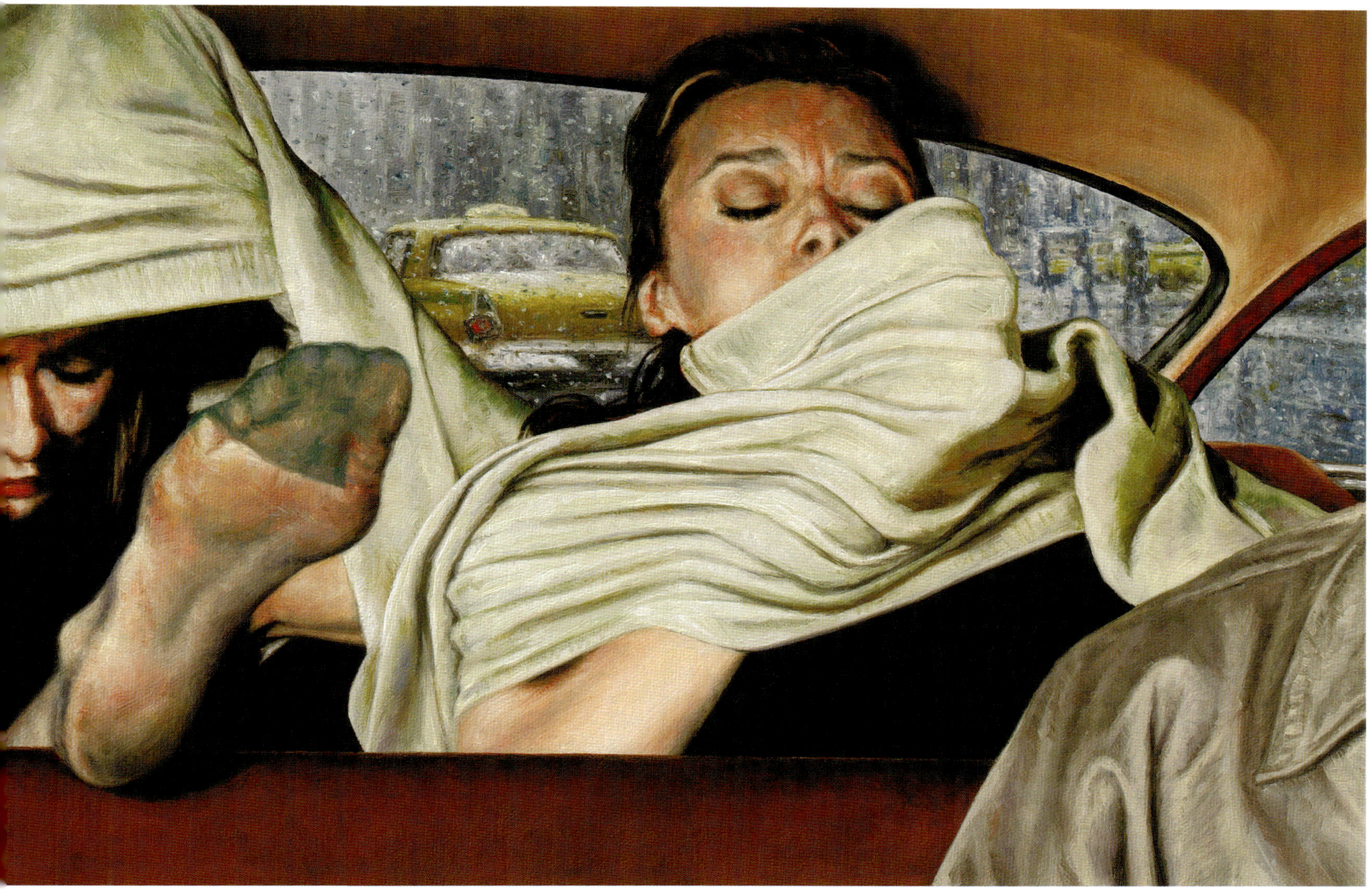

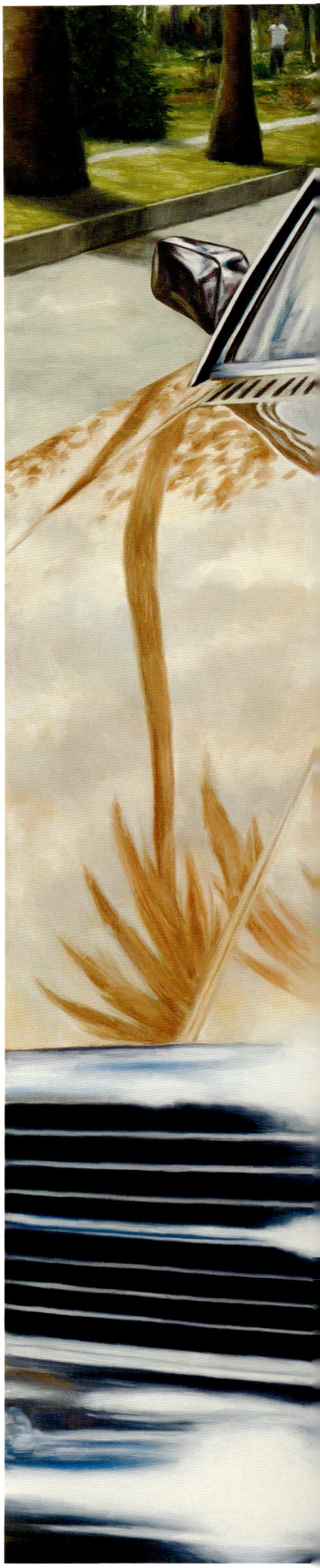

1974 Mercedes-Benz 450 SL (Annie Hall)
2011
Oil on linen
48 x 48 in.

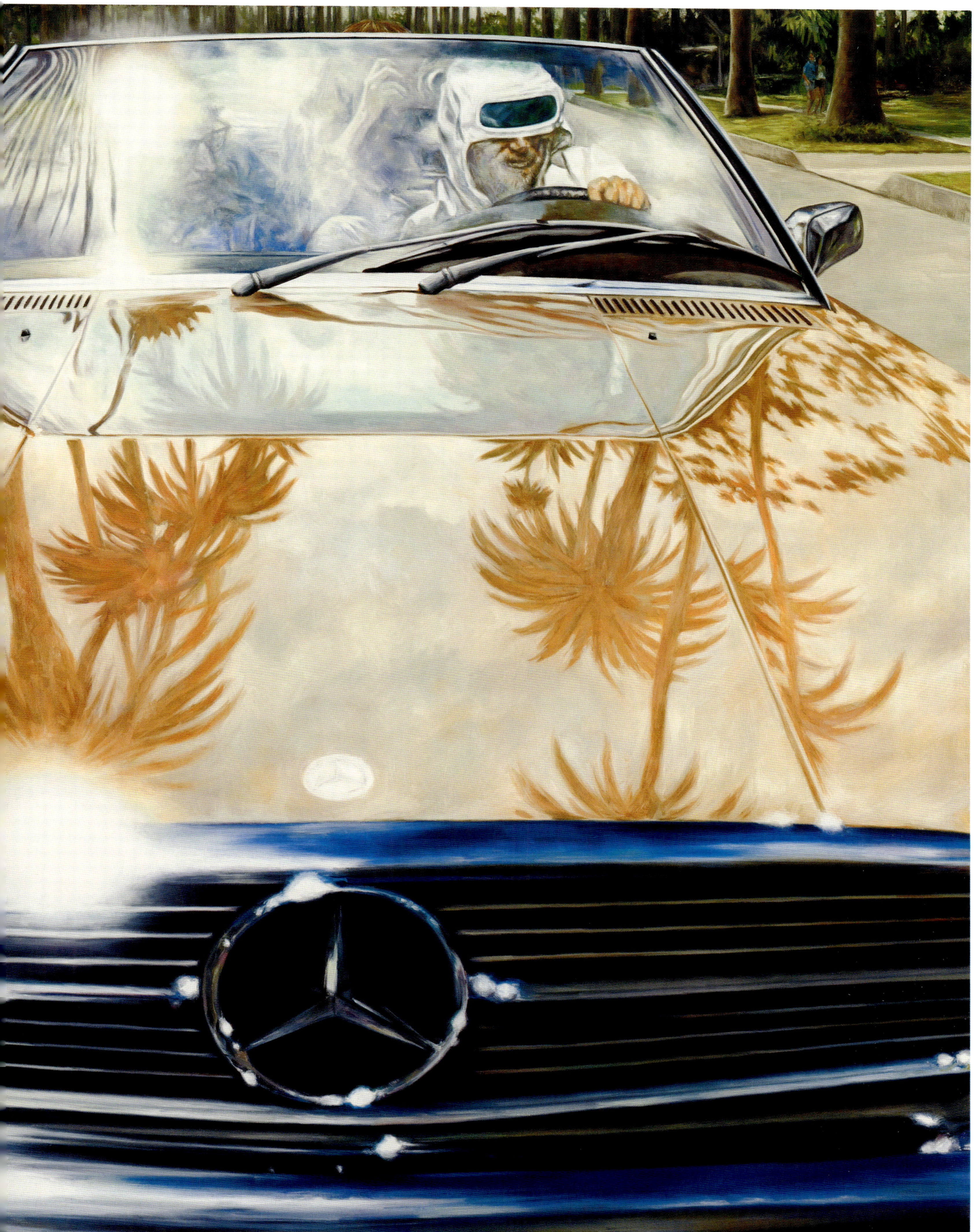

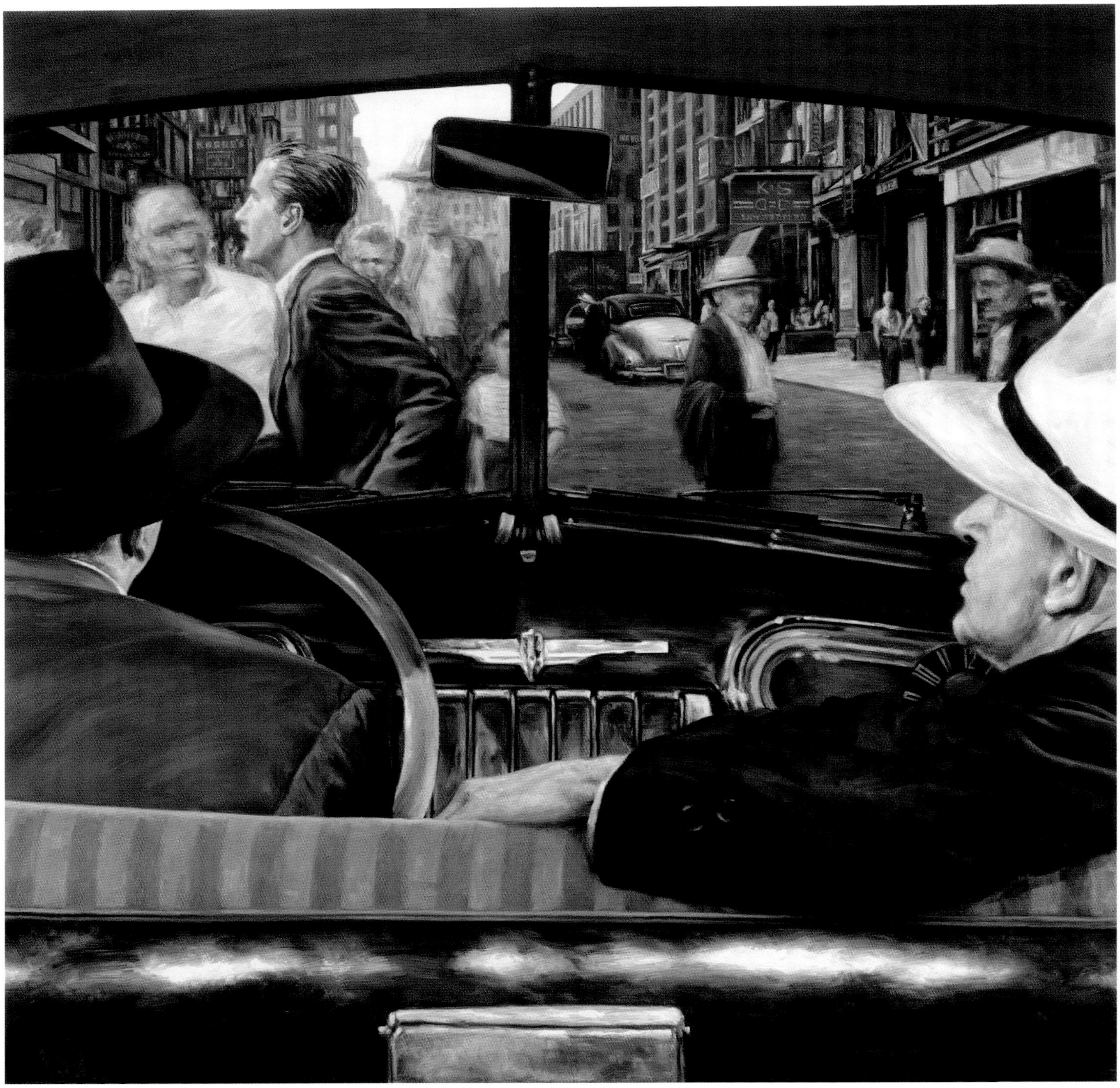

1942 Studebaker Commander Custom Land Cruiser (The Naked City)
2012
Oil on linen
36 x 36 in.

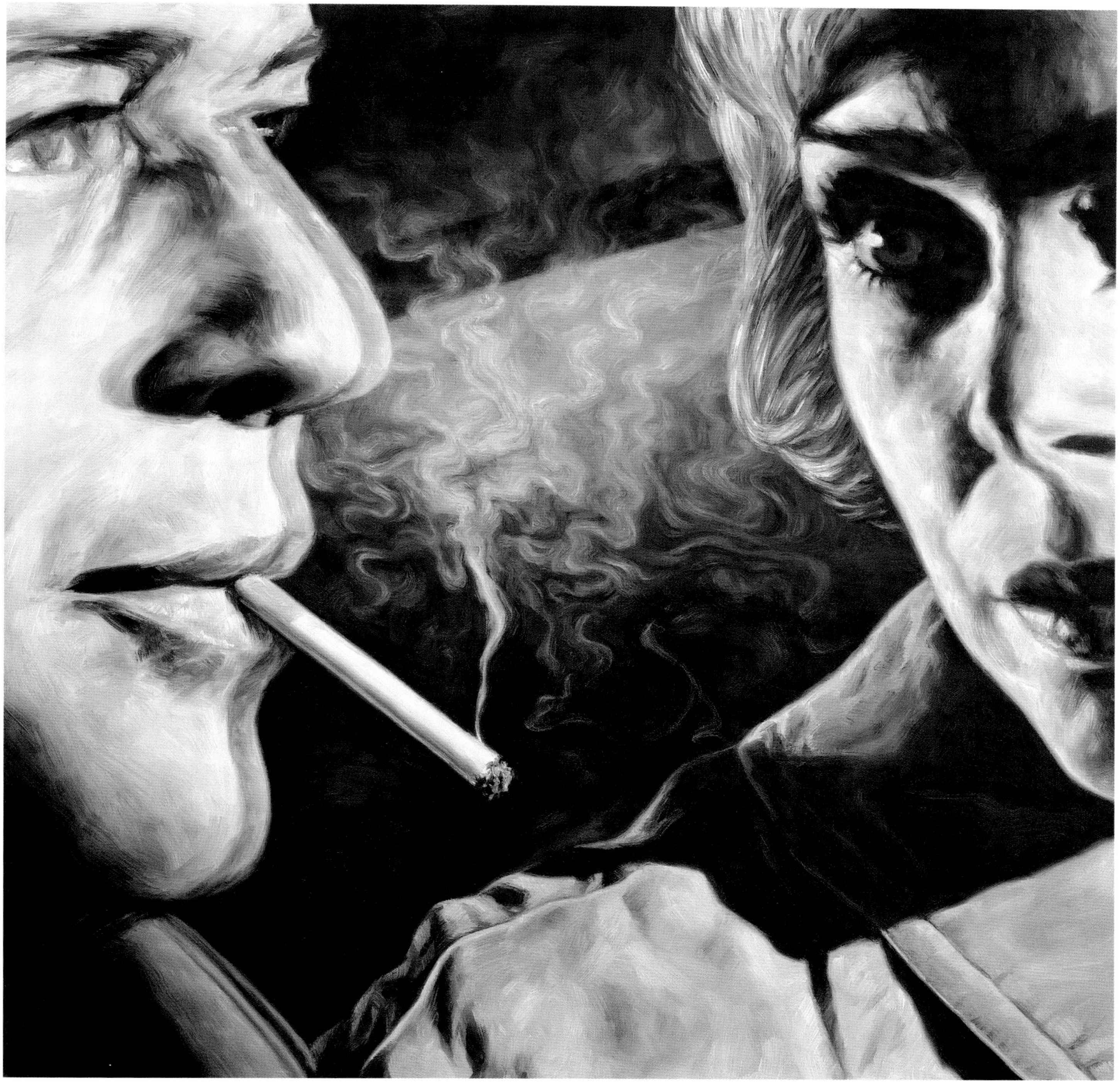

1953 DeSoto Powermaster 8 Passenger Taxicab (The Manchurian Candidate)
2012
Oil on canvas
24 x 24 in.

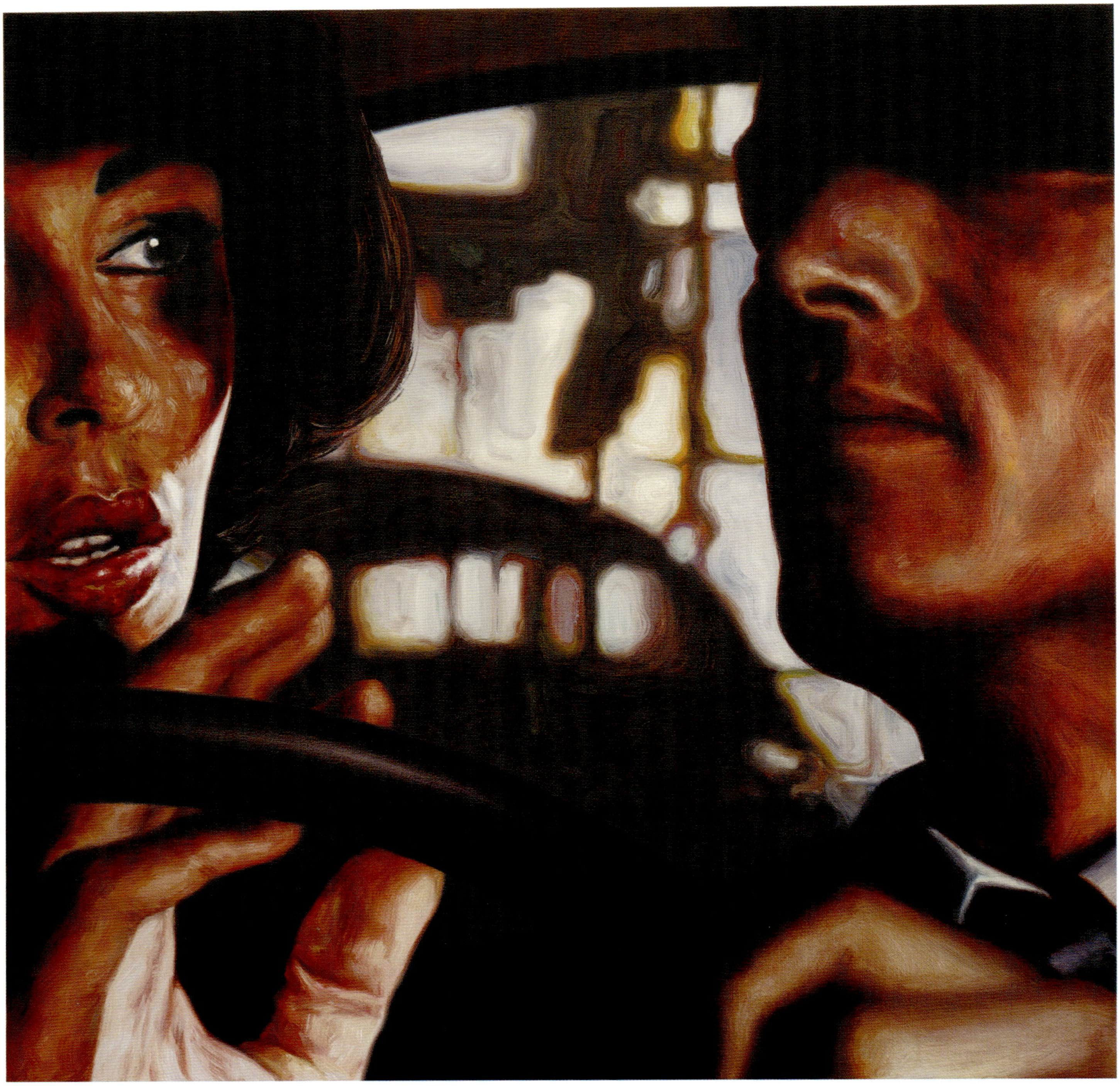

1960 Sunbeam Alpine Sport Series 1 (Butterfield 8)
2012
Oil on linen
24 x 24 in.

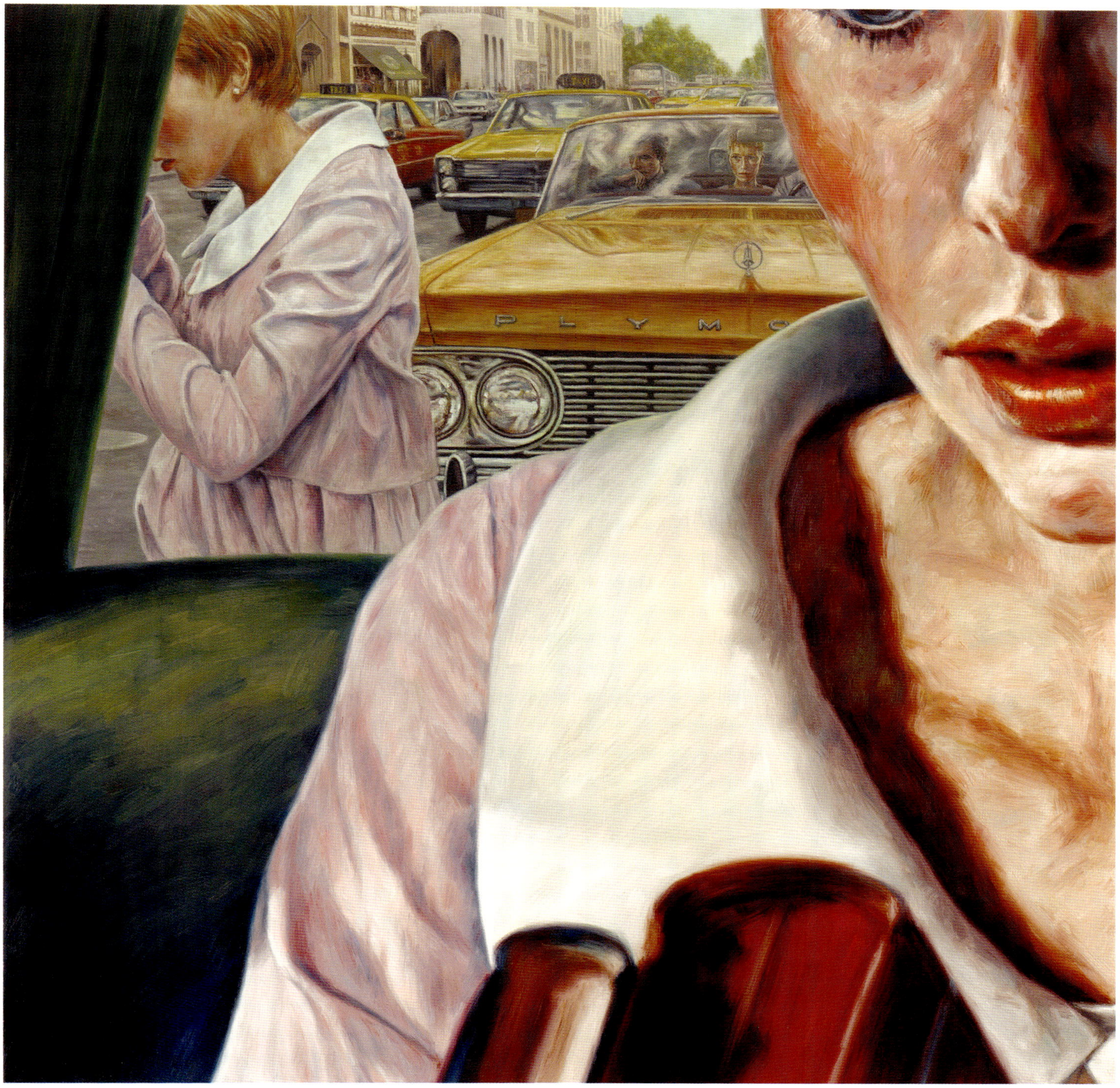

1963 Plymouth Belvedere (Rosemary's Baby)
2012
Oil on linen
36 x 36 in.

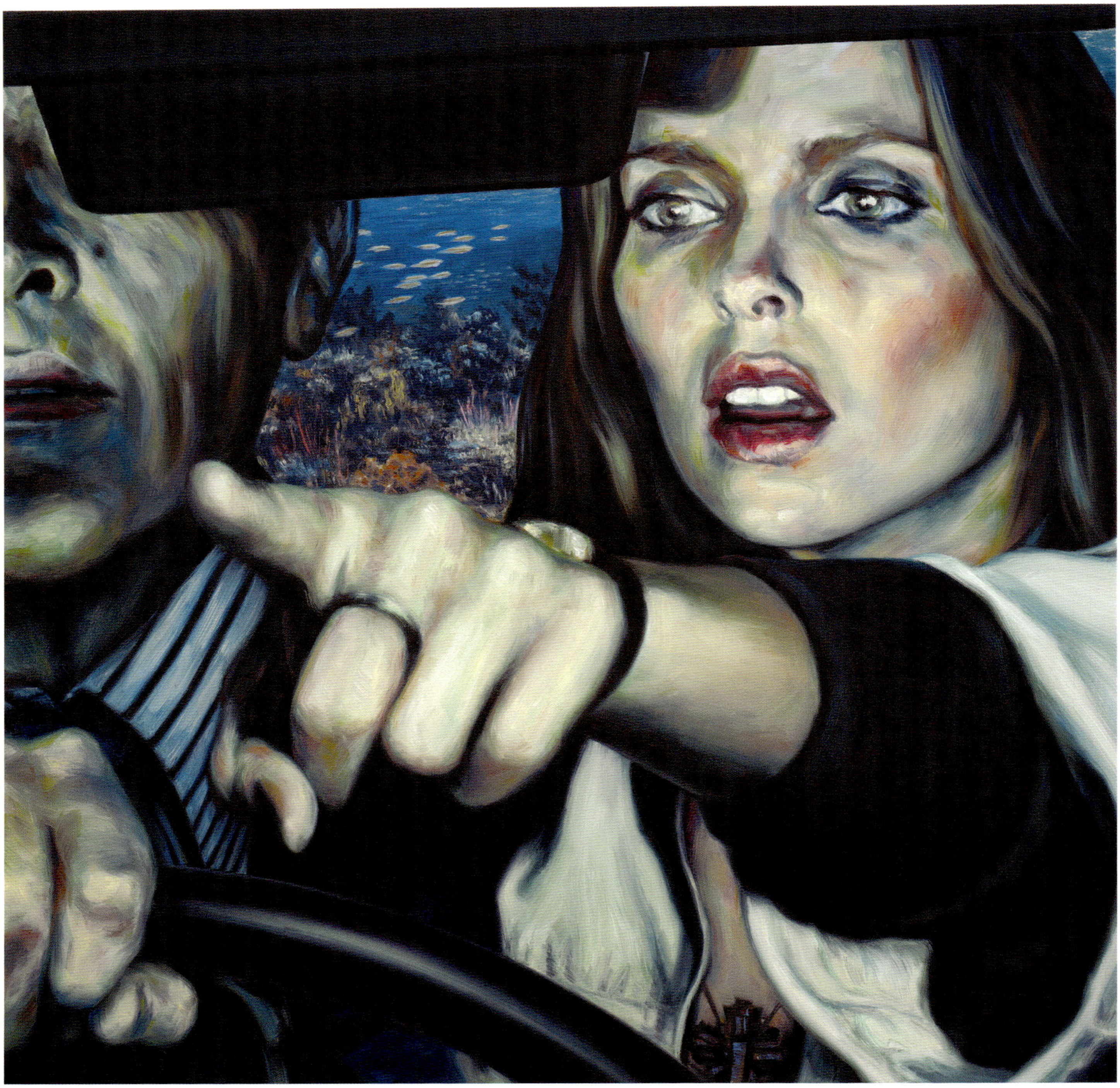

1976 Lotus Esprit Type 79 (The Spy Who Loved Me)
2013
Oil on canvas
24 x 24 in.

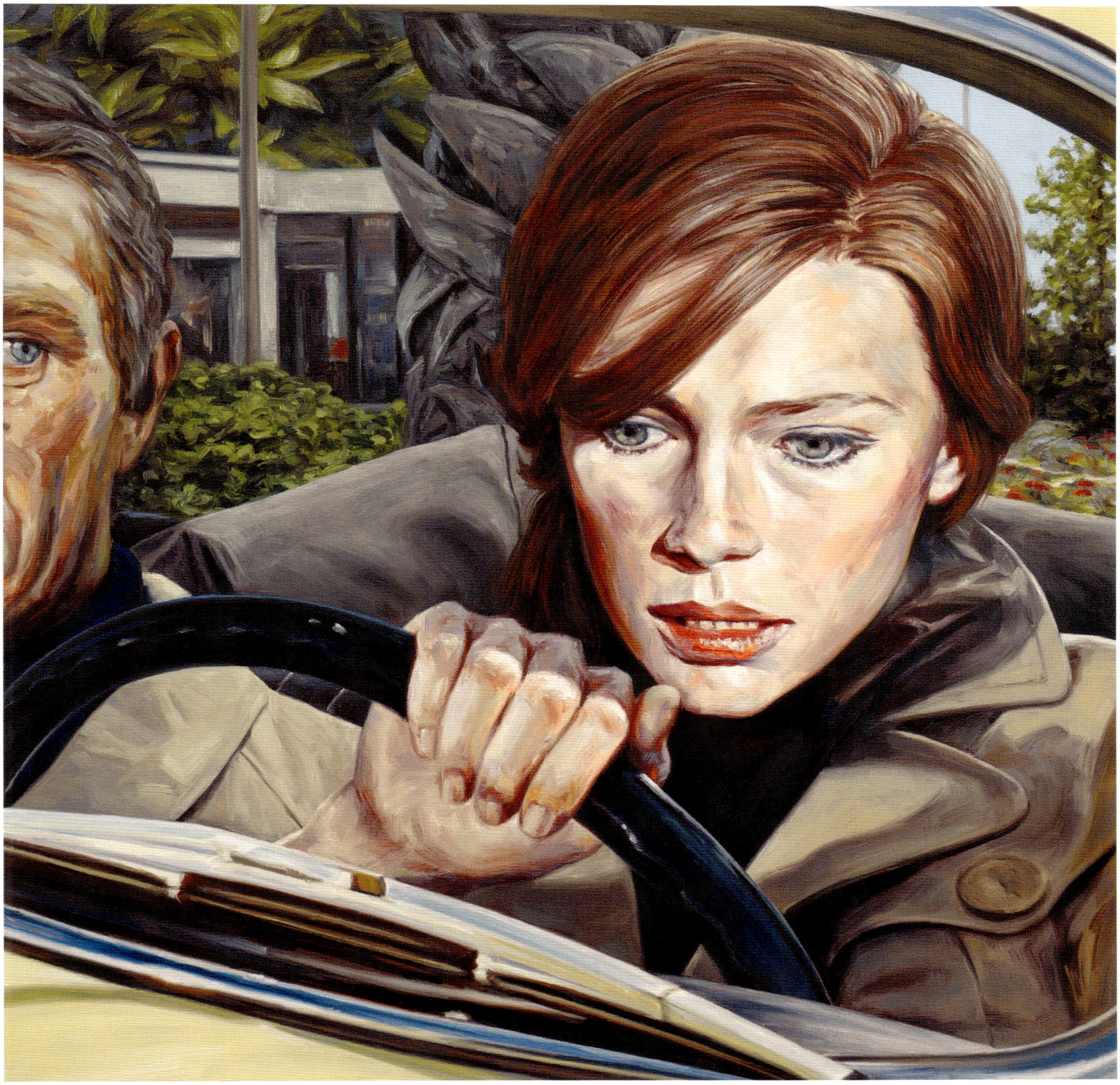

1964 Porsche 356 C Cabriolet T6 (Bullitt)
2013
Oil on canvas
24 x 24 in.

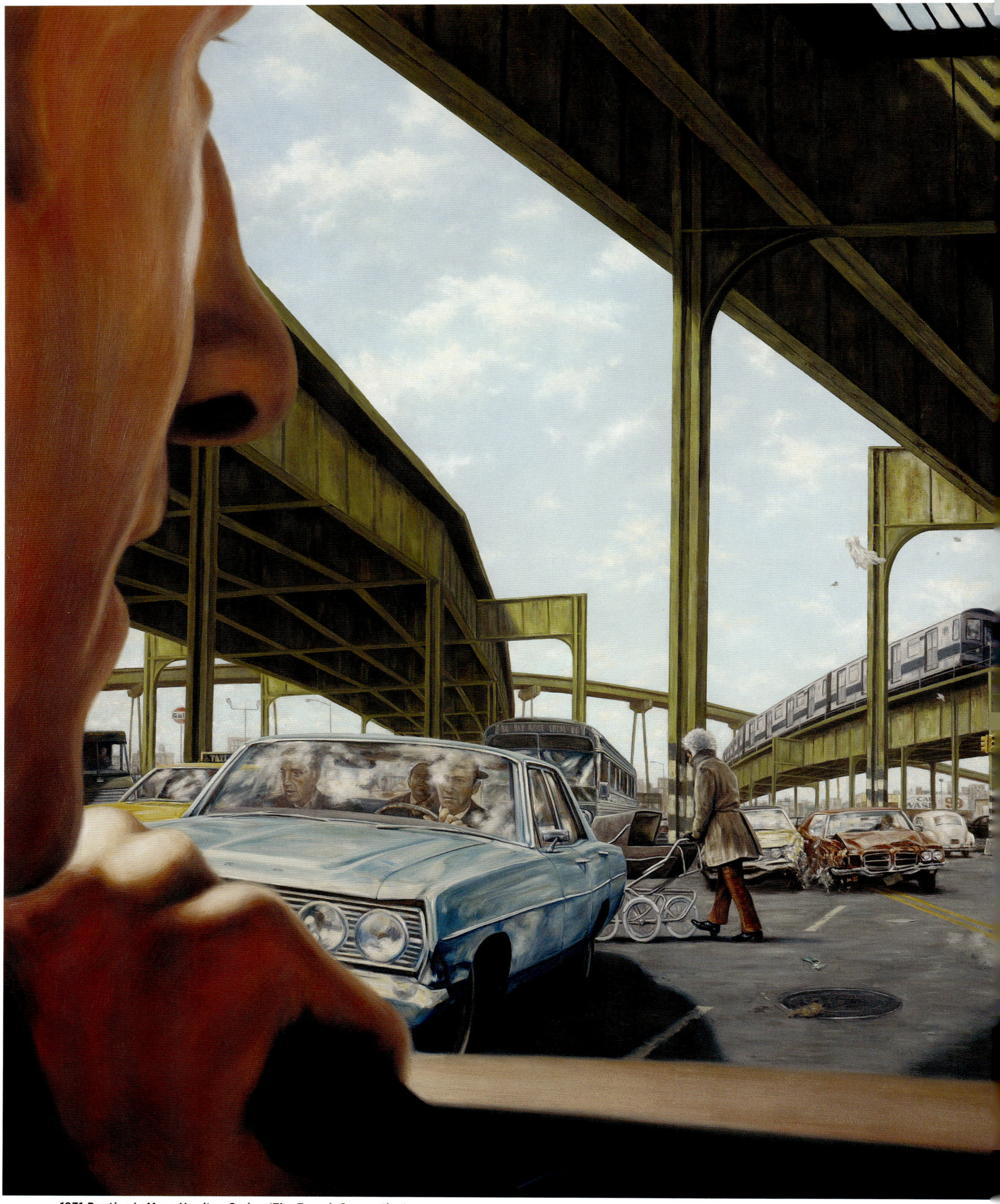

1971 Pontiac LeMans Hardtop Sedan (The French Connection)
(detail on following page)
2012
Oil on canvas
72 x 120 in.

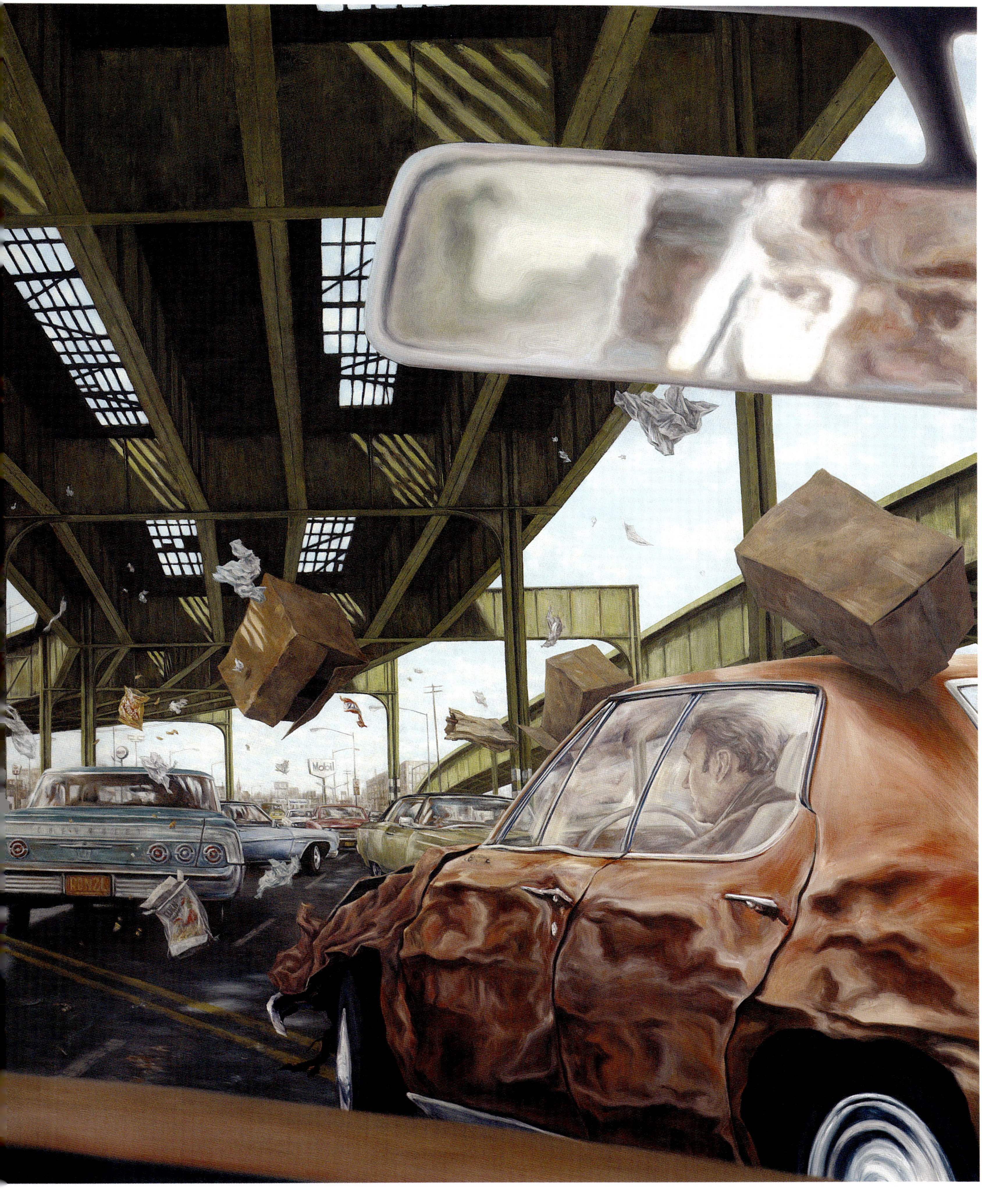
Mobil

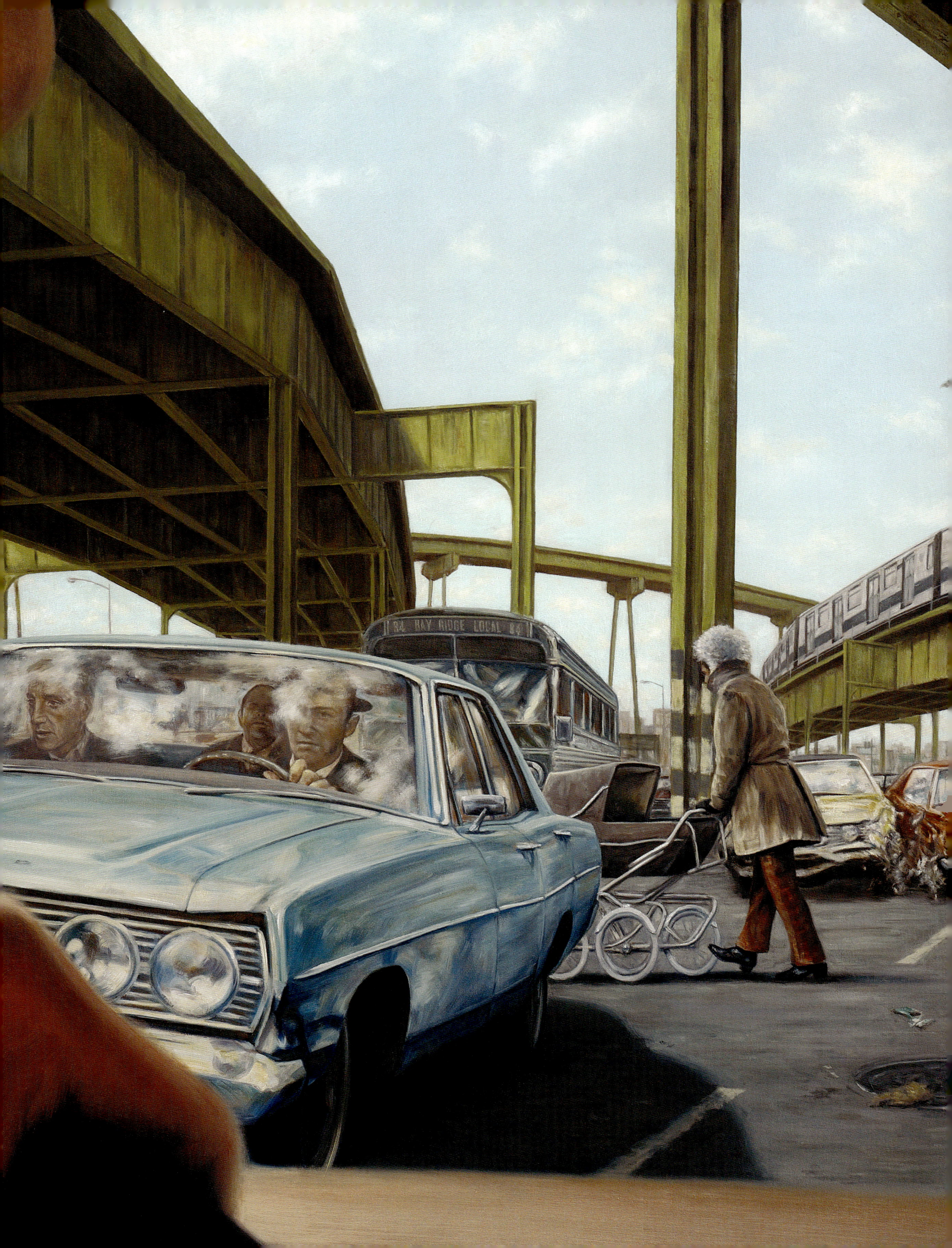
84 BAY RIDGE LOCAL 84

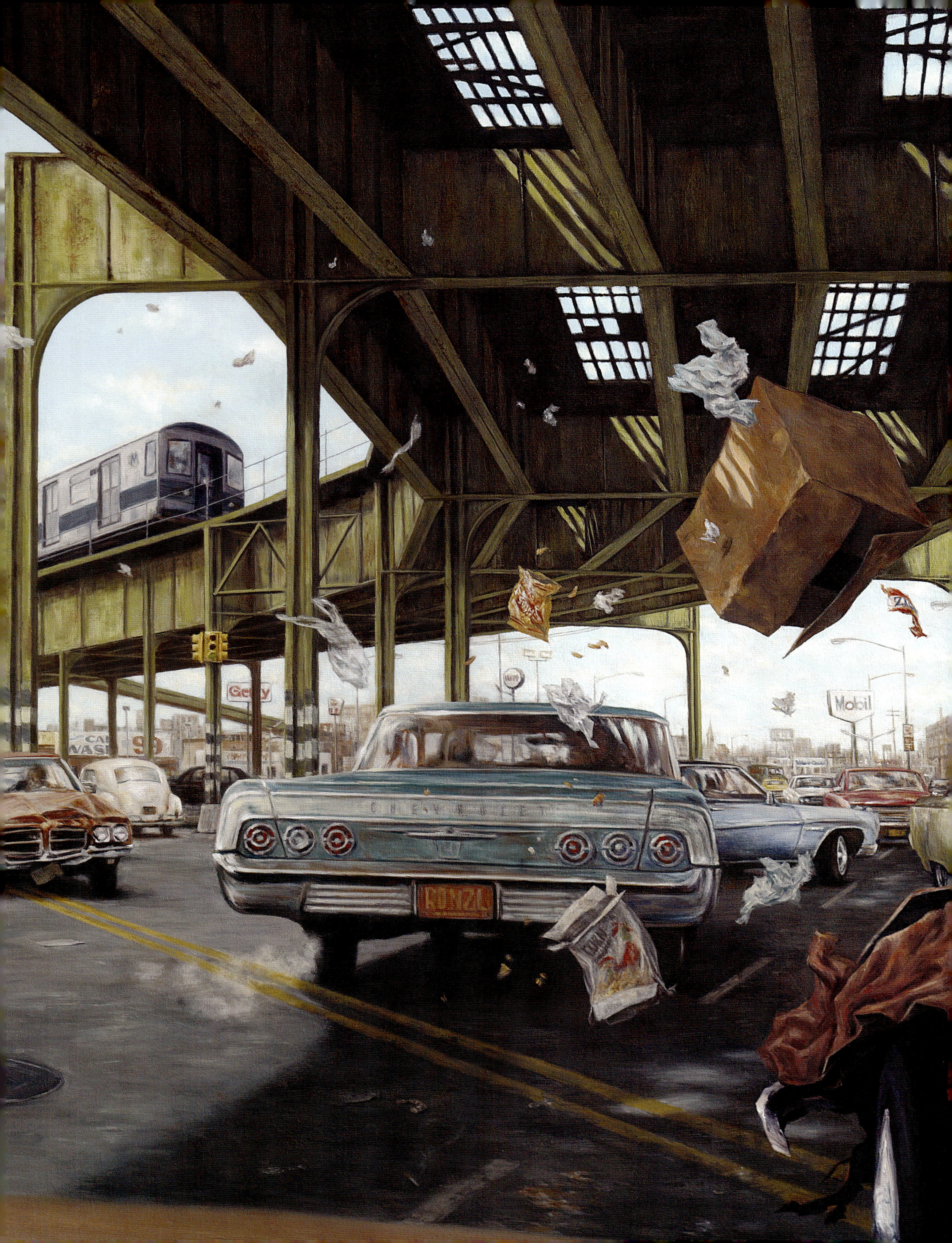
Getty
Mobil
CHEVROLET

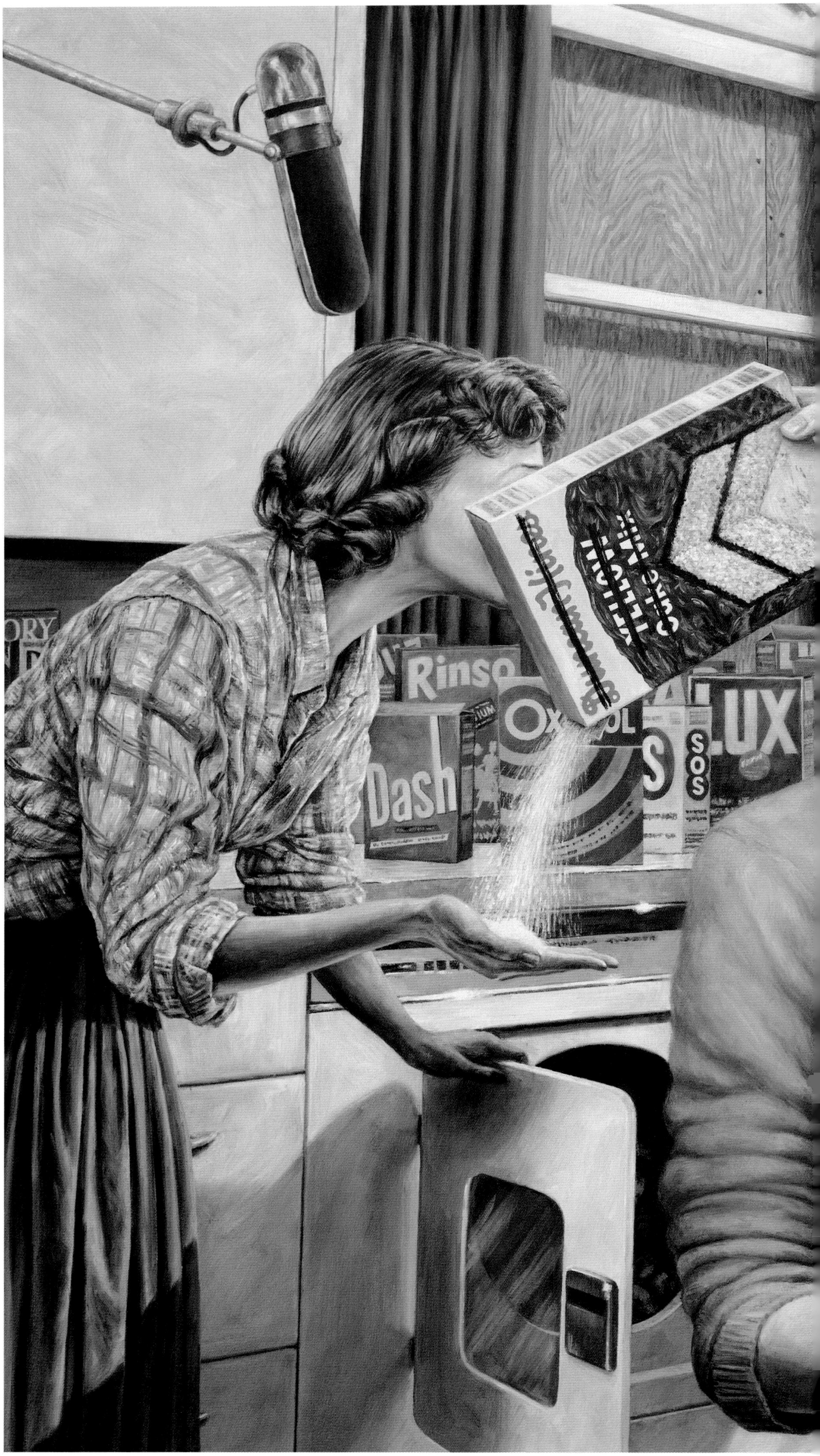

By Committee
2013
Oil on canvas
36 x 48 in.

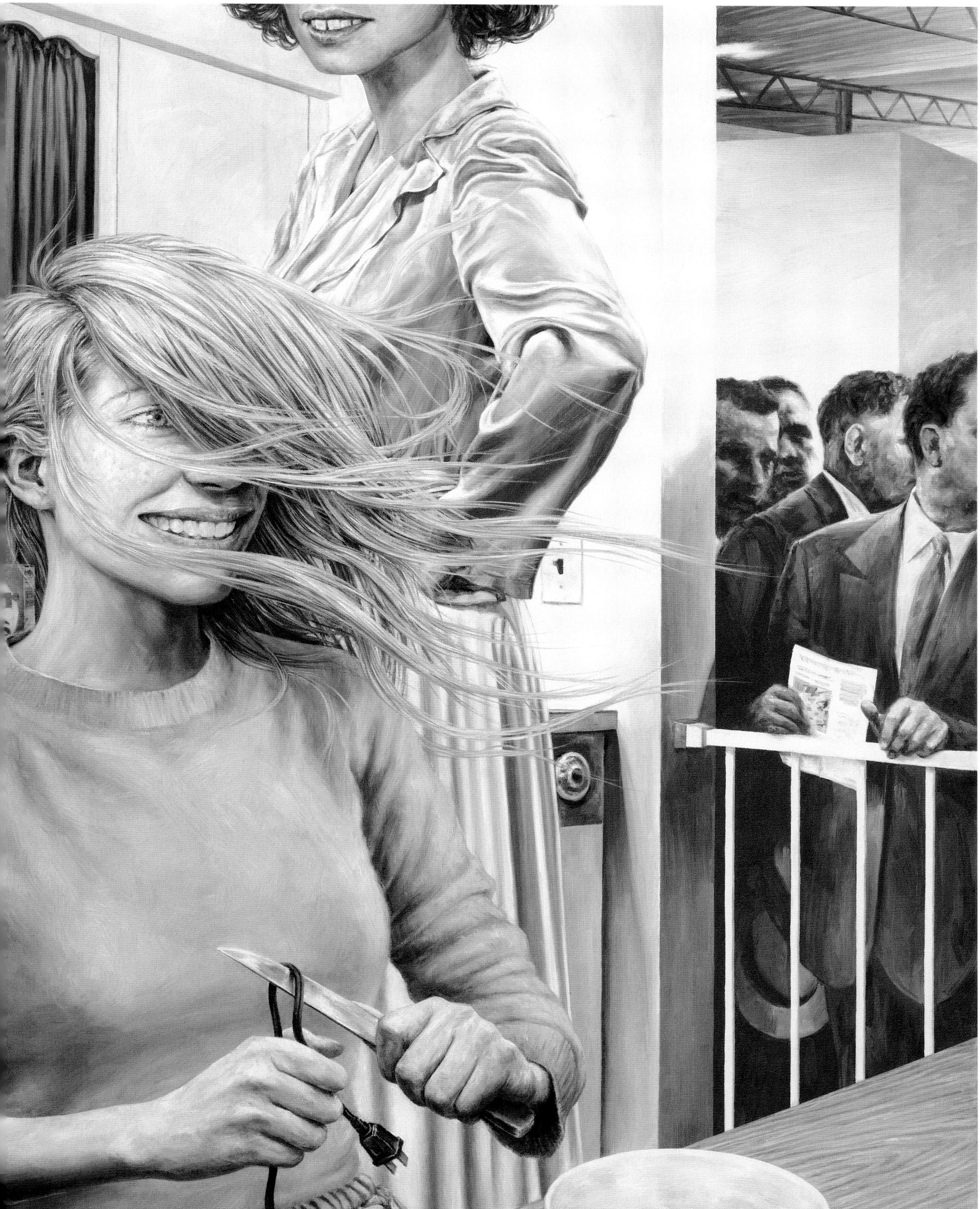

1/3-SCALE RETROSPECTIVE
IVAN QUARONI

The distinction between truth and fiction, authenticity and falsification, is the theme of *1/3-Scale Retrospective*, an installation composed of miniature copies of earlier works by the artist, ordered from Xiamen Unique Oil Painting Co., Ltd., in China. At first glance, what might seem like a self-tribute, a sort of premature "best of," is actually simultaneously an ironic take on the self-congratulation of many contemporary artists and a biting critique of painting in the era of its maximum technical reproducibility. By displaying the reproductions of some of his work made by others, White demonstrates that it is possible to easily fake a painting by using some simple expedients. The miniatures of *1/3-Scale Retrospective* are prints on canvas and retouched by hand, thus a type of art production different from traditional handmade techniques. There are artists today who use this technique—often without admitting to its use—for the sole purpose of concealing their technical ineptitude. *1/3-Scale Retrospective* is a work of protest, an outburst of indignation that amplifies the tricks and ruses found in a certain kind of contemporary art. At the same time, it is a heartfelt praise of authenticity—an act of love of the painter for painting.

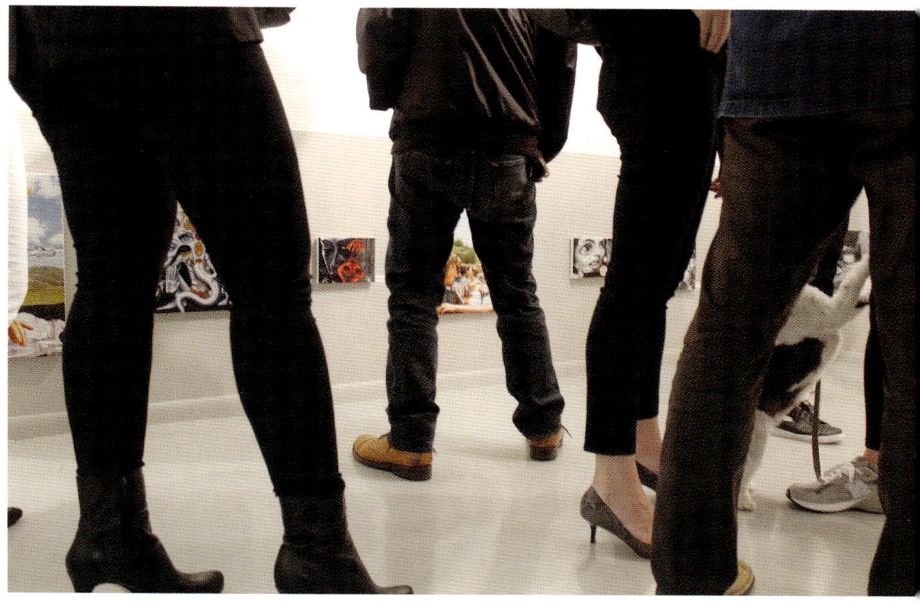

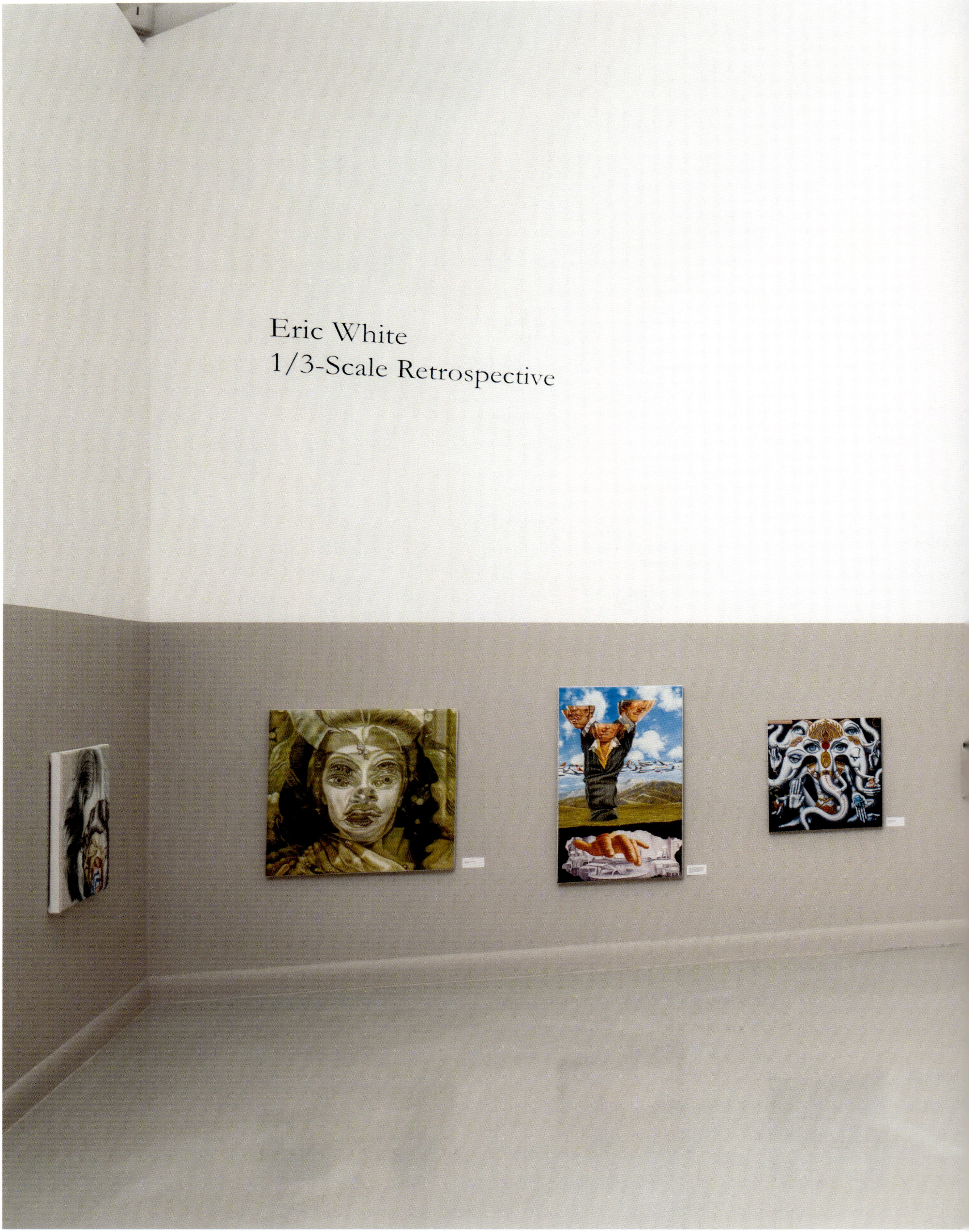
Eric White
1/3-Scale Retrospective

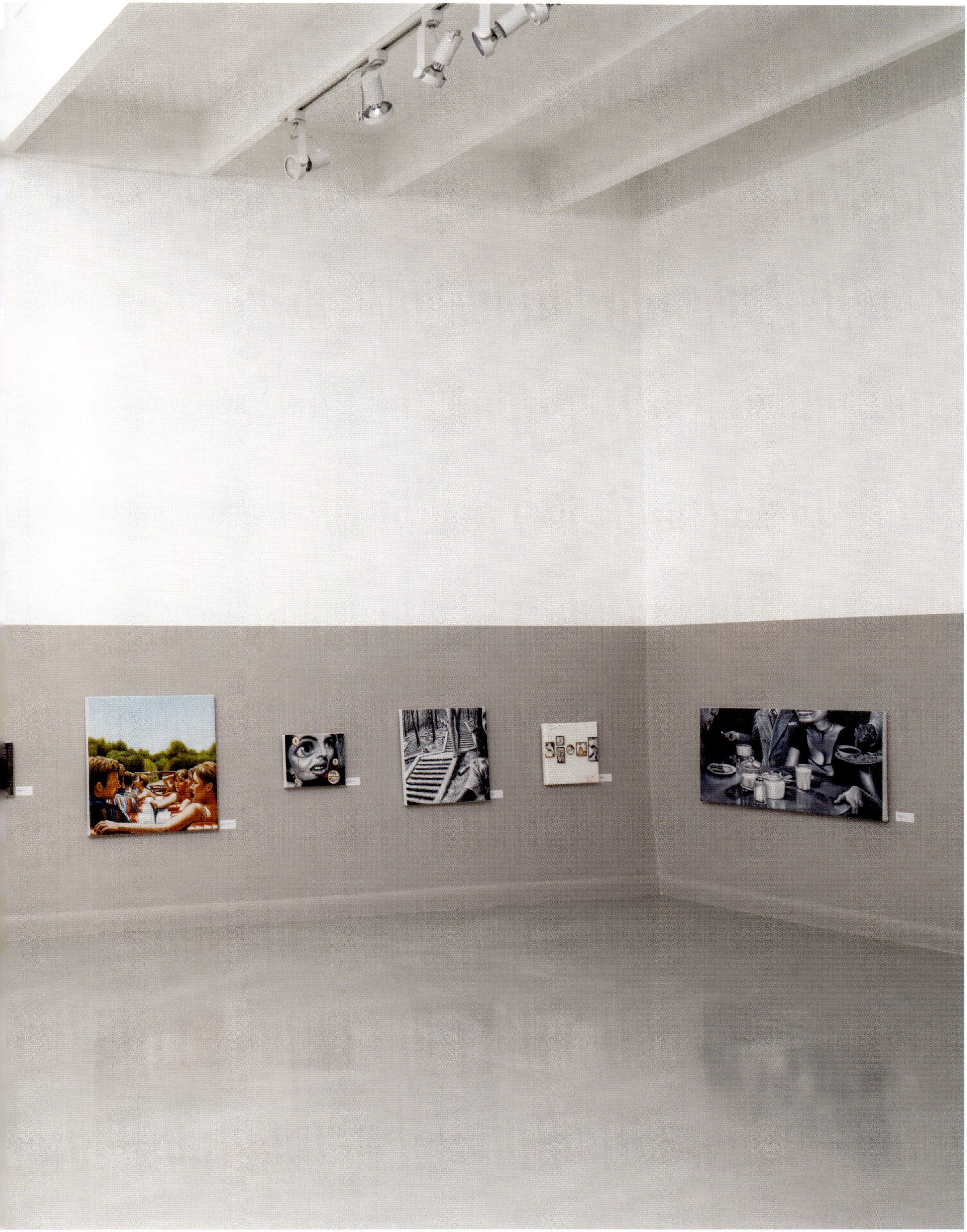

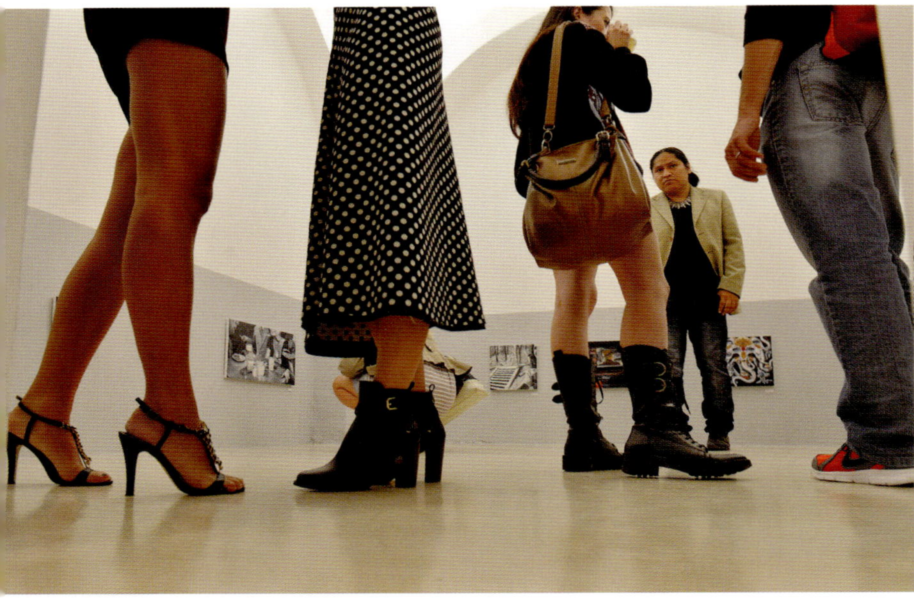

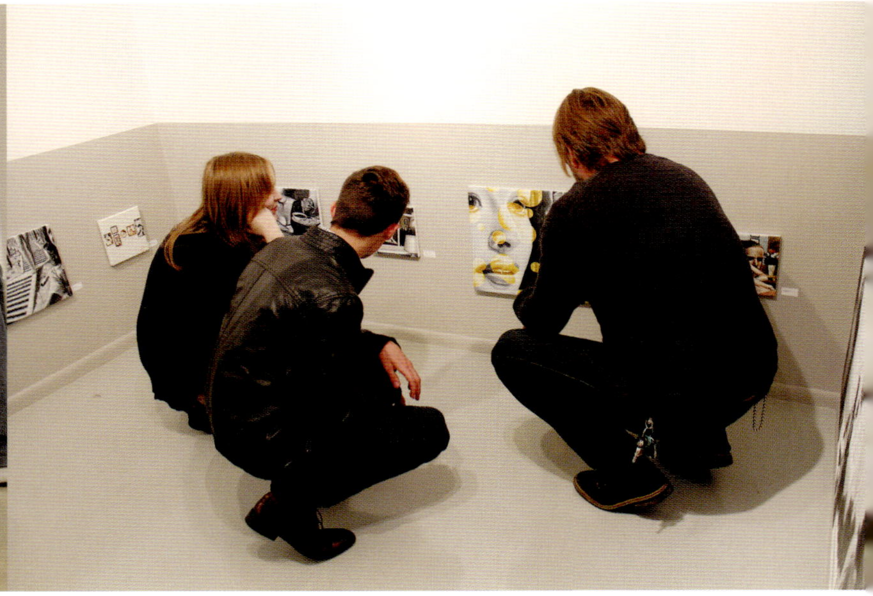

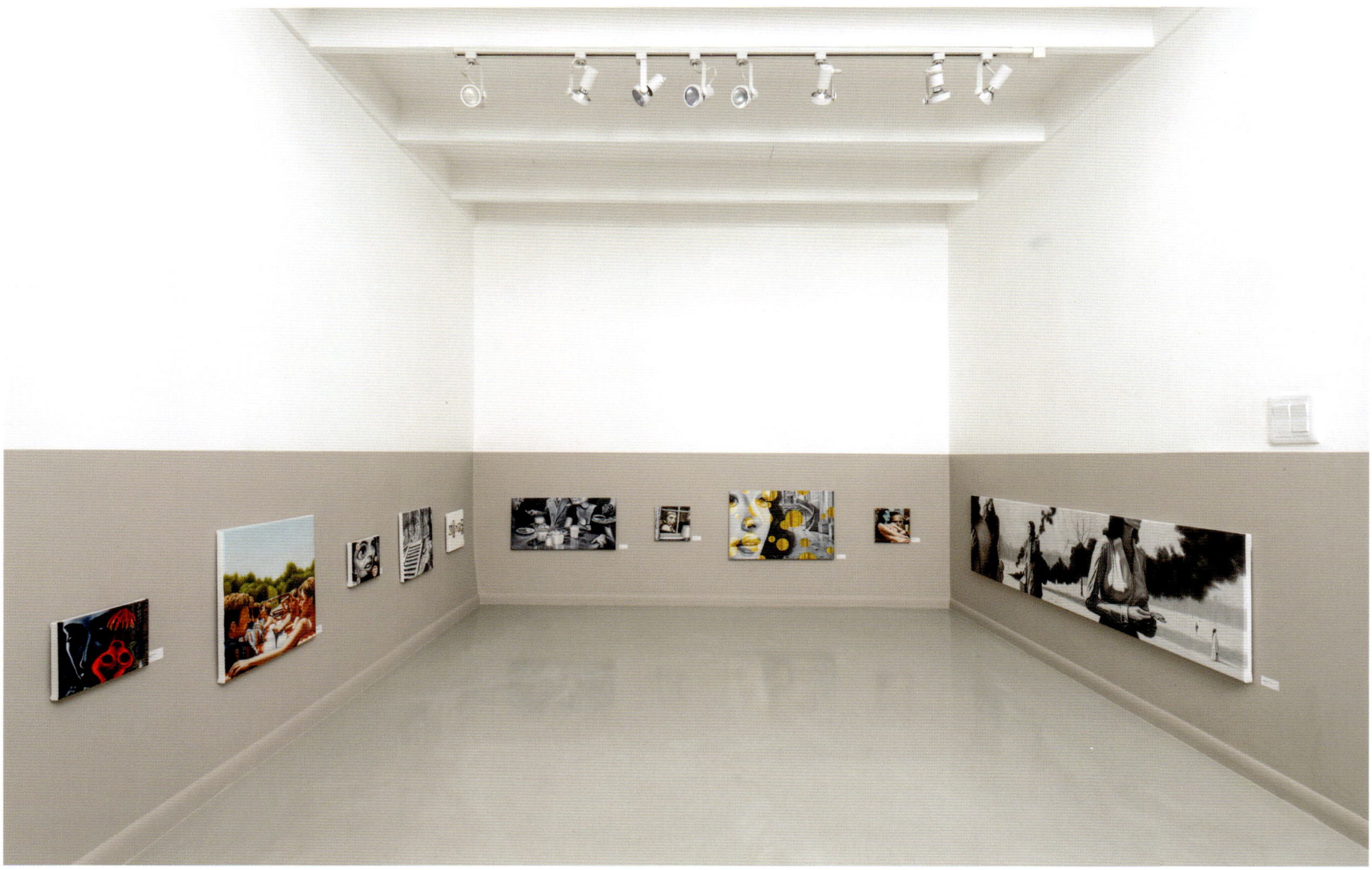

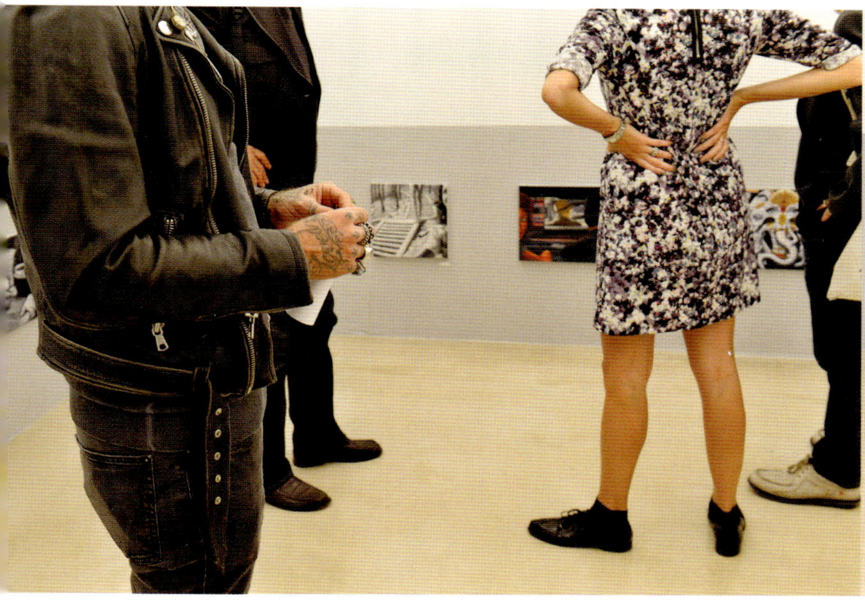

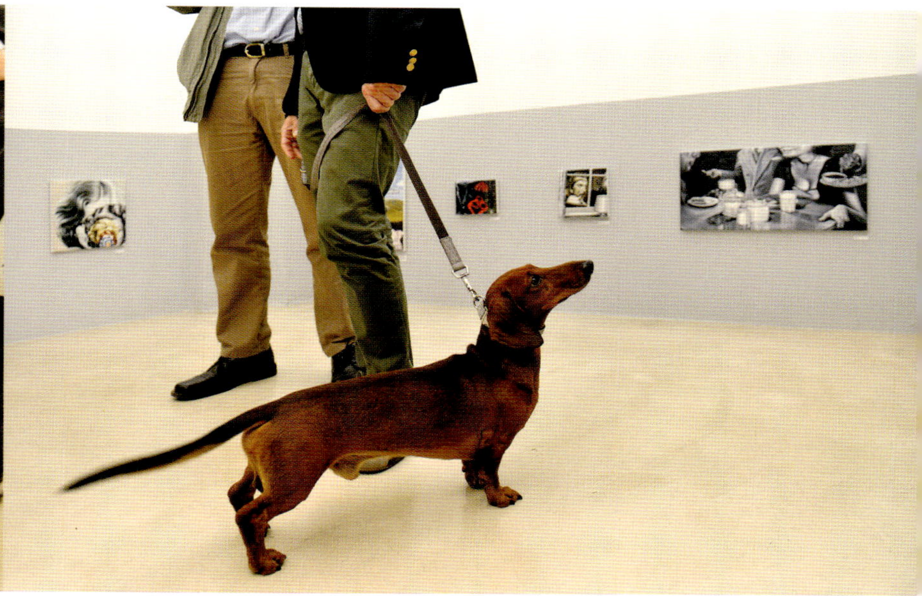

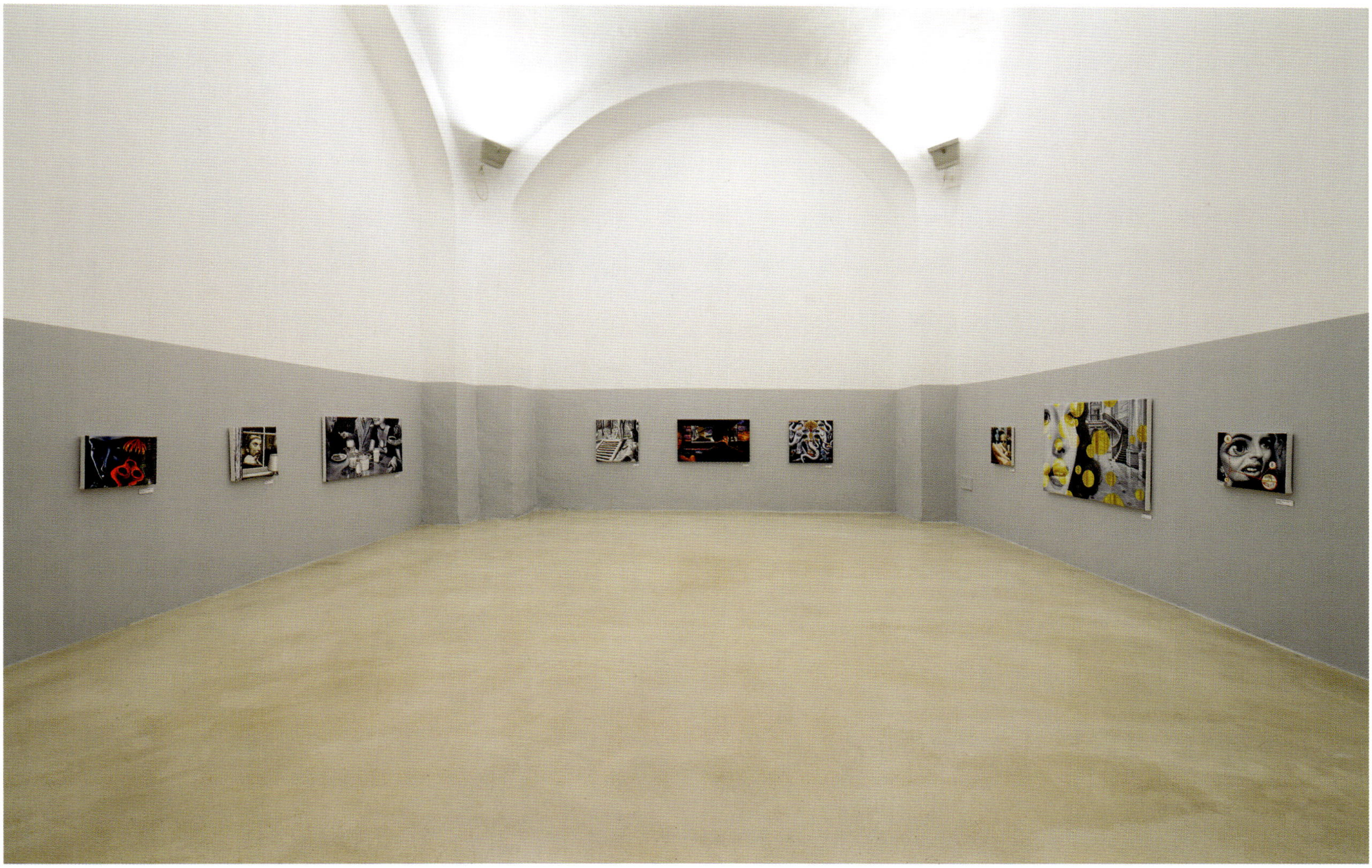

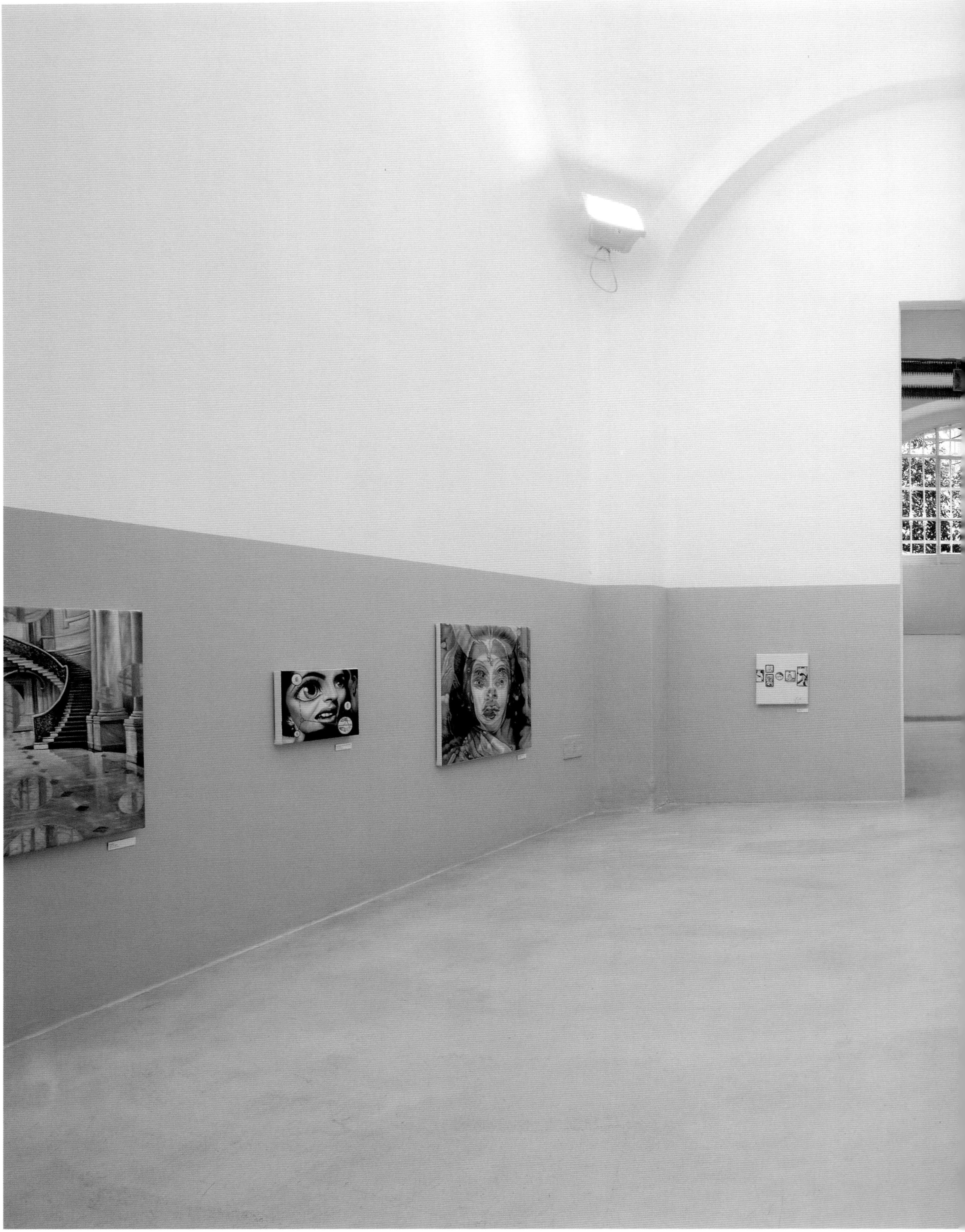

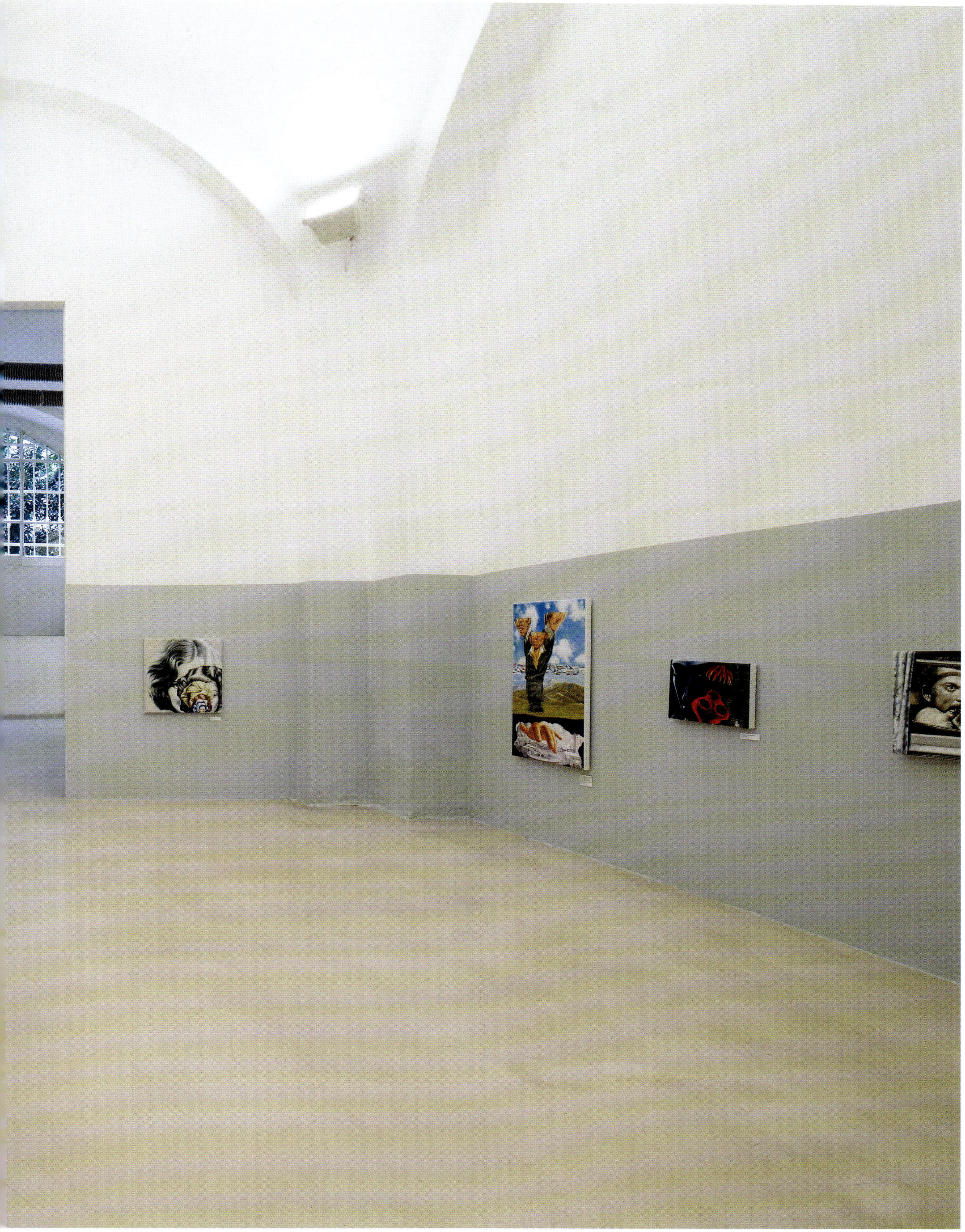

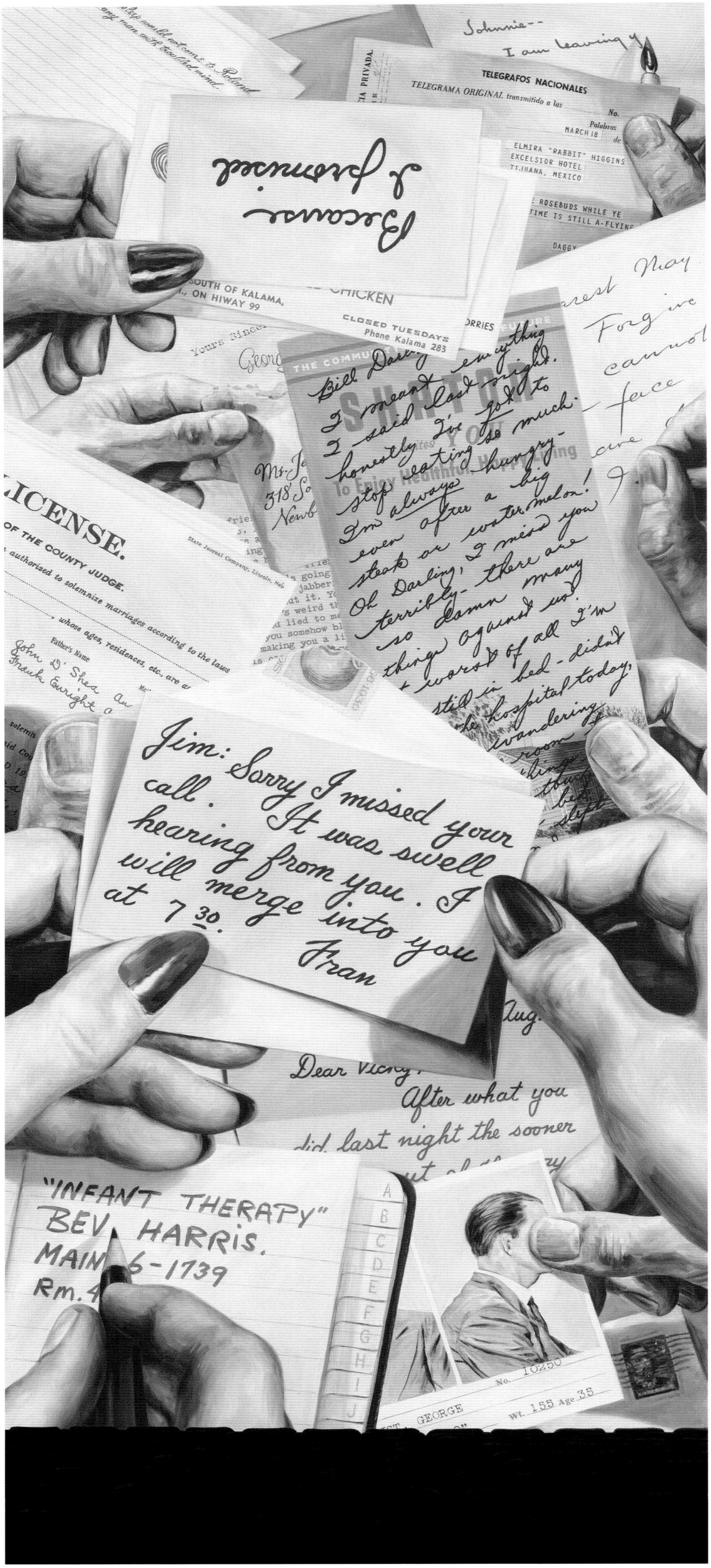

Rom Com
(detail, opposite)
2013
Oil on canvas
96 x 42 in.

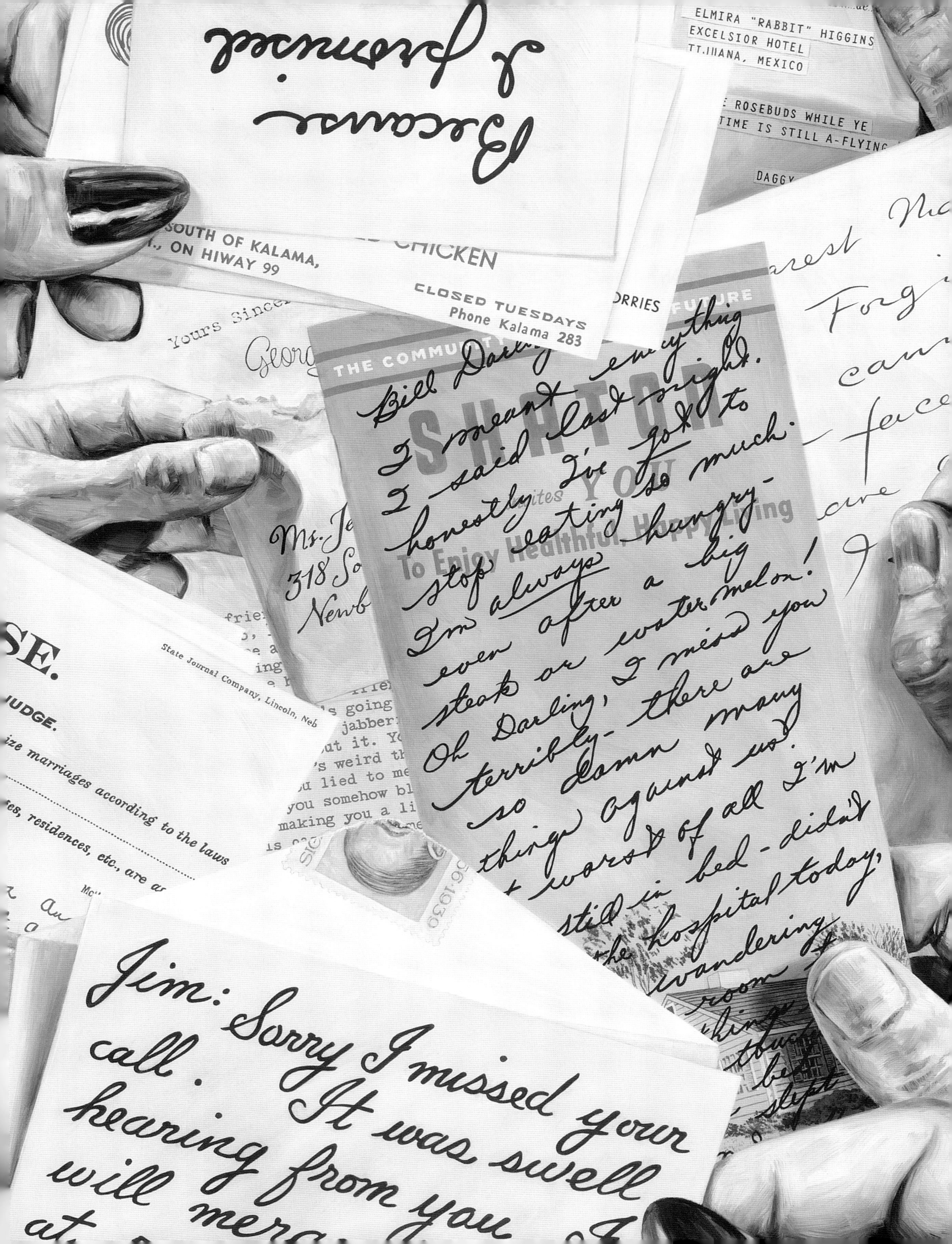

ELMIRA "RABBIT" HIGGINS
EXCELSIOR HOTEL
TIJUANA, MEXICO
ROSEBUDS WHILE YE
TIME IS STILL A-FLYING
DAGGY
SOUTH OF KALAMA,
ON HIWAY 99
CHICKEN
CLOSED TUESDAYS
Phone Kalama 283
Yours Since
THE COMMUNITY
FUTURE
YOU
To Enjoy Healthful, Happy Living
Bill Darling,
I meant everything
I said last night.
honestly I've got to
stop eating so much.
I'm always hungry-
even after a big
steak or watermelon!
Oh Darling, I miss you
terribly - there are
so damn many
things against us.
worst of all I'm
still in bed - didn't
the hospital today,
wandering
room
State Journal Company, Lincoln, Neb
SE.
UDGE.
ize marriages according to the laws
es, residences, etc., are a
's going
jabber
ut it.
you lied to me
you somehow bl
making you a li
Jim: Sorry I missed your
call. It was swell
hearing from you.

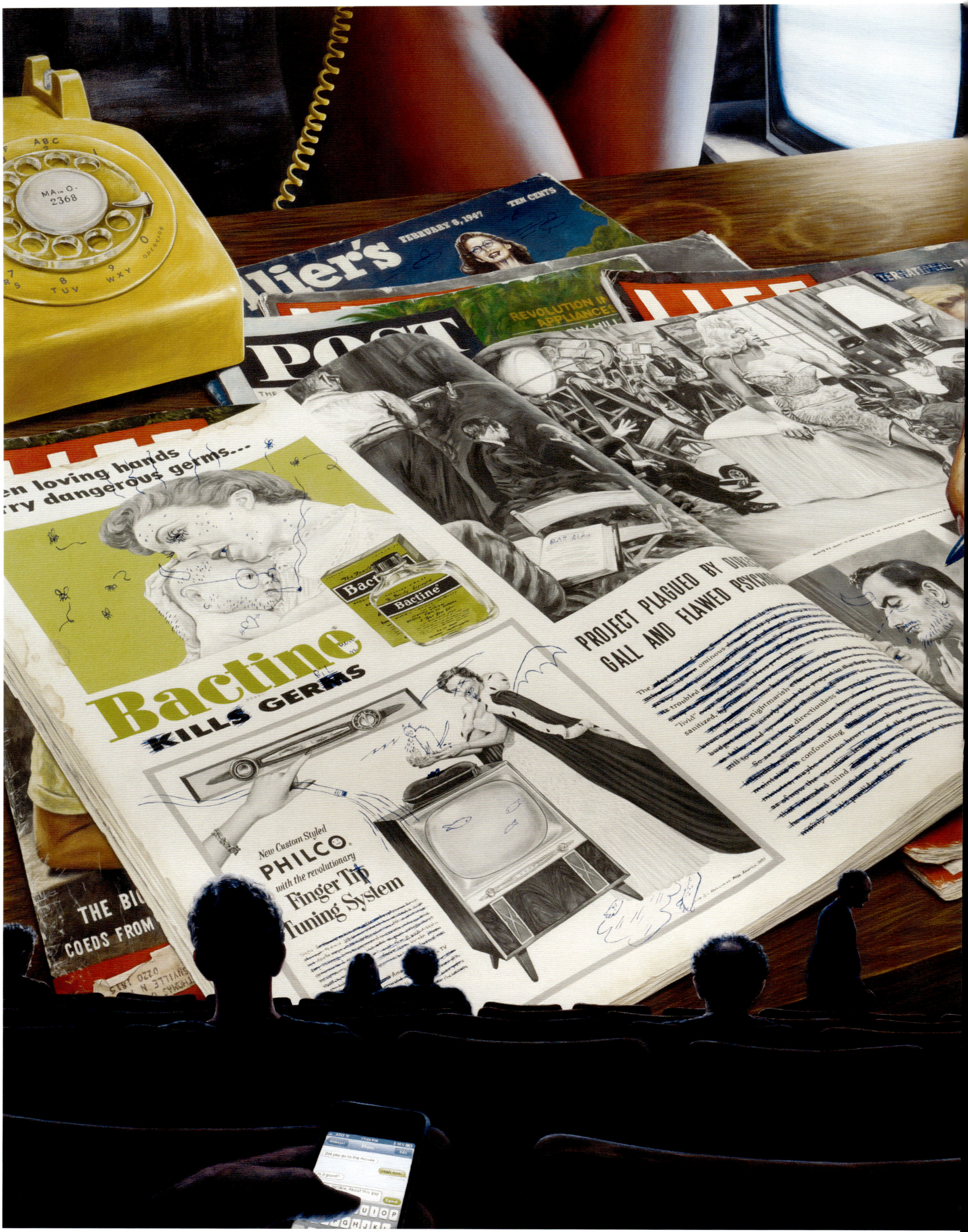

MA O-
2368
FEBRUARY 8, 1947
TEN CENTS
llier's
REVOLUTION IN
APPLIANCE
POST
en loving hands
rry dangerous germs...
Bactine
Bactine
KILLS GERMS
New Custom Styled
PHILCO
with the revolutionary
Finger Tip
Tuning System
PROJECT PLAGUED BY DIR
GALL AND FLAWED PSYCH
THE BI
COEDS FROM

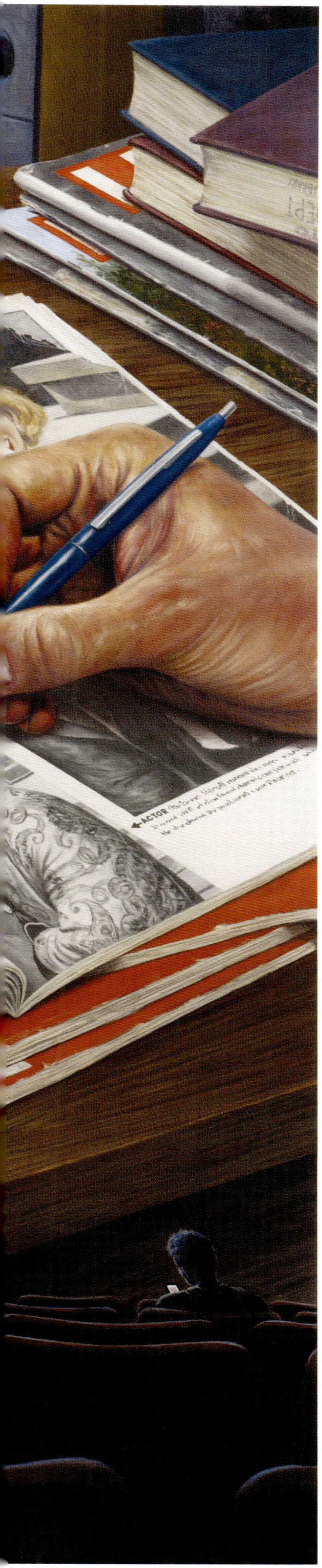

Mommie Issues 2: The Reckoning
(detail on following page)
2013
Oil on canvas
60 x 60 in.

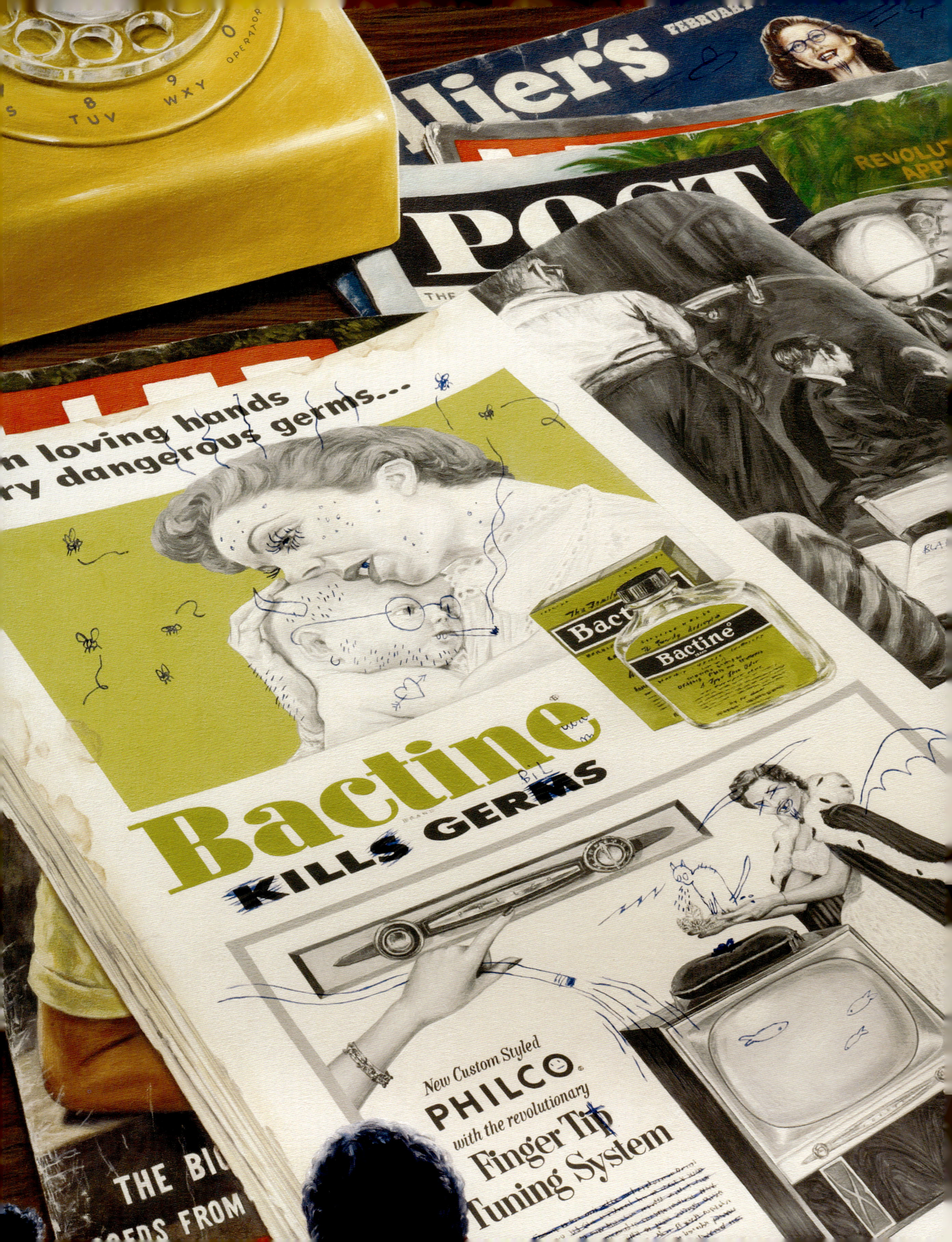

8 TUV
9 WXY
0 OPERATOR
POST
n loving hands
ry dangerous germs...
Bactine
Bactine
KILLS GERMS
New Custom Styled
PHILCO
with the revolutionary
Finger Tip
Tuning System
THE BI

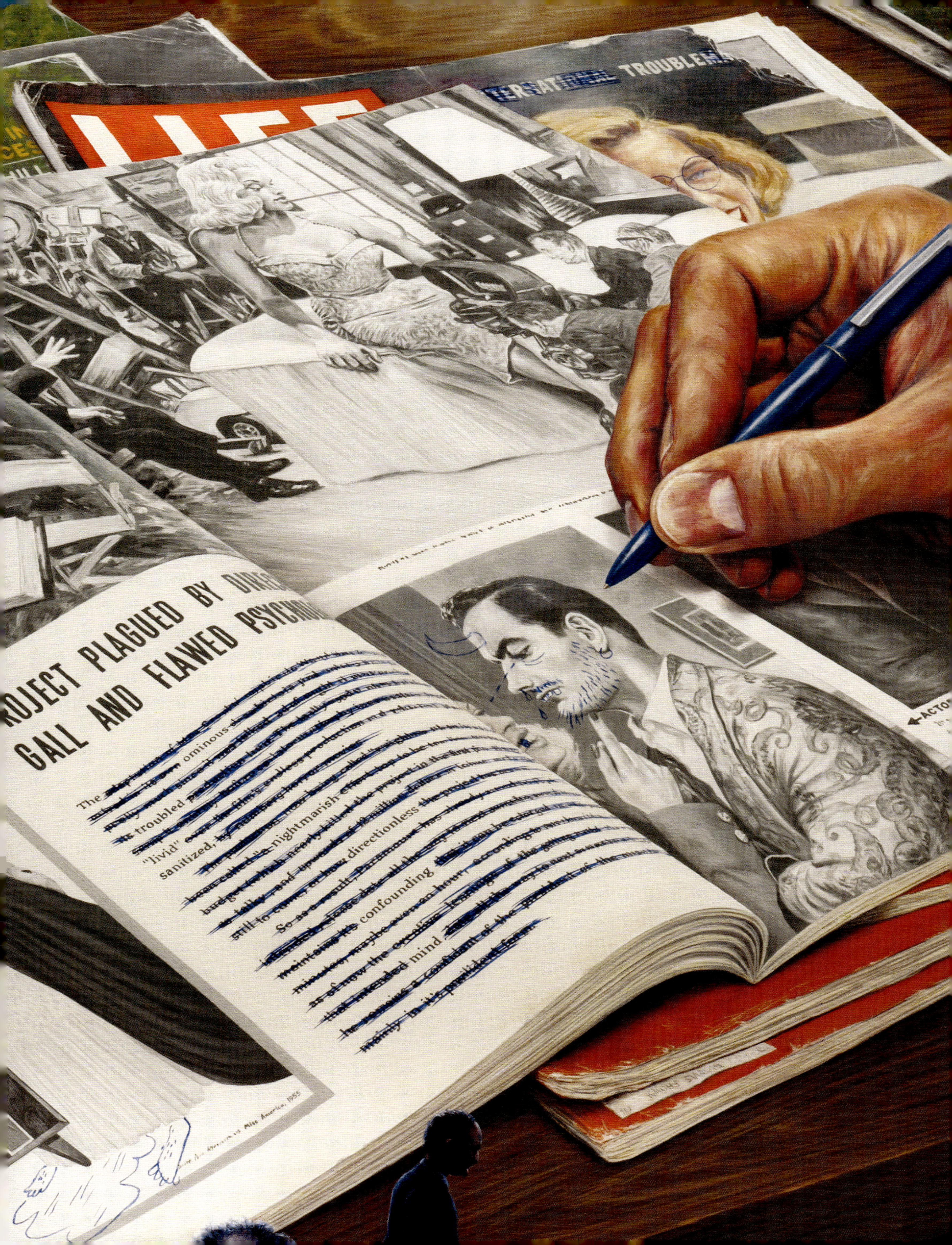

LIFE
TROUBLE
ROJECT PLAGUED BY
GALL AND FLAWED
The
ominous
troubled
"livid"
sanitized,
nightmarish
directionless
confounding
mind
Miss America, 1955

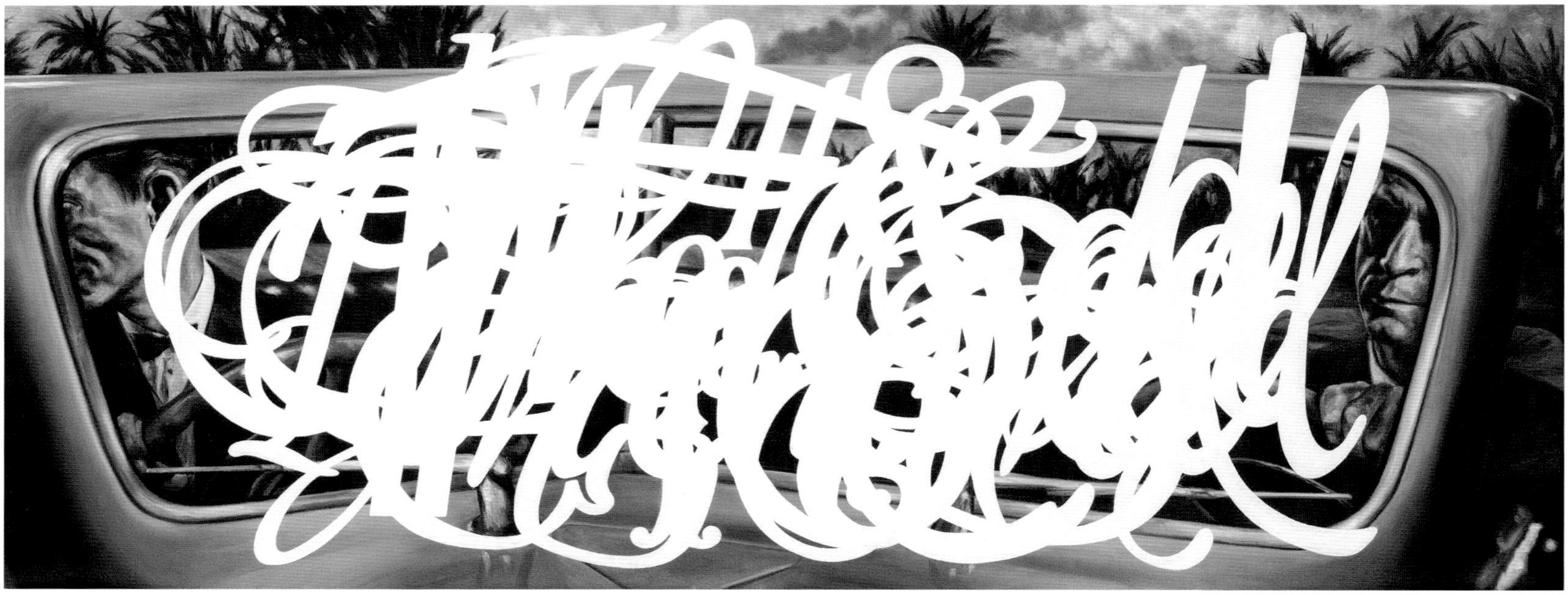

The End (Brute Force)
2013
Oil on canvas
18 x 46 in.

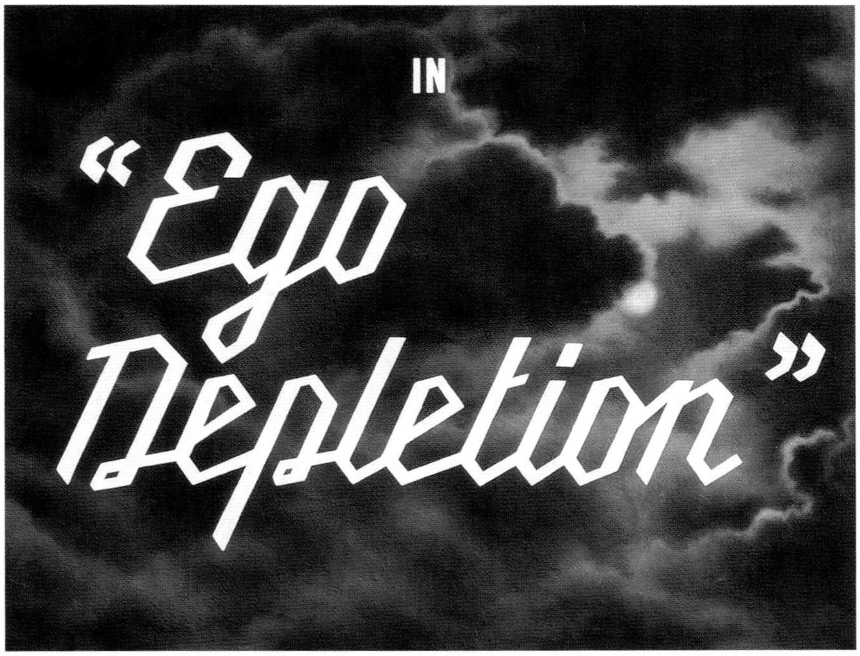

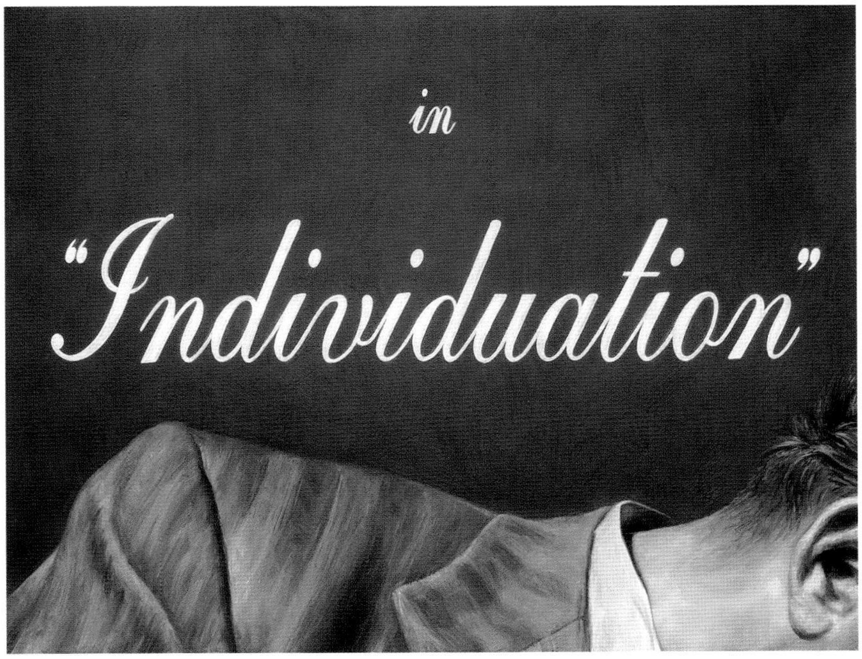

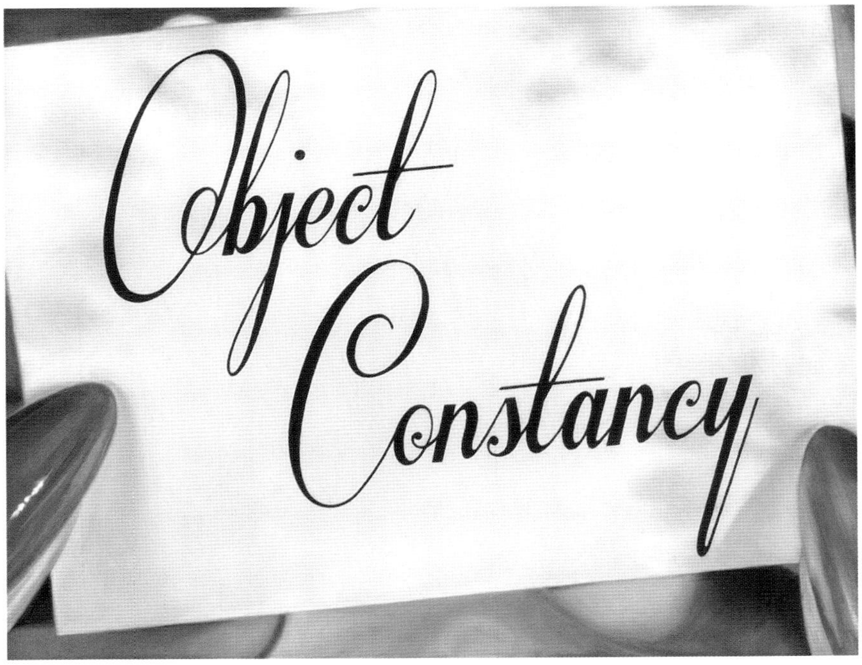

Intertitle (Ego Depletion)
2013
Oil on panel
11 x 14 in.

Intertitle (Individuation)
2013
Oil on panel
11 x 14 in.

Intertitle (Object Constancy)
2013
Oil on panel
11 x 14 in.

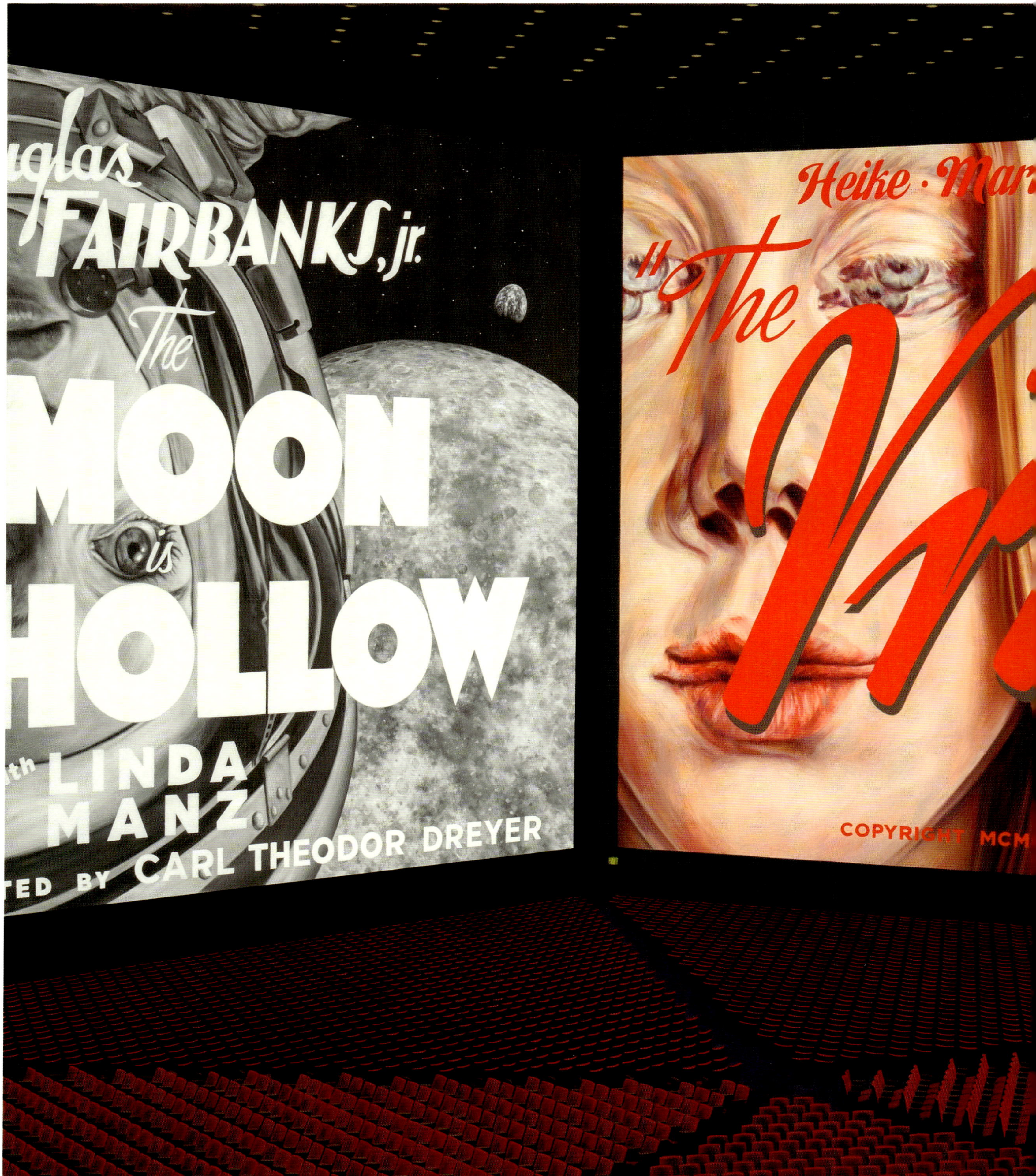

PENTAPLEX: Coming Attractions
(detail on following page)
2013
Oil on canvas
84 x 144 in.

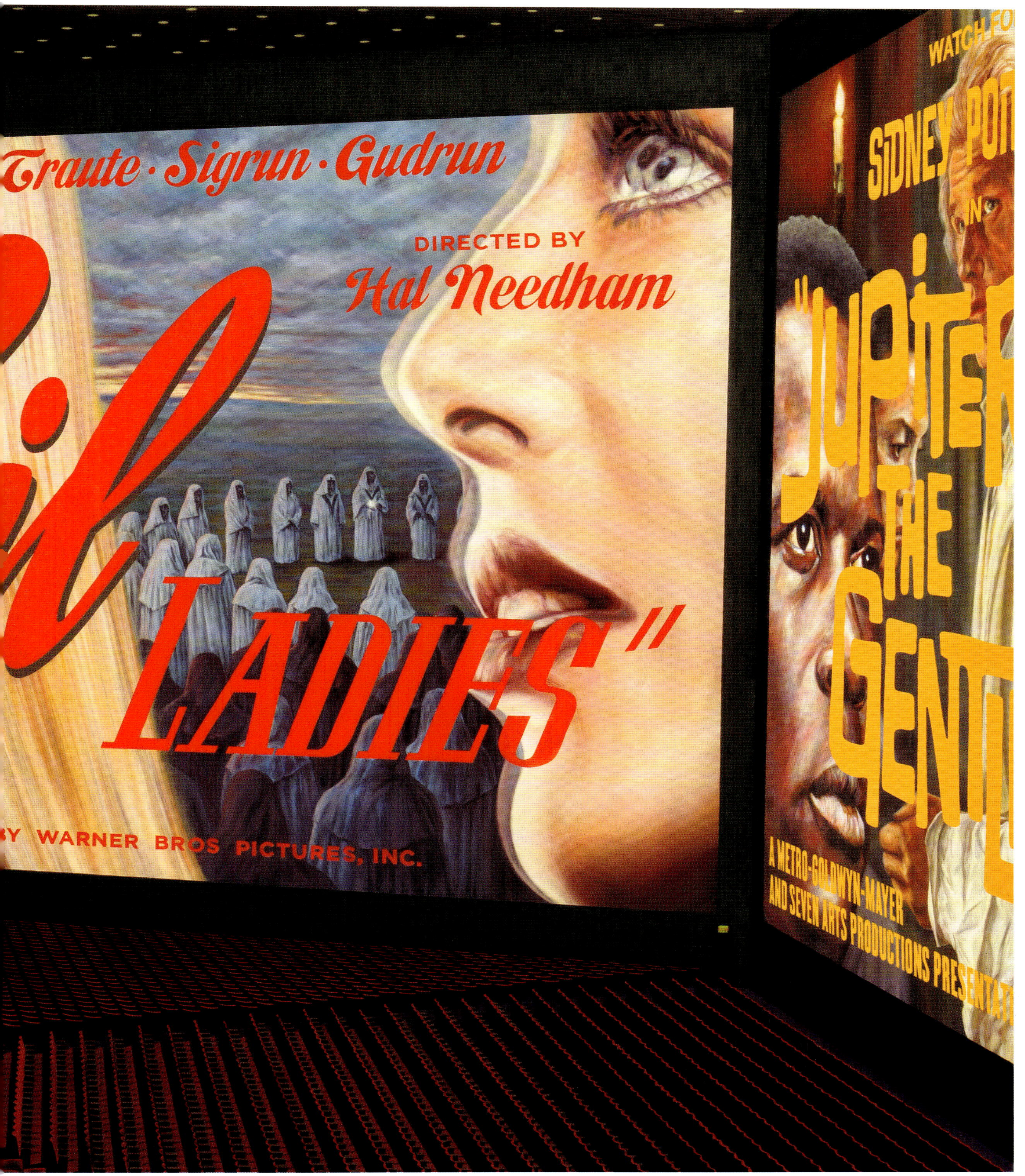
Traute · Sigrun · Gudrun
DIRECTED BY
Hal Needham
LADIES"
WARNER BROS PICTURES, INC.
IN
A METRO-GOLDWYN-MAYER
AND SEVEN ARTS PRODUCTIONS

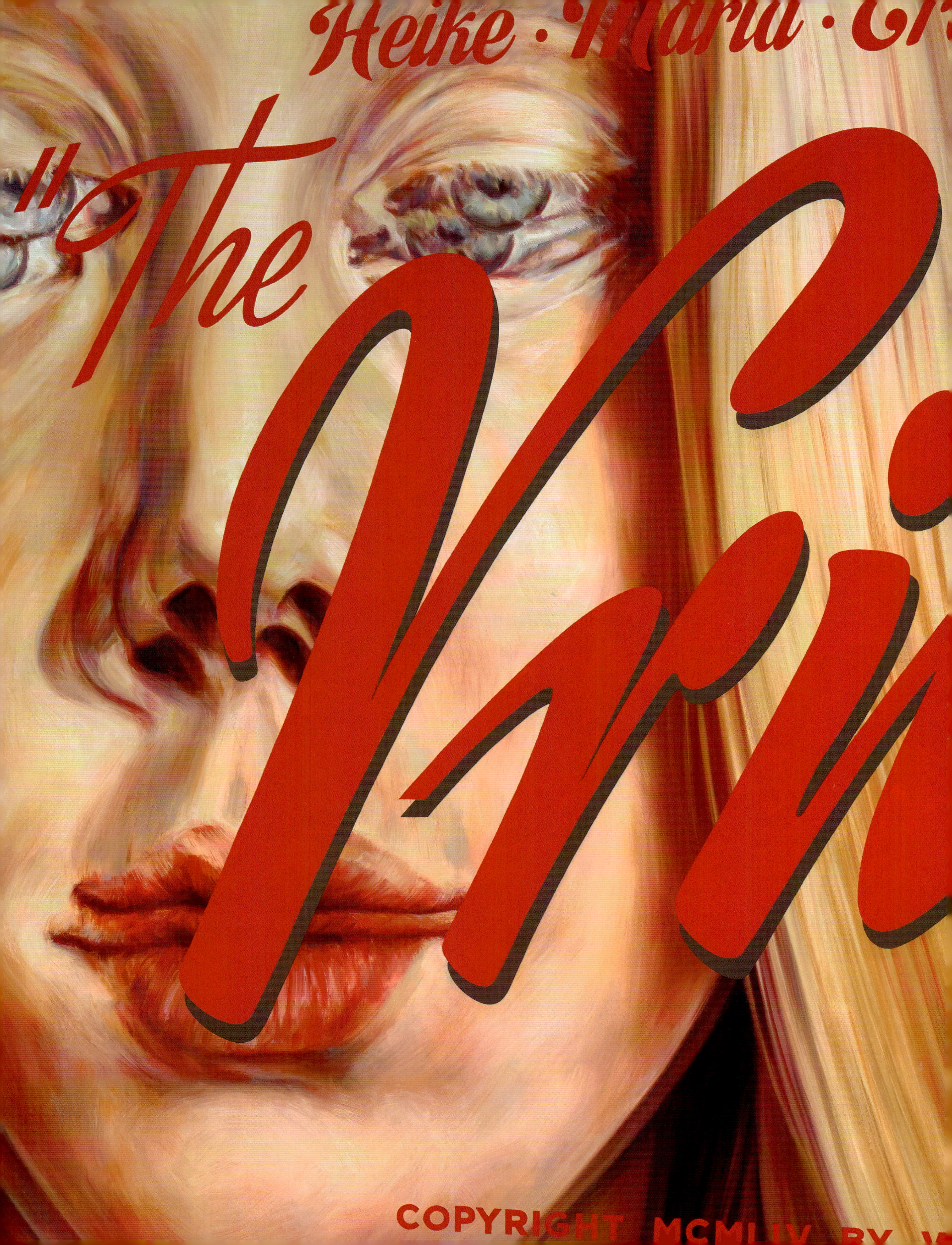
Heike · Maria ·
"The
COPYRIGHT MCMLIV BY

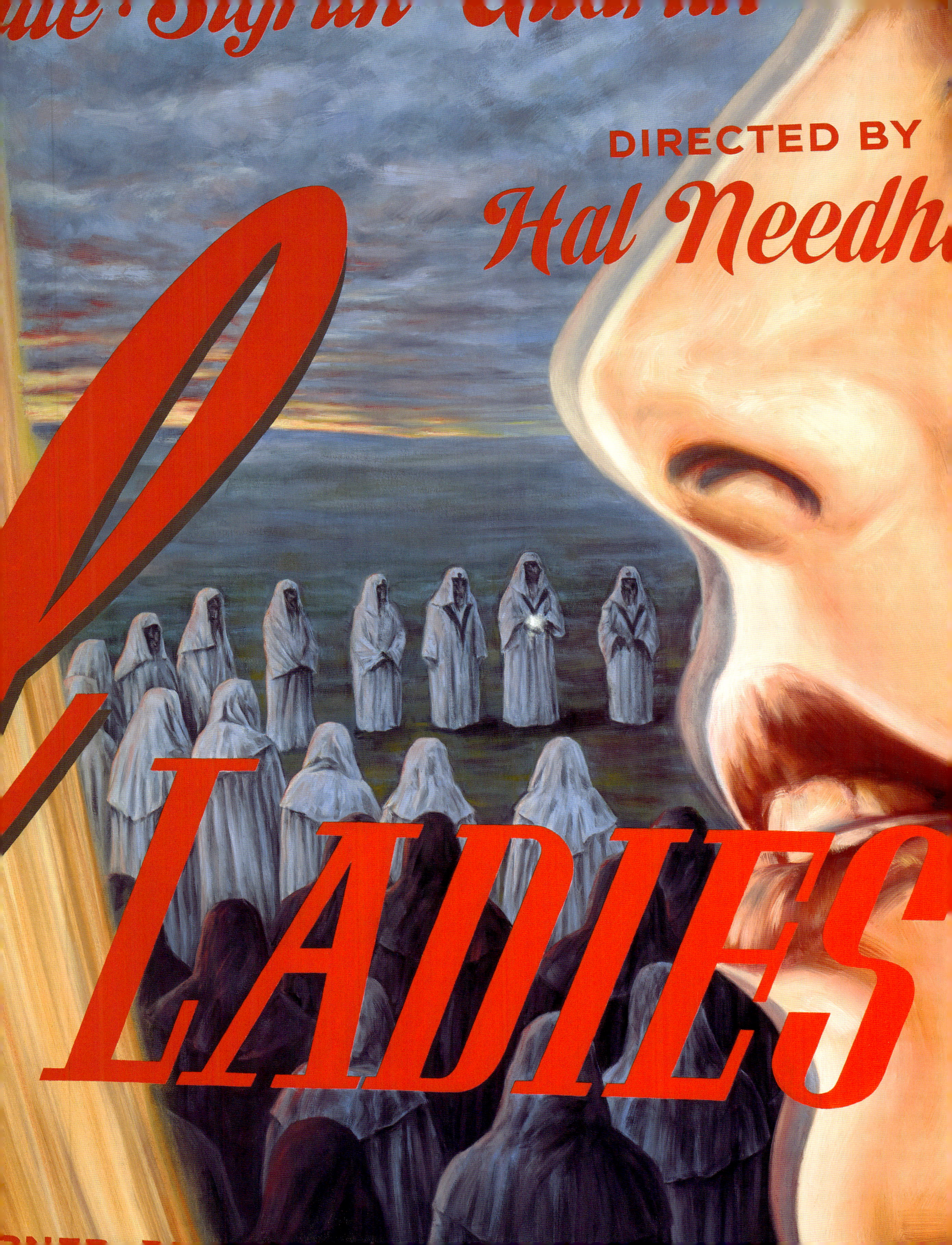
DIRECTED BY
Hal Needh
LADIES

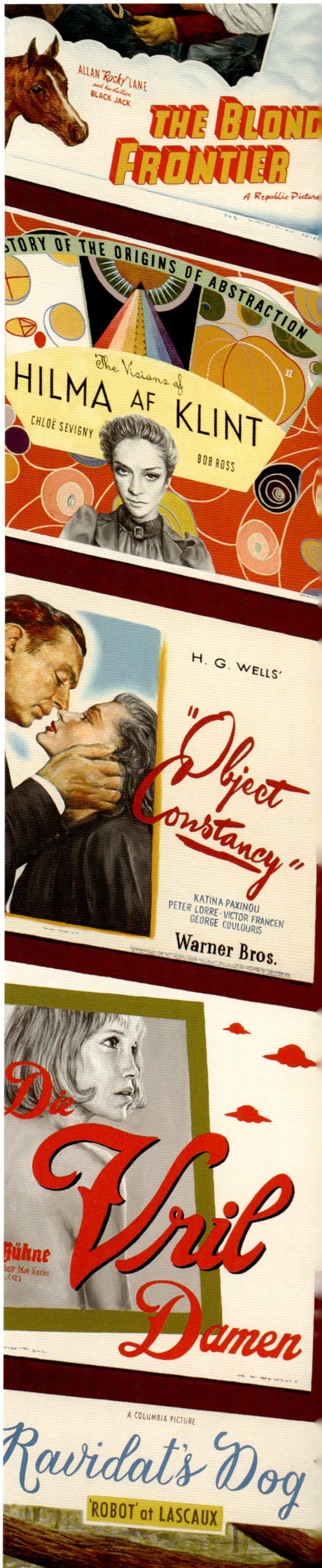

The Lobby
(detail on following page)
2013–2015
Oil on canvas
48 x 48 in.

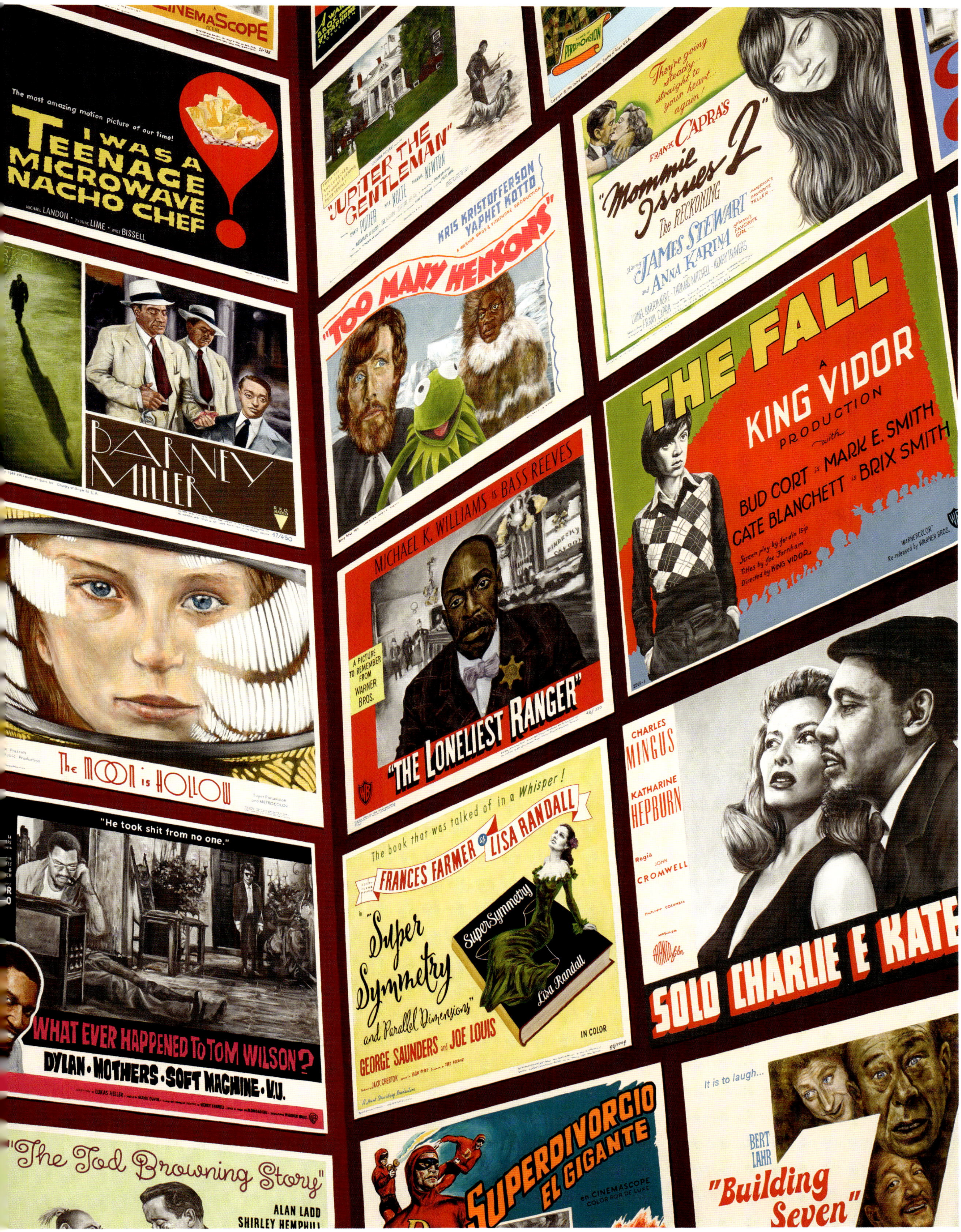

CINEMASCOPE
The most amazing motion picture of our time!
I WAS A TEENAGE MICROWAVE NACHO CHEF
MICHAEL LANDON · LIME · BISSELL
"JUPITER THE GENTLEMAN"
POITIER · NOLTE · NEWTON
They're going steady straight to your heart again!
FRANK CAPRA'S
"Mommie Issues 2"
The RECKONING
JAMES STEWART
ANNA KARINA
LIONEL BARRYMORE · THOMAS MITCHELL · HENRY TRAVERS
KRIS KRISTOFFERSON
YAPHET KOTTO
"TOO MANY HENSONS"
BARNEY MILLER
THE FALL
A KING VIDOR PRODUCTION
with
BUD CORT as MARK E. SMITH
CATE BLANCHETT as BRIX SMITH
Screen play by Jordin Isip
Titles by Joe Farnham
Directed by KING VIDOR
WARNERCOLOR
Re-released by WARNER BROS.
MICHAEL K. WILLIAMS is BASS REEVES
A PICTURE TO REMEMBER FROM WARNER BROS.
"THE LONELIEST RANGER"
The MOON is HOLLOW
CHARLES MINGUS
KATHARINE HEPBURN
Regia JOHN CROMWELL
SOLO CHARLIE E KATE
"He took shit from no one."
WHAT EVER HAPPENED TO TOM WILSON?
DYLAN · MOTHERS · SOFT MACHINE · V.U.
The book that was talked of in a Whisper!
FRANCES FARMER as LISA RANDALL
"Super Symmetry and Parallel Dimensions"
SuperSymmetry
Lisa Randall
GEORGE SAUNDERS and JOE LOUIS
IN COLOR
"The Tod Browning Story"
ALAN LADD
SHIRLEY HEMPHILL
SUPERDIVORCIO EL GIGANTE
en CINEMASCOPE
COLOR POR DE LUXE
It is to laugh...
BERT LAHR
"Building Seven"

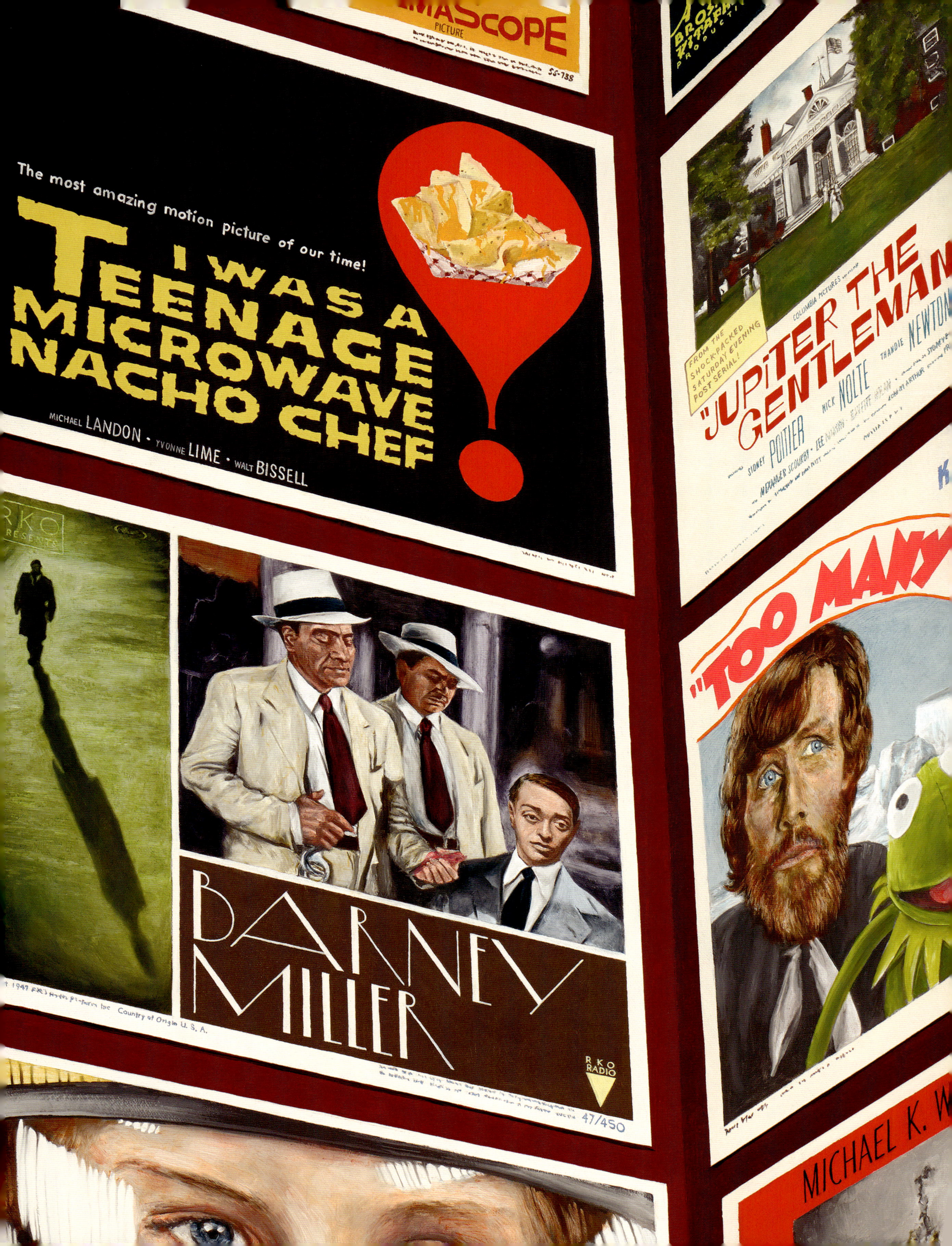
The most amazing motion picture of our time!
I WAS A TEENAGE MICROWAVE NACHO CHEF
MICHAEL LANDON · YVONNE LIME · WALT BISSELL
BARNEY MILLER
RKO RADIO
47/450
Country of Origin U.S.A.
"JUPITER THE GENTLEMAN
FROM THE SHOCKPACKED SATURDAY EVENING POST SERIAL!
SIDNEY POITIER
NICK NOLTE
THANDIE NEWTON
"TOO MANY
MICHAEL K. W

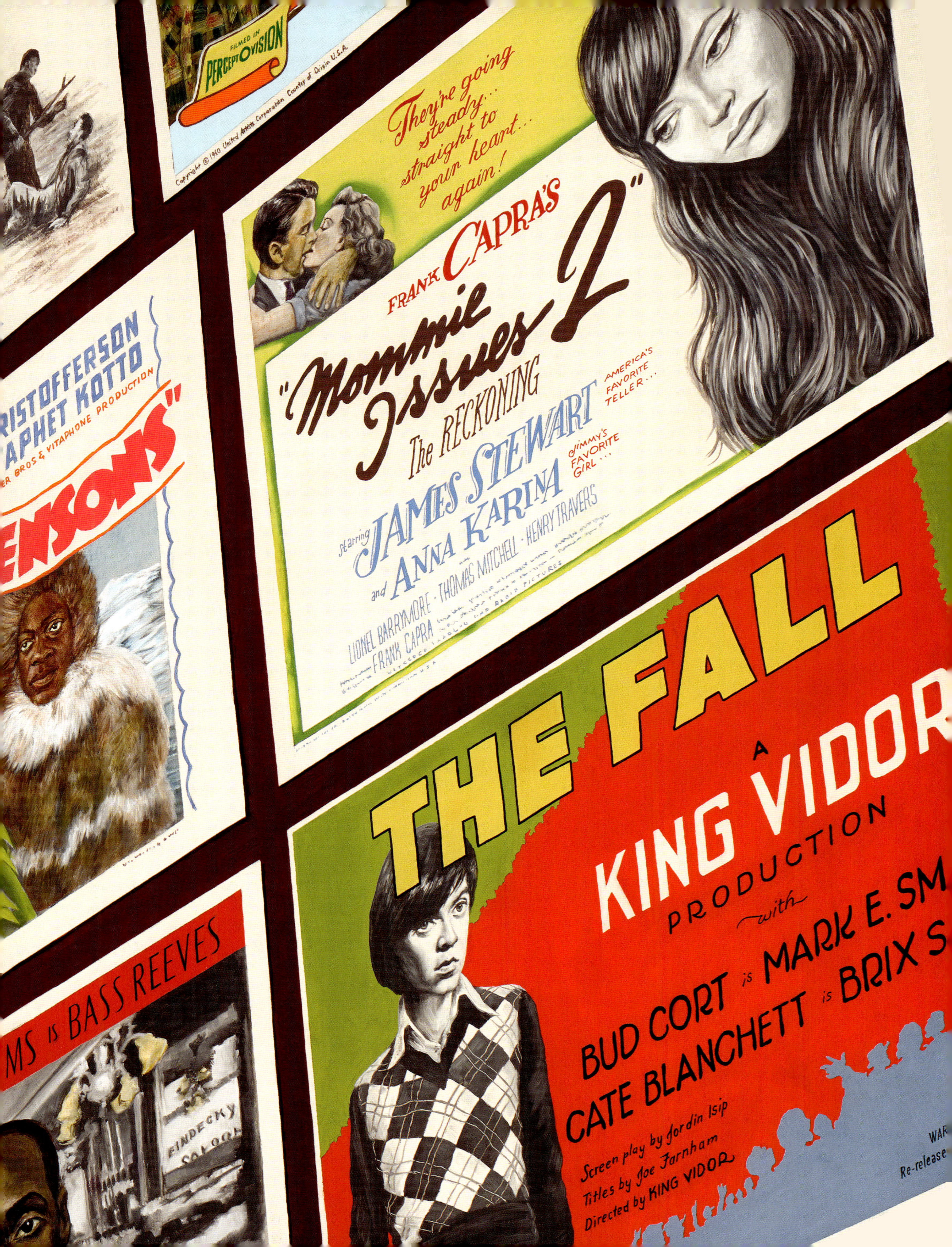
FILMED IN
PERCEPTOVISION
They're going steady... straight to your heart... again!
FRANK CAPRA'S
"Mommie Issues 2"
The RECKONING
starring JAMES STEWART
AMERICA'S FAVORITE TELLER...
and ANNA KARINA
JIMMY'S FAVORITE GIRL...
LIONEL BARRYMORE · THOMAS MITCHELL · HENRY TRAVERS
FRANK CAPRA
RISTOFFERSON
APHET KOTTO
ER BROS & VITAPHONE PRODUCTION
ENSONS"
MS IS BASS REEVES
THE FALL
A KING VIDOR PRODUCTION
with
BUD CORT is MARK E. SM
CATE BLANCHETT is BRIX S
Screen play by Jordin Isip
Titles by Joe Farnham
Directed by KING VIDOR
WAR
Re-release

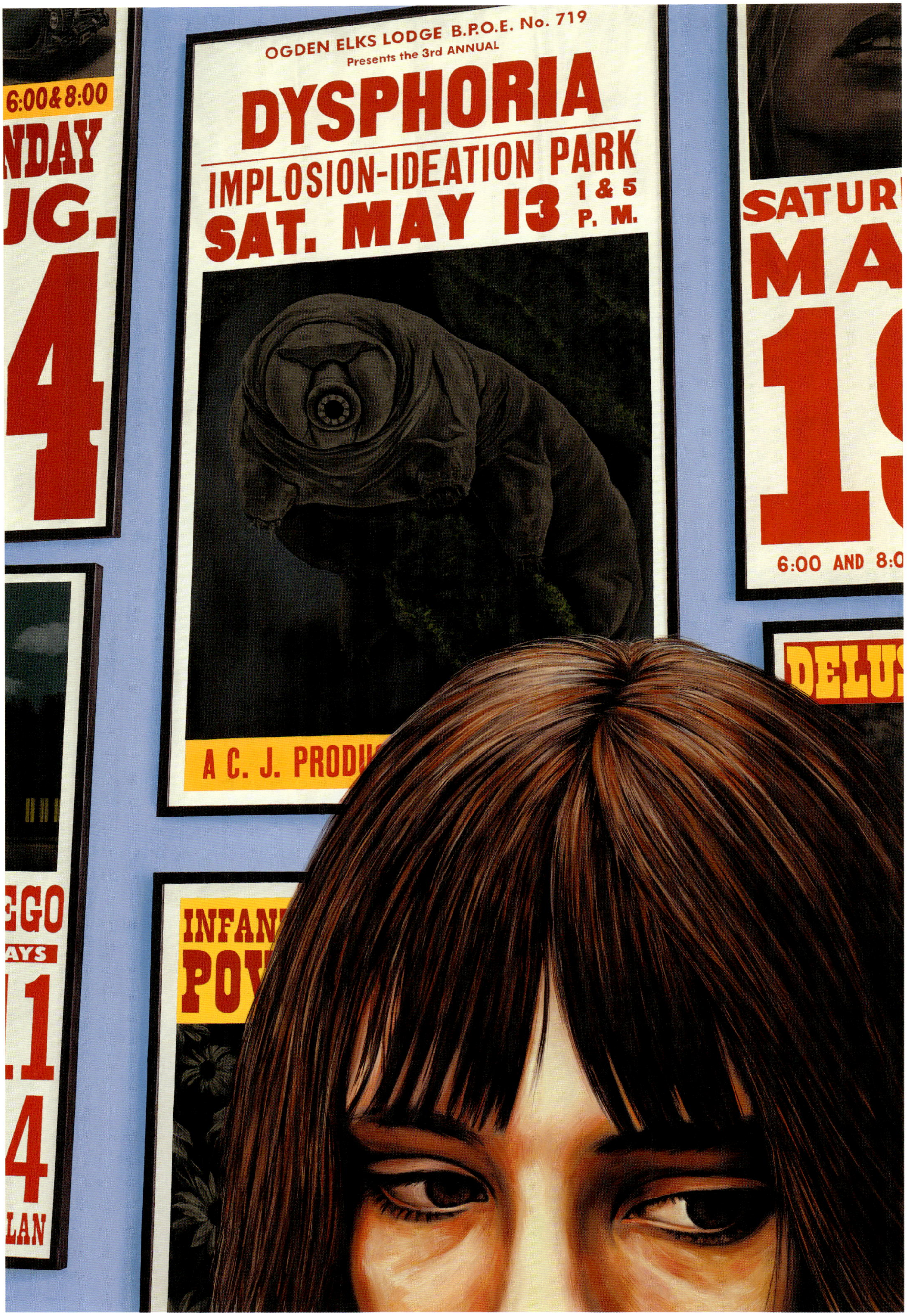

Redacted
2014
Oil on canvas
60 x 40 in.

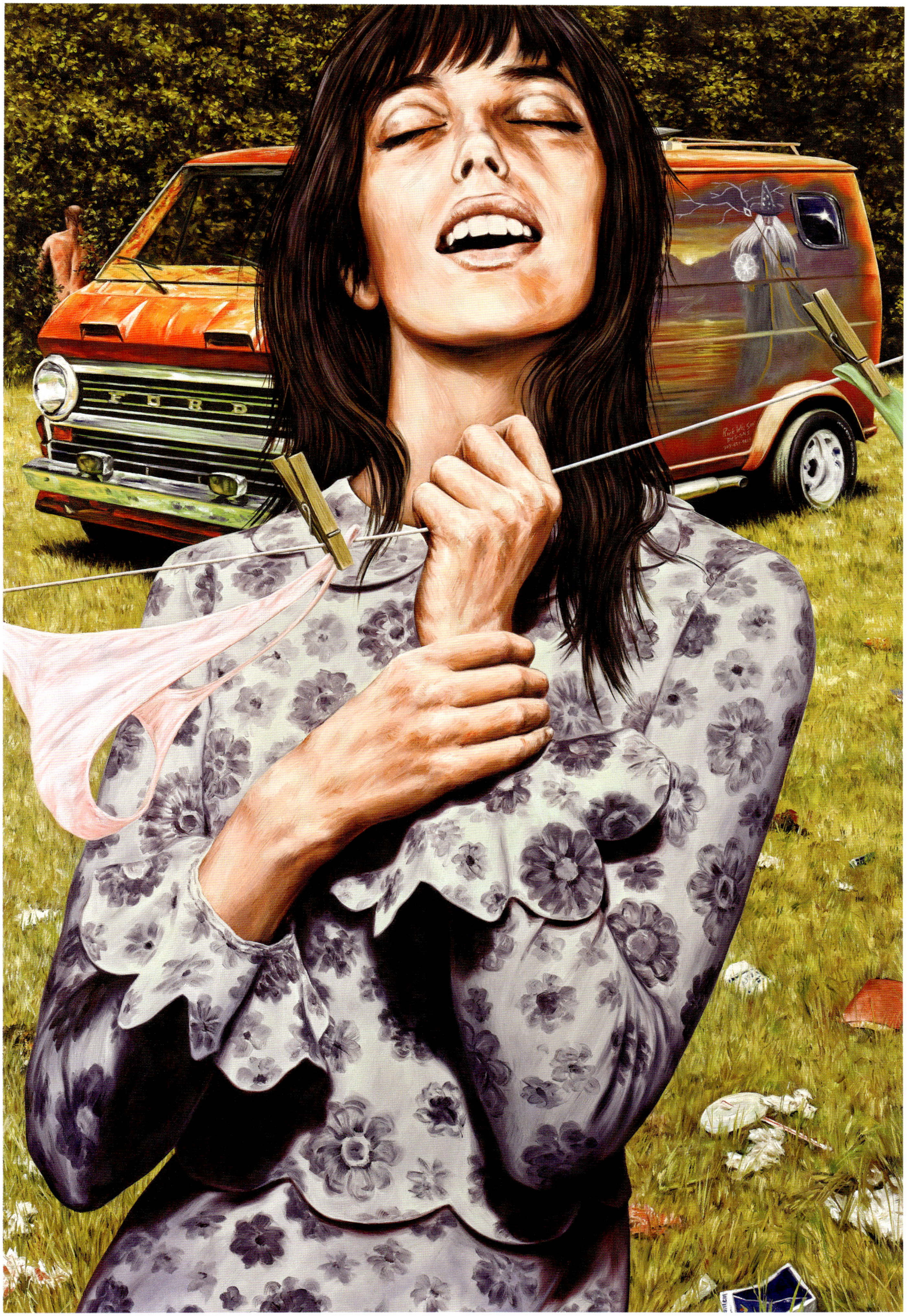

Jane
2014
Oil on canvas
60 x 40 in.

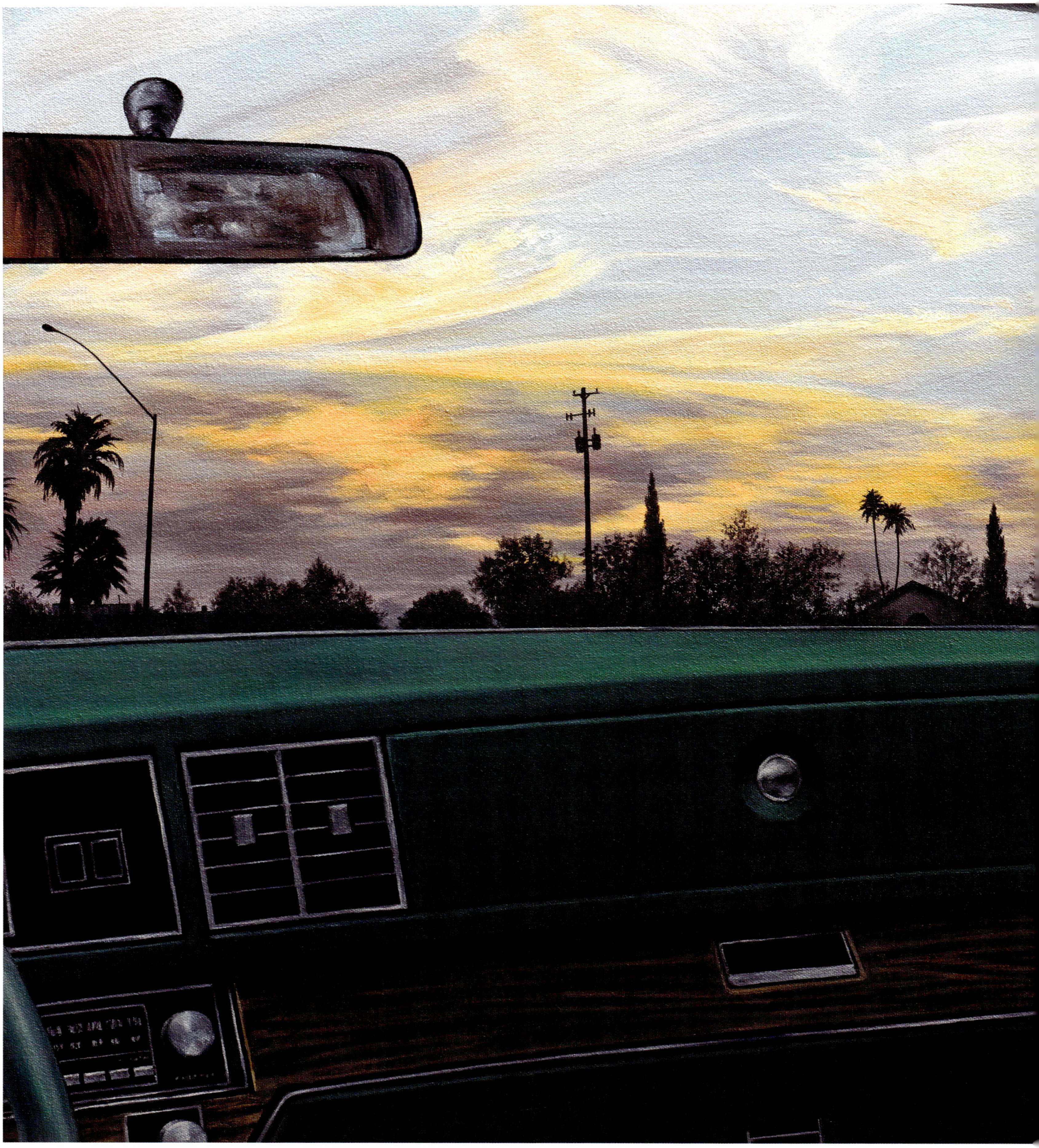

Down In Front: Love In The Afternoon
2014
Oil on canvas
20 x 36 in.

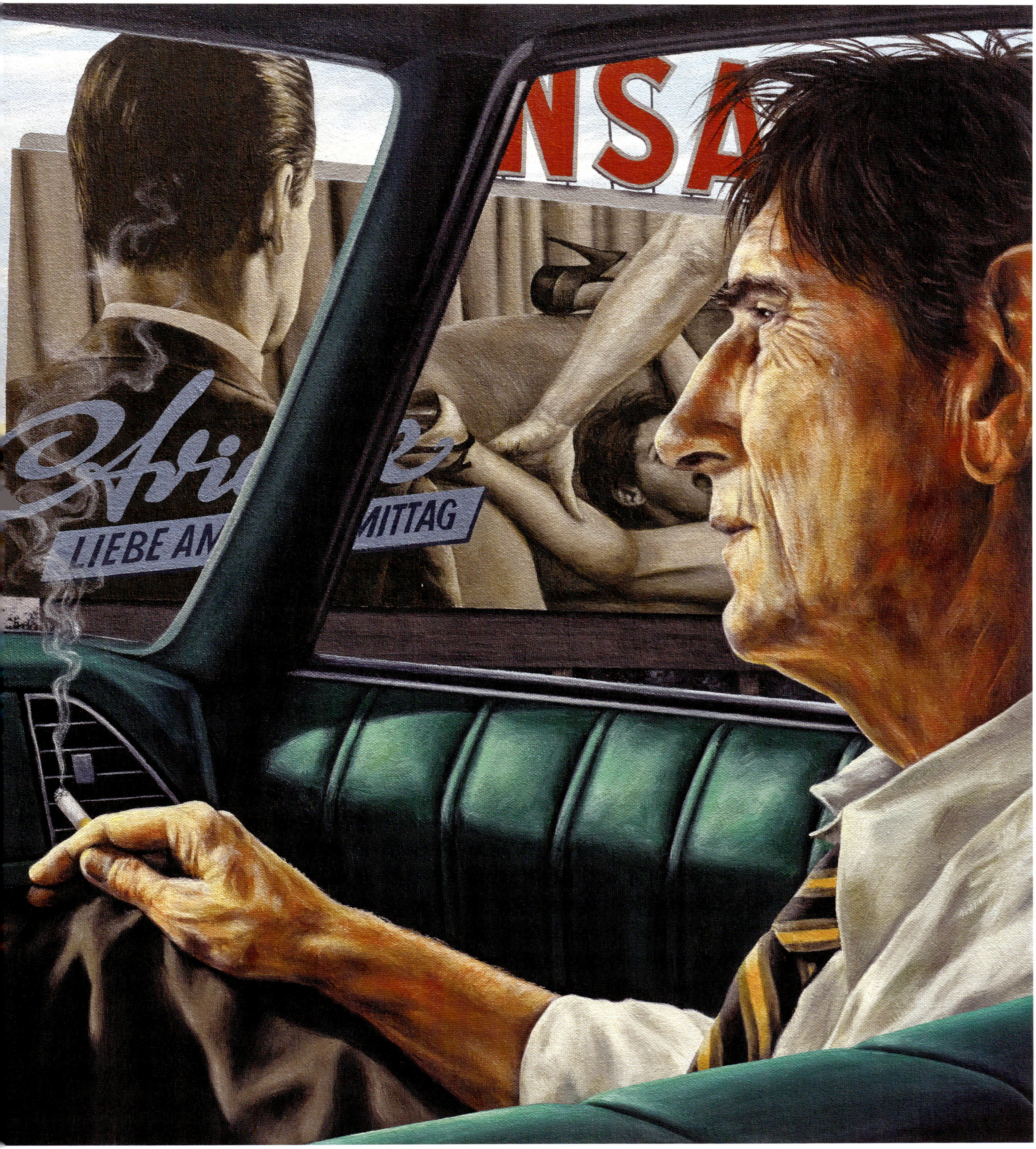
NSA
LIEBE AM
MITTAG

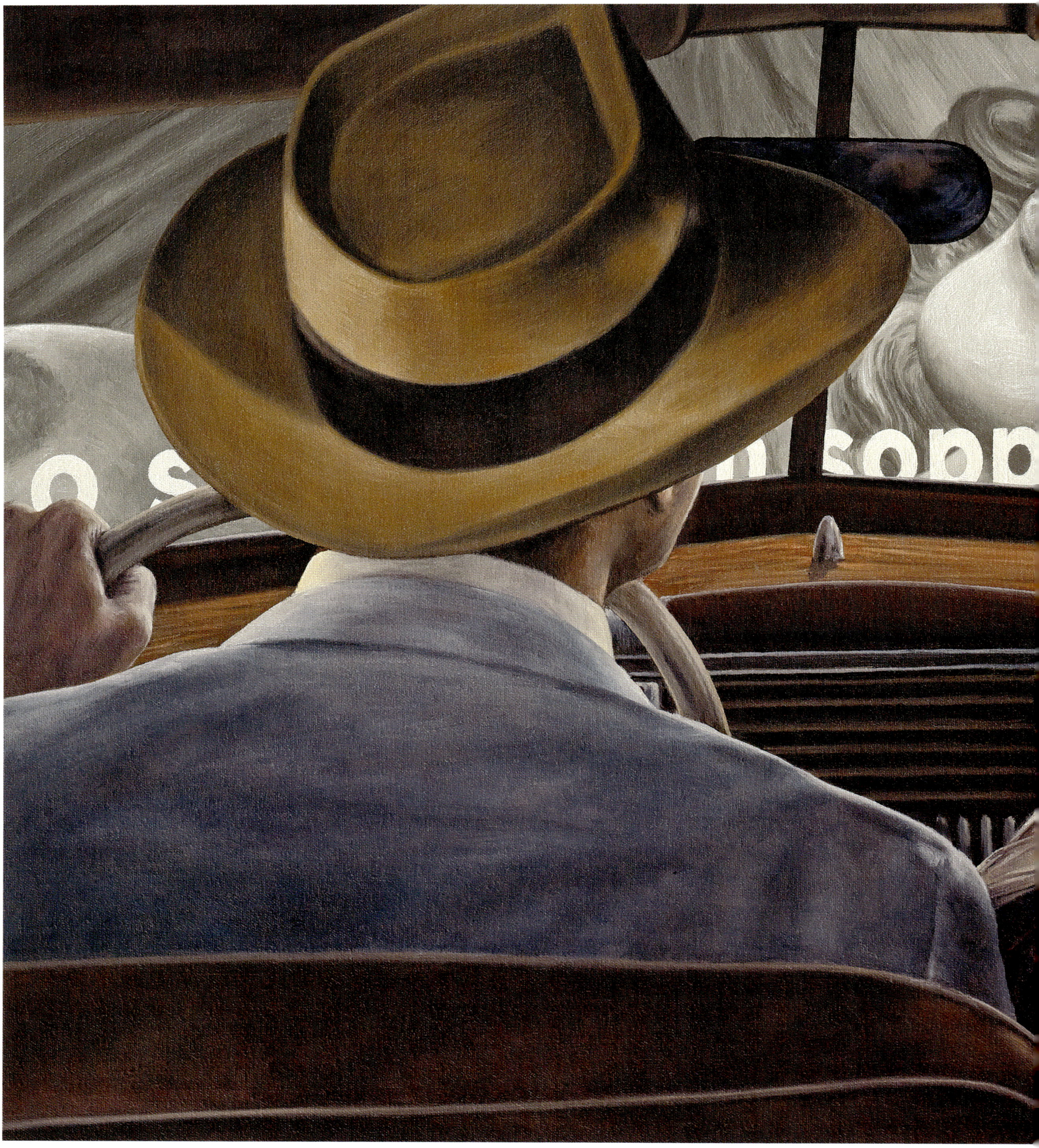

Down In Front: Sedile Posteriore
2014
Oil on canvas
20 x 36 in.

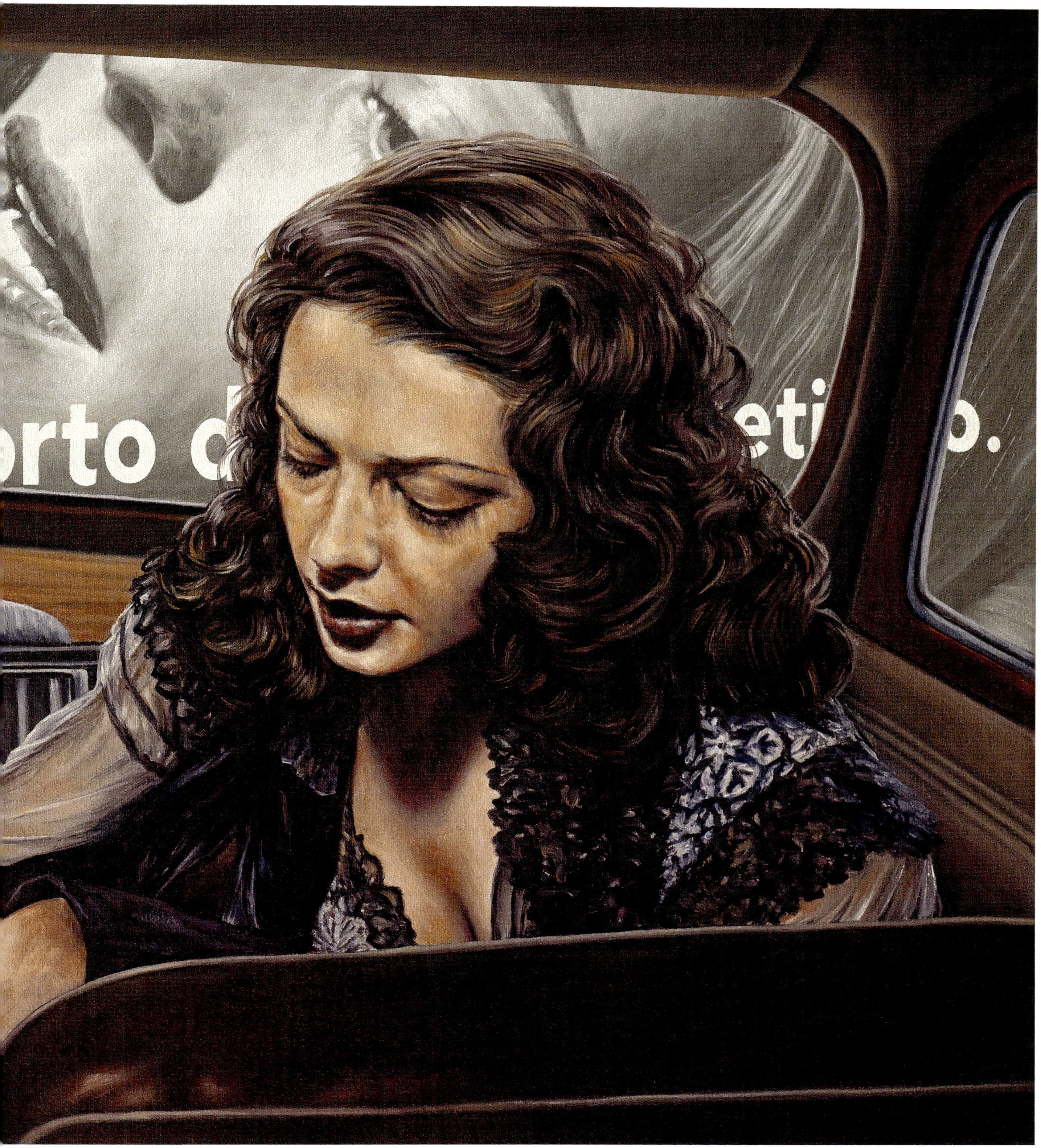

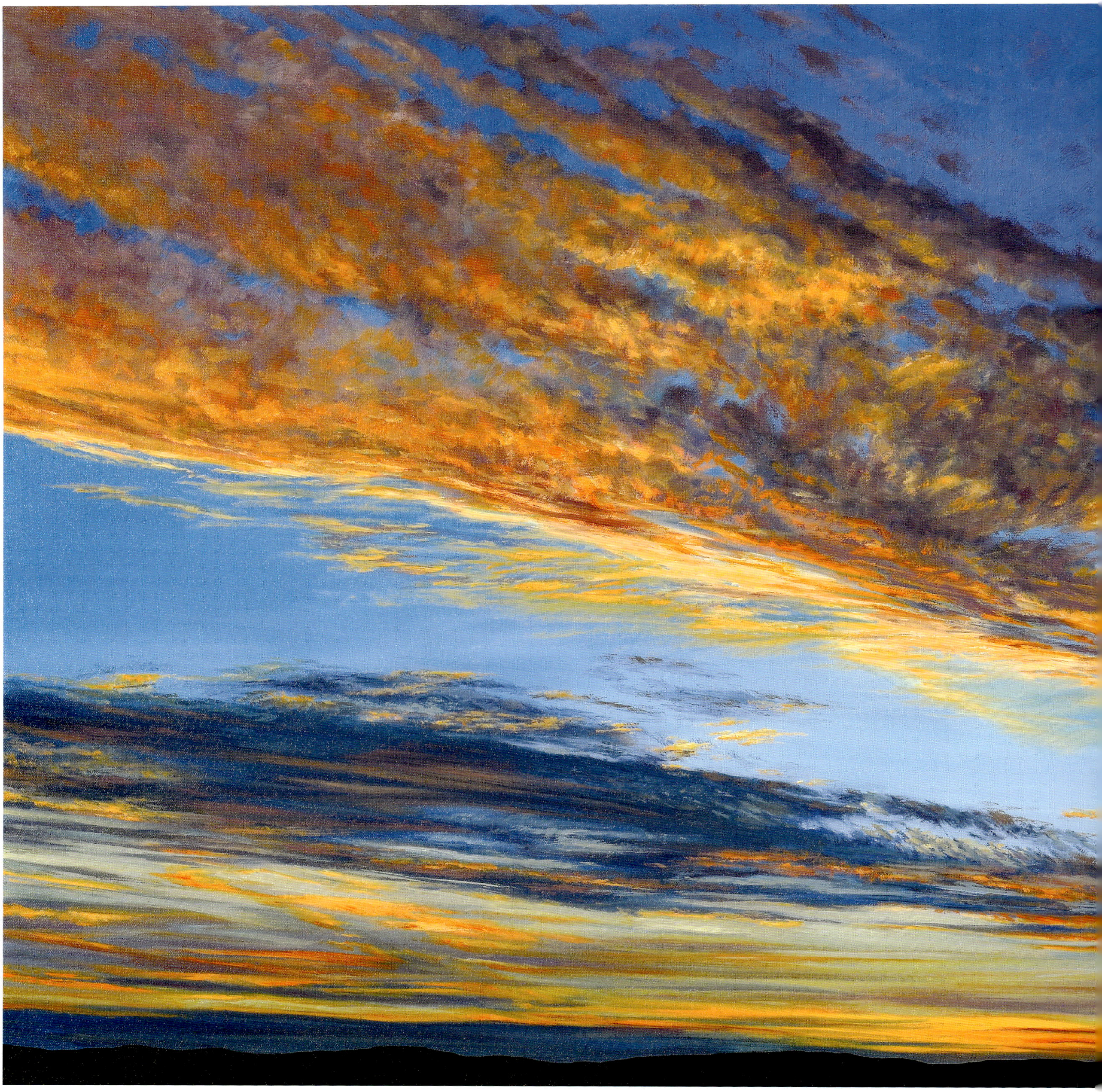

Down In Front: Paramount's
2014
Oil on canvas
24 x 48 in.

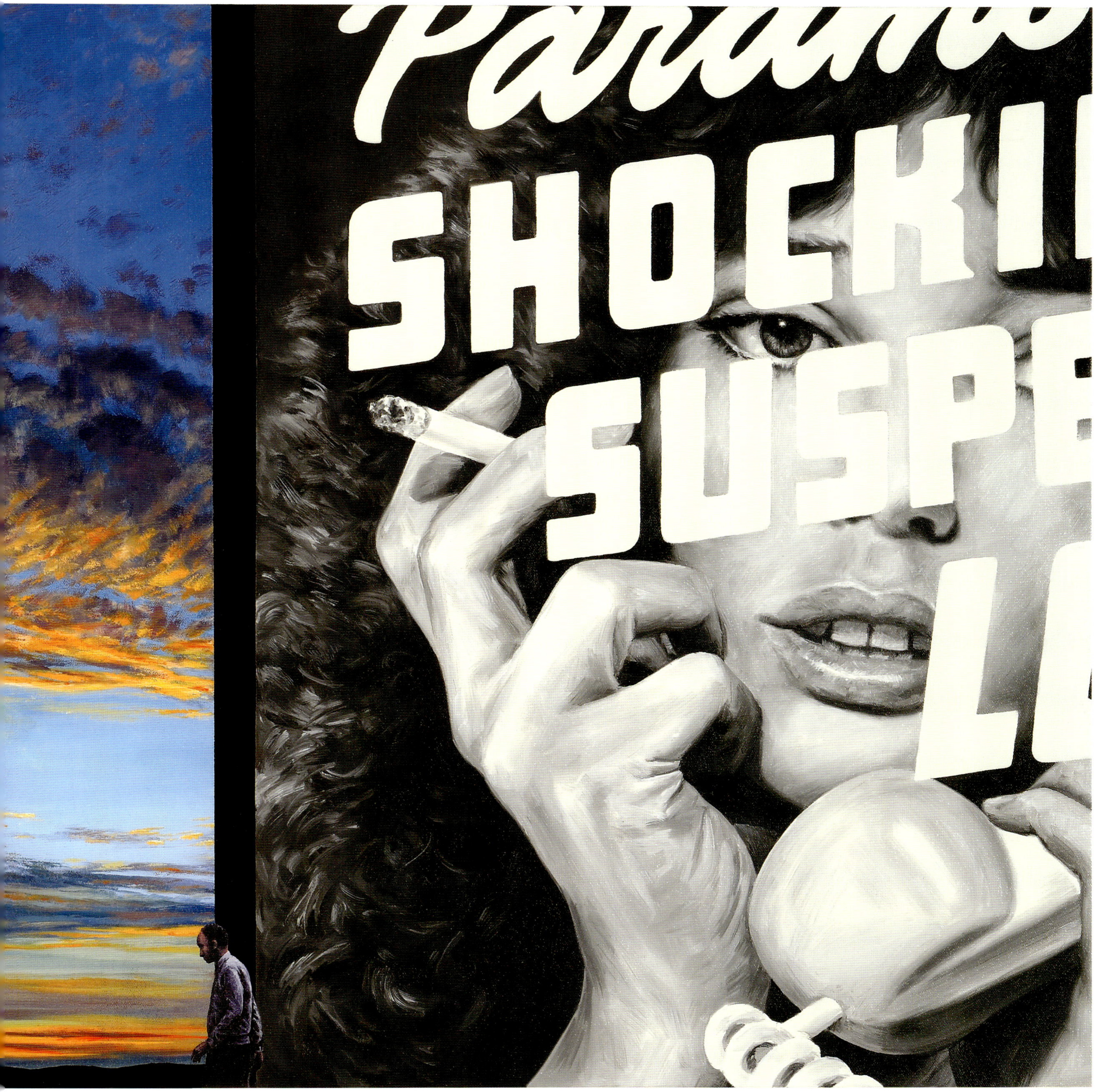

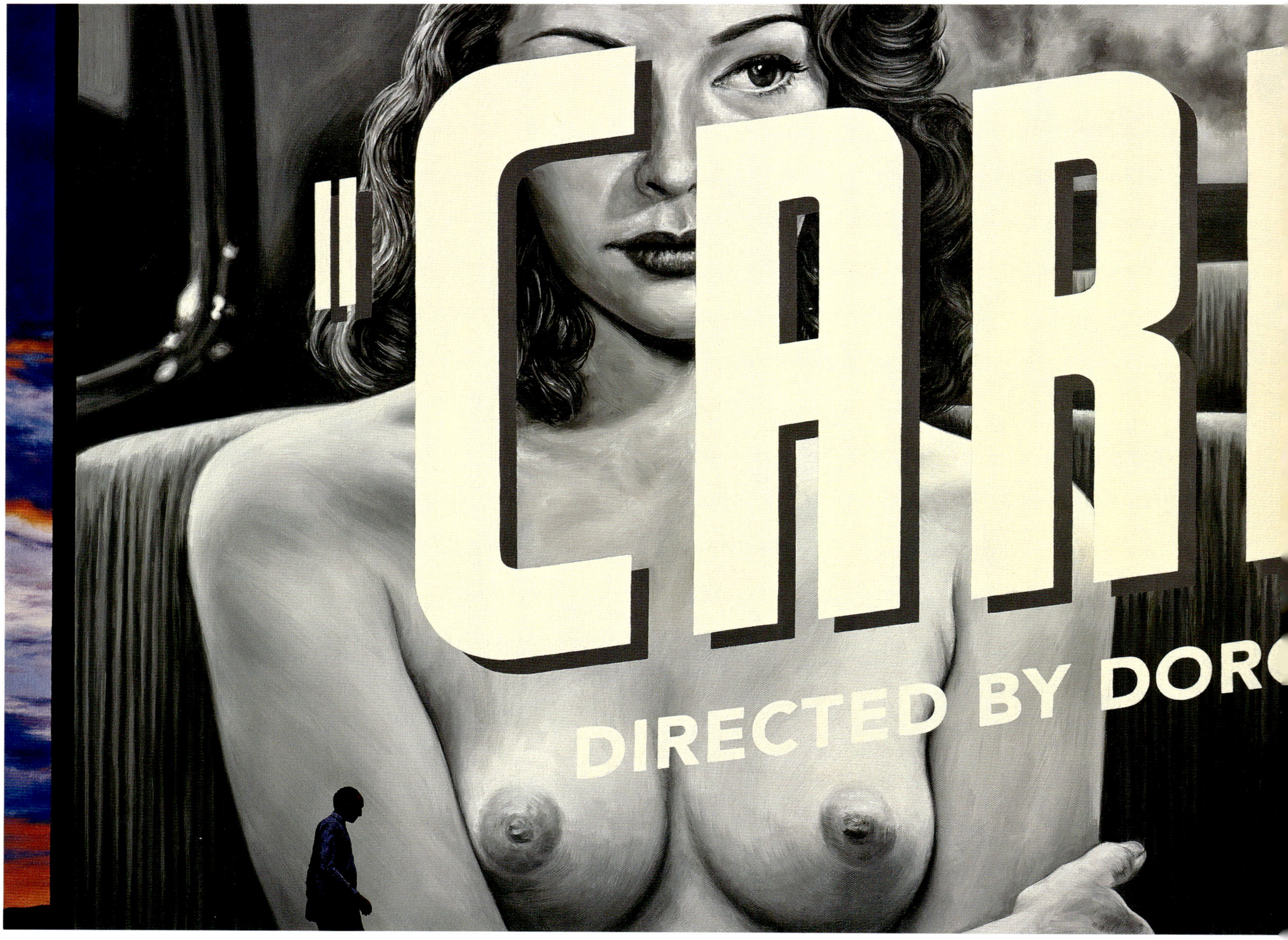

Down In Front: The Company She Keeps
2014
Oil on canvas
22 x 60 in.

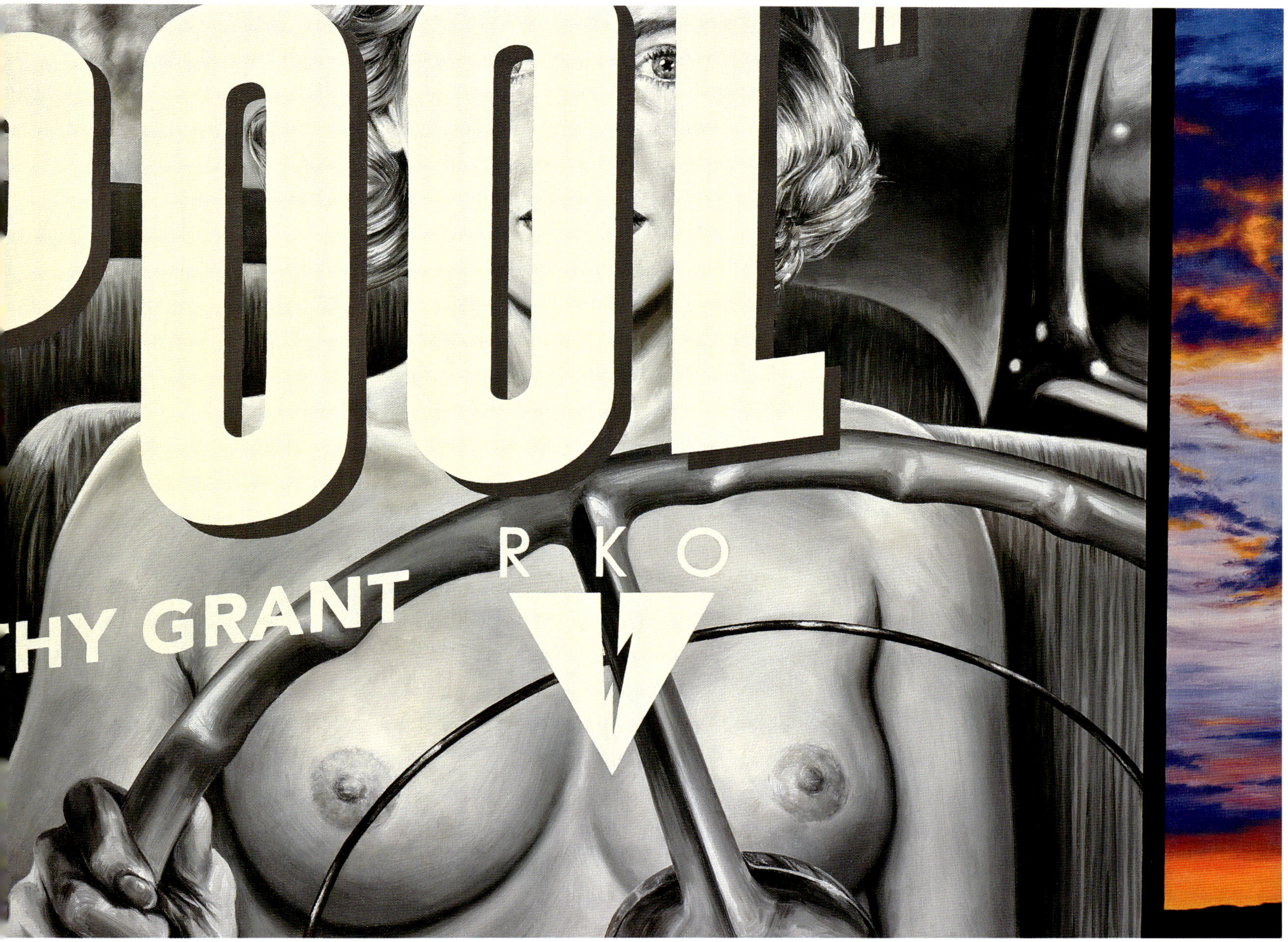
POOL"
HY GRANT
R K O

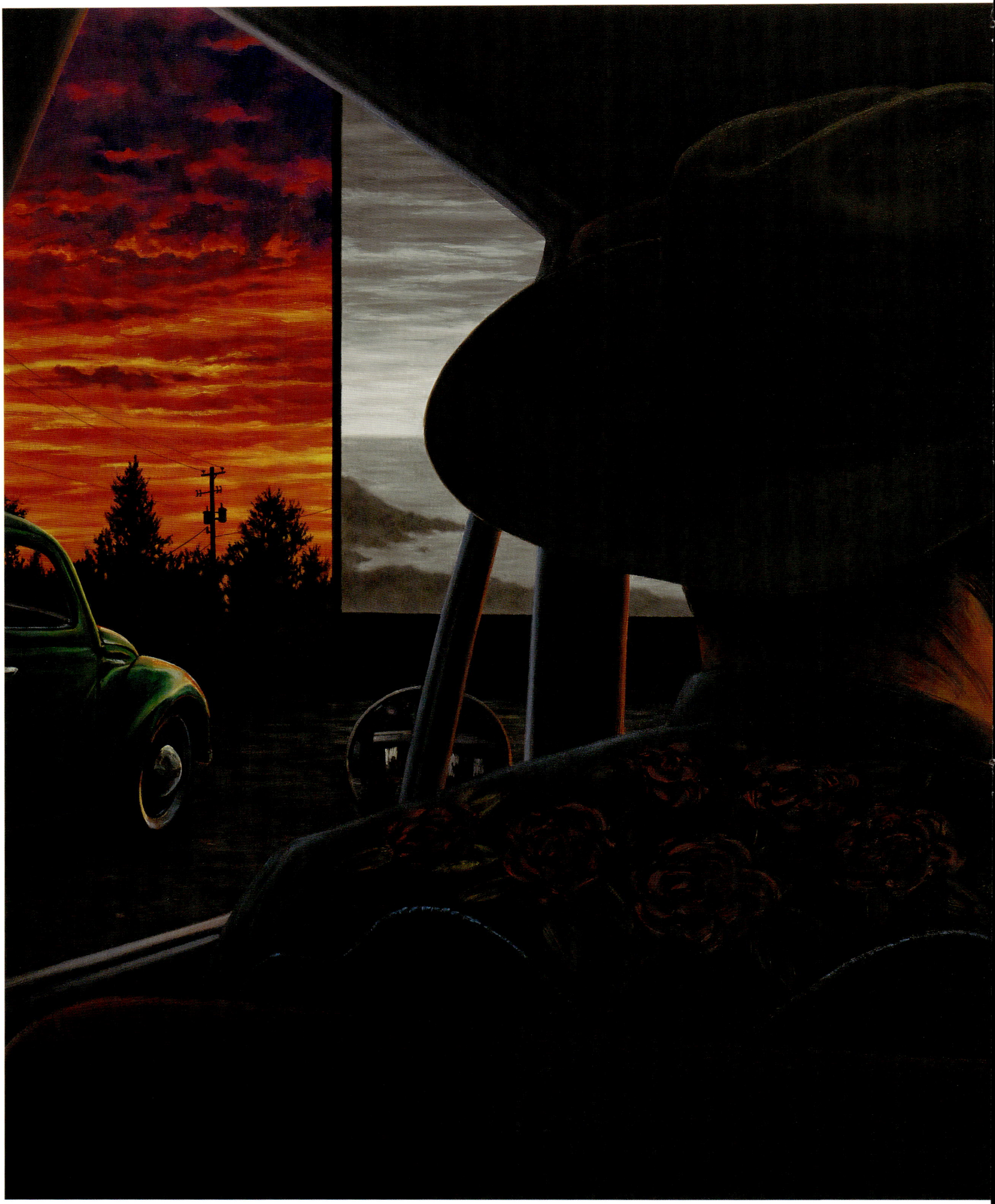

Down In Front: Fresh Air
2014
Oil on canvas
36 x 60 in.

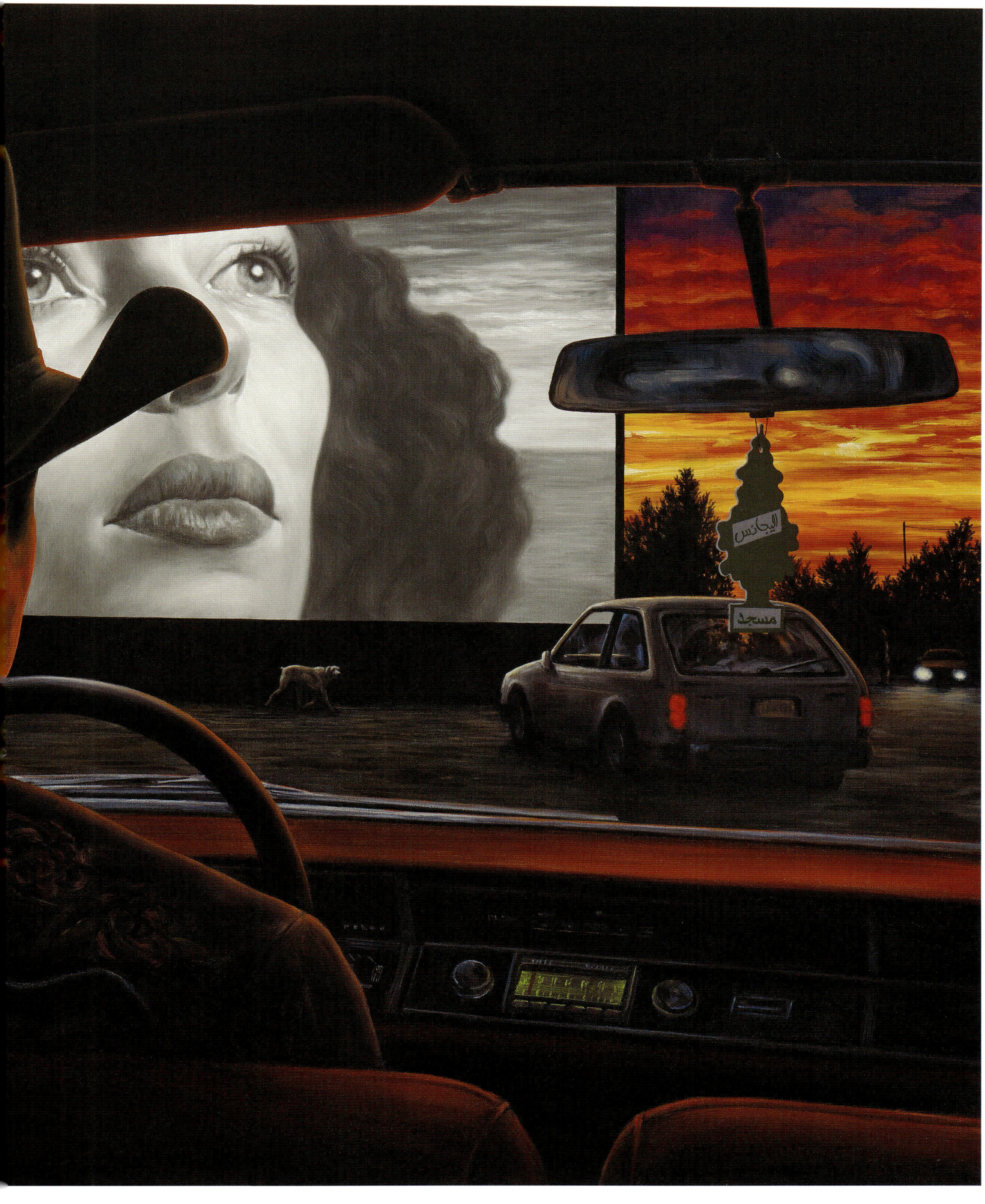
مسجد

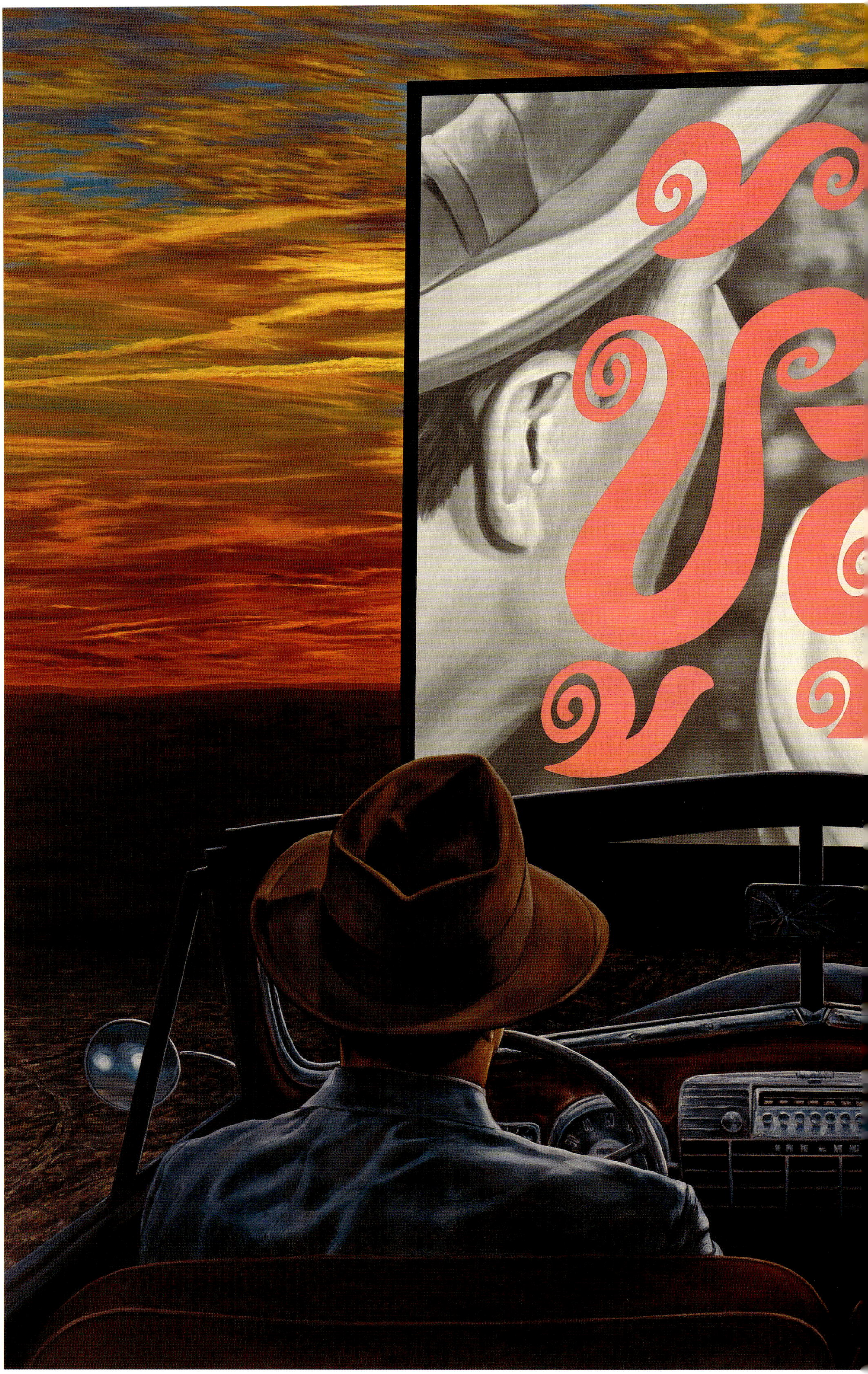

Down In Front
2014
Oil on canvas
60 x 85 in.

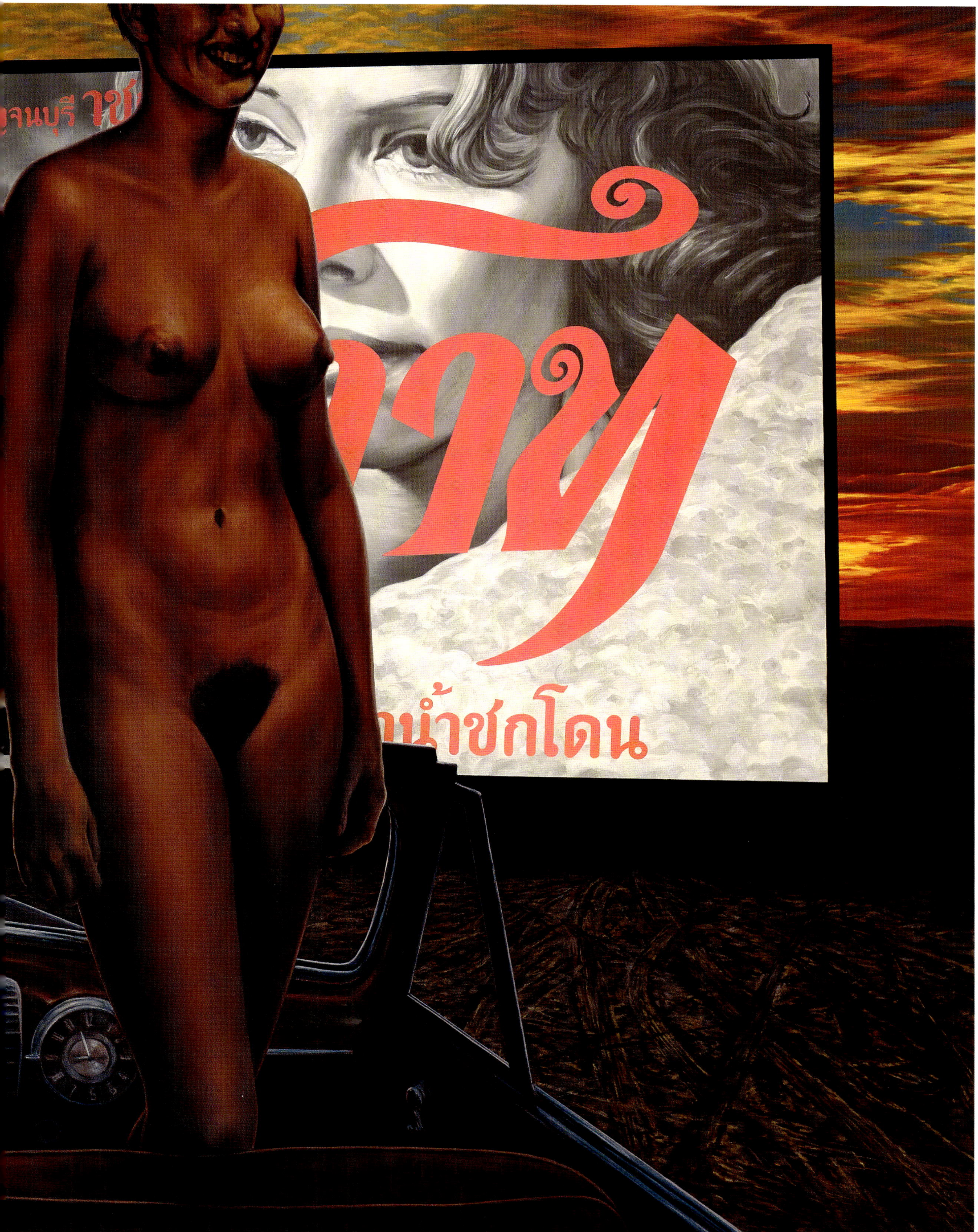

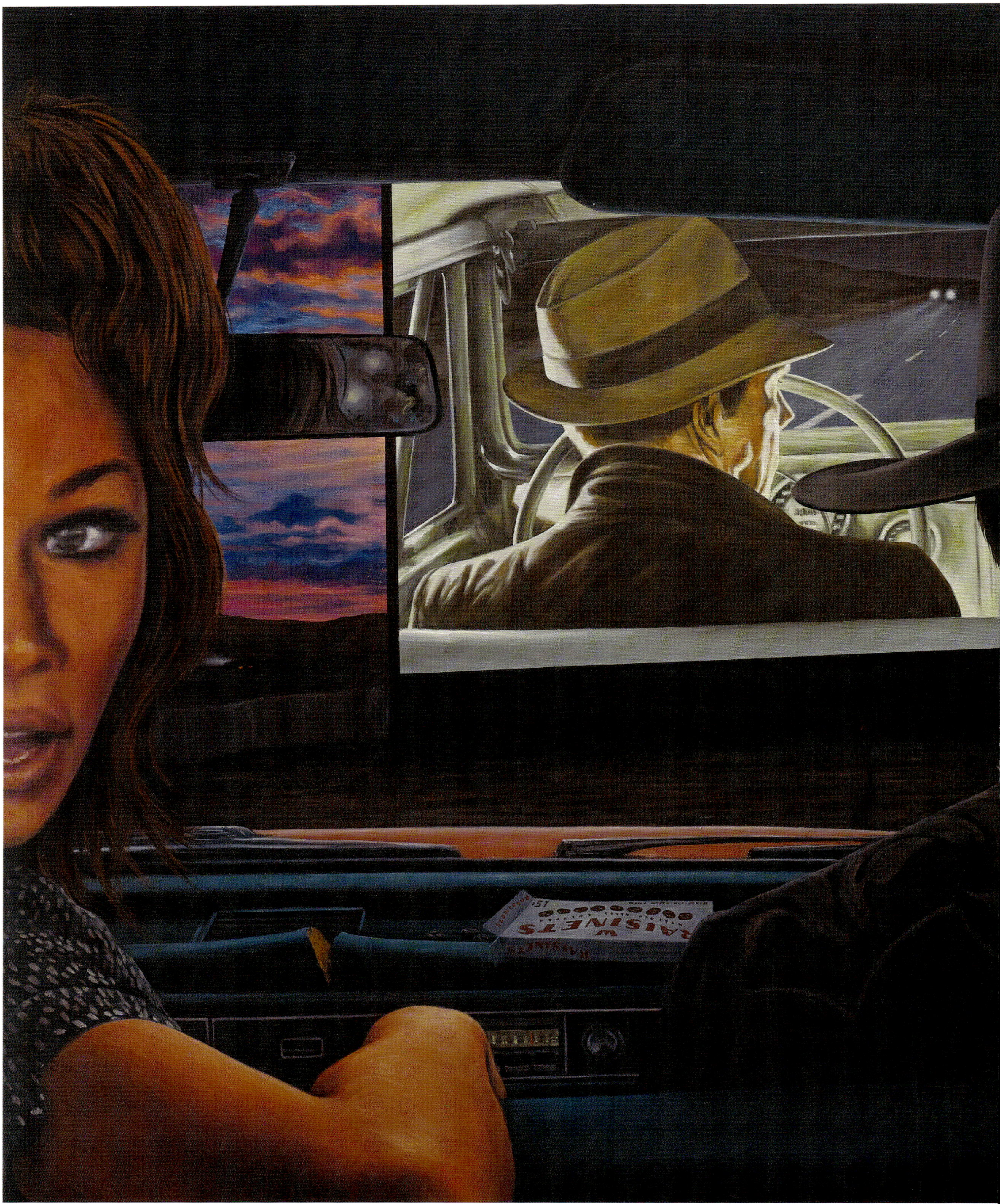

Down In Front: Dead Reckoning
2014
Oil on canvas
36 x 60 in.

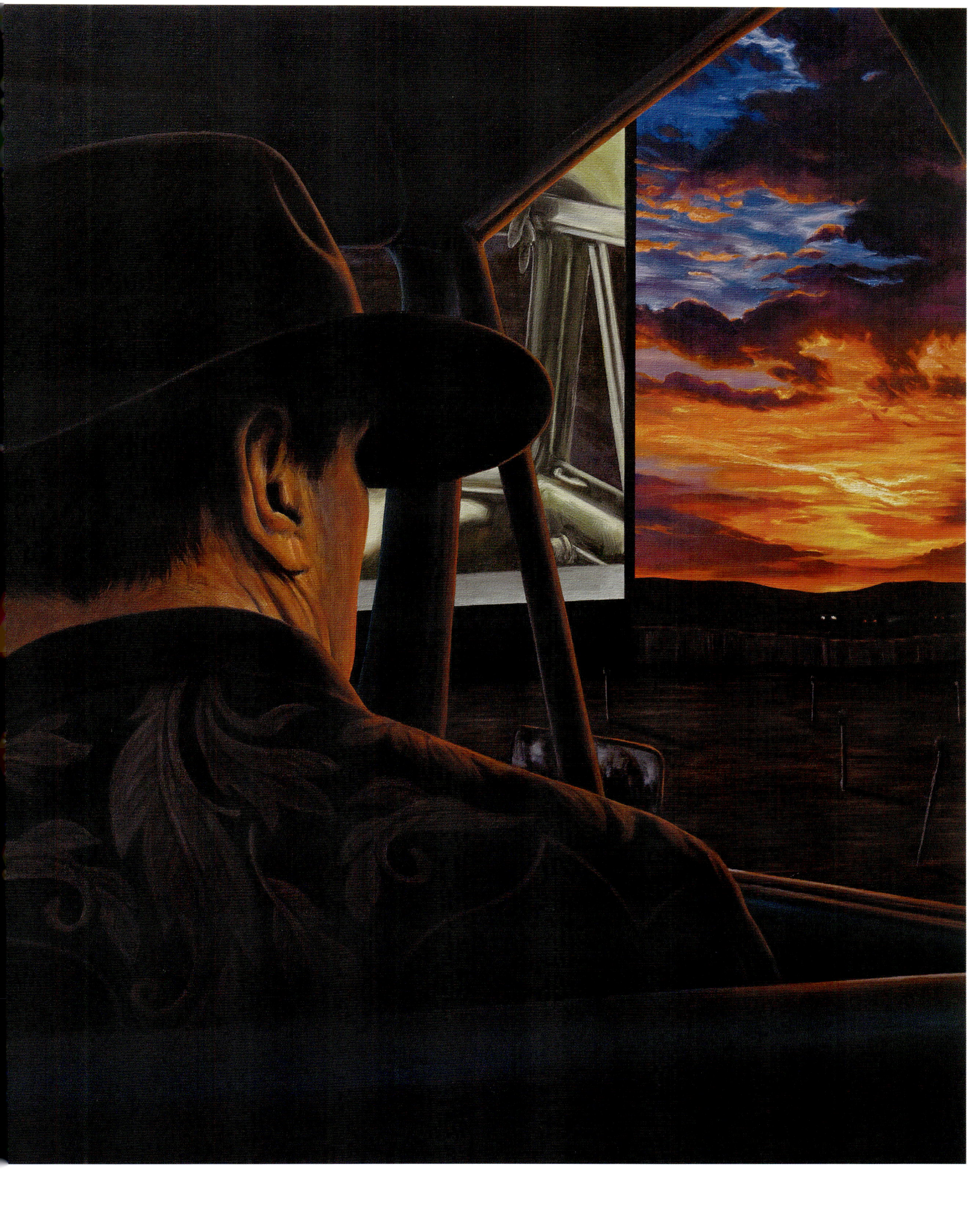

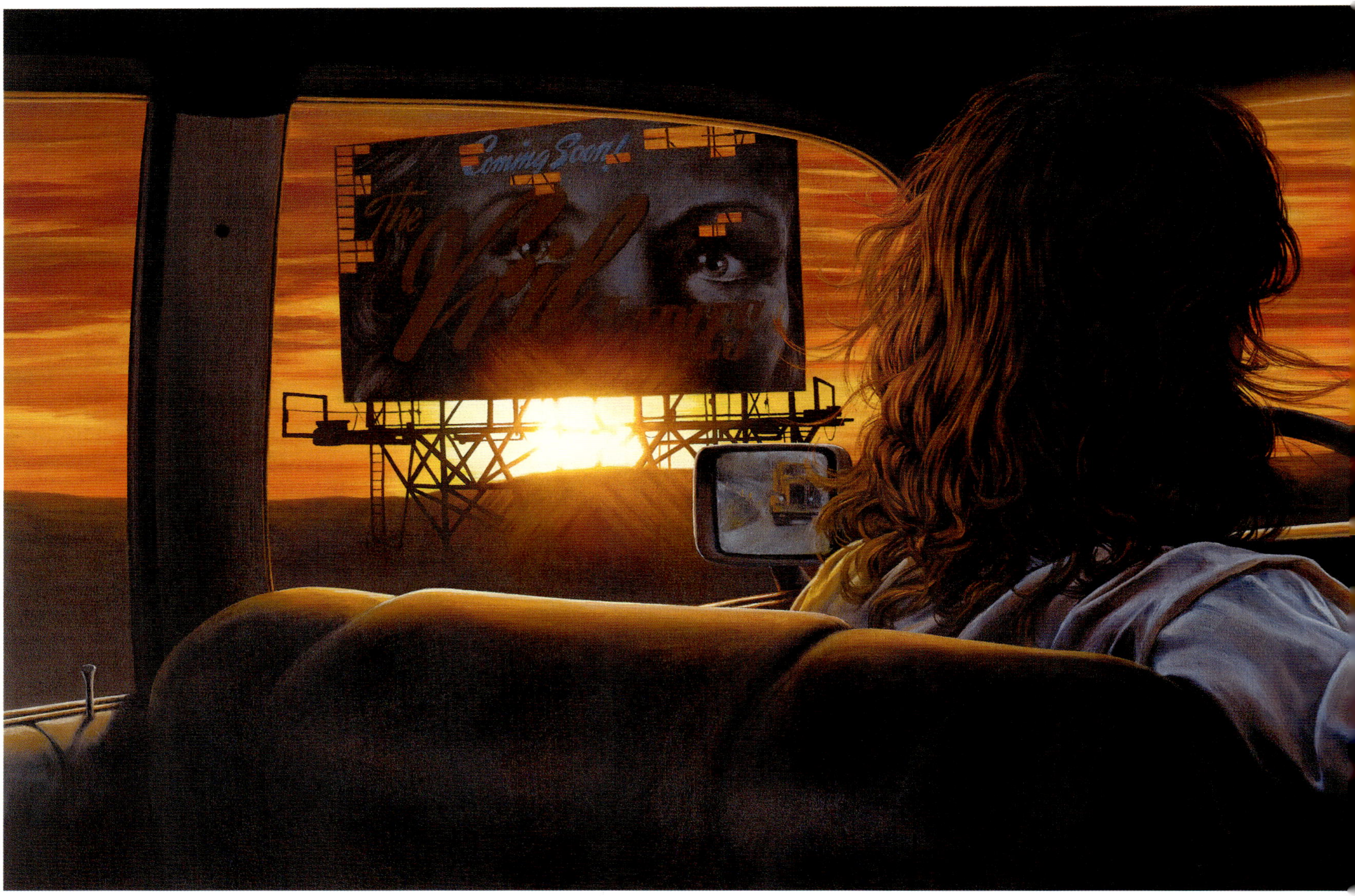

Down In Front: Coming Soon
(detail on following page)
2014
Oil on canvas
26 x 78 in.

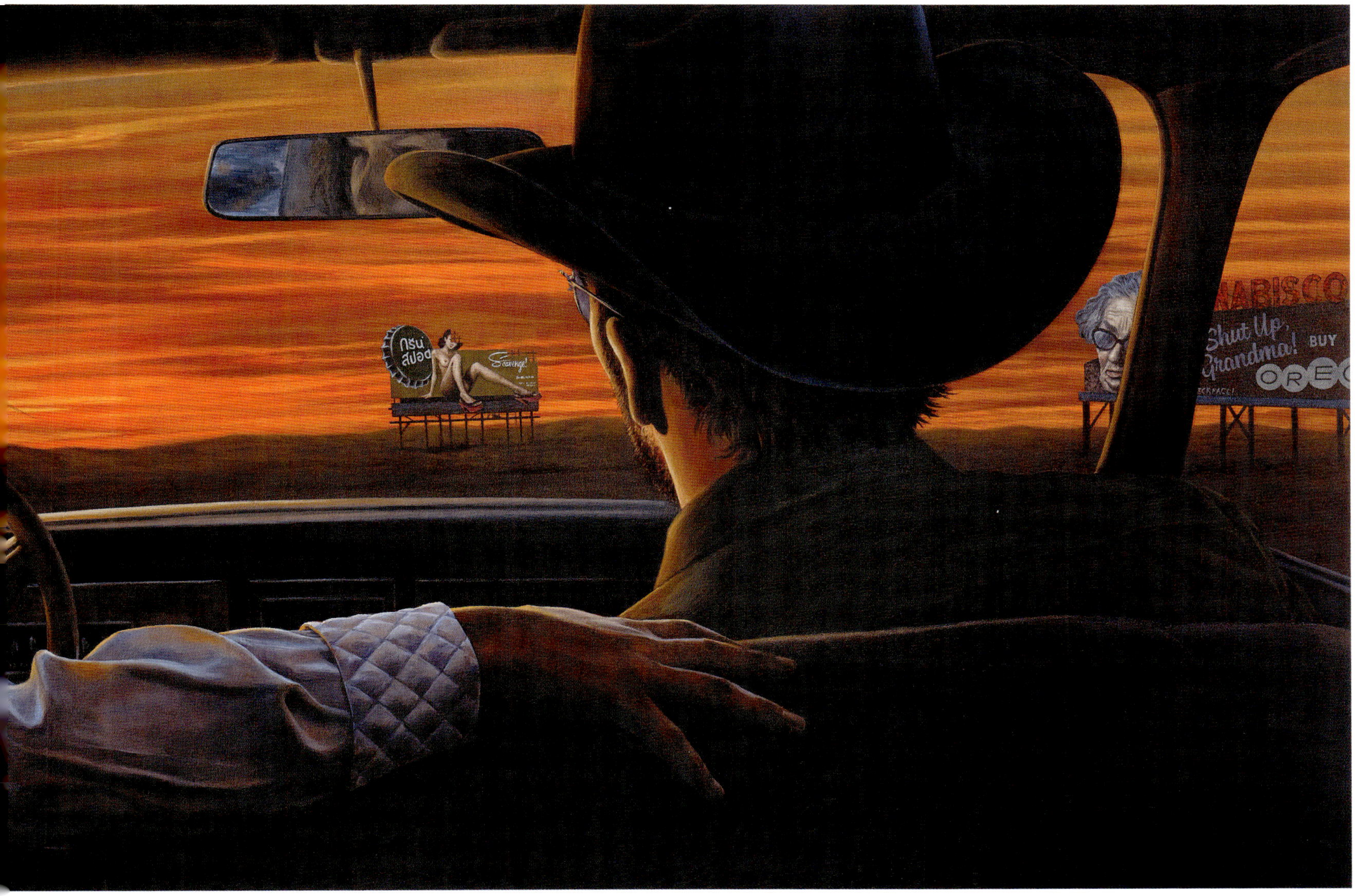

Shut Up, Grandma!
BUY

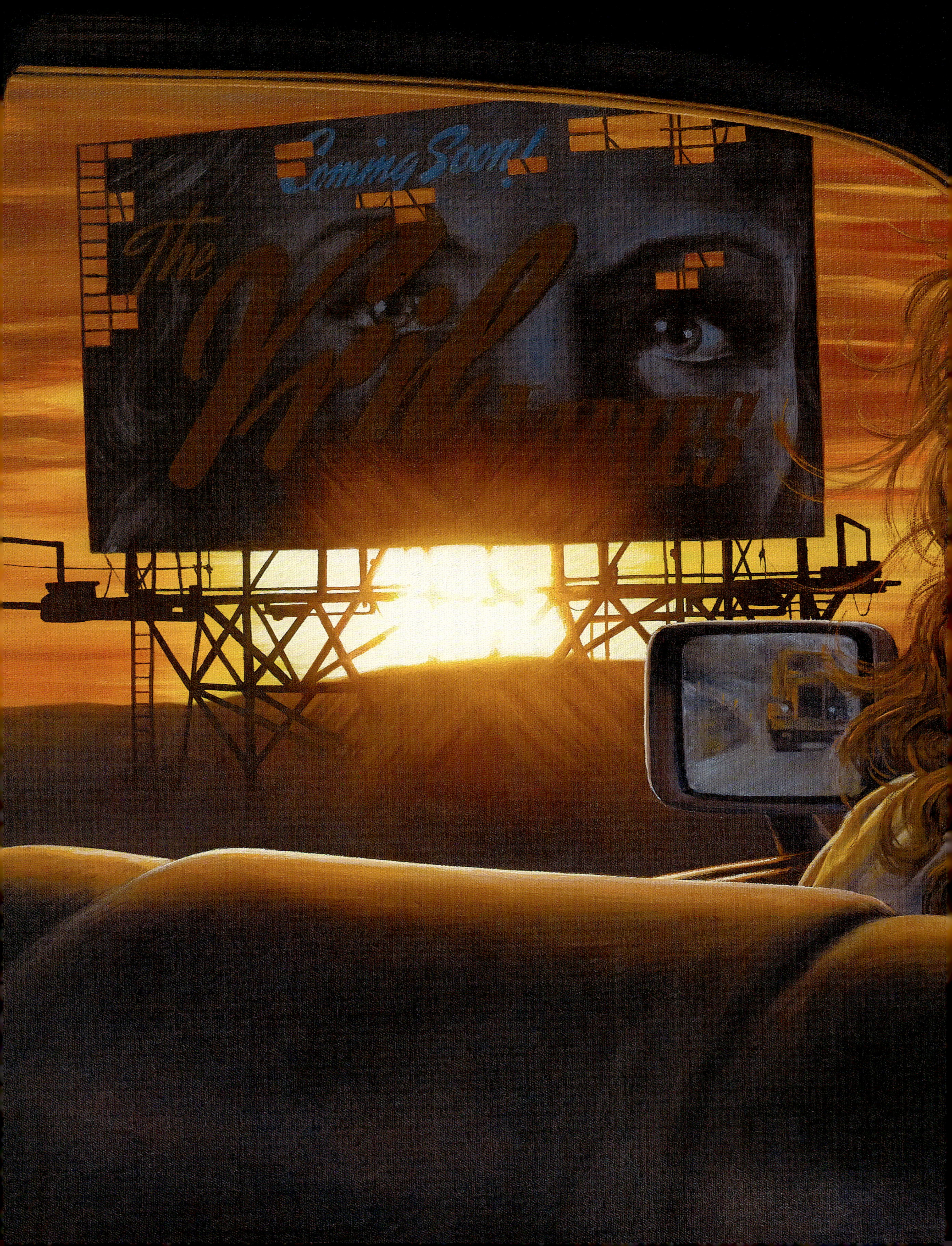
Coming Soon!
The

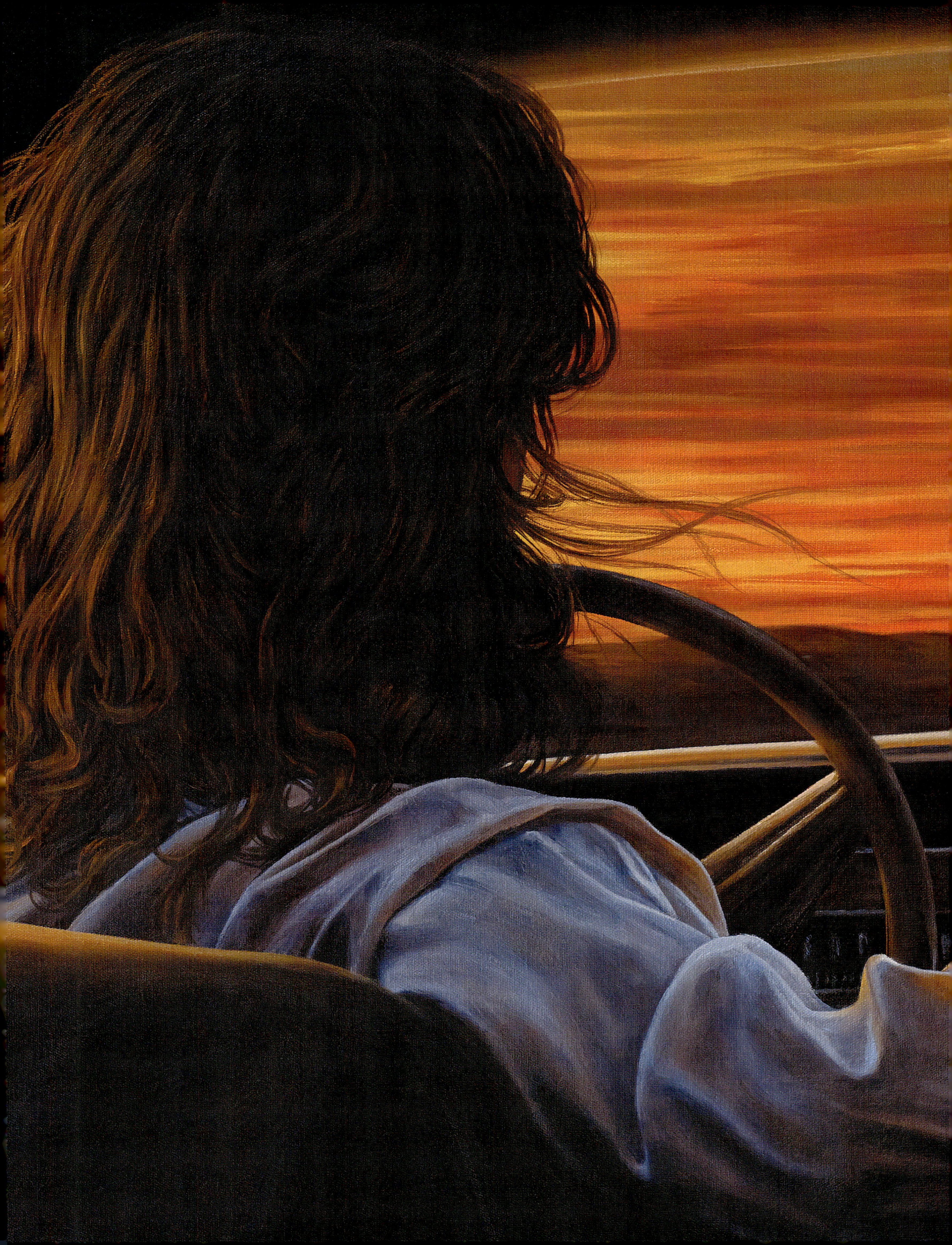

DRAWINGS

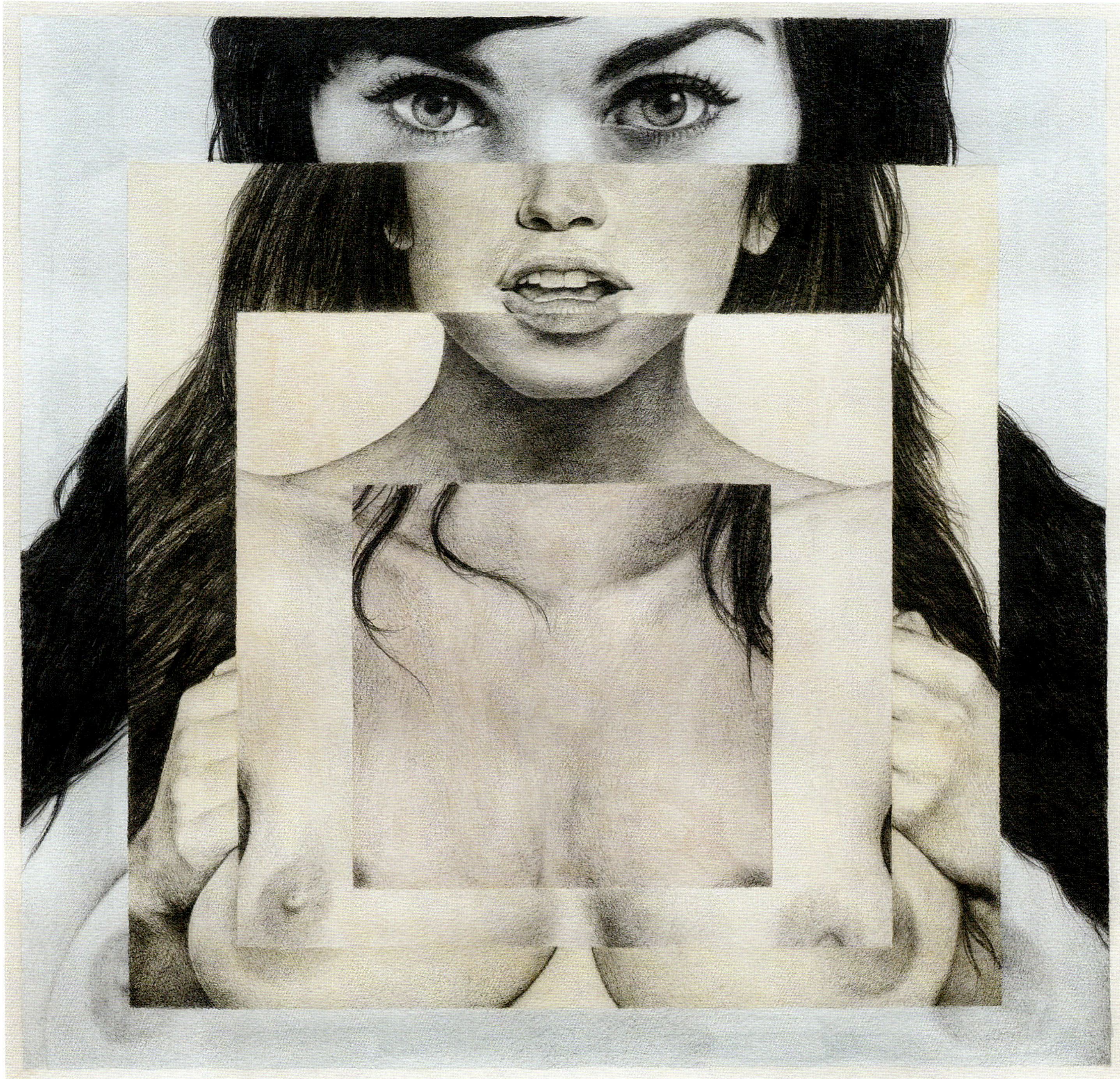

Here(after Albers)
2010
Graphite and acrylic on paper
16 x 16 in.

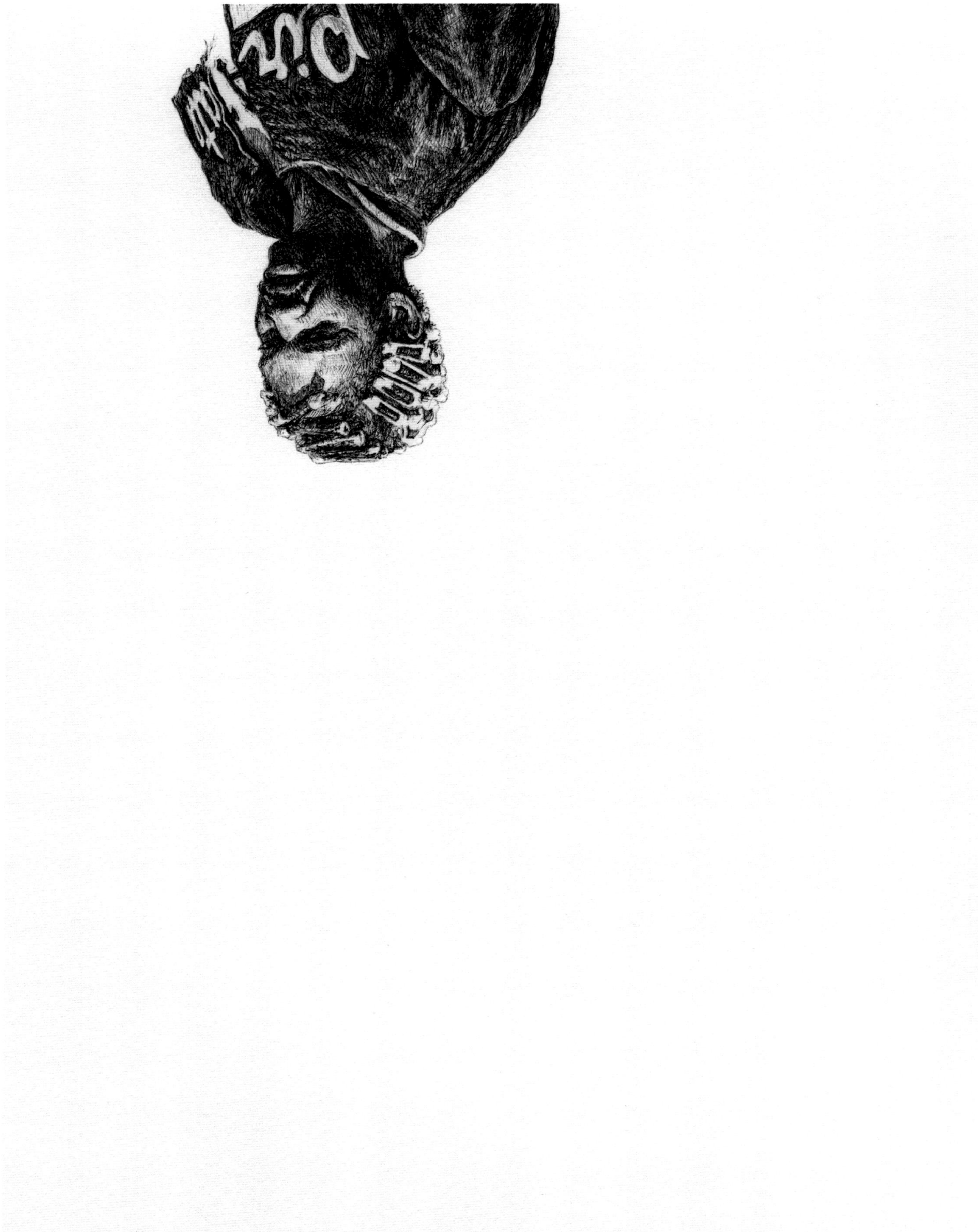

Cease & Desist
2008
Ballpoint pen on paper
11 x 8.5 in.

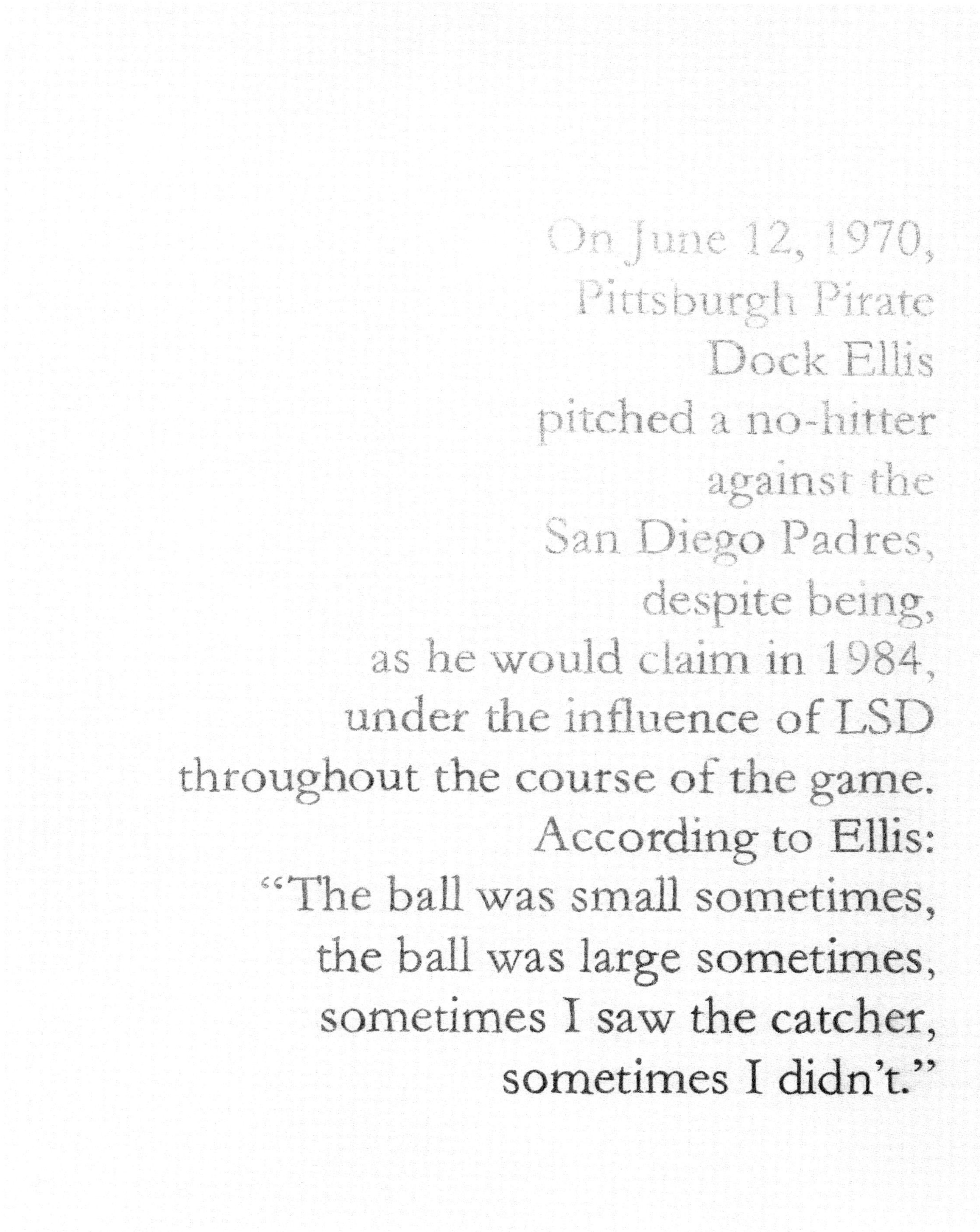

On June 12, 1970,
Pittsburgh Pirate
Dock Ellis
pitched a no-hitter
against the
San Diego Padres,
despite being,
as he would claim in 1984,
under the influence of LSD
throughout the course of the game.
According to Ellis:
"The ball was small sometimes,
the ball was large sometimes,
sometimes I saw the catcher,
sometimes I didn't."

Sometimes I Didn't
2008
Graphite on paper
11 x 8.5 in.

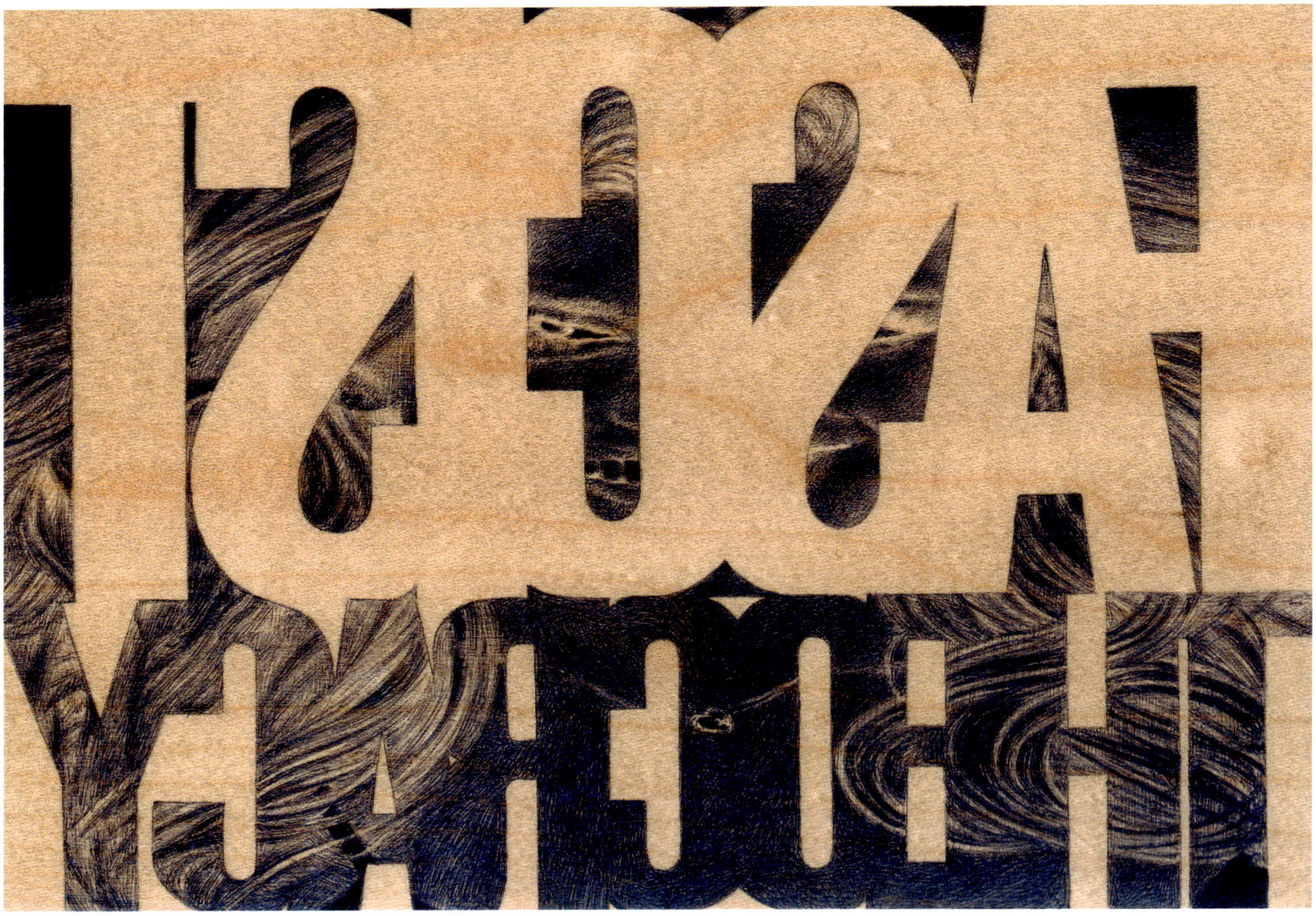

Tsicsaf Ycarcoeht
2008
Ballpoint pen on panel
5 x 7 in.

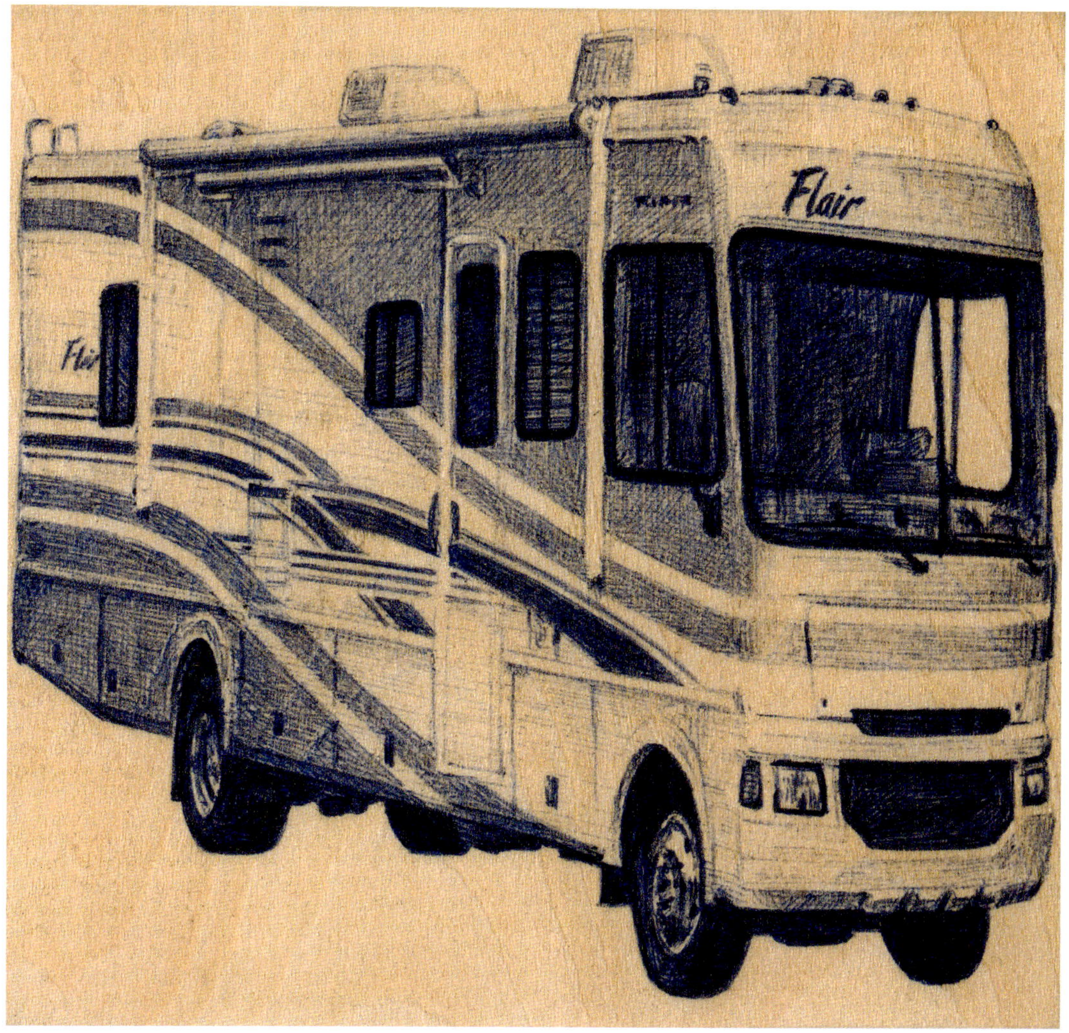

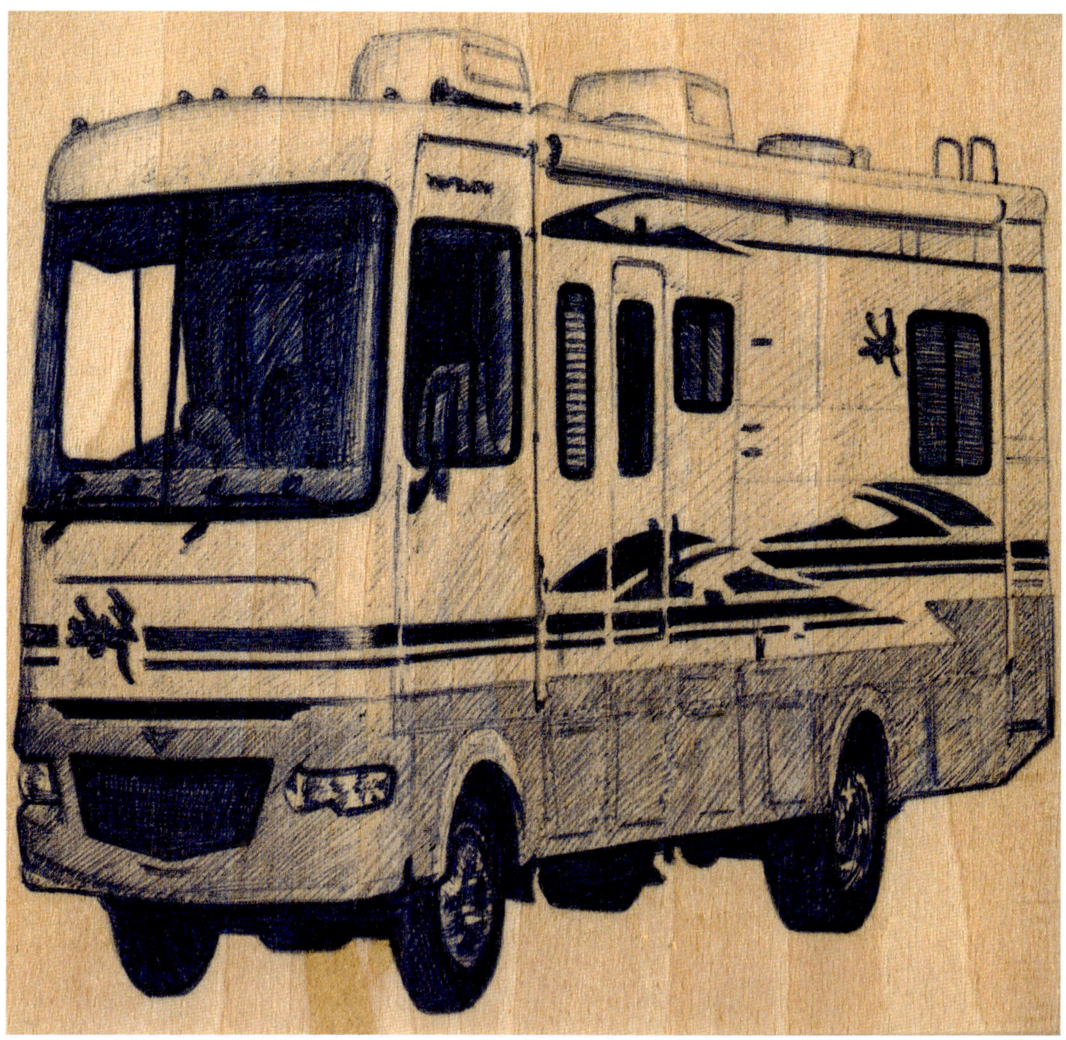

Understand
2008
Ballpoint pen on panel
4 x 4 in.

Understand
2008
Ballpoint pen on panel
4 x 4 in.

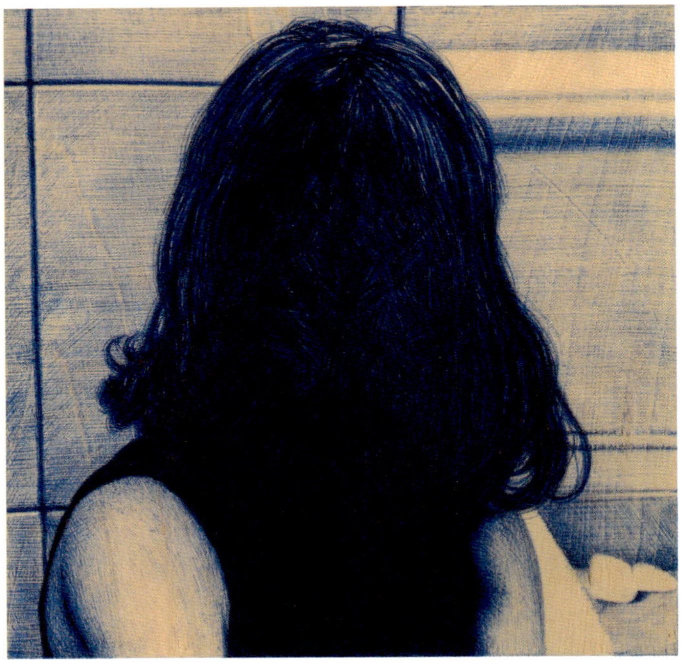

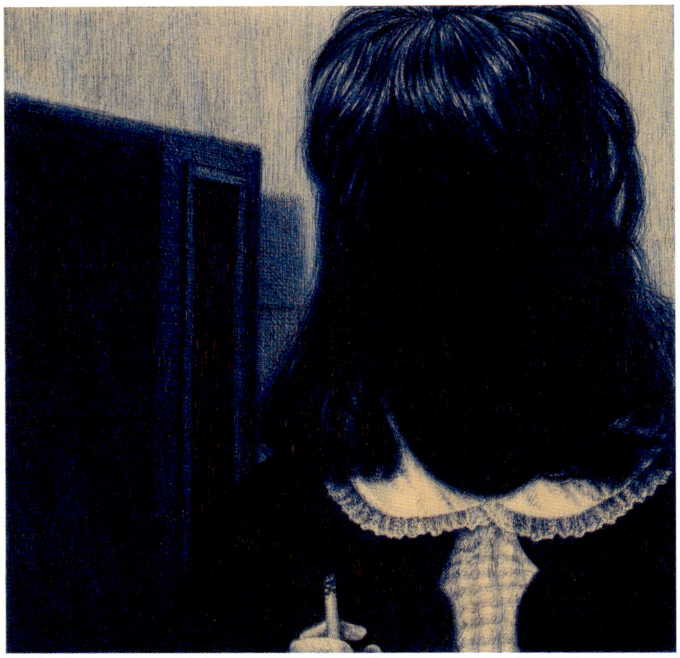

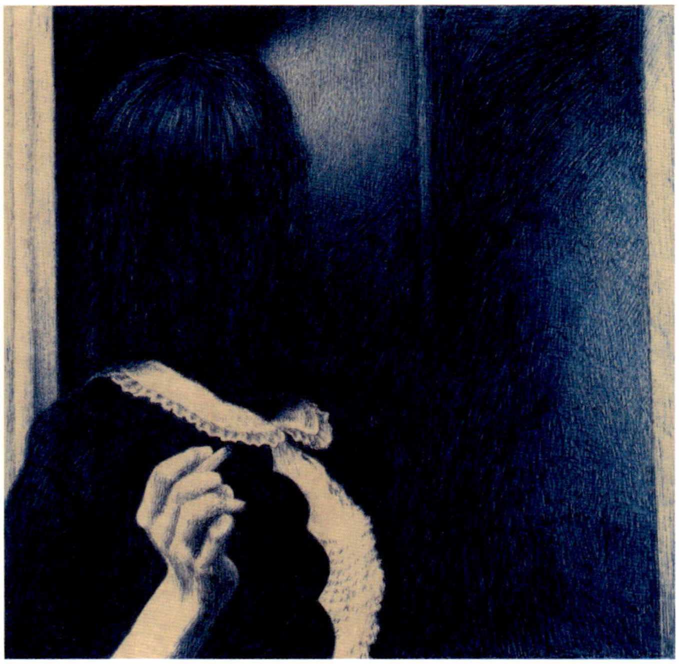

Terribly Wanting To Be Loved
2010
Ballpoint pen on panel
6 x 6 in.

Terribly Wanting To Be Loved
2010
Ballpoint pen on panel
6 x 6 in.

Terribly Wanting To Be Loved
2010
Ballpoint pen on panel
6 x 6 in.

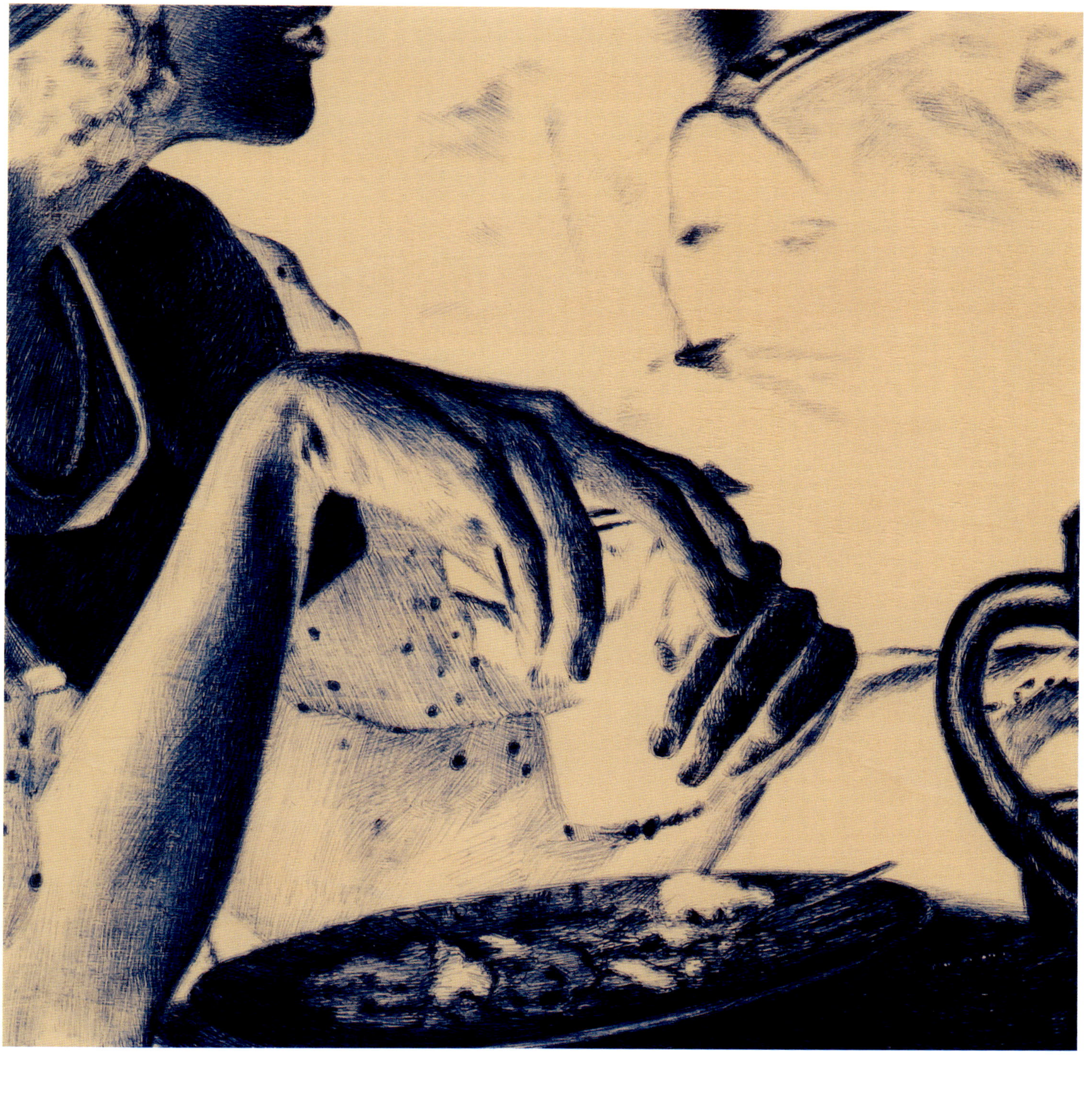

Kay Adams-Corleone and Negative Milk
2009
Ballpoint pen on panel
8 x 8 in.

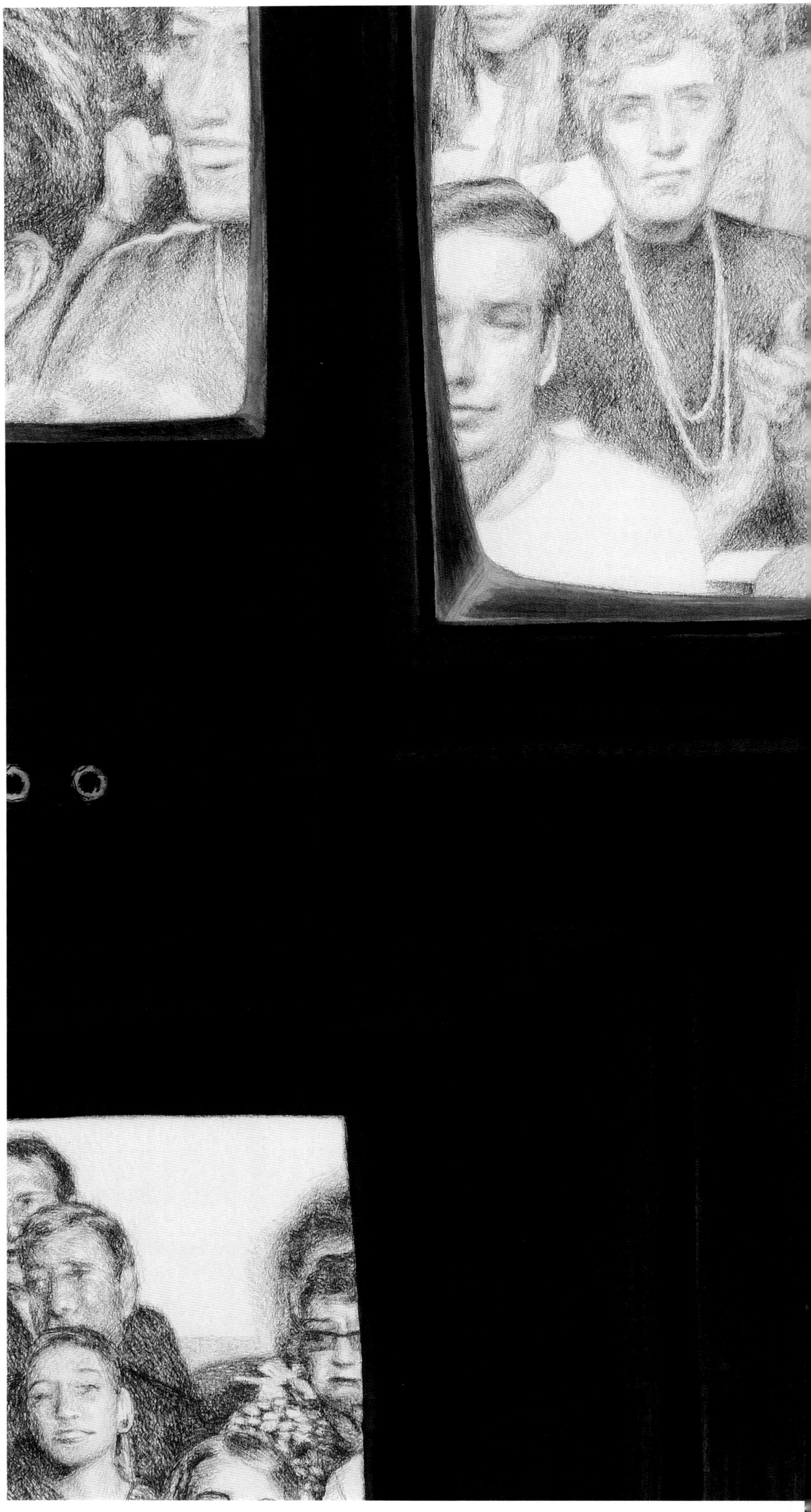

Untitled
2012
Graphite and acrylic on paper
15 x 20 in.

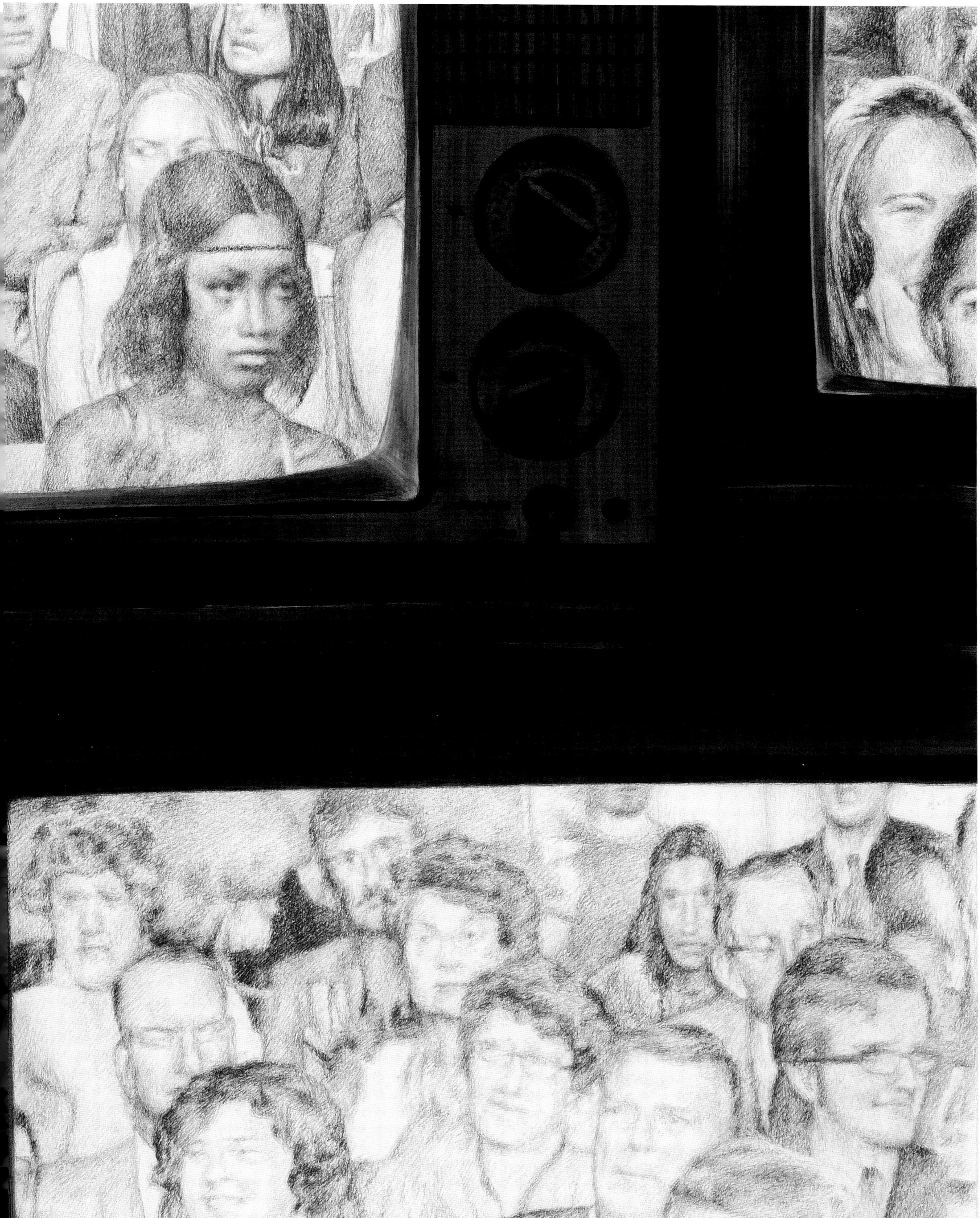

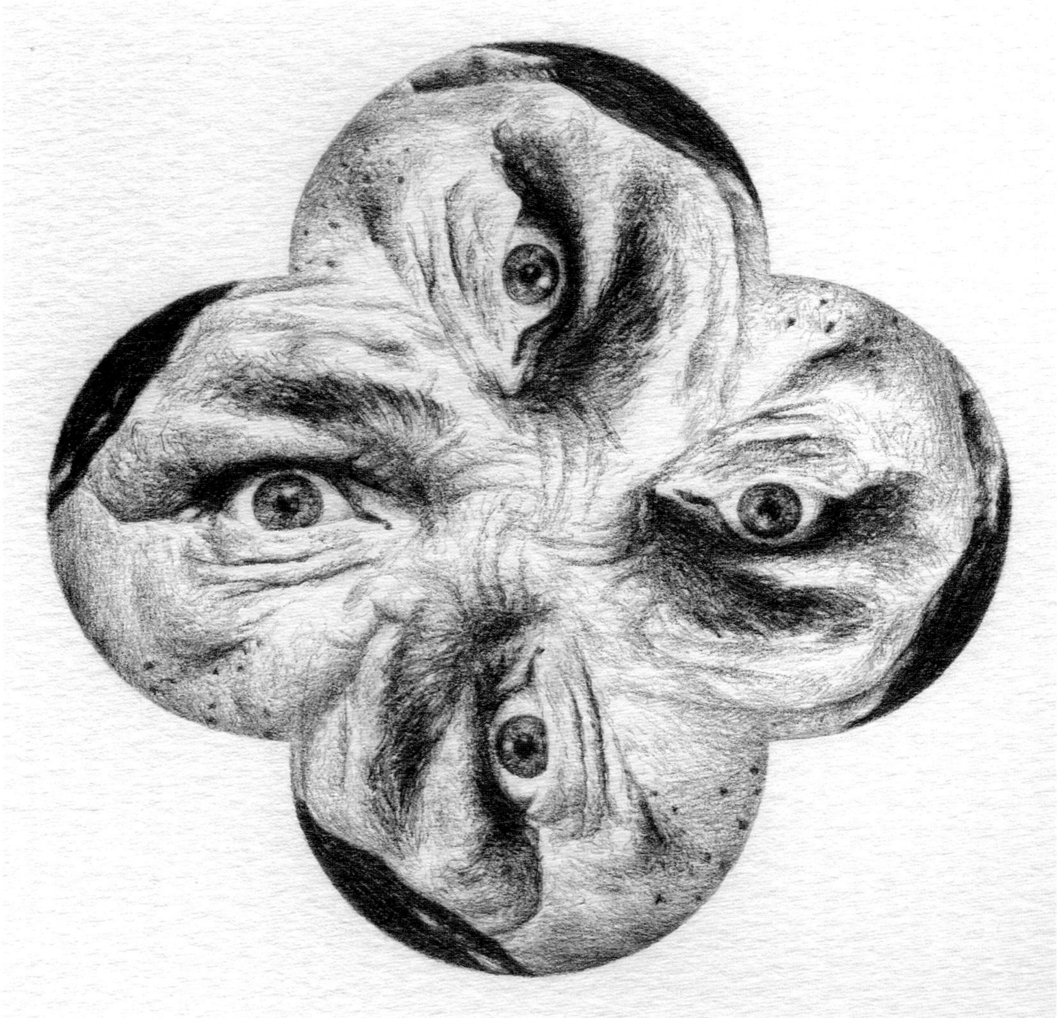

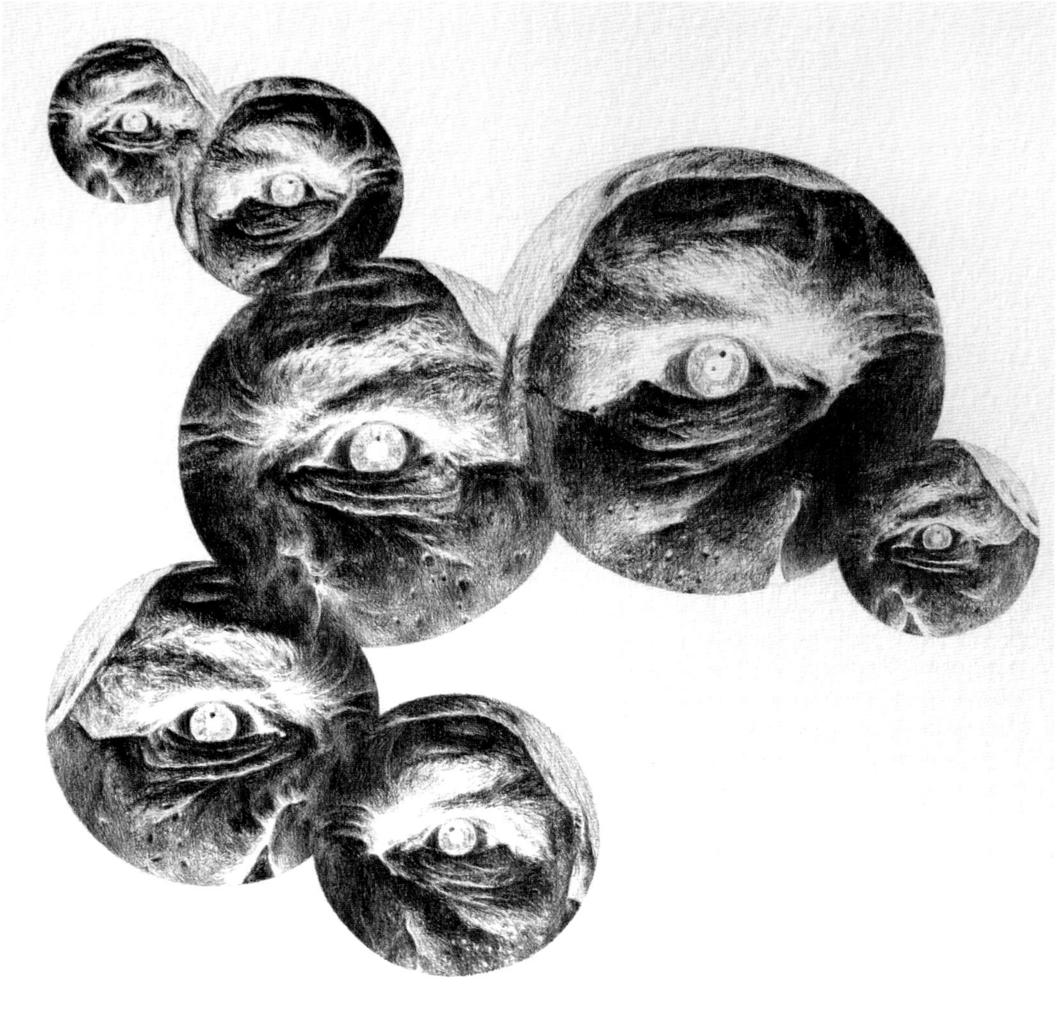

Shemp Eyes
2012
Graphite on paper
9 x 9 in.

Shemp Eyes (Negative)
2012
Graphite on paper
10 x 14 in.

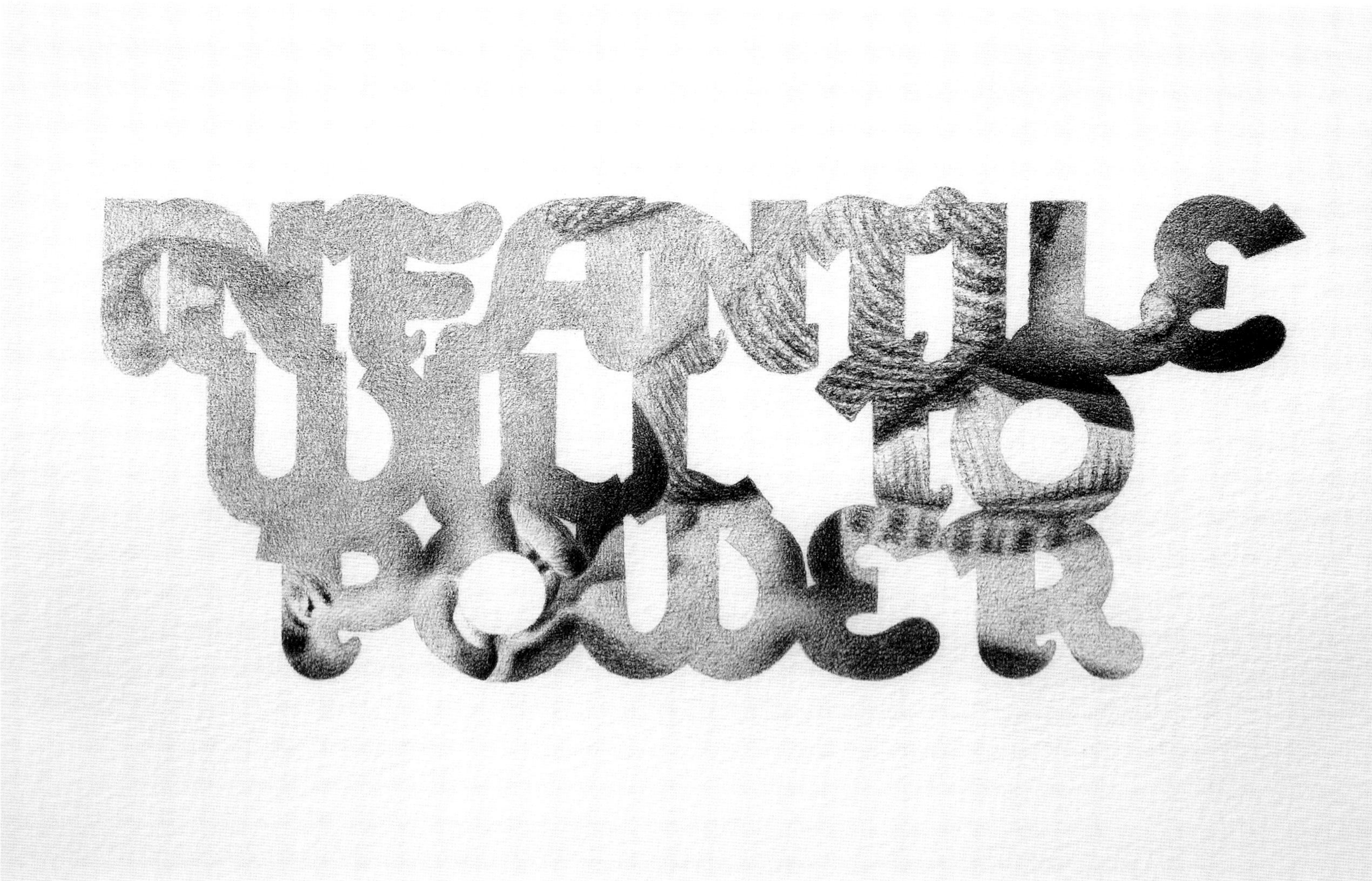

Infantile Will To Power
2012
Graphite on paper
6 x 9 in.

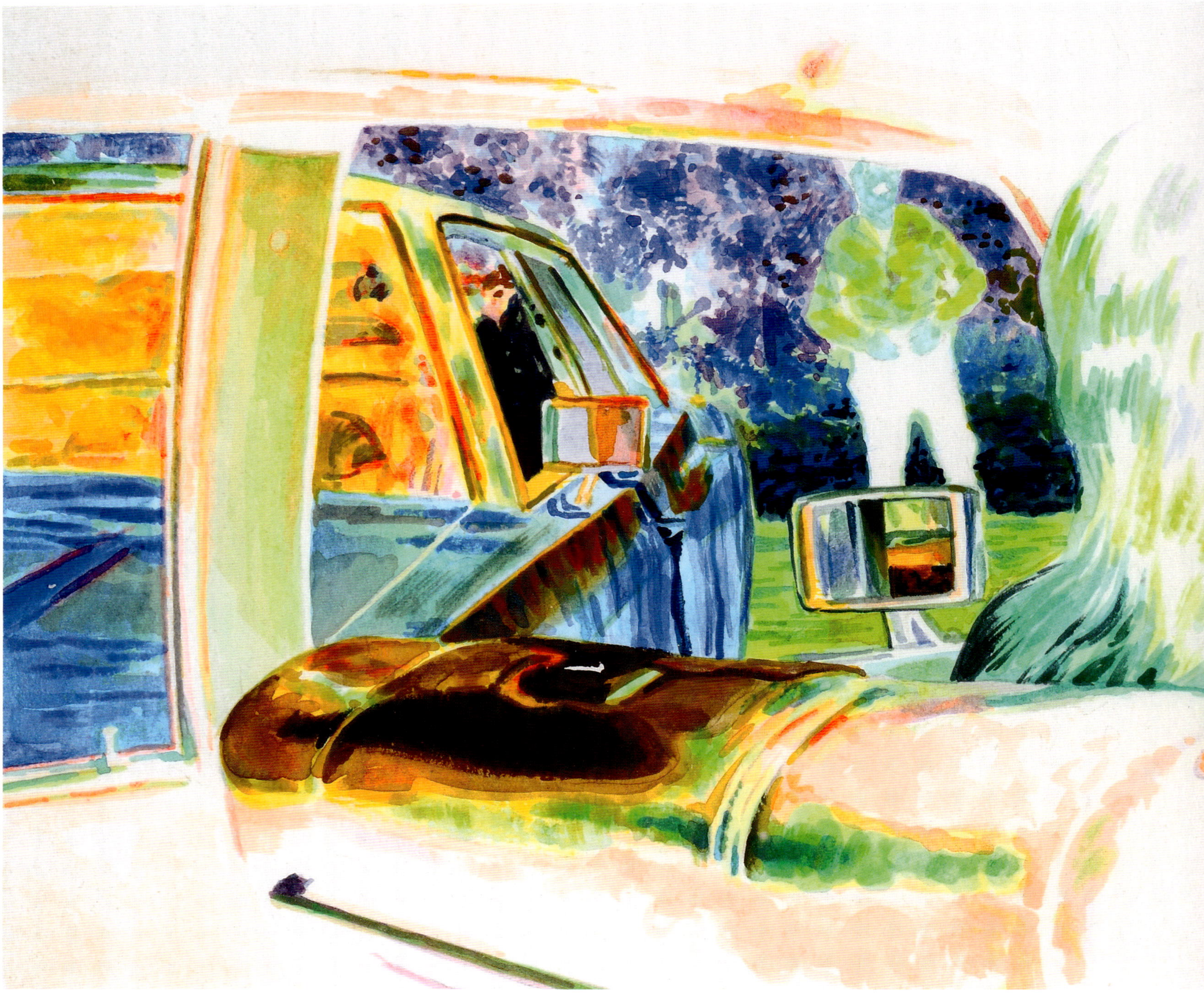

Charley Varick Inverse 1971 Lincoln Continental Backseat
2014
Acrylic gouache on paper
5 x 12 in.

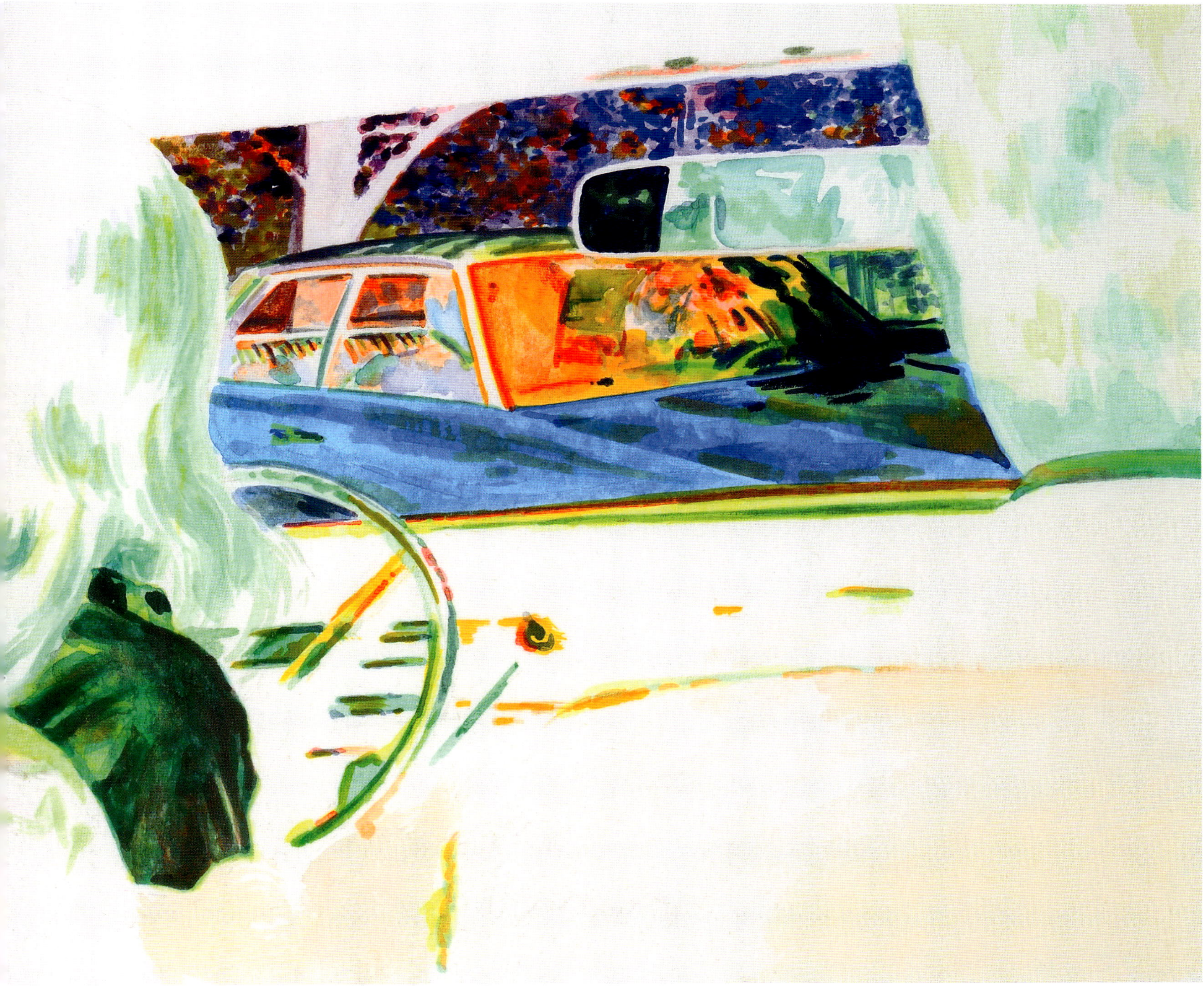

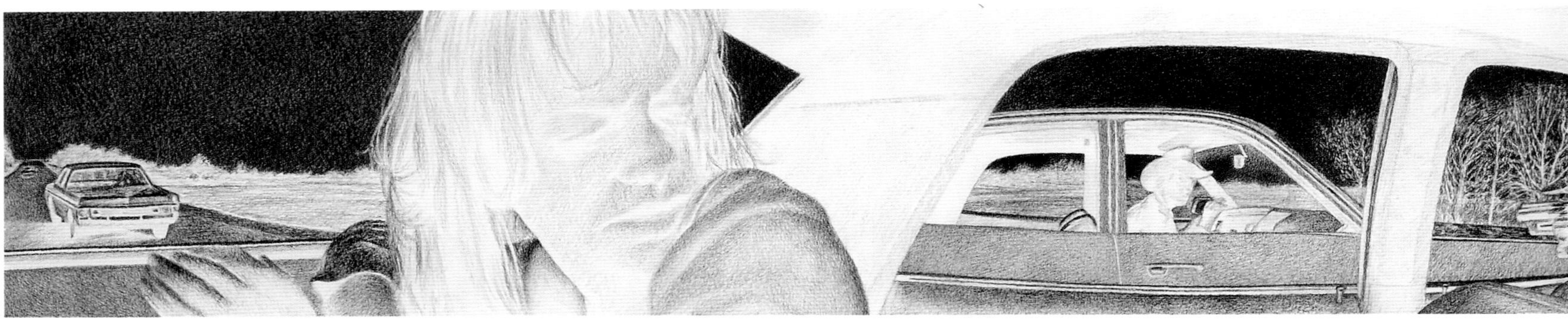

Sugarland Express Inverse Study 1973 Dodge Polara Backseat
2014
Graphite on paper
4 x 40 in.

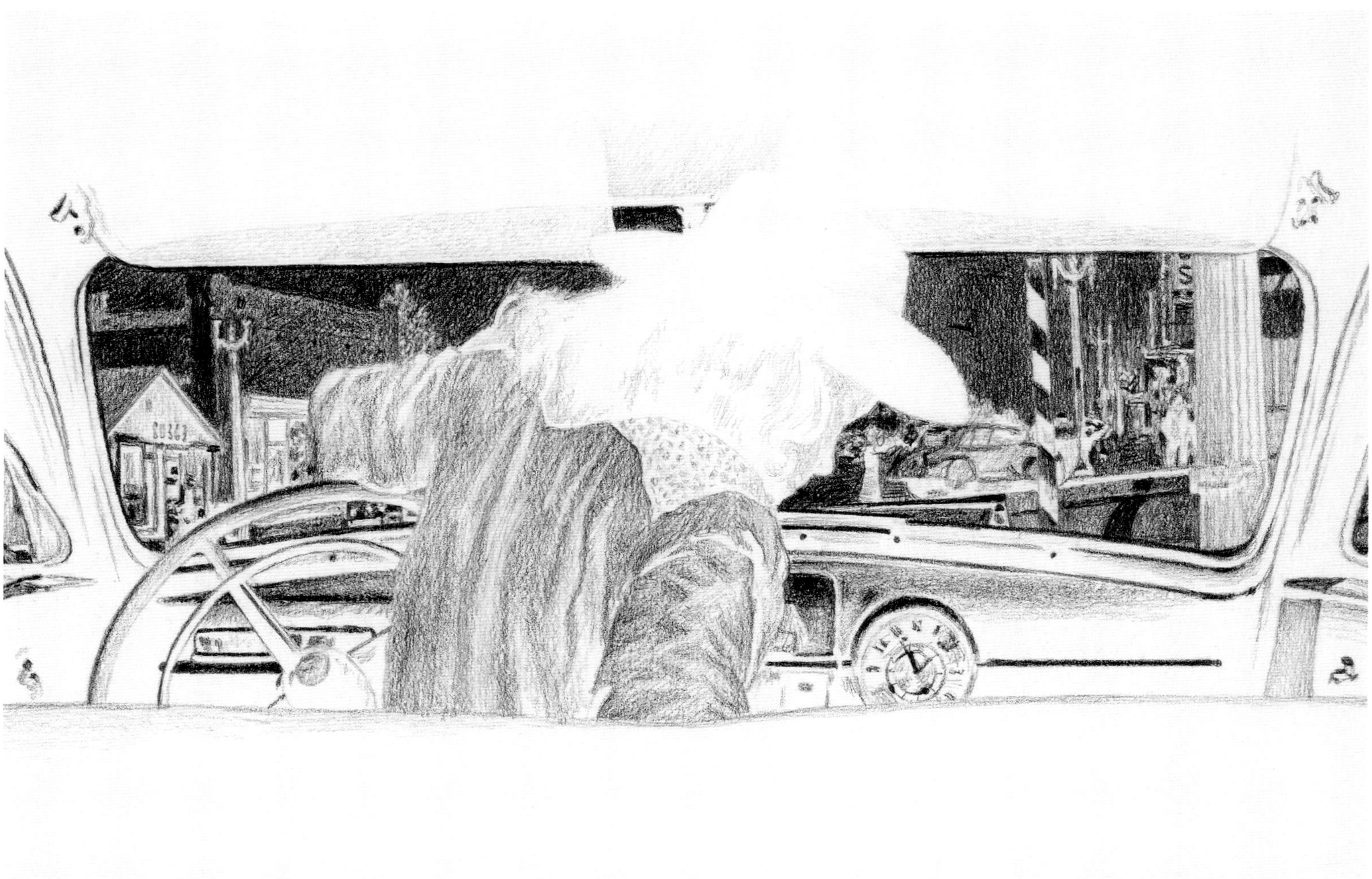

Gun Crazy Inverse 1948 Cadillac Series 62 Cowgirl Backseat
2014
Graphite on paper
6 x 9 in.

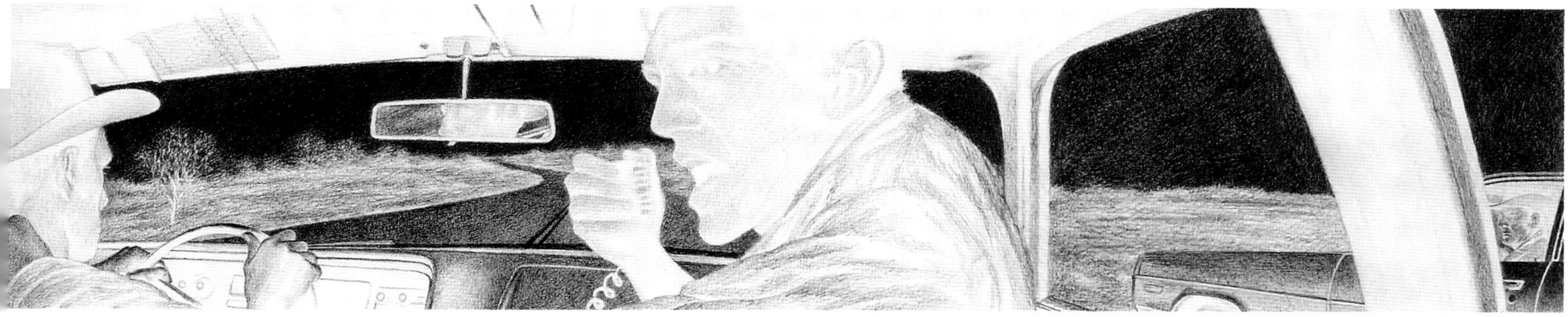

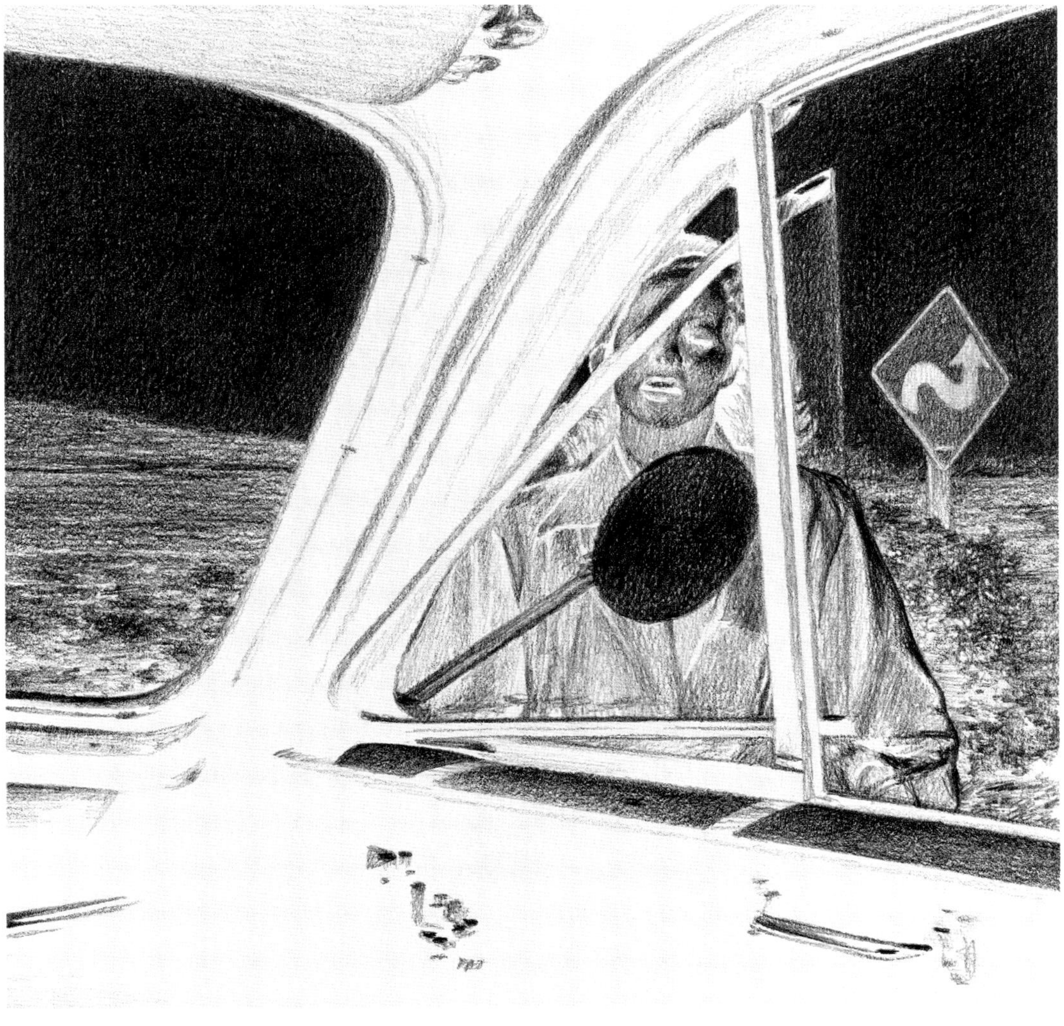

Gun Crazy Inverse 1948 Cadillac Series 62 Backseat
2014
Graphite on paper
7 x 7 in.

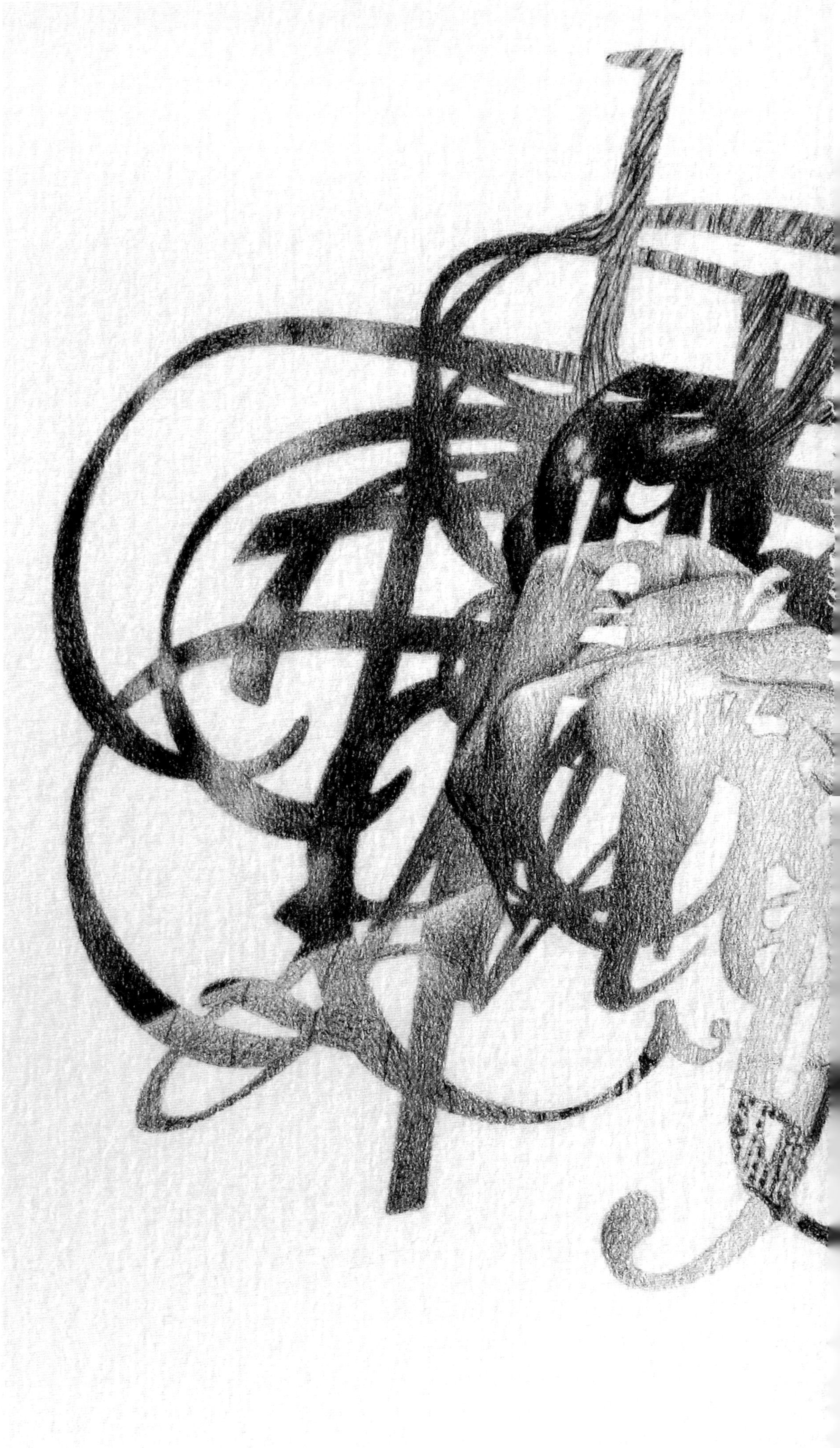

The End
2012
Graphite on paper
10 x 14 in.

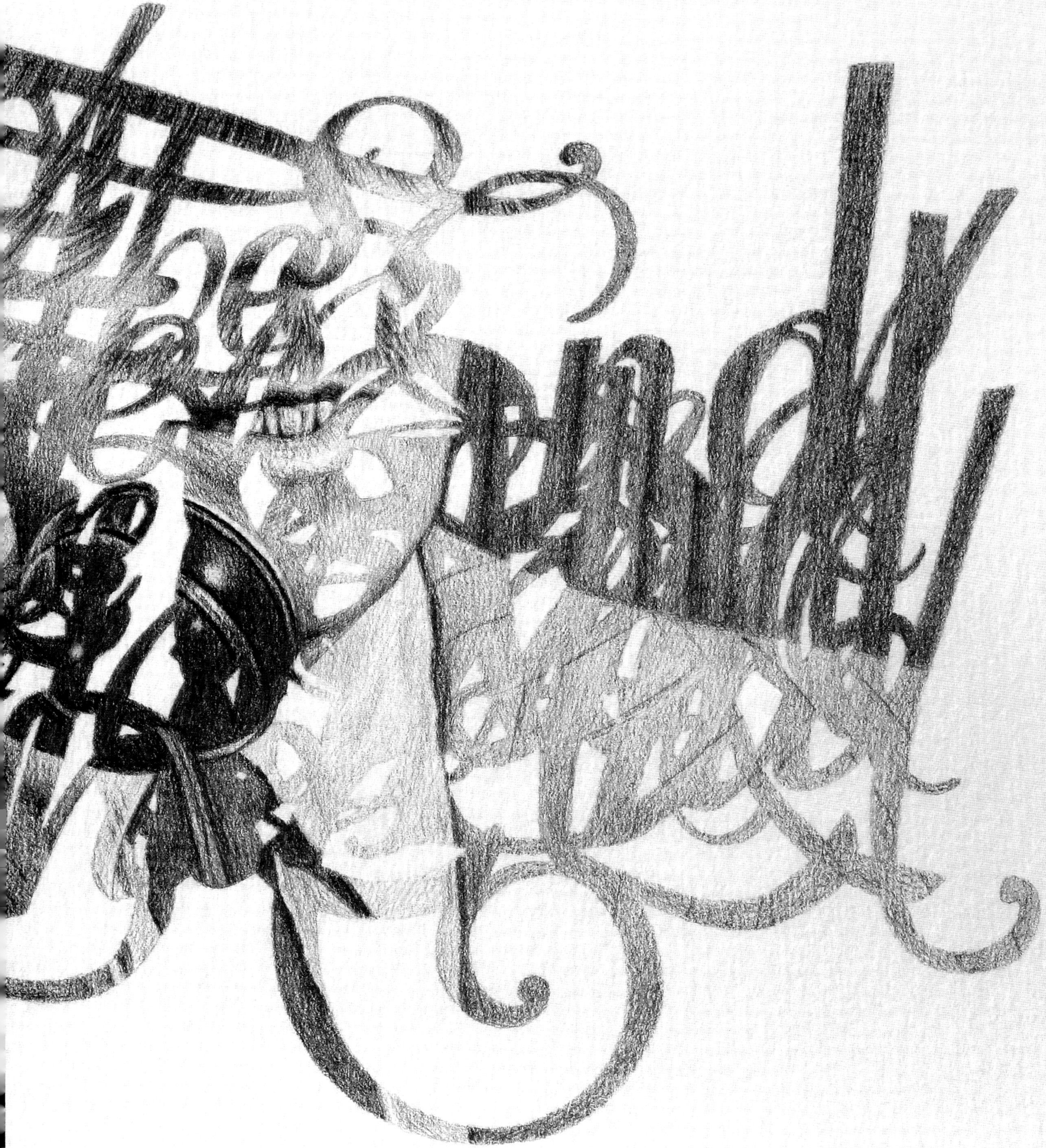

First published in the United States of America in 2015 by
Rizzoli International Publications, Inc.
300 Park Avenue South
New York, NY 10010
www.rizzoliusa.com

2015 2016 2017 2018 2019 / 10 9 8 7 6 5 4 3 2 1

Design by Claudia Brandenburg, Language Arts

Artwork Photography by Paul Felder, Steven Bates, James Dee, Dan Kvicta, Max Yawney, Rachel Pontious, Joshua White, Pier Maulini, Paolo Vandrasch, Daniel Rider

Printed in China

ISBN-13: 978-0-8478-4620-7
Library of Congress Control Number: 2015941520

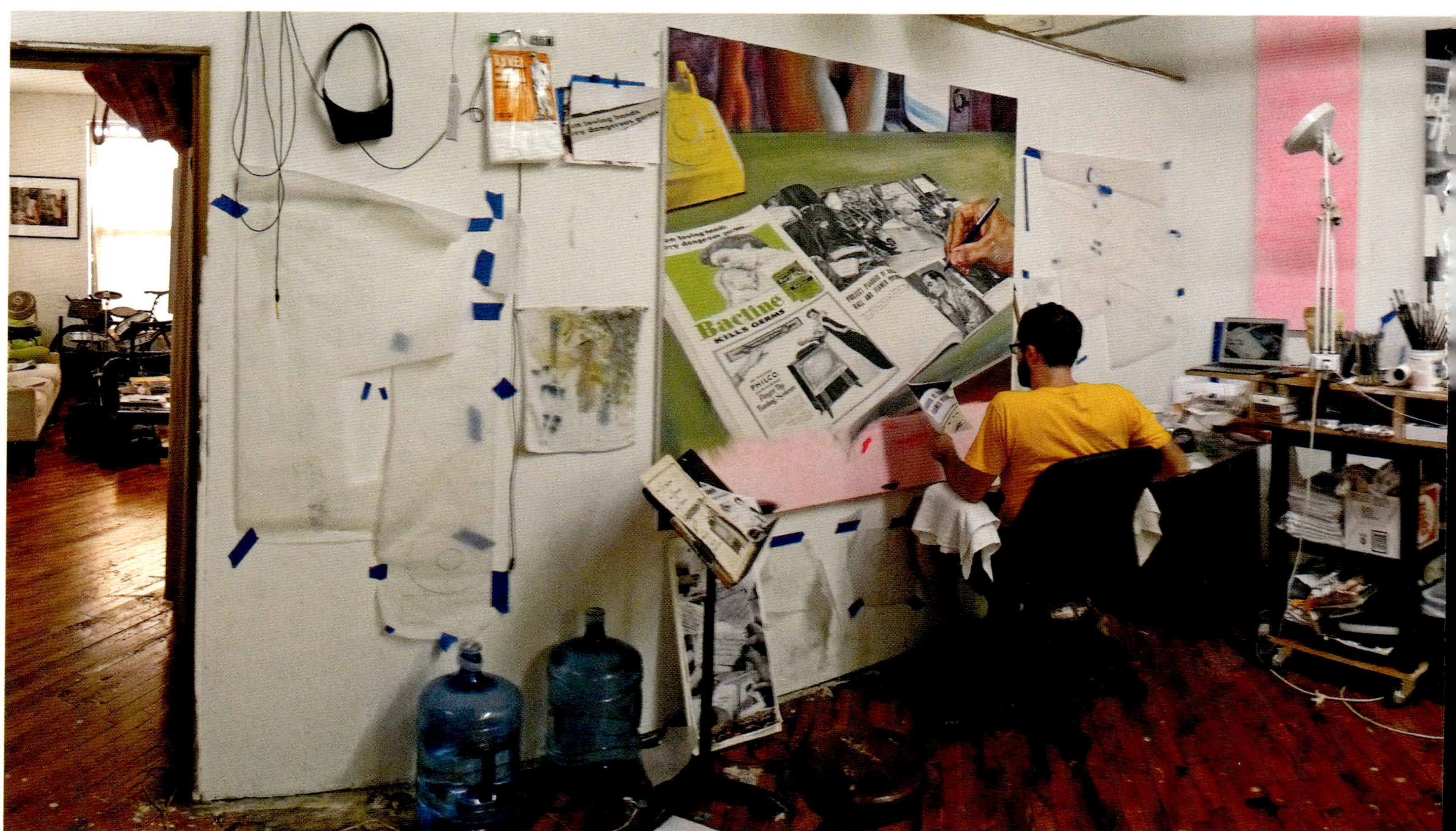

Eric White Studio, Brooklyn, New York, 2013
Photo by Peter Altenberg

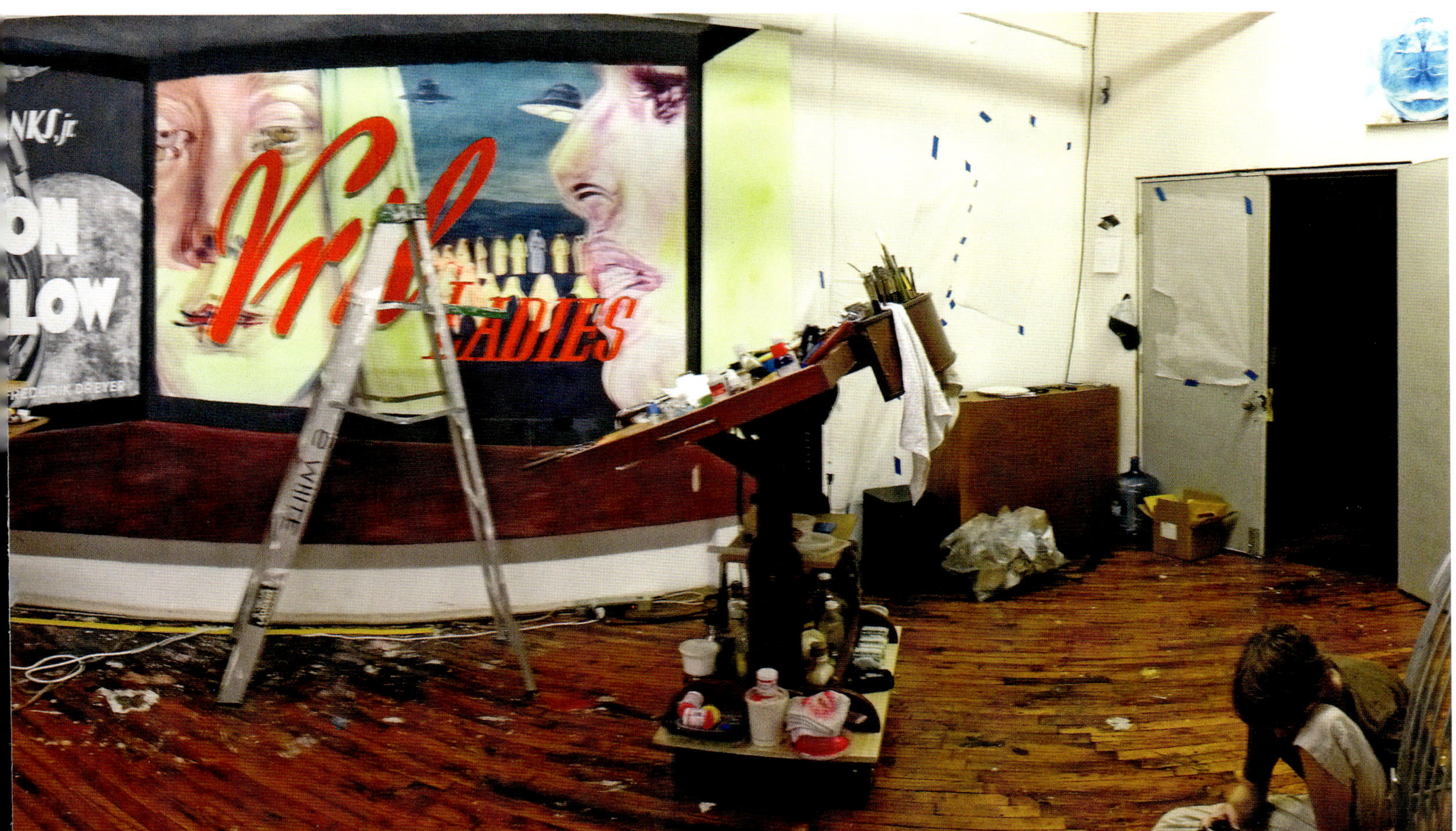
NKS, jr.
ON
LOW
FREDERIK DREYER
LADIES

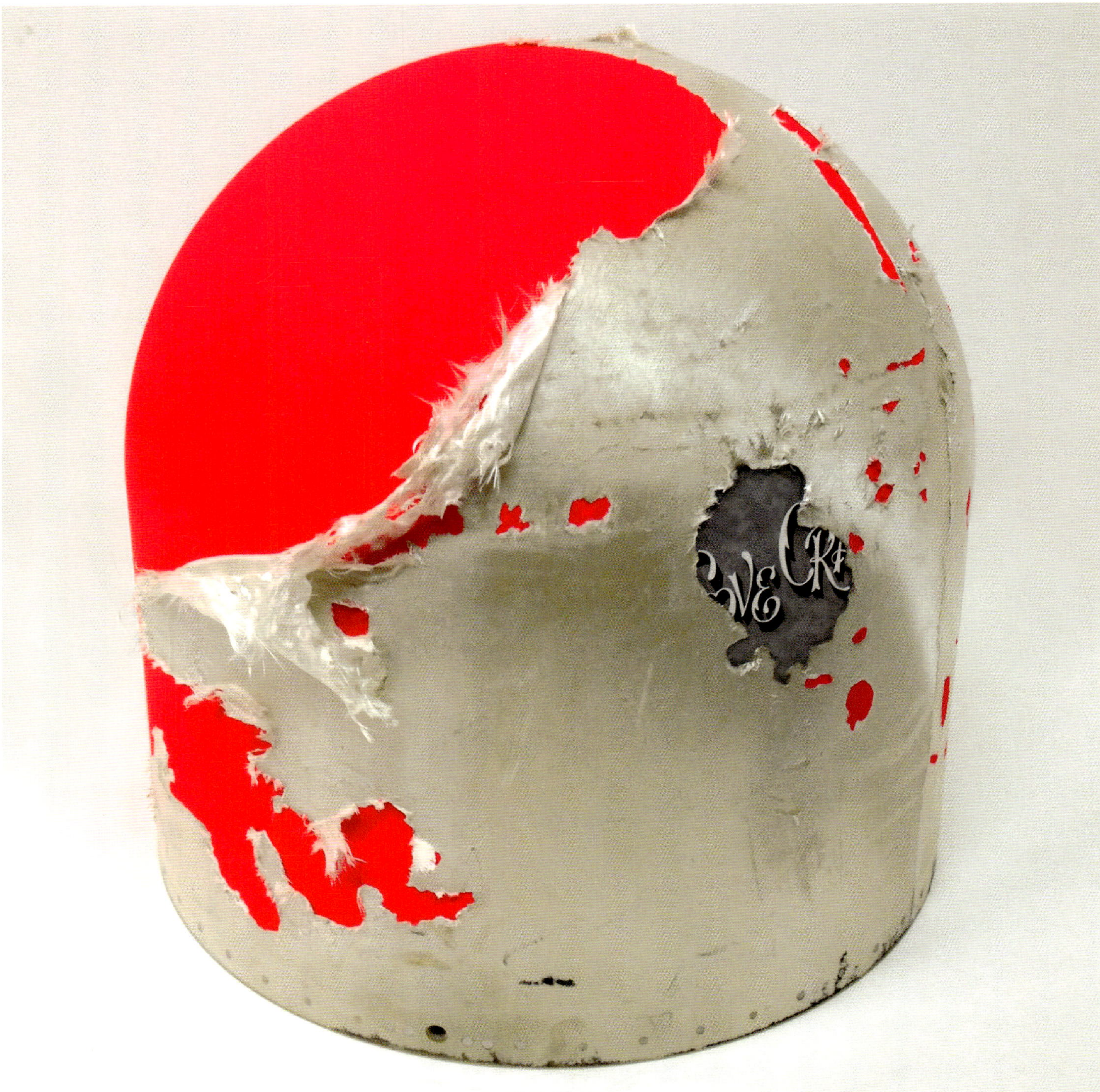

Love Crazy
2012
Acrylic on nosecone
24h x 24 in. diameter